"Andrew Flibbert has written an accessible and thematically grounded overview of Iraq's complex history. He analyzes the impact of individual decision-makers, domestic politics, and the international system on key moments in Iraq's history and the development of state institutions. All who read this book will better understand the contemporary politics and international relations of Iraq."

David Patel, *Crown Center for Middle East Studies, Brandeis University, United States*

IRAQ

Addressing major political developments in Iraq over the past century, this book provides an up-to-date and accessible study of the country, advancing a sympathetic yet balanced understanding of its critical role in the Middle East and North Africa (MENA) region and in global affairs.

The author introduces three concepts to aid in understanding Iraq's historical trajectory: the pursuit of power, the impact of state institutions, and the transformation of social identities. Using this analytical approach, the book illuminates the unique political, economic, and social dimensions of Iraqi national life. In addition to providing comparisons with several MENA countries and the Arab states, the book evaluates Iraqi relations with external actors, including the United States, the European powers, China, and Russia. Though conscious of Iraq's long and complex history, special attention is paid to contemporary events, ranging from Saddam Hussein's invasion of Kuwait in 1990 to the American-led invasion in 2003, and more recent struggles with elections, the Islamic State, and democracy. It is nevertheless argued that, despite its challenges, Iraq's story remains hopeful, moving forward in time.

Both wide-ranging and closely focused, the book is vital reading for students, scholars, and general audiences interested in Iraqi politics, international relations, and political economy.

Andrew J. Flibbert is Associate Professor of Political Science at Trinity College in Hartford, Connecticut, USA, where he teaches Middle East politics, international relations, and foreign policy. His research has addressed the Iraq war, state failure, WMD proliferation, civilian suffering and war-time ethics, human rights in the Middle East, and the political economy of cultural production. He has contributed to edited volumes and published articles in *Political Science Quarterly*, *Middle East Policy*, *Security Studies*, *Middle East Journal*, and *PS: Politics and Political Science*.

THE CONTEMPORARY MIDDLE EAST
Edited by Professor Anoushiravan Ehteshami
Institute for Middle Eastern and Islamic Studies,
University of Durham, United Kingdom

For well over a century now the Middle East and North Africa countries have formed a central plank of the international system. **The Contemporary Middle East Series** provides the first systematic attempt at studying the key actors of this dynamic, complex, and strategically important region. Using an innovative common format – which in each case study provides an easily digestible analysis of the origins of the state, its contemporary politics, economics and international relations – prominent Middle East experts have been brought together to write definitive studies of the MENA region's key countries.

Titles include:

Egypt
A Fragile Power
Eberhard Kienle

Yemen
Poverty and Conflict
Helen Lackner

Iraq
Power, Institutions, and Identities
Andrew J. Flibbert

For more information about this series, please visit: https://www.routledge.com/The-Contemporary-Middle-East/book-series/CME

IRAQ

Power, Institutions, and Identities

Andrew J. Flibbert

LONDON AND NEW YORK

Designed cover image: © Scott Nelson / Getty Images

First published 2023
by Routledge
4 Park Square, Milton Park, Abingdon, Oxon OX14 4RN

and by Routledge
605 Third Avenue, New York, NY 10158

Routledge is an imprint of the Taylor & Francis Group, an informa business

© 2023 Andrew J. Flibbert

The right of Andrew J. Flibbert to be identified as author of this work has been asserted in accordance with sections 77 and 78 of the Copyright, Designs and Patents Act 1988.

All rights reserved. No part of this book may be reprinted or reproduced or utilised in any form or by any electronic, mechanical, or other means, now known or hereafter invented, including photocopying and recording, or in any information storage or retrieval system, without permission in writing from the publishers.

Trademark notice: Product or corporate names may be trademarks or registered trademarks, and are used only for identification and explanation without intent to infringe.

British Library Cataloguing-in-Publication Data
A catalogue record for this book is available from the British Library

Library of Congress Cataloging-in-Publication Data
Names: Flibbert, Andrew J., author.
Title: Iraq : power, institutions, and identities / Andrew J. Flibbert.
Description: First Edition. | New York, NY : Routledge, 2023. |
Series: The contemporary Middle East |
Includes bibliographical references and index.
Identifiers: LCCN 2022043701 (print) | LCCN 2022043702 (ebook) |
Subjects: LCSH: Iraq–Economic conditions–20th century. |
Iraq–Social conditions–20th century. | Iraq–Foreign relations. |
Iraq–Politics and government–20th century.
Classification: LCC HC415.4 .F55 2023 (print) |
LCC HC415.4 (ebook) | DDC 330.9567–dc23/eng/20221028
LC record available at https://lccn.loc.gov/2022043701
LC ebook record available at https://lccn.loc.gov/2022043702

ISBN: 978-0-367-52090-8 (hbk)
ISBN: 978-0-367-52092-2 (pbk)
ISBN: 978-1-003-05644-7 (ebk)

DOI: 10.4324/9781003056447

Typeset in Bembo
by Newgen Publishing UK

To Joseph T. Flibbert

CONTENTS

List of Tables *x*
Acknowledgments *xi*
Note on Transliteration *xii*

    Introduction: Iraq, Old and New   1

1   State Formation, 1914–1958   11

2   From Revolution to Dictatorship, 1958–1988   47

3   From Dictatorship to Troubled Democracy, 1988–2022   84

4   International Relations   114

5   Political Economy   162

    Conclusions   191

Bibliography *200*
Index *209*

TABLES

5.1	GDP—Iraq	165
5.2	MENA country populations	167
5.3	MENA country areas	167
5.4	MENA oil reserves	168
5.5	MENA GDP	168
5.6	MENA GNI, per capita	169
5.7	Population growth—Iraq	170
5.8	Median age in select countries	171

ACKNOWLEDGMENTS

I have accumulated debts over many years of learning about Iraq and writing this book. Most immediately, my sincere thanks to Greg Gause, Michael Herb, John Lee Holmes, Marc Lynch, David Patel, and Bruce Rutherford for their generous and incisive commentary on various parts of the manuscript. In more distant but fundamental ways, a host of Georgetown, Virginia, CASA, and Columbia professors introduced me to Iraqi politics and the larger Middle East, international relations, and the Arabic language. Ambassador Mary Ann Casey and the late Wayne White at the U.S. State Department gave me opportunities and guidance in my early-career work on Iraq and its troubled relationship with the United States. Lisa Anderson and the late Robert Jervis and R. K. Ramazani provided long-time mentoring and new ways of seeing the world. I am grateful to Trinity College, my political science colleagues, and our talented and energetic students, for the privilege of teaching, writing, and learning together. Euan Rice-Coates, Anoush Ehteshami, and Joe Whiting were thoughtful and remarkably efficient in their editorial capacities at Taylor & Francis.

Any serious marathon—writing or running—follows a hard road. I thank Sonia, Alex, and Sammy, whose love and forbearance throughout this and other distance ventures have made it all possible, and worth it. I dedicate this book to my father, Joseph T. Flibbert, who taught American literature at al-Hikma University in Baghdad before I was born, enlivening my childhood with his stories and his example as an inspired teacher and scholar.

NOTE ON TRANSLITERATION

In writing this book for multiple audiences, I use simplified romanization and transliteration for Arabic names and places. I omit nonessential diacritical marks, as well as many initial *ayns* and *hamzas*. For personal or place names, I usually drop the definite article *al-* or, with well-known historical figures, employ the most common usage (e.g., *Nuri al-Sa'id*). For terms like *Ba'ath*, an extra "a" is used for clarity and readability in English. I use *Shi'i* as an adjective and *Shi'a* for the plural noun, presuming the variation is not distracting. While capitalization does not exist in Arabic, it is helpful in romanized names and short phrases.

FIGURE 0.1 Map of Iraq

Source: U.S. Government, 2009.

INTRODUCTION
Iraq, Old and New

A relatively new country in an ancient land, Iraq is a contradiction. It has great oil wealth alongside considerable poverty and deprivation. It has been at the forefront of economic transformation and educational attainment in the Middle East and North Africa (MENA), while its social bonds are tattered and its national community is fragmented. It has experienced one of the most sustained and transformative democratic experiments in the Arab world, but also one of its longest and harshest periods of authoritarian rule. It has been both the focus of global attention and an international pariah with few enduring allies. Its capital, Baghdad, was once a renowned center of science, philosophy, culture, and technology, but the Golden Age of Islam ended over a thousand years ago and the city was all but destroyed by the Mongols in 1258. Its fertile land, vast oil resources, storied history, and human diversity offer exceptional possibility, though achieving and maintaining anything close to Iraq's potential has been elusive.

Over several thousand years, the land that is now Iraq has seen repeated attempts to define, extend, and consolidate political community and authority. The contemporary Iraqi state is the latest such effort, getting its start as a twentieth-century colonial creation. It has changed a great deal from its early establishing years, when it was effectively nonexistent, then underdeveloped and weakly institutionalized, before being transformed by oil revenues, war, and political turmoil. Iraqis themselves are also changing. While there was no Iraqi national community a century ago, one exists today, alongside subnational and supranational identities competing for allegiance. More real than ever, Iraq is torn by a variety of divisions and battered by a difficult history, but it still stands and has been surprisingly resilient.

This book explores Iraq's political life over the past one hundred years. It does so by introducing its most influential leaders and their constituencies, describing

DOI: 10.4324/9781003056447-1

crucial moments in Iraqi state formation and national development, and explaining some of the country's most consequential international actions and challenges. Three concepts are among the master keys to understanding Iraq's trajectory and telling this story: the perennial pursuit of power, the impact of state institutions, and the transformation of social identities. Power, institutions, and identities are relatively timeless constructs that have been present in one form or another throughout history, presenting a useful lens for seeing and investigating the country's social and political life. While not the only forces shaping Iraq, together they form a vital through-line running from the deep past to the present and future.

This basic theoretical claim goes a long way by providing an analytical map to achieve a better understanding of the place and its evolution over the years. The map is schematic and minimalist, not depicting its subject in fine-grained, photographic detail so much as pointing out the most relevant thematic features that require close and sustained attention. This chapter starts with a brief elaboration of these terms of reference, which are used throughout the rest of the book, often implicitly but more directly in some cases. It offers corresponding Iraqi examples, most of which are described more fully and put in context in subsequent chapters. Finally, it gives a short preview of the major issues that each chapter covers and notes a few core findings. The book overall begins narrowly with theoretical and historical issues, widens in its middle chapters to address modern national political life, encompasses international concerns and political economy in its second half, and concludes with a handful of general observations with an eye on Iraq's future prospects.

A Conceptual Framework

A study focused on Iraqi power, institutions, and identities can be conducted on various levels of analysis (LOA), ranging from the country's many individual decision-makers to the domestic contexts in which they operate and the regional or international forces beyond Iraq or the greater Middle East. Such a three-tiered, LOA framework is a way to organize arguments and evidence in the political domain, and it has a long history, especially in the study of international relations.[1] Implicit in the framework is an epistemological dilemma from social theory: knowing the relative causal weight of agents and structures in any political outcome. That is, the framework asks whether, to understand political life in Iraq or any country, it is most useful to focus on decision-makers and their many choices, the national context driving social and political actions, or the regional and international forces pushing in various directions and shaping all outcomes measurably.

Rather than choosing one level, this book finds an analytical balance between attention to the dynamic, purposive actors in politics and the structural constraints and enablers that move such actors. As a single-country study, it has the advantage of encompassing multiple levels, with minimal risk of being overwhelmed by too much data. No doubt, Iraq has had several important decision-makers, and its state and national development have been complex, interactive processes involving numerous institutions and social actors. The country also exists in a pressure-filled regional environment and has faced the active engagement of multiple neighbors, regional adversaries, and great powers. Yet, a streamlined focus on power, institutions, and identities cuts through some of this complexity and simplifies Iraq's story sufficiently—as good theory often does—to make it legible and coherent. It encompasses the most salient factors affecting modern Iraqi life. A brief review of the three key terms of reference reveals how much ground they cover together.

Power

In Iraq, as elsewhere, power operates on all levels of society and is such a general concept that it verges on being banal or devoid of particular usefulness. Yet, it is the coin of the political realm, and its pursuit is a basic human impulse. It is sought and deployed by a wide range of actors, from individuals and organized domestic groups to national states and international entities of all kinds. It consists most fundamentally of a capacity to bend others to one's will. It can be used to solve collective problems and manage the largest social and economic challenges and grievances, or for narrower and more selfish pursuits like individual aggrandizement. As a capacity, both latent and exercised, power manifests in many forms, including in a material or physical sense but also in less obvious ways like agenda setting, issue framing, normative influence, or structural power. Even when originating in material forms, power can have intangible effects, such as when rising power generates increased ambition on the part of those who command it. Power allows actors to do what they otherwise could not do and changes political interactions.[2]

In considering the role of power in an Iraqi context, the individual decision-makers at the helm are especially important. Power politics in some contexts is little more than personal politics, as individuals compete with others and strive for dominance or, just as often, for political and even personal survival. By this logic, a study of Iraq will focus often on the specific people ruling the country or attempting to do so. While a close examination of the lives and pursuits of leaders like King Faisal I, Nuri al-Sa'id, Abd al-Karim Qasim, or Saddam Hussein may seem like a form of excessive analytical personalization, the focus is not so much on their personal histories as their pursuit and wielding of power. This also allows us to see both their choices and how their agency is surprisingly limited at times by the institutional constraints and political incentives in their environments, as well as to assess the relevance of their decision-making in relation to these structural factors. Even the most powerful leader in any social context has to contend with pressures that limit their actions and thwart their plans.

The presence of contending power centers like external actors or dominant social groups complicates matters further. In early-twentieth-century Iraq, as we will see, power dynamics between British colonial authorities, the Hashemite monarchy, and social elites limited early state-building in ways that frustrated King Faisal and inhibited his effort to construct a new national community. Likewise, mid-century Prime Minister Nuri al-Sa'id's relentless pursuit of power, both successful and failed, left its mark on Iraq's political trajectory by weakening the organized opposition, and it may have aborted the possibility of reformist change in a country barreling toward revolution. Much later, Saddam Hussein's autocratic rule displayed elements of totalitarian power in mobilizing Iraqis from all walks of life, who had little choice but to follow a leader bent on plans that proved reckless and destructive to all, including himself. Similarly, attention to power dynamics reveals how Saddam's authority—or legitimated power—diminished after blunders in Iran and Kuwait forced him to narrow the social bases of his regime. Even dictators have constituencies to placate, paying a price when they misspend their power resources.

Institutions

While power is a core element in any national story, institutions are a second and vital feature. Most fundamentally, institutions are the rules, practices, norms, and shared understandings that shape and shove political choices and actions. Institutions are informal and abstract when embedded in everyday activities like voting or democratic engagement, making them ubiquitous but hard to isolate and distinguish usefully in the social sciences. They are formal and more fully evident when written into rules and codified into laws. They can be concretized or made material in the establishment of an organization, agency, bureaucracy, party, or electoral system, all of which typically are easy to identify but hard to characterize in general terms. The analytical value of institutions—they are everywhere and take many forms—can also pose a challenge because of the difficulty of identifying which are most relevant and consequential.[3]

Political institutions are an important structural feature of politics in Iraq, as elsewhere, on both the state and societal sides of the state–society divide. State institutions, as elaborated in Chapter 1, are especially relevant and are created by intentional political efforts at state-building, as well as by the more gradual, historically driven processes of state formation. They are the instruments and vessels for large-scale, modern political engagement and activity, channeling human initiative in many directions, though their absences and failures can have an equally dramatic effect. They provide a mechanism for expressing the choices of political actors and a means to achieve any number of objectives. Societal institutions, likewise, are fundamental and have multiple origins, encompassing associational life on all levels and sometimes becoming active, relevant features of the political landscape.

Iraqi state and societal institutions have appeared, developed, atrophied, and been transformed by the political actors and entrepreneurs who shape and deploy them. They work with a kind of structural power or agency of their own to incentivize these same actors. Iraq's Ba'ath Party, for example, played a significant role in connecting the Iraqi state to the larger population, mobilizing people in the service of regime objectives. Institutions tend to be sufficiently durable in that they have a political life of their own and a resilience that defies reducing them to the individuals who constitute them.[4] Once created, they sometimes endure and remain in place long after becoming dysfunctional, obsolete, or even destructive or anachronistic.

Again, the Baʿath Party in Iraq began as an underground movement in the 1950s, helped to organize coup plotters in the 1960s, governed in the 1970s and 1980s, atrophied in real power in the 1990s, and returned to the underground opposition as an insurgency in the 2000s after Saddam's deposal. Some party activists remain engaged today, even joining the Islamic State in recent efforts to retake control of the country.

Identities

Finally, if power and institutions have material aspects and real-world consequences, other factors like identity are equally important in shaping social and political outcomes. Identities are socially shared senses of self, constructed out of the available physical and ideational resources in any context. While identities can be made and unmade, they tend to have an enduring, persistent quality that defies their immediate transformation or dissipation. Individuals and the groups they cohere into hold many overlapping identities rather than being reducible to one-dimensional figures. The significance or salience of specific identities is a direct function of the political environment and provides a basis for mobilization and activism.[5] The context-dependent relevance of identities requires close attention in Iraq, where ethnic, sectarian, tribal, extended family, or regional affiliation matters, though only sometimes. The actions of people identified as Iraqi nationals in one context—for immigration or citizenship purposes, for example—might be better understood in another context as driven by their ethnic, sectarian, or tribal identity. Membership in the Al-Bu Nasir tribe, for example, at times came with great benefits, given Saddam Hussein's reliance on family and tribal ties to protect his rule.

Apart from community-related identity issues, other nonmaterial factors like norms and ideologies sometimes matter a great deal too. Socially shared beliefs, common ideological commitments, and mutually negotiated normative standards can have important consequences for group actions and choices. All these elements are "social facts," as opposed to brute material realities, and as such they have a capacity to shape and even coerce individual actions, with great political consequence.[6] We know, for example, that an obstacle to Iraqi political change has been the weakness of democratic norms, or standards of behavior, regarding the use of power. Even if such norms do not necessarily require centuries to emerge and are not culturally bound, positive political change like democratization requires a normative shift in Iraq, which is especially difficult in the aftermath of decades of authoritarian rule. Tracking these changes, or lack thereof, throughout the past century tells us something about the country's problems and prospects.

All three of these core elements—power, institutions, and identities—operate on both the national and international levels, including in domains ranging from authoritarian regime maintenance and electoral politics to decision-making in foreign policy and international relations. Nationally, they are implicated in a wide variety of actions, such as the pursuit of power and self-interest by individuals and groups, the emergence and collapse of state and societal institutions, and the activation and transformation of social identities. Internationally, they encompass the quest for power, security, and the national interest under anarchy, the call and interplay of common social identities across borders, and the construction and deconstruction of international institutional mechanisms that mitigate conflict and permit cooperation. A framework focused on these dynamics has analytical space for the human agency at the center of political initiative and activism, along with the structural influences that inform and incentivize their decisions. In the coming pages, a focus on Iraq itself will show how this happens.

Plan and Organization

This book follows a thematically guided structure, with an historical account of critical events in Iraq, focused largely—if often implicitly—on the three themes of power, institutions, and identities. These themes point in particular directions and merit emphasis, though they are sufficiently broad in conceptualization to avoid constraining the narrative with an overly rigid formula. Other relevant themes are given due attention as necessary, including, for example, the nature of civil–military relations and changing norms of political violence. Building on this framework, the rest of the book proceeds with a foundational chapter; two chapters devoted to modern, postrevolutionary politics; a chapter on Iraqi international relations; a chapter covering contemporary issues in political economy; and a conclusion.

Accordingly, Chapter 1 focuses on the early, incipient Iraqi state and nation. It acknowledges the community's ancient origins in Mesopotamia, but emphasizes the period from Britain's post–First World War mandate to Iraq's formal independence in 1932 and the eventual July 1958 revolution. Drawing on the comparative political concepts of state formation and state-building, it delineates the establishment of Iraq's coercive, administrative, lawmaking, and extractive institutions in all their variability and occasional dysfunctionality in the country's first few decades. The energetic but foreign-born founding king, Faisal I, oversaw the creation of the first state institutions, as well as efforts to reconfigure Iraqi politics around a national sense of community. He had very limited success and struggled, as a weakly empowered monarch, with the new country's divergent social groups and political players, including British authorities. In effect, in these early years, the Iraqi state and nation had yet to be created. As King Faisal declared in a confidential memo, there was "no Iraqi people but unimaginable masses of human beings, devoid of any patriotic idea, imbued with religious traditions and absurdities, connected by no common tie, giving ear to evil, prone to anarchy and perpetually ready to rise against any government whatever."[7]

Faisal's early death in 1933 left Iraq in the hands of a less capable son, Ghazi, along with a series of ambitious civilian and military leaders with their own ideas and interests. State coercive institutions developed all too fully, as army Colonel Bakr Sidqi launched Iraq's first military coup in 1936, and the Second World War drew the Rashid Ali government into a confrontation with Britain. With Ghazi having died in a car crash before the war and the Regent Abd al-Ilah managing the crown, civilian politicians regained influence but had little latitude in governance. A postwar respite proved short-lived, as pro-British, eight-time Prime Minister Nuri al-Sa'id proved unwilling to cultivate democratic institutions, while Nasserist-inspired Free Officers organized underground. The July 1958 revolution seemed to offer a fresh start, but powerful, mobilized groups of nationalists, Ba'athists, and communists were ready to take advantage of Iraqi institutional weakness and communal incoherence.

Chapter 2 examines key events, junctures, and trends in national-level politics from 1958 to the end of the war with Iran in 1988. It starts with the pivotal few years after the July revolution led by Abd al-Karim Qasim, whose plans were undone by his incapacity to manage the wildly disparate political forces mobilized by the revolution. Qasim was a contradictory figure. He had inclusive instincts regarding the national community and permitted some liberalization of the artistic and scholarly domains, such as the continued operation of an American-style academic institution, al-Hikma University. Yet, he also became fully dictatorial and isolated when facing almost immediate threats and challenges from across the political spectrum, attempting but failing to balance them against each other. An ensuing February 1963 coup was orchestrated by a mixed group of Ba'athists and their military allies, who ousted Qasim and then squabbled and turned on each other. This prompted a November 1963 takeover by the Arif brothers and nearly five years of military rule, which only served to harden authoritarian tendencies, extend patronage networks, and establish a transactional basis for political loyalty.

The eventual result was a July 1968 Ba'athist coup, which installed a more durable regime under Ahmed Hassan al-Bakr and his young but ambitious lieutenant, Saddam Hussein. Saddam found myriad ways to consolidate his own position, shape oil and Kurdish policy, expand state security institutions, and cultivate an extensive kinship-based patronage system. He had organizational talent, cunning political skills, close family and tribal ties, and a carefully managed patronage network, all of which allowed him to defend against numerous regime threats and eliminate his enemies. Saddam sent Bakr into retirement and claimed the presidency in 1979, building a fearsome *mukhabarat* state that included a powerful domestic security apparatus, near-totalitarian demands on the population, and a cult of personality. Fearful that revolutionary Iran would move Iraq's Shi'a to rebellion, Saddam's regime soon launched a defensive and opportunistic invasion of its neighbor. The war quickly drained Iraq's newfound national wealth and descended into a long war of attrition that ended in a bitter stalemate in 1988.

Chapter 3 addresses domestic politics in the remaining period from 1989 to the present. It starts after the Iran–Iraq War, with the fleeting window of opportunity to reassess, rebuild, and turn the page. Facing mounting domestic and international pressures, Saddam missed the opening and elected to launch a new, disastrous foray into neighboring Kuwait. Despite a trouncing at the hands of a U.S.-led international coalition, the regime survived, only to face intensifying international sanctions targeting its WMD programs, along with episodic troubles from domestic and international opponents. Saddam himself did not seem to be long for this world, but he muddled through the 1990s, having coup-proofed the regime by narrowing its support base and relying heavily on extended family, kinsmen, and close associates. Iraq overall did not fare well and was hollowed out in this period by the twin pressures of international sanctions and brutal authoritarianism.

The regime's success at surviving came to an abrupt end after a six-week invasion launched by the United States in 2003. This was followed by an American occupation, weak and largely incompetent temporary governance by the U.S. Coalition Provisional Authority (CPA), and a set of more permanent domestic transformations wrought by slow institution-building in the face of an insurgency and quasi-civil war. Iraq held parliamentary elections in 2005 and then witnessed a period of restored sovereignty, state reassertion, and a shift toward sectarian rule under Prime Minister Nouri al-Maliki. A long-time Shi'a activist and Da'wa party leader, Maliki managed to stay at the helm through the 2010 elections—which his party technically lost—until an additional defeat at the polls in 2014, and, more importantly, an invasion from Islamic State forces rendered his continued tenure impossible. Subsequent events included the temporary loss of control over 40% of Iraq's territory during the Islamic State's military campaign from 2014 to 2017; further national elections in 2018 and 2021; and more recent civil discontent and turmoil associated with the *Tishreen* protest movement.

While the first few chapters, by necessity, reference the many foreign influences on Iraqi national politics, Chapter 4 is devoted more directly to Iraqi international relations. It starts with the early years under British dominance and ranges through the revolution and Abd al-Karim Qasim's threat to Kuwait, followed by the oil-induced transformations of the 1970s and the subsequent three decades of intense conflict with neighboring states and the international community. The chapter devotes special attention to two seminal contemporary events: Iraq's invasion of Kuwait in August 1990, and the American invasion of Iraq in March 2003. Theoretical insights from a range of perspectives shed light on these developments, including the power of ideas to shape state action and the importance of regime survival calculations. Saddam's decisions vis-à-vis Iran, Kuwait, and international sanctions and inspections had substantial domestic determinants. While it can be difficult to distinguish underlying causes from precipitating events, attention to both in Iraq's case—as well as leadership analysis—shows that Saddam's only priority was remaining in power.[8]

The latter part of Chapter 4 reviews Iraqi foreign relations after it regained sovereignty in 2004. Its initial efforts to reengage with the Arab world had mixed success, as most countries had relatively little to gain from a close relationship with Baghdad, along with residual concerns about Iraq's past and potential future role in the Middle East. Instability from multiple sources—terrorism, domestic insurgents, the pressures of the Arab Spring, the Islamic State—also made it harder for Iraq to put its foreign relations back on track. It made eventual progress in the Arab world, and it also sought to improve its complex and fraught relationships with the non-Arab states of Turkey and especially Iran, though it remained steadfast in its opposition to normalization with Israel. No longer the object of international sanctions or weapons inspections, Iraq engaged with the European powers, especially France, Britain, and Germany, as well as newly significant international powers like Russia, China, and India, which served as hedges against an overreliance on the United States and Europe.

Chapter 5 steps back to take a wider look at contemporary Iraq from the perspective of political economy. The first half summarizes the core features of Iraq's economy and resource endowments, along with a set of important demographic and social factors like population growth, gender inequality, sectarianism, and the ethnic divide. It also offers comparisons to other MENA states to contextualize Iraq's position in the region. Importantly, Iraq is potentially dominant among the Arab states, due to a combination of factors that include its relatively large population, geographic size, oil reserves, and gross domestic product. At the same time, it faces political and economic challenges from Iran, Turkey, and Israel. Domestically, while Iraq's ethnic and sectarian divides have gained much attention over the years, its fast-growing and exceptionally youthful population is a major looming challenge. The country has doubled in population since the late 1990s, and it now has a median age of 21, which is roughly half that of the European and American medians and a decade younger than those of neighboring Turkey, Iran, and Saudi Arabia.

None of these young people remember Saddam Hussein, and all of them will make demands as well as contributions, both political and economic. The remainder of the chapter focuses on several major features of the Iraqi political economy that might be available to address their needs and the country's broader prospects. These include oil and external rents, industrial development, Tigris and Euphrates River resources, agriculture, international trade, labor migration, earnings remittances, and foreign assistance. Like the earlier chapters, Chapter 5 follows a thematic track, emphasizing the dynamic, reciprocal influence of politics and economics in contemporary Iraq, where having almost 10% of the world's proven oil reserves has not translated into corresponding developmental gains. It might still do so, depending in large part on the country's capacity to make simultaneous progress in the political, economic, and social domains.

The Conclusion offers several general observations about Iraqi political life. Iraq faces what might be called a "middle-state dilemma," due mainly to its regional position. Attention to this dilemma, and the incentives and temptations it generates in foreign policy, is a useful counterpoint to the excessive analytical personalization common in studies of Iraqi international relations. Relatedly, Iraq's remarkable oil endowment has obvious benefits and a seemingly unavoidable set of potential costs in enabling regionally destabilizing behavior. The ongoing energy transition from fossil fuels is not likely to remedy oil's impact on Iraq, for better or worse, though there is nothing inherent in the natural resource itself that obligates states to misuse their endowments. More generally, to manage the host of political challenges associated with oil, development, and foreign policy, Iraq has a new, quasi-democratic set of institutions at its disposal—if it can keep them. A problematic ethnosectarian power-sharing arrangement in the electoral system, however, has failed to deliver broadly satisfactory results so far, replicating earlier patterns of elite dominance and patronage politics.

Failure in the governance domain is likely to affect all other areas of Iraqi life, demonstrating how deficiencies in Iraqi state formation and nation-building have been difficult to escape in the contemporary era. Still-normalized patronage politics, long-time military politicization, and persistent ethnosectarian mobilization and violence are hard to leave behind. That said, the book concludes by emphasizing Iraq's relative success in surviving as a polity, perhaps against the odds, into the twenty-first century, with a high likelihood that it will remain an important actor in the MENA region for years to come. Other than Kurdish nationalists and residual Islamist militants, few if any major domestic or international parties are interested in challenging Iraq's place in a world of national states. Now more than a hundred years old and having survived several extraordinary ordeals, Iraq is likely to persist well into the future.

Notes

1 Waltz (1959).
2 Lukes (2021); Baldwin (2016); Gaventa (1982).
3 Rhodes et al. (2006).
4 North (1990); Mahoney (2000).
5 Telhami and Barnett (2002).
6 Durkheim (1964), 60.
7 Batatu (1978), 25.
8 On the social science challenges, see Przeworski (1991), 97.

1
STATE FORMATION, 1914–1958

The first modern humans evolved from their predecessors over 200,000 years ago, eventually migrating from Africa to Asia, the Middle East, Europe, and beyond. Archeological sites like Shanidar Cave in Kurdistan contain skeletal evidence of a human presence there 35,000–65,000 years ago.[1] Iraq itself emerged as a distinctive place more than 5000 years ago, with the rise of permanent settled communities on the flat, alluvial floodplain of the Tigris and Euphrates Rivers. These communities came into existence during the prehistoric Neolithic period, when nomadic hunter-gatherers descended from the northern mountains and foothills of Asia Minor following the river systems flowing to the southeast. The rivers provided abundant water and fertile soil for year-round cultivation beyond the immediate needs of local populations. This allowed for the accumulation of food reserves, which contributed to population growth, urbanization, economic diversification, social stratification, legal and institutional innovation, and what eventually would be known as civilization.

These early developments occurred both in parallel and sequentially in only a few places on earth, mostly a function of fundamental geographic and material conditions that created the opportunities and incentives driving major changes. The Tigris and Euphrates thereby have an originating significance comparable to the Nile, Yellow, and Indus Rivers, which produced the storied civilizations of Egypt, China, and India. Their settlements were among humanity's first large gatherings of people. The earliest communities did not have significant political reach across extensive territory, in no way resembling the national-scale territorial states of the world in later millennia. But as distinct entities, with substantial populations, agricultural development, and new forms of governance, they constitute direct and significant precursors to what was to come. Ancient Ubaid, Uruk, Sumer, Akkad, Babylon, Nineveh, and Assyria were the initial kernels of the polities and societies established in what eventually would be called Mesopotamia, much of which was brought together to form Iraq thousands of years later.[2]

Iraq's earliest history is deeply consequential in several areas that have been profoundly important to the world. These include significant contributions to an array of human achievements, including the beginning of agriculture, the invention of new technology like the wheel, the creation of writing systems permitting the accumulation of knowledge, the establishment of the rule of law, the advancement of mathematics and astronomy, and the organization of military forces.[3] Ancient Iraqis did not invent sliced bread, but almost: bread itself was first made by the Natufians in nearby contemporary eastern Jordan, spreading eventually to what was then Mesopotamia.[4] As one of the "cradles of civilization" on par with just a few others, it left a mark on the entire world, in addition to having consequences for modern politics and society.

Aside from the fact that modern Iraqis descend from ancient peoples who were major early contributors to human progress, a vital legacy of this long history lies in the realm of the political and social imagination. Even if their world has been wholly transformed over the millennia, Iraqis in the twenty-first century have a communal self-awareness of vastly long ties to a specific piece of territory, something that does not exist in most of the world. In a manner not too different from how modern Egyptians refer to Egypt as *Umm al-Dunya*, or "Mother of the Earth," many contemporary Iraqis have at least some awareness of their connection to ancient Iraq.[5] Over the millennia, this connection has been established, affirmed, all but erased, and reconstituted by political authorities many times. It is available for mobilization and deployment by contemporary leaders, as Saddam Hussein discovered in the late 1960s when he began using Iraq's ancient Mesopotamian identity as a basis for national community-building.[6]

What matters most about the Iraqi past, therefore, is that it is not past—it remains in people's minds, and its legacies shape their behavior today. Some of the oldest communal remnants of the distant past still provide a basis for group affinity, as well as a source of resentment and hostility. Iraq's small but distinctive and self-aware Assyrian community, for example, originated nearly 5000 years ago in ancient Mesopotamia but endured through the years and was caught up in the rough and tumble of Iraqi politics in the early 1930s, when it rebelled and was repressed with great brutality by the fledgling Iraqi military.[7] More recently, the Assyrians were given a seat on the Iraqi Governing Council in June 2003 and were targeted specifically by invading Islamic State forces from 2014 to 2016. In all these dynamics, it is not that Iraqis or other Middle Easterners have unusually long memories or dwell unnecessarily on the past. It is that the region itself has an unmistakably long if sometimes tumultuous history, and that history is still impactful to this day.

History's importance notwithstanding, it is not necessary to give equal and uniform consideration to the long train of events in the territory over several thousand years. This chapter instead focuses on the twin processes of Iraqi state formation and national development, highlighting the most consequential political, communal, and institutional changes that have occurred over many years in the country's unfolding history. It emphasizes the recurring pursuit of power, the transformed institutional contexts in the territory, and the changing nature of social and political identity. Taking independent Iraq's establishment by Great Britain as a point of departure, it examines the creation and evolution of new state institutions, along with the construction of a shared sense of national identity beginning in the 1920s and continuing to today. In addressing both the institutional and communal aspects of Iraqi development, the chapter shows how Iraqi leaders pursued these dual tasks, doing so in a complex and challenging regional environment. After a brief conceptual discussion of state formation and nation-building, the chapter begins with the Britain's establishment of a mandate after the First World War and follows a thematically guided chronological order.

State Formation and Nation-Building

We live in a world of national states, an institutional model created mostly by Europeans and exported over time through colonial and imperial expansion, along with political emulation.[8] Modern state formation itself is the process of creating, consolidating, and extending a state, or an organization of legitimate domination over a population, in a given territory. It is an historical process, taking decades if not centuries. State formation in Europe entailed local and national actors engaging each other over time, with this interaction leading to the creation of a larger, more organized, centralized political authority. Whether in its original Weberian form in Europe or in newer versions elsewhere, state formation tends to be violent, lengthy, and costly. It typically involves establishing a definition of political authority that differs from what already exists, and it entails a struggle for internal control, political unification, and external security. Further interrelated elements include the consolidation of political power, the establishment of a unified legal system, the achievement of territorial contiguity, the propagation of legitimacy doctrines, and the creation and maintenance of coalitions of domestic support for the state.[9]

State formation affects everything from political institutions and economic development to social organization and the cultural landscape. It changes relationships and transforms identities in ways only achievable by large-scale human processes, for better or worse.[10] In the political domain, for example, without a functioning state, there can be no unified, national-scale government authority, much less a democracy, since state institutions provide the foundation for all such political activity.[11] When a state is only nominally real and is limited to formal, juridical recognition but has no matching empirical capacity, political instability is highly likely. This might occur when state boundaries are established by external powers, when rulers are installed by outside actors, or when institutions are created by actors beyond the immediate political ecosystem. War-making and state formation are organically connected, but in most cases, domestic actors must drive the process for the result to be durable.[12]

For Iraq, the most important era in the initial creation of the modern state was during and just after the First World War, when the European powers, especially

14 State Formation, 1914–1958

Britain, established Iraq's formal borders, gave it a new kind of coherence as a monarchy, and granted it a measure of independence. Most of the initial upheaval and violence in its early state formation, before its declaration as a new mandate, occurred between British and Ottoman military forces—both outsiders to the heart of the MENA region. The British were a colonizing power and, in fact, delegated most of the fighting to the British Indian Army, with troops largely from the South Asian subcontinent. Even a good number of the earliest bureaucrats of Iraq were drawn from India. The Ottomans, for their part, had Arab officers, but the latter were not typically in the uppermost ranks. In short, the major antagonists in the Mesopotamian campaign of the First World War were Indian soldiers fighting Ottoman Turks, a conflict that led the winner to establish an institution—a fledgling national state—reflecting its own understanding of the best political order for the territory. Iraqis themselves had little to do with it.

Despite the British victory, this dynamic did not even remotely resemble European state formation or have the same effect on Iraq as events in the European context had in various states. It was a much faster process in terms of timescale, with a great deal happening in the ten years from 1914 to 1924 alone. It was a much more internationalized process, involving not only the European powers but also countries from as far afield as Russia and even the United States—via Wilsonian notions of self-determination and the League of Nations. And it was mostly dedicated to developing the formal, juridical, externally oriented attributes of the state rather than its substantive, empirical, and internally capable institutions. While Iraq's rich history complicates the social context in which modern state formation and statebuilding occurred, the Iraqi state itself is a modern, twentieth-century creation of British colonial authorities. Whether it would evolve into something lasting was an open question at the time.

The MENA regional environment in Iraq's early decades was quickly evolving and intensely interactive, as more than a dozen newly independent political entities came into being through a variety of paths. Some were established in processes that paralleled aspects of Iraq's experience, with countries like Transjordan, Syria, and Lebanon created almost out of whole cloth and shaped to accommodate the ideas, needs, and preferences of the colonial powers. Others resulted from vicious struggles between contending nationalist movements, as was the case in Israel and Palestine, each following their own distinctive trajectories but only one emerging successfully. Some states had deep roots but were led by nationalist movements that needed to assert themselves to obtain actual or truer independence: Egypt and the North African countries of Morocco, Algeria, Tunisia, and Libya, with Algeria waging a war of national liberation. A few did not gain full independence for decades, until postwar sovereignty norms made remaining outside the club of states undesirable: the UAE, Bahrain, Qatar, and even Kuwait. Saudi Arabia emerged from conquest and the rising dominance of the Al Sa'ud, joined to a conservative social movement led by Wahabi Islamists. The larger, non-Arab states of Iran and Turkey had their own massive upheaval and travails. Iraq's experience was intimately connected to the rest of the region but had idiosyncrasies that merit elaboration.

British Conquest and Occupation

Great Britain launched the Mesopotamian campaign in November 1914, shortly after the start of the First World War. It already had dispatched a small force to protect an important new oil refinery in nearby Abadan, Iran, at the outset of hostilities in the Great War. The campaign itself marked the start of a four-year military venture and more than four decades of active engagement in a region it had come to see as vital to its global interests. After a short naval bombardment of the old, Ottoman-held fortress on the Fao peninsula, the Sixth (Poona) Division of the Indian Expeditionary Force D (IEFD) landed there on November 6, 1914. It was telling and consequential that invading British troops were mostly part of the vast British Indian Army, organized and directed at the outset by the India Office and under the command of expatriate British officers. The IEFD pushed back the small Ottoman force and moved up the *Shatt al-Arab* waterway to safeguard British oil facilities at Basra within a few short weeks. The campaign had begun, along with all it portended for the region and its people.[13]

For nearly 400 years, Ottoman Iraq had been a relatively low priority for Istanbul, only loosely controlled via a fluctuating series of local authorities or proxies traversing several provinces and administrative units.[14] In fact, imperial authority and territorial control had become more rigid and formalized after the modernizing reforms of the Tanzimat period in the nineteenth century, which were designed to address both internal and external threats to the Empire by building stronger identities, more capable institutions, and enhanced state power. Even more consequentially for the MENA region, the Ottomans had joined Imperial Germany in beginning work on the Baghdad Railway, part of a larger effort to link Berlin to Istanbul, and Istanbul to Baghdad. This rail connection was to extend eventually to Basra and a new port to be constructed on the Persian Gulf. All told, this would provide Germany with improved access to suspected oil reserves in Ottoman Iraq, along with a way to circumvent the British-controlled Suez Canal. The Ottomans hoped to strengthen their hold on the Arabian Peninsula and reassert themselves in the region, situating there the headquarters of the Sixth Army Corps. This effort to connect Istanbul to Baghdad and beyond became part of a series of transformative challenges and responses that affected both the MENA region itself, already restive with a percolating sense of shifting identities, and the larger geostrategic concerns of the major imperial powers of Britain, France, Germany, and Russia.

Britain, for its part, viewed the region through the interrelated lenses of India, oil, and great power rivalry. Its first priority was defending and maintaining British India, and for this it dispatched troops and colonial administrators from India itself, imbued with an unreconstructed White Man's Burden mentality. Its abiding interest in India, however, was accompanied by a need to protect its rapidly emerging oil interests while defending its regional position in Persia against possible incursion by Czarist Russia. British attention to the possibilities of Persian oil began at the turn-of-the-century Paris Exhibition in 1901, when Antoine Ketābči Khan, Persia's representative at the exhibition, began soliciting European investment in a Persian oil concession. Ketābči met British entrepreneur and investor William Knox D'Arcy, who traveled to Tehran in April 1901 to begin negotiations with the government of Mozaffar al-Din Shah, which led to a 60-year oil concession in May 1901.

D'Arcy's subsequent exploration efforts on the ground teetered on the brink of failure, but critical investment from Burma Oil and a shift in location to southwestern Persia at Maidan-e-Naftan led to a breakthrough discovery in late May 1908. The discovery saved the failing Anglo-Persian Oil Company, which went public in April 1909. Lord of the Admiralty Winston Churchill's decision to convert the British Navy's warships from coal- to oil-burning engines in June 1913 required the securing of reliable oil sources. Oil, it was now evident, was available in Persia and, in all likelihood, in Ottoman Iraq.[15] At Churchill's prompting, Britain acquired majority holdings in the Anglo-Persian Oil Company, a move that was presented to the House of Commons in June 1914 and formalized in August 1914, just at the start of the First World War.[16] Oil interests were not a fundamental cause of the First World War, but the war's impact on the mechanization and industrialization of warfare made oil a critical strategic asset from then on.

Britain therefore sent troops to Abadan and up the Fao peninsula in November 1914, committing itself to a substantially expanded regional role and challenging Ottoman dominance both directly and militarily. It henceforth would not ignore any potential threats or give any thought to the interests, identities, or future aspirations of the MENA region's inhabitants. Inherent in this initiative, moreover, was the likelihood that defeating its Ottoman rival would undermine a longstanding if loosely defined imperial order that had prevailed in much of the Middle East and North Africa. Ottoman imperial arrangements—a set of power relations, institutions, and associated identities—would be replaced by a system and array of national states in the region. It is not without irony that the latter system of national states in the MENA region was to become wholly inconsistent with long-term British colonial or imperial control. Britain, the imperial change agent, was also Britain, the target of newly energized national challengers.

The Mesopotamian campaign itself proved long and difficult. After the landing on Fao, the IEFD made a rapid initial advance up the Tigris and through Ottoman-held territory to Basra and Qurna in 1914, before being bogged down by stronger resistance from the Iraq Area Command of the Ottoman Army. From 1915 onward, despite a series of command changes, military reorganizations, and multiple initiatives by both sides, the Mesopotamian campaign proceeded slowly and painfully, not substantially unlike the rest of the war in Europe. It was not a minor set of skirmishes. The campaign involved hundreds of thousands of combatants; cost tens of thousands of lives; saw the introduction of air, artillery, and armored elements; and lasted nearly four years. It included, among others, battles at Shaiba in April 1915, Nasiriyya in July 1915, Ctesiphon a few months later in November 1915, and a long siege of British forces at Kut from December 1915 to April 1916. After a major initiative to retrain, reequip, and reconfigure its leadership, British forces finally took Baghdad, setting out in January and reaching the city by March 1917.

This success was followed by final efforts in October 1918 to consolidate its position ahead of an impending armistice.[17]

Tellingly, a majority of the fighting forces on both sides were not indigenous to the region: Ottoman Turkish troops fought a range of Indian units under British command. On the British side, the India Office and Indian Army were largely responsible in the early years of the campaign, owing to the extent to which British planners linked concerns about Ottoman Iraq to the defense of India, including keeping a wary eye on Indian Muslim popular opinion. For the Ottomans, the Fourth Army did most of the fighting, as one of the Empire's major military formations, having been constituted in the mid-nineteenth century under Ottoman military reforms. While its XII Corps included troops from Syria and Palestine, the defenders of the Empire hailed from all over the MENA region and beyond, including commanders like the Bulgarian-born Fakhri Pasha. There was nominal involvement by Shi'i Arab tribesmen pledged to the Ottoman Empire, but their numbers were few, their impact on the course of the campaign was limited, and their loyalties shifted by the end of the war, as it became clear that the Ottomans would not prevail.

Fighting in Mesopotamia ended with Ottoman agreement to the Armistice of Mudros in October 1918, which required the surrender to Allied troops of all Ottoman garrisons outside Anatolia. British ground forces from the Indian Cavalry Brigade took advantage of the cessation of hostilities to extend Britain's de facto control to Mosul in November 1918, despite howls of protest from the Ottoman governor, who noted that Mosul was neither part of Mesopotamia nor subject to the withdrawal provisions of the Armistice. It was a fateful move, and the governor's assertion went unheeded because Mosul was prized not only for its oil but also as an entrée to the north and—given the region's geography—as a strategic necessity for defending the low-lying territory of the Tigris–Euphrates valley to the south. Later efforts by French authorities to keep Mosul out of the British orbit proved fruitless.[18]

From Mandate to Uprising

With the Ottoman territory in hand, Britain and the Allies reached further armistices in Europe and proceeded to the Paris Peace Conference meetings of 1919 and 1920, signing the Treaty of Versailles ending the First World War in June 1919. They also convened an additional, parallel series of separate meetings and peace conferences with the other Central Powers, first in San Remo, Italy, in April 1920. San Remo was most noteworthy for marking the beginning of the formal dismemberment of non-Turkish Ottoman territories, which were parceled out to the winning powers largely in accordance with a secret framework reached previously by Britain and France under the Sykes–Picot agreement of 1916, which had started the process of dividing up anticipated postwar territorial gains. San Remo issued a resolution under the auspices of the newly constituted League of Nations, which allocated to Britain under Article 22 certain Class "A" mandates to administer what were, at the time, the imprecisely defined Ottoman territories of "Mesopotamia" and "Palestine." France gained control of the mandates of "Syria" and "Lebanon."[19]

Shortly thereafter, on August 10, 1920, the Treaty of Sèvres gave away large parts of the Ottoman Empire to Britain, France, Italy, and Greece, also including provisions for a Kurdish state of sorts. Sèvres itself proved untenable, with even harsher conditions imposed on the Ottomans than those dealt to Germany at Versailles. It sparked immediate Turkish nationalist opposition and mobilization, led by Mustafa Kemal, and helped to prompt a Turkish war of independence in Anatolia to accompany the collapse of the Ottoman Empire. The war and all its associated upheaval and violence was a complex, prolonged, and multifaceted affair on several fronts, as it pitted Turkish nationalists against the European powers and a fledgling, short-lived Republic of Armenia. It accompanied the abolition of the Ottoman Sultanate and ushered in the birth of the secular, ethnonationalist Turkish state, though it also was implicated in the Armenian Genocide. As the former metropolitan core of the Ottoman Empire, modern Turkey emerged from the wreckage of the First World War better positioned than its smaller, less unified, provincial counterpart in Ottoman Iraq, which pursued somewhat similar objectives in the form of an independent national existence but lacked the wherewithal to achieve them.

Even before the Mesopotamian campaign and the First World War ended, both popular and elite sentiment in Ottoman Iraq had shifted in favor of independence. Activists created a number of organizations and clandestine societies to mobilize various segments of the population and press demands for independence in the Ottoman territories. These groups included the secretive Guardians of Independence (*Haras al-Istiqlal*), which formed after British authorities denied Iraqis an opportunity to attend the Versailles peace conference and called for the establishment of a democratic constitutional monarchy. Shi'i *'ulama*, like the Ayatollah Muhammad Taqi al-Shirazi, issued a *fatwa* rejecting service in any British-run administration under the auspices of the newly conceived but widely distrusted Mandate for Mesopotamia. The Mandate was seen as colonial rule by another name despite British claims that it was intended as a mutually beneficial compromise. Iraqis were having none of it, finding the idea patronizing and dismissive of their capacities.

While there was no unified Iraqi national sense of self at this moment, Iraqis had little interest in swapping one imperial overlord for another or being guided to eventual independence by yet another outsider. The abiding skepticism about British rule was also fueled by Britain's obvious reliance on an outmoded India model, both informally in its thinking and materially in how it constructed its colonial arrangements. Britain deployed administrators from the India Office and displayed a White Man's Burden mentality that flew in the face of new Wilsonian ideas about self-determination. It replaced Ottoman-era rules and laws, dismissed any Arab capacity for self-government, denied Iraqis leadership positions, and placed Indians in key roles in the army and police.[20] It even designated the Indian rupee as the country's fiat currency. From the Iraqi perspective, Britain was creating a colony out of another colony.

Britain's relative success in organizing India's institutions may have led it to underestimate the challenge of doing much the same in Iraq. India, after all, from the British perspective, was much larger and more socially diverse than Iraq, with incomparable linguistic and even religious heterogeneity compared to the seemingly lesser incompatibilities in Iraq. Officials in British India seconded to Iraq might have presumed the task would be easier in the former Ottoman territories, accustomed as they were to an outsider presence. This presumption might have influenced initial British decision-making, including its willingness to add Mosul and the Kurdish north to a newly constructed Iraqi state in the early 1920s and to grant Iraq independence under an artificial but functioning monarchy by the early 1930s. Then again, Britain's 1947 partition of India and Pakistan emanated from a realization that some social schisms were too profound, at least in certain political contexts, to be managed so easily. But this was years after Iraq was already set on its course.[21]

The result was the Great Uprising of 1920, a critical early episode in Iraqi state and national development, both institutionally and in nationalist thought and mythology. Shortly after San Remo ended and word got out that Iraq would not be granted independence, opposition groups coalesced and mobilized, including nationalists, Shi'i *'ulama*, and disaffected tribal leaders, who gathered in May 1920. Shi'i tribes in the mid-Euphrates valley began the actual rebellion in June, triggered partly by the heavy-handed arrest of Ayatollah Shirazi's son for a refusal to pay taxes. The revolt spread along the valley in short order and gained Sunni support, especially in the form of religious declarations by the *'ulama*, though it remained relatively disorganized and decentralized, and it was waged mostly in the countryside but not particularly in the cities. Using field artillery and the recently elevated Mesopotamian Group of the Royal Air Force to lower the financial cost, the British were able to put the revolt down by October. Still, the human toll was striking: 6000 Iraqi dead, along with 500 British and Indian soldiers.[22]

While relatively brief, the revolt was not without consequences. Aside from the lessons it taught Iraqis about the significance of military power, it eventually dissuaded Britain from maintaining the formal mandate it had been awarded by the League of Nations at San Remo in April. In this sense, it helped to shift the British approach from a strategy of direct rule to indirect control via an indigenous governing structure. While initially and somewhat incongruously Britain continued to pursue colonial domination in the region by signing the Treaty of Sèvres in the middle of the Uprising, events on the ground led Britain to conclude that direct rule under a mandate was not tenable and prompted it to search for alternatives. The cost in manpower and treasure was too high, especially when it could get what it wanted—mostly oil and geostrategic position—more cheaply through another mechanism.

The Sharifian Solution

As a result, Sir Percy Cox was dispatched to Baghdad in October 1920 as high commissioner and consul general, replacing acting Civil Commissioner for Mesopotamia Captain Arnold T. Wilson and tasked with the assignment of creating a unified monarchy. Toward this end, in March 1921, the new Colonial Secretary Winston Churchill convened a vitally important conference in Cairo to address the disposition of all of Britain's holdings in the MENA region, including Mesopotamia. Attendees included Churchill, other British officials like Sir Percy Cox, the now-famous Arab Revolt organizer T. E. Lawrence, the equally influential and colorful Oriental Secretary Gertrude Bell, a handful of military service chiefs, and the future Iraqi Prime Minister Ja'far al-Askari. In the end, Churchill opted at the Cairo conference for a version of T. E. Lawrence's Sharifian solution: giving two sons of Hussein bin Ali al-Hashemi, the Sharif of Mecca and leader of the Arab Revolt, nominal control of two Middle Eastern territories. Iraq would become a monarchy and have a king.

Accordingly, High Commissioner Cox first appointed Sayyid Abd al-Rahman al-Kailani to be head of a Council of Ministers under British supervision. Kailani was from an influential, highly esteemed Sunni family of *ashrafs*, descendants of the Prophet Mohammed. He formed a new government body of 21 leading Iraqis from all three former Ottoman provinces, though it was predominantly comprised of Sunni Arabs, plus a few Shi'a and Christians, and one Jewish member. For their role in fighting the Ottomans, the British gave Sunnis—especially the urban elites—most of the prominent positions in what became a self-evidently unbalanced system. A few Kurds managed to enter military service and, in some cases, rose to prominence eventually. To placate Iraqis unhappy with the earlier turn to India Office colonial-style governing structures, the council restored some Ottoman-era administrative units and added municipal councils overseen by Iraqis, with British advisors. Few posts went to Shi'i administrators, who typically had not been included in the Ottoman state and therefore lacked administrative experience. More to the point, the Shi'a were seen as suspect for their role in the Great Uprising and faced a broader British distrust of their political reliability.

Britain's choice of a king for Iraq was a simplifying move, taken to address a complex array of problems and interests. Choosing the sons of Hussein, the Sharif of Mecca, made sense to British planners. One son, Faisal bin al-Hussein al-Hashemi, or Faisal I, was designated to rule Iraq once approved in the country by a national plebiscite, while his older brother, Abdullah bin al-Hussein, was to be installed as the emir of Transjordan. These actions, in conjunction with initiatives to deal with the even thornier issue of Palestine, were intended to protect Britain's strategic interests while meeting its competing and sometimes contradictory obligations to various parties, both in the MENA region and internationally. The British approach was imperial, calculated, arrogant, and to no small extent deceitful, but it accorded with Britain's sense of self and a perceived entitlement to manage its affairs—and those of others—in the way it saw fit.

Eventually, the MENA region would be brimming with monarchies created by British and French colonial authorities. The colonial powers somewhat mistakenly assumed monarchy to be a natural match to the region, but more shrewdly saw it as the most effective institutional form for maintaining postcolonial control from a respectable, even deniable, distance. Most MENA monarchies were not historically rooted or endemic, and the idea of monarchy itself had a vaguely illicit, illegitimate European association that all but doomed them. The only eventual exceptions were those with unusually substantial symbolic, financial, or strategic resources available to protect and perpetuate their rule. Iraq in its early years had none of the wherewithal of its Saudi, Jordanian, or Moroccan counterparts, and a great many liabilities.[23]

For this reason, creating a monarchy in Iraq with Faisal on the throne was a risky and even audacious gambit. Not only did Iraq have no history of monarchy, but Faisal himself had never even been to Iraq, nor did he understand its particular subtleties and challenges. He was born in the mountain town of Ta'if, 50 miles southeast of Mecca, raised in Istanbul, and had spent most of his recent years either in Arabia or in Syria as the head of a small Arab army and pursuing a throne of his own, after his father was declared king of the Hejaz.[24] The previous July of 1920, the French army had removed him from Damascus, where Syrian nationalists had installed him, with British military support, as the head of a self-proclaimed and short-lived Arab Kingdom of Syria, just before France obtained a mandate for Syria and Lebanon at San Remo. Other than among a small number of Iraqis following international events, he was utterly unknown on a popular level in the country itself. Upon hearing the news of his impending arrival, Iraqis tended to be skeptical and resentful of a distant cousin and ousted monarch associated with Britain coming for a second chance at being a king. In fact, he had little in common with most Iraqis. Even his faith, as a minority Sunni Arab, was suspect in the eyes of Iraq's emerging Shi'i majority. He was not unaware of all these obstacles or of the fact that he had little to work with by way of an Iraqi sense of national self.

Nonetheless, Britain expected Faisal, the third son of Hussein, to be a good choice for Iraq, which was sparsely populated in 1920, with only about 3 million people.[25] At age 36, Faisal was an energetic, charismatic, experienced leader, seemingly open to British influence and certainly aware of the precariousness of his position. Given his prior experience in Syria, no doubt he understood the ease with which a new Middle Eastern king might be removed from the throne by a European power. His vulnerability combined with a sense of gratitude and even indebtedness to Britain for their shared success against the Ottomans. He had the support of Percy Cox, Gertrude Bell, and T. E. Lawrence for his contributions to the fight against the Ottomans, and he benefited from their assessment that he would be most successful in uniting Iraq's Sunnis and Shi'a. His close relationship with T. E. Lawrence in particular, developed during the two-year revolt, gave him insight into British thinking. His aristocratic lineage as a Sharifian—a direct descendant of the Prophet Mohammed[26]—and as a son of Hussein, newly enthroned king of the Hejaz, made him as natural a royal as possible in a region where monarchy and royalty had risky connotations.[27] He brought with him a loyal cadre of Sharifian veterans of the Arab Revolt, though this cut both ways, as his Sunni Arab entourage engendered resentment with locally born Iraqis and would come to put nationalist pressure on Faisal to defy Britain in ways that did not seem tenable to the new king.[28]

Shortly after the Cairo conference in March 1921, Britain dispatched Faisal on a countrywide tour to win the acquiescence of the Iraqi people and thereby secure a veneer of legitimacy for his rule. He was introduced at gatherings organized by local officials, who lauded him to relatively small audiences and then asked if there were any objections to his becoming king. Obviously, the decision to install him on the throne had already been made, and typically few if anyone in attendance objected—other than some clear and telling dissent in Kurdistan—because no serious alternative was offered. Participants were instructed to sign loyalty oaths to seal the deal, and the results of this tour eventually were presented to the world as a kind of popular referendum. Faisal was enthroned in Baghdad on August 23, 1921.[29]

The Hashemite Kingdom

The resulting state and monarchy were far from perfect and could easily be characterized as unnatural and arbitrarily constructed. British authorities had assembled modern Iraq out of three former Ottoman provinces centered on Baghdad, Basra, and Mosul. The shared Ottoman origins and relatively close proximity of these provinces did give them commonalities that provided a basis for association.[30] Yet, assembling Iraq was not like gluing together pieces of broken china. In fact, the three united provinces were only under weak Ottoman control by the early twentieth century, and they varied in the nature of their governance. They also differed in their levels of integration into the empire and were not similar in the direction of their orientation to the rest of the world. Given its significance in Arab history, Baghdad not surprisingly looked toward the Arab world. Basra's position at the confluence of the Tigris and Euphrates connected it more naturally to the Persian Gulf. Mosul's northerly location and historical trade routes linked it to the Anatolian peninsula. The ground-level perspectives from Baghdad, Basra, and Mosul were very different from the bird's eye views of the colonial and imperial powers. Nominal control of the territory by an external, culturally distinctive Ottoman power never transformed any of these perspectives or their associated self-conceptions.

Iraq as ultimately constructed, moreover, did not even entirely reflect Ottoman-era borders and boundaries. Substantial geographic spaces beyond the three designated Ottoman provinces were enclosed and included in the modern state, thereby adding a fair amount of non-Ottoman territory to the provinces to create Iraq's final borders in the 1920s. This territory—mostly sparsely populated lands bordering the Arabian Peninsula and Syrian desert—was inhabited by tribal, nomadic, or semi-itinerant Arab populations. Most of the tribes were Shi'i, and they moved seasonally throughout the region. Some of these tribes had staged intermittent rebellions against Ottoman authority, though some also had thrown in with the Ottomans as the changing geopolitical situation warranted. None of the populations enclosed in the new territory saw the state or nation as natural, inevitable political forms designed to help them realize their aspirations or reflect their core identities. Citizenship and all the trappings of the modern national state were alien concepts.[31]

In terms of identities, the establishment of fixed borders locked in place a difficult demographic mix. Iraq's population in 1920 was approximately 3 million.[32] Of that, just over 50% were Shi'i Arabs, compared with 20% Sunni Arabs, 20% mostly Sunni Kurds, and the remaining 10% primarily Christians, Jews, Yazidis, Sabaeans, and Turkmens. None were especially responsive to European-originated norms of sovereignty, territoriality, and state centralization, especially where they were accustomed to Ottoman-era norms of decentralization and looser political control. For this reason, the relatively sudden shift toward an aspiring centralized state engendered great distrust, particularly among the tribes. It did not help that the new state was to be dominated by Sunni urban elites who were privileged by virtue of having been allied to Britain against the Ottomans. In general, this larger additional factor—nonterritorialized populations in what would become the Iraqi space—provided yet another challenge for state- and nation-building in Iraq, as these populations eventually would need incorporation and accommodation.

In general, the early Iraqi state was led by a new king who faced enormous constraints, most immediately in the form of British insistence on formal arrangements to assure its de facto control of matters it deemed essential. Britain's technical status as the mandate power, along with its military presence and its success in putting Faisal on the throne, provided the necessary leverage for it to secure favorable treaty arrangements with Iraq. After brief negotiations, these arrangements took the form of a Treaty of Alliance between Great Britain and Iraq, signed on October 10, 1922.[33] The Anglo–Iraqi Treaty limited Iraqi sovereignty, gave Britain power over military and foreign affairs, and allowed London to staff the Iraqi state bureaucracy, which it did with officials largely seconded from the India Office. Article 3 of the Treaty obligated King Faisal to create an "Organic Law" for Iraq—essentially a new constitution—while stipulating that this new constitution "shall contain nothing contrary to the provisions of the present treaty."[34] This is how Britain transitioned, somewhat improbably, from interested outside power to invading army, to military occupier, to mandate holder in the face of a national rebellion, and then to architect of a new and only nominally independent monarchy.

Early State-Building

Once King Faisal was on the throne and the Anglo–Iraqi Treaty was signed, more substantial state-building could occur. The first order of business was a constituent assembly, or parliament, which was deemed necessary to ratify the treaty and to draft and ratify a new constitution as well. In fact, a Council of Ministers had been in place in Iraq since 1920, with a government headed by Sayyid Abd al-Rahman al-Kailani. But a more formal parliament was necessary to give Iraq at least the trappings of self-government and thereby fulfill Britain's obligations as the nominal mandate power. Elections for the assembly were held over an exceptionally extended time period, between October 24, 1922, and February 25, 1924. The resulting legislative body was less a partner in actual governance with King Faisal than an intermittent challenger and a source of political pressure. It operated frequently in an oppositional mode, with Kailani resigning over King Faisal's enthronement and having serious reservations about the Anglo–Iraqi Treaty. It did provide some political experience for a few young Iraqi political figures who would rise to prominence later.[35]

Internationally, Britain continued to vie with France and other rivals for an advantageous position in the MENA region. The Treaty of Lausanne in July 1923 replaced the Treaty of Sèvres, which was rejected by Mustafa Kemal's reconfigured and newly capable post-Ottoman Turkish state. Lausanne annulled most of Sèvres' harshest provisions and reneged on its commitment to a small, separate, independent Kurdish state. In March 1925, an International Commission of Inquiry set up by the League of Nations established a permanent border with Turkey and awarded Mosul and the surrounding *vilayet* once and for all to Iraq—despite Mosul having a Kurdish majority and a large Turkmen population that would be difficult to assimilate into a national project rooted in an ethnonationalist identity.

No doubt, this moment marked a shift in the prospects for, and the status of, the Kurdish region. It gave Britain colonial control not only of the Ottoman provinces or *vilayets* of Baghdad and Basra and their various *sanjaks*, but also of a territory with closer cultural and historical connections to the north than to the south. It reconceived of Kurdistan as permanently divided, with its northern reaches incorporated into eastern Turkey and most of its southern territory, especially in the Mosul area, integrated de facto into a newly configured Iraq under British control. Most of the Kurdish population from this period onward was fatally divided between the four MENA states of Iraq, Iran, Turkey, and Syria. In each individual state, the Kurdish population was too large to be eliminated or assimilated easily, yet too small compared to the dominant ethnonationalist population to press successfully for independence. The result was a decades-long oscillation between Kurdish national self-assertion and state-led oppression in most of these countries.[36]

France, for its part, relented on its claims to Mosul by 1925, and Russia—now forming the core of the postrevolutionary Soviet Union—was entirely excluded from a direct role in the immediate region, though it had acquired control over neighboring Armenia in 1920 and remained interested in extending its influence southward toward the warm waters of the Persian Gulf. The interwar period brought a complex combination of military exhaustion, social distraction, Allied exhilaration at having achieved a victory, however costly and narrow, and some *schadenfreude* vis-à-vis Germany that would prove deeply destructive in the years ahead. Britain had lost its late nineteenth-century global dominance in monetary and military affairs, though it remained seemingly unaware of the new realities of the twentieth century and strove to retain control of its colonial possessions even when all indications were of the futility of such efforts.

The new Iraqi monarchy's political structure had clear elements of constitutional constraint, though the explicit legal and institutional limitations on King Faisal were quite weak, and his formally designated powers were impressively strong in relation to other state actors as they existed at the moment. Aside from having the full backing of Britain—admittedly a double-edged sword if ever there were one—the new king's powers flowed directly from the constitution of July 10, 1924, as amended in July 1925.[37] The constitution was passed by the constituent assembly with difficulty, but provided the framework for all domestic political activity until 1958, including by establishing a bicameral legislature with an elected lower-house Chamber of Deputies (*Majlis al-Nuwwab*) and an appointed upper-house Senate (*Majlis al-'Ayan*).[38]

The king's authority under the constitution was formally sufficient to enable him to act in many domains and with few limitations, rooting some of his powers in the use of the Royal *Irada* (Will or Command). He had the power to promulgate, confirm, and implement laws. He was permitted to initiate elections and then to convene, suspend, prorogue, or even dissolve parliament. He could issue legally binding commands when parliament was not in session and had discretionary spending authority beyond the normal state budget. The king chose the prime minister, who served at his pleasure and in later years could be dismissed at will.[39] While the constitution gave the Iraqi people sovereignty, it did not let them keep it or 'have the last word,' stating: "The sovereignty of the constitutional Kingdom of Iraq resides in the people. It is a trust confided by them to King Faisal, son of Husain, and to his heirs after him."[40]

This early period of Iraqi state formation put in place new institutions that changed power dynamics and mobilized identities not easily demobilized in the years to come. As strong as the monarchy was vis-à-vis the constituent assembly, the state itself was weak and dependent. Britain retained two airbases at Habbaniya to the west of Baghdad and Shu'aiba near Basra, had unfettered access to key sensitive sites, and, under the terms of the new Anglo–Iraqi Treaty, controlled the training, advising, and equipping of the military. While Iraqi elites concluded after the 1920 revolt that the country needed a stronger capacity to defend itself and established a Royal Military College in July 1921, acquiring genuine defense capability took time. The military itself was headed by Minister of Defense Ja'afar al-Askari, an Ottoman officer from Baghdad who had fought for King Faisal's father, Hussein al-Hashemi, in the Arab Revolt and attended the Cairo conference with Churchill the previous March 1921. Initially, Askari commanded a small force of about 3000 men, including several hundred veterans of the Arab Revolt who had been with Faisal at Damascus. The army attracted relatively few recruits in its first few months because many young Iraqis inclined toward this vocation joined the better-paid British-sponsored force, the Levies.[41] Recruit numbers improved eventually, growing several fold to over 10,000 troops within a few years and then more in short order.[42]

More consequential than recruiting numbers in these early years was the organizational culture, political orientation, and self-defined mission of the new Iraqi military. The military was implicated in ethnosectarian politics from the very beginning, with a Sunni Arab–dominated officer corps and mostly Shi'i recruits among the enlisted.[43] It did attract a small number of Kurds, including future strongman Bakr Sidqi, who, like others, had been an Ottoman-era officer. But these were exceptions to the rule of Sunni privilege, which had begun with the Ottomans for their own reasons, even if this did not translate into support for Sunni Arab independence.[44]

Ideologically, the officer corps was imbued with a strongly nationalist ethos directed against all threats, both foreign and domestic. Its self-definition was more influenced by Kemalism from neighboring Turkey than by norms of strict professionalism or apoliticism that might have emerged from Iraq's brief but intense exposure to British military practices and training. The new Iraqi military saw itself as a political actor and a national defender, not only responsible for the protection of borders from foreign adversaries but also dedicated to the construction of a shared national sense of self, typically defined in pan-Arab terms. Despite all the international threats to Iraq when it came into being, this potentially lethal state institution was directed at domestic politics and the challenges of identity construction in an unformed national community.[45]

As for the new party system, it displayed a contradictory mix of weakness and modest progress, like much else in Iraq. On the one hand, it contained an underdeveloped array of parties, many of which were single-issue-oriented, ideologically incoherent, or directionless compared to their European counterparts.[46] The existing parties were only loosely connected to elections for the constituent assembly and the filling of the office of the prime minister. The assembly was little more than an Ottoman-style collection of notables, who used their positions to protect their individual economic interests. On the other hand, Iraq's early years did witness a growing acceptance of the idea of interparty competition, organized political opposition, and the formal articulation of public policies favored by various groups. Operating in parties and competing in elections provided new political experiences and shifted expectations regarding how to challenge authority, articulate interests, and channel grievances toward peaceful resolution. In what can be read as both a strength and a weakness, Iraq had regular political turnover in its early years—perhaps too much, but better than none at all—with nearly a dozen different prime ministers in the years of the formal British mandate from 1920 to 1932.[47]

Faisal did his best to work with what he had, though he faced tremendous headwinds, not least of which came from communal and institutional weakness. As historian Charles Tripp put it, "He was the sovereign of a state that was itself not sovereign."[48] He did have modest success in establishing the formal institutions of statehood—the army, police, bureaucracy, various government authorities, and the educational system. And Britain found him useful because he was both responsive to British wishes and reasonably effective in getting things done in Iraq. But national community-building in the face of Iraqi social heterogeneity proved wholly elusive and discouraging to the king. As Faisal wrote in 1933, a dozen years after ascending to the throne and with his country at least nominally independent, "there is still—and I say this with a heart full of sorrow—no Iraqi people but unimaginable masses of human beings, devoid of any patriotic idea, imbued with religious traditions and absurdities, connected by no common tie, giving ear to evil, prone to anarchy, and perpetually ready to rise against any government whatever."[49]

Independence under the Hashemite Monarchy

Iraq gained fuller national autonomy on October 3, 1932, when it became the first mandate to be granted independence and membership in the League of Nations, years before the others. The premise of the mandate system, patronizing at best, was that new countries needed time to develop national solidarity, authoritative government, and a well-functioning political system. While Iraq had none of these, the prevailing view was that it was moving in the right direction under King Faisal, and Britain would maintain a measure of control under the terms of the renegotiated Anglo–Iraqi Treaty of November 1930. Even if independence was supposed to usher in a new era for the country, Britain prioritized political order and its strategic interest in oil over democracy, individual rights, or government accountability. Faisal, as the head of a traditionalist monarchy with increasingly viable state institutions and some of the trappings of representative government, was expected to deliver the stability Britain demanded.[50]

But time was not on his side. Faisal's deteriorating health led him to Switzerland for treatment, where he died of a heart ailment on September 8, 1933, at the age of 48.[51] He left the crown and country to his inexperienced 21-year-old son, Ghazi, who was not the steady hand needed. Unlike his father, Ghazi lacked the personal qualities, intelligence, and political skill that had allowed Iraq's first king to make modest headway in building state institutions and drawing people into patronage networks, reorienting them toward the Iraqi state in politically constructive ways. Ghazi despised and resented the British, generally disliked politics, and tended to side with younger, nationalist-minded military officers, resentful of an overbearing older generation that questioned his judgment and political acumen. His weakness and immaturity destabilized political life and contributed to the politicization of the military, with consequences that would last for generations, if not forever in changing Iraq's trajectory.

At the time of Ghazi's ascent to the throne, the Iraqi state and nation did not yet exist for most ordinary Iraqis in an immediate, everyday sense. State- and nation-building were new, elite-dominated political projects, foreign constructs that did not have their attention and loyalty. Most people saw other institutions and identities as more relevant and significant, whether in helpful ways or as potential threats in what continued to be a vaguely anarchic order. Iraq's social landscape was divided between urban dwellers and formidable, geographically dispersed tribes in the rural areas. Kinship was generally as important as any other social cleavage. The urban centers were well established, some having prominent families and commercial connections beyond themselves. The tribes were situated outside every city and controlled travel routes throughout the country, dominating most of the territory under the mandate. Tribal affiliation was still a key identity that could not be ignored and was hard to overestimate in political significance. Tribal outlooks, values, and social mores remained dominant, as did loyalties to extended family and clan more than any form of national identity or state affiliation, even in the cities. The tribes themselves were heavily armed, by one estimate having over 100,000 riflemen on hand in 1933, just after formal independence, compared to government forces several times smaller.[52]

Nonetheless, independence and a new king did mark the beginning of a sea change in Iraqi lives. Most prominently, the growing reach, autonomy, and ambition of the state and its rulers were becoming increasingly evident and, to some, troublesome. The state, for example, finally promulgated a long-sought conscription law in 1934, seeking to extend its authority outward from Baghdad and curb the power of the rural sheikhs. The new law provoked a series of tribal rebellions along the middle Euphrates in the spring of 1935 and into 1936, which were put down definitively in short order. A Yazidi revolt at Mount Sinjar in 1935 and earlier Kurdish uprisings in the north, such as one by Ahmed Barzani in 1931, had met similar fates. While the army could do little to protect the country against external powers like a still-domineering Britain, it was becoming effective at targeting perceived internal adversaries. These included not only the Shi'i tribes and the Kurds but also the Assyrians, who had pressed for political autonomy in August 1933 and were massacred by the hundreds, including in the northern town of Simele in a brief, brutal campaign that made world headlines. The Simele massacre was led by a rising Kurdish-born, British- and Ottoman-trained military officer, Colonel Bakr Sidqi. Sidqi was declared a hero in 1933 and paraded through Baghdad with the prime minister for his success in repressing the Assyrian rebellion.[53]

The larger region was no stranger to upheaval, but political violence came early to newly independent Iraq, driven by a changing political order that rewarded ambition and opportunism on the part of aspiring leaders. Having a stronger state but a weaker monarch created opportunities for new political figures struggling for position in the expanding political terrain. State institutional strength itself was largely a function of the efforts and ambitions of individual personalities, who created organizations to suit their specific purposes, such as independence from Britain or opposition to the monarchy, but which would not prove to be enduring. Such a relatively unstructured, unstable political system favored personalistic politics, as organized groups and aspiring individuals jockeyed for position at the top of a growing set of state institutions. In some cases, these figures orchestrated their rise by taking advantage of Iraq's unformed national community.

As a general matter, state formation almost always includes painful episodes of dominant organized powers taking on social actors in a wide range of areas, such as membership in the national community, loyalty to the state, taxation, conscription, social mores, access to patronage, and resource allocation. In Iraq's case, this was the first time in its independent political life that state–society engagement pitted one major Iraqi actor—the emerging security institutions—against other Iraqis without the involvement of external parties like Britain or the Ottoman Empire. The violent suppression of tribal, sectarian, and ethnic rebellions would persist intermittently for decades thereafter. It would have internal and external dimensions, now more fully in local hands.

The timeframe for this process was both vastly extended and heavily compressed. It was extended in that Iraq, as a settled and identifiable territory, had existed for thousands of years, even if its name and governing authorities changed. It carried the legacies of a long history, including exceptional ethnic and communal diversity. It was compressed, however, in that the country had been under a rapidly changing series of rulers since the early twentieth century: longtime Ottoman rule until 1914, then a contested war zone for a few years, British military occupation until 1921, a formal British mandate for more than a decade after that, and a nominally independent kingdom beginning in 1932. As a result, fundamental questions of state authority, territorial borders, and the bases for national identity were thrown open and left either unresolved or contested. Unsurprisingly, all this uncertainty and upheaval contributed to further political mobilization and activism.

The Sidqi Coup

On October 29, 1936, in the midst of the tumult, Iraq experienced the first coup d'état in the modern Arab world. The event also marked the most substantial and overt involvement of the Iraqi officer corps in national political life. It occurred at a time of rising international pressures from resurgent European military and nationalist competition. While European rivalries echoed in the MENA region, which continued to serve as a battleground for the great powers, it was mostly the actions of Iraq's leadership that precipitated this first turn toward using the state apparatus against itself.

Former Interior Minister and cabinet official Hikmat Sulayman played a central role in orchestrating the coup against Prime Minister Yasin al-Hashimi, especially by convincing Bakr Sidqi to participate.[54] Sidqi had risen to the rank of brigadier general but was serving as commander of the second division in his hometown of Kirkuk. Al-Hashimi's autocratic tendencies were growing, and his cultivation of the police and security services under Interior Minister Rashid Ali al-Gaylani had alienated both young King Ghazi and a range of political figures, including Sulayman and the secular, liberal-minded *Ahali* ("Peoples") association of reformists under Ja'afar Abu al-Timman.[55] The highly ambitious and well-known General Sidqi was persuaded to join the plot, having been denied the position of chief of staff in favor of Prime Minister al-Hashimi's brother, Taha, who was less committed to a strong and modernized military.

The coup itself was mostly bloodless, though General Sidqi did have Defense Minister Ja'afar al-Askari assassinated in the process. Sidqi organized the action with a handful of military and civilian associates, marching on Baghdad after leafleting the city with a proclamation he signed as "Chief of the National Reform Force."[56]

A nervously hesitant King Ghazi met with his advisors at Zuhur Palace and then acquiesced to the coup leaders' demands by asking Sulayman to form a new government, which included liberal *Ahali* reformers like Abu al-Timman. General Sidqi, for his part, chose to serve as military chief of staff, refused a cabinet portfolio, appointed allies to key positions, and established himself as de facto ruler of the regime. Abu al-Timman and his young, reformist associates quickly regretted their actions and resigned within months, soon finding themselves exiled or imprisoned.

The government formed after the Sidqi coup did have limited, superficial promise in its socially diverse leadership, which included Sidqi (a Kurd), Sulayman (a Turkmen), and Abu al-Timman (a Shi'i Arab). More Shi'a were participating in political life than before. The regime's ideological leaning toward an Iraq-centered view of the nation helped to reinforce the country's recognized, if problematic, territorial boundaries and subsume its social cleavages into a more inclusive non-sectarian national identity. Sidqi himself was more interested in building the military than joining forces with other Arab territories or reconfiguring the wider Middle East. He would have preferred fashioning ties to non-Arab countries like Kemalist Turkey and Pahlavi Iran, which seemed to offer successful models for political transformation and economic development.

It did not take long, however, before alienated Arab nationalist military officers took action against Sidqi, who was assassinated in August 1937 as he was passing through Mosul en route to Turkey, less than a year after taking power. While the details remain contested, some observers saw a conspiratorial British hand in the involvement of former Prime Minister Nuri al-Sa'id, who had been ousted from the al-Hashimi cabinet and taken refuge in the British embassy before fleeing to Cairo. Others emphasize the contending nationalist visions of Sidqi and his pan-Arabist counterparts, who had concerns including fears of favoritism toward Kurds in military recruitment.[57] Regardless of motives, both the Sidqi coup and his subsequent removal contributed to an emerging pattern of violence, military intervention, extraconstitutional activity, and personalistic politics.[58]

After eliminating the upstart Sidqi and bringing down the government, a handful of senior military officers—Husain Fawzi, Amin al-'Umari, Salah al-Din al-Sabbagh, Kamil Shabib, 'Aziz Yamulki, and Fahmi Sa'id—were positioned to play dominant roles in political life.[59] These officers were pan-Arabists in how they saw themselves and their country, unmoved by alternative visions of an Iraq-centric national community. Aside from ideological questions, their primary political focus was on developing strong, personally rewarding patronage networks and protecting their positions from the many perceived risks of a weakly institutionalized environment.

Throughout this period, the monarchy had lost the initiative and suffered from diminished authority, having opened the door to military participation in governance. As if to put an exclamation mark on royal aimlessness, a drunken King Ghazi crashed his car into an electric pole and died under suspicious circumstances in early April 1939. His three-year-old son took his place on the throne as Faisal II, though, in accordance with Article 22 of the Constitution, a regent was appointed—26-year-old Prince Abd al-Ilah. The regent was the late King Ghazi's brother-in-law, young Faisal II's uncle, and a son of the former King Ali ibn Hussein of the Hijaz. Abd al-Ilah changed the balance of power between the monarchy, military, Britain, and the political elite. He had a disdainful, condescending view of the Arab nationalists but was indecisive and lacked charisma and political skill. This made it easier for civilian politicians like Nuri al-Sa'id to operate successfully in tandem with senior military commanders. The latter included the four "Golden Square" colonels: Salah al-Din al-Sabbagh, Fahmi Sa'id, Mahmud Salman, and Kamil Shabib. These military figures were on the rise in Iraq.[60]

The Second World War and Rashid Ali Coup

Regional and world events had great consequences for Iraq from the mid-1930s onward, when British repression of the Arab Revolt in Palestine created an additional grievance for Arab nationalists and Baghdad experienced a series of bombings and demonstrations in support of Palestine.[61] The start of the Second World War in September 1939 led Britain to demand that Iraq break ties with Germany and contribute to the war effort, as obligated under Article 4 of the 1930 Anglo–Iraqi Treaty of Alliance. Nuri al-Sa'id, the pro-British prime minister who penned the latter treaty and had been back in office since late 1938, was amenable to complying. He initiated stepped-up censorship, rationing, and the requisitioning of war materiel, though he did not have Iraq declare war on Germany. He was in a delicate position, as the Iraqi military was growing in size and influence. With conscription in place since 1934, troop numbers rose from 20,000 in 1936 to 28,000 in 1939 and 47,000 by 1941.[62] Initially, the military's leadership tolerated supporting Britain and the Allies. This included the Circle of Seven, a powerful clique of pan-Arabist officers.[63] In time, however, British–Iraqi relations became so strained that it divided the cabinet, with the Regent Abd al-Ilah caught between a coalition of assertive and increasingly capable domestic groups and a beleaguered but determined international power.

A British–Iraqi confrontation became more likely in late March 1940, when a strident nationalist, Rashid Ali al-Gaylani, replaced Nuri al-Sa'id as prime minister. Rashid Ali was a lawyer and politician from a distinguished Sunni family, who had previously served as prime minister, interior minister, and first president of the Chamber of Deputies. In returning as prime minister, he resisted wartime cooperation with Britain by not allowing Allied troop transit through the country and refusing to cut ties with Fascist Italy when it entered the war in June 1940. This eventually led Britain to demand his removal, which proved difficult and did not occur until early February 1941 but drove him to begin plotting the regent's demise with his Golden Square military allies.[64] The latter group already had strong anti-British sentiment, was under the influence of German Ambassador Fritz Grobba, and some members may have started cooperating with German intelligence. Their politics were more oppositional to Britain than sympathetic to Nazi Germany, which was an ally of convenience with a shared adversary.[65]

Rashid Ali finally seized power in a coup supported by Salah al-Din al-Sabbagh and the Golden Square colonels on April 1, 1941, deposing Prime Minister Taha al-Hashimi and frightening the Regent Abd al-Ilah into exile. He appointed a new and more pliant regent and proclaiming himself the head of a "National Defense Government." Rashid Ali and his coconspirators believed Britain to be too weak and distracted by the war in Europe to resist forcefully, anticipating a likely Nazi victory in the wake of early German successes and expecting to secure a negotiated British departure from Iraq. British forces were indeed spread thin, and with the United States sitting largely on the sidelines and Stalin's Soviet Union still adhering to a nonaggression pact, Nazi Germany seemed unstoppable.

The Churchill government responded nonetheless in early May 1941 with a month-long campaign, the Anglo–Iraqi War. The main military engagement of the war was the British airbase at Habbaniya, 55 miles west of Baghdad along the Euphrates, to which Rashid Ali had dispatched a substantial Iraqi force to occupy an escarpment overlooking the small squadron stationed there. Britain declared this a violation of the 1930 treaty and an act of war, eventually launching airstrikes on Iraqi forces and driving them from the area. With very limited German and Italian assistance to the Iraqis, British land forces mobilized from India and Transjordan made their way toward Baghdad by late May and were poised to retake the city, prompting the government to collapse. Rashid Ali fled the country and subsequently three of four of the Golden Square colonels were put to death in courts martial. Britain restored the Regent Abd al-Ilah in 1941, but remained in occupation of Iraq until after the Second World War in 1947.[66]

For a short time, British intervention had interrupted the pattern of military dominance in politics, shrinking the size of the Iraqi military by half and permitting a return to civilian rule. It could not, however, entirely eliminate the norms and ideas that had taken hold regarding the potential role of the military in governance and the associated impulse to intervene in politics to achieve desirable outcomes. In fact, its victory may have taught the opposite lesson by demonstrating the efficacy of military force, whether wielded by a domestic player or an international power. Force had become the ultimate arbiter in Iraq when existing political institutions failed to channel individual and group interests and impulses in peaceful directions. At a minimum, the coup demonstrated the changing role of the officer corps, having transitioned from occasional supporter of various political factions to powerful independent actor in its own right. Other parties also performed on the same stage and were coming into their own in this same period.[67]

The Postwar Era

In the short term, the postwar era saw a return to civilian-dominated politics, with the lifting of martial law and relaxation of press censorship, all with palace support. A softer authoritarianism and the redevelopment of party politics created new space for political activism right after the war, as the organized opposition emerged in 1946 under Prime Minister Tawfiq al-Suwaidi. Newly legalized parties like Kamil Chadirchi's left-leaning, *Ahali*-based National Democratic Party (*Hizb al-Watani al-Dimuqrati*) sought socialist reform, while the moderately Arab nationalist Independence Party (*Hizb al-Istiqlal*) set its sights primarily on foreign policy. Small socialist parties formed, at least briefly, though most failed to develop broad appeal beyond intellectuals and notables or to reach and mobilize much of the middle class. While the Iraqi Communist Party (ICP), founded in Baghdad a decade earlier in 1935, did not win government approval, it recruited and organized students, cultivated contacts with the Soviet Union, and created parallel organizations in Kurdistan.[68]

At the same time, rising Arab nationalist sentiment diminished the political salience of sectarian identity, enhanced the integration of the Shi'a, and created political opportunities for national-level Shi'i leaders not seen before. The percentage of Shi'i cabinet members more than doubled in this period compared to what it was during the monarchy's inaugural decade in the 1920s. For the first time, a series of Shi'i politicians occupied the office of the prime minister, starting with Salih Jabr in March 1947, who was the first Shi'a in the position. People paid a little less attention to sectarian identity, as other forms of social and political association rose in prominence to form the basis for mobilization and activism.

This seeming openness and quasi-democratic competition notwithstanding, differences in power, participation, and economic opportunity remained very real across the country. Sunni Arab politicians held a solid majority of seats in the Chamber of Deputies, despite being a smallish minority of perhaps 20% of the Iraqi population. In many locations, Sunni politicians represented majority-Shi'i populations not only in the national chamber but also as the mayors of predominantly Shi'i cities.[69] The postwar economy, for its part, was so damaged that most Iraqis at this time were much worse off than before the war. Rationing, triple-digit inflation, high unemployment, food shortages, stagnant wages, and crop deficiencies hit ordinary Iraqis hard, including workers and salaried employees, with an especially heavy toll in the Kurdish north. This included the Kirkuk area, where the ICP organized a major strike at the Iraq Petroleum Company refinery in July 1946, which was repressed by the Arshad al-Umari government and ended with an unfavorable mix of minor wage concessions and major police brutality.

The challenge of engaging, much less integrating, the Kurdish population had been pushed aside in the previous two decades and was never addressed to any party's satisfaction. Political uncertainty and ambiguity, born of the rapidly changing domestic and international environments, combined unhelpfully with the dispersal of Kurds across state boundaries that were quickly becoming settled into apparent permanence. Politics, geography, and a few colorful personalities together generated a series of on-again, off-again rebellions, false starts, and efforts at achieving Kurdish statehood—or holding on to it, in the case of Mahmud Barzanji's semi-independent entity after the First World War. In the game of Middle Eastern musical chairs, the Kurds seemed badly positioned and out of luck, with a recurring pattern of disappointment followed by rebellion, leading to partial if temporary and grudging accommodation and an eventual renewal of conflict and, against the odds, hope for a better outcome. In this context, the ICP had established a Kurdish branch in the mid-1930s, and a group of young professionals and urban intellectuals led by historian and writer Rafiq Hilmi created *Hiwa* (Hope), a moderately left-leaning Kurdish nationalist organization in Kirkuk in 1938.[70]

The challenge for the Kurds only became more acute after the war, as the vise-like pressures of political oppression and economic deprivation grew stronger. Kurdish activists responded by founding the Kurdish Democratic Party (KDP) in August 1946 and convening in Baghdad to promote *kurdayeti*—a kind of quasi-nationalist solidarity.[71] The KDP had partial roots in *Rizgari Kurd* (Liberation of Kurds), which itself had origins in the ICP and grew during the brief existence of the Soviet-sponsored *Mahabad* Republic, located at the intersection of Azerbaijan, Iran, and Turkey until *Mahabad*'s collapse in 1947.[72] The KDP was organized by Barzani allies, and he was its first president, though still in exile. It sought to unite the tribal, rural Kurds from the Bahdinan region (including Dohuk, Amediye, and Barzan) with the more educated, left-leaning urban Kurds from Sulaimaniyya and Erbil. The mountainous Kurdish areas were incorporated into Iraq and subject to state authority but were never integrated or fully dominated. As the largest ethnic group in the MENA region without a political entity of their own, the Kurds were too numerous to be assimilated or eliminated, but not sufficiently strong or politically unified to carve out an independent state. Without a state of their own, they suffered, with lower levels of economic development and educational attainment than other groups.[73]

The *Wathbah* and Nationalist Impulse

Beyond Kurdistan, the combination of deteriorating economic conditions and rising nationalism exploded in January 1948, with a month-long uprising in Baghdad that came to be called the *Wathbah* ("The Leap"). Primarily taking the form of spontaneous or semi-organized urban unrest, the event was sparked by rumors of an impending renegotiation of the Anglo–Iraqi Treaty of 1930. Foreign Minister Fadil al-Jamali, in fact, had negotiated a secret new security agreement with Britain, signed at Portsmouth on January 15, 1948, on behalf of King Faisal II and the Saleh Jabr government. The Portsmouth Treaty would provide for a British withdrawal of troops occupying Iraq since the 1941 Anglo–Iraqi War, but it left Britain fully in charge of Iraqi defense and foreign affairs for a period long surpassing the 25-year expiration of the earlier 1930 treaty. A wide array of Iraqis rejected any such treaty constraints, and the response from a coalition of students, workers, and the urban poor was rapid. Not surprisingly, it met with a brutal police response that cost hundreds of lives.[74] The immediate crisis ended in late January when the Regent Abd al-Ilah replaced Prime Minister Jabr with a long-time Shi'i political figure, Mohammed al-Sadr, and abandoned Portsmouth. Rail and port strikes and protests, led mostly by the ICP and fed by broader grievances, restarted between March and May. The upheaval only ended when the government declared martial law over the war in Palestine in May 1948.[75]

The Palestine war went badly for the Arab states and even worse for the Palestinian people, though the stakes were lower and the impact was more indirect for Iraqis. The 1948 war and the Palestinian *nakba* did contribute to a heightened sense of nationalist fervor and political radicalization. It also exacerbated domestic sectarian tensions between Iraq's Muslim majority and its substantial, 2000-year-old Jewish community. The Iraqi Jewish population had ancient origins in the Babylonian era of the seventh century BCE and was considered fully part of the emerging national community.[76] By the late 1940s, it exceeded 100,000 people out of a total population of about 5.5 million.[77] With mixed feelings that included ambivalence and apprehensiveness, Iraqi Jews began to depart en masse for Israel in 1950, motivated by a range of factors, from increasingly open sectarian discrimination and the promulgation of a new, property-confiscating emigration law in Iraq, to the active assistance of the Israeli government and Zionist organizations.

In this sense, the nationalist idea taking shape in Iraq was a project of inclusion and exclusion, and it interacted with other such projects in the Middle East. The result was a process of interactive state formation and nation-building. This process had little tolerance for disempowered groups in territories where they were a numerical minority: the Jewish and Kurdish communities of Hashemite Iraq; or where they faced determined, externally aided adversaries, as with the Palestinian Arab population of Mandatory Palestine. The connection between the two emerging states of Iraq and Israel/Palestine was real and consequential, because the loss of the Palestine war embittered many Iraqi military officers and inflamed the larger Iraqi population not yet fully committed, normatively, to a MENA region of segmented, individual states. The larger regional impact was brought home with the July 1951 assassination of Abdullah I, founder of the Hashemite Kingdom of Jordan and second son of Hussein, the Emir of Mecca. Britain had granted Jordan independence in 1946, but it remained in the British orbit and saw its Iraqi cousins as part of the same regional undertaking. State formation—or failure—in one corner affected all others.

More immediately if indirectly, events in Palestine contributed to moving Colonel Gamal Abd el-Nasser and Egypt's Free Officers to stage a coup in July 1952 ending the Egyptian monarchy. This action reverberated throughout the region for more than a decade, beginning in Iraq with a series of national strikes and protests from late August 1952 onward, known later as the Iraqi *Intifada*. Nasser's actions, and the nationalist efforts of Iran's Mohammed Mosaddeq, soon inspired Iraqi officers, led initially by Rif'at al-Hajj Sirri, to form their own Free Officers group. The Egyptian revolution thereby served as a model and precedent for Iraqi military officers to follow in Egyptian footsteps several years later.

Before the final denouement, however, King Faisal II assumed the full power of the throne in May 1953 when he came of age in turning 18. As part of the process, Abd al-Ilah lost the title of regent and became crown prince, maintaining some influence in a more limited role. Whether due to Faisal II's age and inexperience, or temperament and talent, or the swirling, unmanageable political currents of the postwar Middle East, the young king was never fully in command of his country.

Iraq remained in the throes of a more radicalized moment, with the rising power and broader acceptance of nationalist and communist movements that were at odds with the old-school traditionalism and conservative paternalism of the monarchy. Ironically, the Hashemite monarchy was too novel and young to have taken root in just a few decades. This was even the case in a literal sense: having a teenaged, out-of-touch king, with or without an experienced regent, was ill-suited to an international environment still stunned by the brutality of the Second World War and hurtling toward a global conflict between superpowers, who already had fought an inconclusive proxy war on the Korean peninsula.

Given that Faisal II's youth left him unprepared to govern, the real power in Iraq for much of the 1950s was the experienced and ever-present Nuri al-Sa'id. A fixture in national politics for nearly 40 years, Nuri served as prime minister on eight different occasions between 1930 and 1958, forming 14 different cabinets, in addition to waiting in the wings behind other government leaders like Tawfiq al-Suwaidi at various times. He was a Baghdad-born Sunni and an Ottoman-era army officer, captured in Egypt during the First World War and turned to the British side to fight in the Arab Revolt in 1916. Nuri had followed Faisal to Damascus in 1918 and on to Baghdad in 1920, where he assumed a long series of leadership positions in government service. Supremely confident and a consummate political operator, he was skilled at cultivating personal allies but also drawn to conspiracy and paternalistic, authoritarian politics.

In this sense, the strength of his political experience was also a debilitating weakness in that he displayed an endless capacity to remain in power, but less ability to adapt to changing national and international circumstances. Despite his political talents and accomplishments, he struggled to address any of Iraq's serious social and economic problems, acquired numerous enemies, was accused of involvement in King Ghazi's death, and had to flee the country twice during military coups d'état. Forebodingly, when appointed defense minister in the Midfa'i government of January 1953, he succeeded in restoring discipline and loyalty in the senior military leadership, but failed to connect with the lower ranks or junior officer corps, who were taken by events transpiring in Egypt and beyond. Reluctant about democracy and more comfortable constructing a single-party regime modeled loosely on Ataturk's vision for Turkey, he formed the Constitutional Union Party (CUP; *Hizb al-Ittihad al-Dusturi*) in November 1949 as a vehicle for liberal, prowestern, elite-oriented reformists, but only ended up banning it alongside all other parties in 1954.[78]

Aside from Nuri al-Sa'id, other domestic actors grew in importance in the early to mid-1950s. The ICP waxed and waned in power and relevance.[79] On the one hand, it came into existence before most of the large nationalist parties, and it displayed an early capacity to mobilize supporters on the streets and in protests like the Iraq Petroleum Company strike in 1946. Its ideological appeal to both the intelligentsia and workers exceeded that of the Free Officers and the Ba'athists in this period.[80] It also had intensely dedicated leaders, who did not promote the party simply as a vehicle for their own ambitions and were willing to endure prison sentences and government repression to further their cause. It was not a rigidly dogmatic Marxist–Leninist party so much as a group of social reformers seeking to end exploitative work conditions and social injustice.

On the other hand, the communist party suffered from political infighting in its leadership, faced constant rivalry with left-leaning fellow travelers, and experienced ideological drift verging on incoherence. It also made serious tactical political mistakes, such as backing the Rashid Ali al-Gaylani regime for a time in 1941 or, worse yet, parroting the Soviet Union's recognition of the State of Israel in 1948, which discredited it with the emerging nationalist movement. One critical party leader, Yusuf Salman Yusuf, hewed too closely to Stalinism even after the Soviet leader's excesses were apparent to all. Added to this, the party was subject to frequent and especially harsh political repression, with its entire leadership executed in February 1949, dimming its prospects at a moment when the left was otherwise ascendant throughout the MENA region.[81]

Another political party on the rise, and one that would come to play a central role in Iraqi politics, was the Ba'ath (Renaissance), or more formally the Arab Ba'ath Socialist Party. The Ba'ath was founded in Damascus in the 1940s and brought to Baghdad in 1949 by Syrian students. The party had no substantial following initially, but in 1951, a Shi'i engineer from Nasiriyya named Fu'ad al-Rikabi began quietly organizing meetings to discuss ideas and plans. By the mid-1950s, the group still had only a few hundred members, but it was an opportune moment for expansion. Its members, like many Iraqis, were energized by secular Arab nationalist ideas harnessed to reformist socialism and anticolonialism, having grown deeply skeptical about old-school conservative, elite-dominated politics under a foreign-imposed monarchy. Like the communist party, a substantial number of early Ba'athists were Shi'i students, unmoved by the clerical establishment and attracted to the party's initial inclusivity and nonsectarian identity. Unlike the communists, who became beholden to the Soviet Union, the early Ba'athists were not atheists and had more ideological space for the particular concerns of the Arab world, such as land ownership patterns that differed from what had evolved elsewhere. The party's growth both paralleled and was propelled by MENA regional changes, particularly in Nasser's Egypt after 1952, which had substantial influence and drove a number of seminal changes.[82]

The End of the Monarchy and the 1958 Revolution

The Iraqi monarchy itself was threatened by revolutionary forces at home and throughout the MENA region. Developments in its last few years all but sealed its fate, especially when combined with the pressures of larger regional changes. While the regent lost formal standing when Faisal came of age in 1953, the king himself was unable to manage what would have been a difficult challenge for even a more experienced ruler. At the same time, Nuri al-Sa'id's authoritarianism became more rigid, as neither he nor the national zeitgeist could sustain even a modestly liberal political order. A decisive shift began in 1954, when Nuri dissolved all political parties on the grounds that they had turned to violence in the September 1954 election. This included his own Constitutional Union Party and was rationalized by the claim that the country needed national unity more than a variety of political parties expressing differences or declaring affiliations. The call for unity was unconvincing, however, because the ban included not just parties but all political clubs and societies, totaling a staggering 458 organizations.[83] With Nuri's controlling tendencies and a new government brooking no dissent, there were fewer and fewer regular, institutionalized channels for opposing ideas and interests, incentivizing underground activism and conspiracy.

By relying so heavily on the security services and electoral manipulation, the government missed an opportunity to take a softer, savvier political approach to managing its adversaries and maintaining power. Oil revenues were rising substantially in this period, giving the state more resources to shape the social and political environment and to make progress in implementing its development agenda. With more confidence in its capacity to make bold strides forward and elicit a favorable political reaction, the government might have expanded its support by broadening its ruling coalition to include more elements from the popular classes. It also might have touted its achievements better by publicizing its successes. For example, it had successfully addressed the flooding and irrigation problems plaguing the land for centuries, but it did little to see that this achievement was widely recognized. The Iraqi political elite, led by Nuri and including the monarchy, proved unable to transition from an older form of politics that combined patronage and repression to a newer approach entailing the broad-based delivery of government services in exchange for political support or even acquiescence.

Iraqi opposition parties, large and small, generally were still willing to work within the existing institutional arrangements, flawed and limiting as the system was. Only a handful of antisystem groups sought to destroy the political order entirely.[84] Iraqis themselves were drawn to opposition parties because the government itself did little to compete with the opposition for popular support, despite having tremendous advantages that might have enabled it to succeed in open electoral contests. The crown already was constitutionally empowered under Article 26 to form and dismiss governments, so ruling authority was not at risk and therefore there was little direct incentive to cultivate popular support.[85] Yet, the government still failed to create any regular institutional mechanisms to channel political opposition in constructive directions, relying instead on the police and security services to arrest and intimidate its way to social peace while manipulating the electoral process to achieve desirable outcomes via a submissive parliament.[86] The organized political opposition also shared some of the blame, being unwilling to agree on anything other than general statements of anticolonialism and unable to insert itself constructively into the flawed political process. The growth of radio broadcasts and newspaper circulation amplified pressures from an increasingly educated population, which the political parties—whether legalized or not—could mobilize to strike, demonstrate, or even riot. Ironically, the regime's progress in improving the education system and literacy rates worked against it by creating more capable and willing opponents.[87]

It is conceivable, nonetheless, that no political intervention and activism by the government could have altered Iraq's eventual trajectory. By the 1950s, the historical and structural forces arrayed against the monarchy and the old elites were immense. It was a transformational moment in national politics, economy, and society, but very few of the changes worked in favor of regime continuity. And the government itself seemed to have little interest in exercising whatever agency it had to negotiate a challenging set of circumstances. Between its authoritarianism, its resistance to new ideas, its insistence on staying loyal to the older generation of elites, and its persistence in following a foreign policy rejected by most Iraqis, the monarchy found itself increasingly isolated.

The large MENA monarchies that survived the transformations of the postcolonial period—Saudi Arabia, Jordan, and Morocco—all had special attributes unavailable to Iraq: powerful and rising foreign allies, smaller and more manageable populations, a peripheral location in one case, and unique symbolic resources like direct control over the most important holy sites in Islam in another case. The Hashemite king of Jordan had somewhat easier domestic political circumstances than the Hashemite king of Iraq. Saudi kings, from the founder Abdulaziz onward, had more resources and were under longstanding American protection. The Moroccan monarchy had both external support from France, its former colonial power, and internal capacities that enhanced its chances of survival through the early postcolonial years. The same could not be said of the kings of Egypt and Iraq—or, in later years, the various monarchs of Libya, Iran, and Yemen—all to be swept away with seeming inevitability.

On the ground in Iraq, the major opposition parties joined together to create an underground United National Front in February 1957. This unusually diverse alliance included the National Democratic Party, the Istiqlal Party, the ICP, and the relatively new and rising Ba'ath Party. While the political differences between left-leaning communists and right-leaning Ba'athists were striking, the basis for their cooperation was a common adversary in the monarchy and its external patron. The communist party had been subjected to steady, years-long repression that induced them to work with other parties, and the Ba'athists were still finding their way in the street and benefited from a cooperative arrangement with more established groups. Together, they called for an end to martial law and an opening up of the political system, along with a termination of the Baghdad Pact.

The Front and its supporters had numerous personal connections to the military, most importantly the Free Officers. Created in the wake of Nasser's rise, Iraq's Free Officers were distinguished from their Egyptian counterparts in being somewhat more varied politically. Their leadership formed a supreme committee of 11 key figures, along with a set of working-level committees to implement their plans. Ranging in rank from major to brigadier general, most members were colonels, a group most commonly associated worldwide with coup-plotting in postcolonial states. While the Free Officers were politically diverse, members did tend to be disproportionately mid-ranking, middle-aged Sunni Arabs who had graduated from the Iraqi Military Academy in the late 1930s.[88] To chair the leadership committee, they recruited a relatively senior general officer, 43-year-old Brigadier General Abd al-Karim Qasim, while Colonel Abd al-Salam Arif joined the group and provided a link to the more junior officers. Together, the Free Officers planned for Iraq's future and decided that the country should be organized as a republic and run by military officers under the auspices of a Revolutionary Command Council (RCC). The old elite was to be put on trial for collaborating with the imperialist enemy.[89]

The interaction of domestic and international events altered Iraq's political direction, with the impetus to change often originating beyond its formal boundaries, either nearby in the MENA region or from more distant sources in a world of great power competition. If Egypt's Nasserist revolution in 1952 inspired specific and consequential efforts toward revolutionary changes in Iraq, the next most important event to trigger Iraq's transformation was Nasser's creation of the United Arab Republic (UAR) in February 1958. The UAR unified Egypt and Syria politically and, when seen from Baghdad and Amman, posed an existential threat to the neighboring, traditionally ordered monarchies of Iraq and Jordan. As a political model and an alternative to Iraq's governance institutions, the UAR had wide appeal to ordinary Iraqis, but especially to those in the Sunni-dominated military already organizing for direct action.

To counter the potential internal impact of the UAR and shore up their external defenses, Iraq and Jordan responded with political unification plans of their own, forming the Arab Union in February 1958. Accordingly, parliament was dissolved, new and opposition-free elections for a Chamber of Deputies were held in May, the government was changed, the constitution amended, and Nuri al-Sa'id stepped back in as prime minister. Both Hashemite kings retained their positions, but under the new arrangement, Iraq had overarching responsibility in all areas of governance except defense and foreign policy, which were shared between the two countries. The Iraqi government's capacity to reinvent itself was on full display, since it could launch such reforms via royal decree and a handful of cooperative government ministers. This very freedom of action, and the commitment it entailed, created an opportunity for regime opponents to take the initiative when the time was right.

14 July 1958

The July revolution of 1958 was not immediately revolutionary in itself, though it brought profound changes to Iraqi politics and society in due course. In one sense, it had a kind of inevitability, as it stemmed from a double conspiracy—the combined effects of a determined group of military officers and larger circumstances moving the country inexorably in the direction of dramatic change. The latter included a growing authoritarianism on the part of the old regime, the empowerment and further politicization of the military, the disillusionment of the middle class, the incapacity of the monarchy, and the perceived arrogance of British authorities. With so many of the MENA monarchies resting on flimsy foundations and major changes already afoot in Egypt, Syria, Lebanon, Tunisia, and Algeria, it would have been surprising if the Hashemite regime had survived much longer.

Seeming inevitability aside, the July revolution's orchestrators had longstanding, carefully considered plans to take power by the end of 1958. As it turned out, external events permitted an acceleration of the conspirators' timeline. With a serious political crisis breaking out in Lebanon in May 1958 and mounting pressure from the UAR in July, Prime Minister Nuri al-Sa'id responded to Jordanian King Hussein's request for help by dispatching Iraqi troops to the Jordanian border. Under the cover of these orders on the night of July 13–14, two leading Free Officers—Abd al-Karim Qasim and Abd al-Salam Arif—began moving troops from the east to the west via Baghdad, diverting loyal units to take control of key strategic locations.

Early in the morning on July 14, air units bombed al-Rihab Palace to elicit the surrender of the Royal Guard, which quickly recognized the futility of its position. King Faisal II and Crown Prince Abd al-Ilah hurried out of the back of the burning building to the garden, where they were promptly shot, along with most of their family.[90] It is not clear whether their deaths were planned and ordered from above or were at the hands of zealous junior officers. Regardless, Abd al-Karim Qasim took the ministry of defense a few hours later and the monarchy was over. Nuri al-Sa'id managed to escape and survive one more day, but he was caught in the street disguised as a woman and executed on the spot by a mob reportedly so agitated that it drove a car repeatedly over his body.[91]

Assessing the Hashemite Monarchy

Iraq's nearly four decades of monarchy in the first half of the twentieth century left a mixed legacy of accomplishment and failure. On one level, its achievements were noteworthy. Iraq had been nonexistent as a unified political entity at the end of the First World War. In a few short decades, it acquired a new, coherent political form—however arbitrary and awkward—with a fledgling state bureaucracy, a professionalized military, a lawmaking assembly, and tax-collecting capacity. The country had a veneer of stability and was governed by an established political class, generally supported by the military. It held elections, had a measure of pluralism and competition among elites, witnessed the creation of political parties, and saw the expression of contending visions of its future. Iraqis began to reorient themselves around these new institutions of the state, feeling the gravitational pull of its power and the allure of its capacity to launch initiatives larger than what any more modest institution could achieve.[92] More broadly, Iraq achieved social gains, expanding the number of students in secondary and higher education to an extraordinary degree, and made significant developmental improvements, with increased spending on infrastructure.[93] At least some Iraqis also began to acquire a new dimension to their identities, seeing themselves in national terms to an extent never experienced before, even if the nature of this particular identity remained fluid and contested.

42 State Formation, 1914–1958

Overall, power aggregated toward Baghdad, state institutions came to reshape societal activities, and a national identity began to form.

These achievements and broader social changes notwithstanding, the Iraqi cup was also at least half empty, especially regarding social support for the Hashemite regime. No doubt, a great majority of ordinary Iraqis welcomed the end of the monarchy, which they rejected for its close association with a foreign power, its corruption, and its indifference to their needs and preferences. The country clamored for political reform, if not revolutionary transformation, and got tired of being governed by essentially the same people who had ruled since shortly after the First World War and were mostly oriented toward advancing the interests of the privileged. The peasantry and urban poor in particular were happy to be rid of the royals, who favored both the older landowning sheikhs with parliamentary privileges allowing them to limit land reform and the newer urban elites enriched by rising oil wealth. The same held for most students, bureaucrats, and business owners, who felt excluded and had a modern outlook that rejected the very institution of monarchy, which they saw as both backward-looking and foreign. Military officers at the highest ranks were more ambivalent about changing a political order that rewarded them, though mid-level officers and below saw things differently and in some cases were sufficiently taken by pan-Arabism to support a major change.[94]

Viewed through an institutional lens, Iraq's mixed development under the monarchy retained positive elements, but every major institution was marred by evident flaws. The military's growing strength and professionalization was compromised by its repeated intervention in domestic politics, its normalization of violence against the civilian opposition, and its complicity in corrupt practices keeping elites in power. The constitution gave the king extraordinary powers that required a degree of restraint seldom demonstrated by the palace in its later years. The emerging legal system was undermined by the recurring use of martial and emergency laws. The electoral and party system produced nothing by way of engagement and compromise between regime and opposition, with the opposition existing in a parallel universe of essentially powerless, ornamental dissent. No genuine circulation of elites occurred, other than the occasional swapping of positions or turn-taking in the office of the prime minister, with Nuri al-Sa'id and Jamil al-Midfa'i in office dozens of times. The state bureaucracy and civil service expanded considerably while remaining helpless in the face of stronger actors wielding relatively arbitrary power. Tax authorities grew in capacity, but taxation was constructed so as to minimize liability for those in positions to shape it.

As for fundamental questions of national identity at the end of the monarchy, Iraqis themselves remained fragmented and conflicted. Being Iraqi was an unfinished project. No doubt, the Hashemites had tapped into a live ideological current of immense possibility in the form of a nationalist impulse. Yet, the divide was growing between the advocates of an Iraq-centric identity and the pan-Arabists of various stripes. Even more troubling was the ever-present antipathy between Iraq's Arab majority and its Kurdish minority, with the former showing no interest in accommodating Kurdish rights and the latter resorting to intermittent rebellion while failing to imagine itself as part of an expansively defined Iraqi nation. This fatal flaw was built into the country's demographics and even its geography, and increasingly it called into question the viability of all the available models of national transformation. Each route to a unified, stable, modern polity with a responsive, accountable government seemed to foreclose another path sought by at least one major group. If the first few decades of Hashemite rule were a time of open possibility for nation-building, that door was closing more loudly with every act of repression against minority ethnic or sectarian groups. The squandered decades of Iraq's early years had a seemingly irreversible path-dependent impact on national possibilities that would limit available choices thereafter.

Finally, international influences on Hashemite Iraq continued to be decisive if not determinative, having meaningful consequences for the country right up to the 1958 revolution. Britain's controlling, even domineering tendencies had found an exceptionally compliant partner in the king, regent, and government. Yet, despite Baghdad's cooperation, London did little to make life easier for the palace, insisting on restrictive bilateral treaty arrangements and inflaming nationalist sentiments by abdicating responsibility in Palestine and recklessly invading Egypt in 1956. Declining British power on the world stage did not soften its Iraq policy or reduce its demands for a close partnership, unwanted by most Iraqis on both popular and elite levels. The postwar global ascendance of the United States only added the Cold War rivalry to international constraints on Iraqi actions. Neither Britain nor the United States concerned themselves with Iraqi democratic development, especially when their vital strategic and economic interests were affected.

Likewise, in the international economic domain, the explosive growth of state revenues from oil exports—a nearly 40-fold increase in the last decade of the monarchy—and the emergence of Iraq's rentier state did nothing to improve the responsiveness and accountability of its political leadership.[95] Oil rents from abroad filled state coffers, but inhibited the regime's sense of restraint and obligation to its citizens at home while introducing an additional source of social tension from newly wealthy elites and resentful urban dwellers. Unlike Jordan's Hashemites, the Iraqi monarchy primarily followed Nuri al-Sa'id's vision and imagined its oil wealth as an instrument of power that would allow it to play an outsized role in the region. It was an aspiration never realized under the monarchy, with oil in itself proving insufficient to ensure the regime's survival.

On the surface, the architects of the July revolution were ready to move Iraq past all these troubles and into a new era. Change was in the air, and the Free Officers were united, at least in what they did not want: royalty, notables, and foreign domination. They would be rid of it all, while retaining at least some of the more helpful elements of the new Iraqi state, from its army to its growing civil service, oil wealth, and a newfound capacity to assert itself independently in the world. The hope was that Iraq would transition from old to new, from dominated quasi-colony to sovereign independent state, from poor to rich, and from prewar antiquity to postwar modernity. It would forge a shared future based on common ideals, a reconstituted identity, and the reclaimed power of its freedom.

It was easier to break the old order, however, than to make a new one, especially given the contending visions and interests of various groups and their leaders. In taking down some institutions of the nascent state, others went with it. Absent the monarchy, with its constitutionally mandated control of the government, the military had no regulator or institutional counterpart to check its actions. The Iraqi army, an inherently strict hierarchy in form and function, channeled power upward to its senior echelons. Iraqi state formation henceforth skewed heavily toward personalized coercive authority at the expense of the rule of law and administration in the public interest. The ending of the monarchy seemed to offer endless possibilities for the recreation of Iraq on more solid foundations. While the Iraqi people could write their own history from then on, they could not do so, as the revolutionary regime would find, under circumstances of their choosing.[96]

Notes

1 Owen Edwards, "The Skeletons of Shanidar Cave," *Smithsonian*, March 2010; Roux (1992), 37–39.
2 "Mesopotamia" was an ancient Greek designation for "(the land) between the rivers."
3 Roux (1992), 1–3, 423–428; Stansfield (2016), 14–15.
4 Helen Briggs, "Prehistorical bake-off: Scientists discover oldest evidence of bread," BBC News, July 17, 2018.
5 The Egyptian association with its ancient self is somewhat stronger, possibly due to the more substantial physical legacies of ancient Egypt throughout the country, along with geographic features like the relative unity and isolation of the Nile Valley.
6 Baram (1991).
7 On the complexity of modern Assyrian identity, see Benjamen (2022).
8 Spruyt (1994).
9 Callaghy (1984); Tilly (1992); Herbst (2000); Rogan (2019).
10 Scott (1998).
11 Flibbert (2003).
12 Tilly (1985).
13 Longrigg (1953), 75.
14 These included provinces (*vilayets*, formerly called *eyalets*) and districts (*sanjaks*). Huber (1899).
15 Dahl (2001).
16 Yergin (2008).
17 Longrigg (1953), 75–98.
18 Johnson (2016); Cleveland and Bunton (2013).
19 Dodge (2003) addresses what British colonial administrators thought they were doing.
20 Stansfield (2016).
21 Sluglett (2007).
22 Tripp (2007), 43.
23 Anderson (1991); Herb (1999).
24 Allawi (2014), 9.
25 www.statista.com/statistics/1066952/population-iraq-historical. The UK population was 37 million in 1921. www.statista.com/statistics/263754/total-population-of-the-united-kingdom.

26 There were 38 generations between Faisal and the Prophet Mohammed. Khadduri (1960), Appendix I, "The Hashimi Family," n.p.
27 The European association of monarchy with divinity risked committing *shirk* in Islam, or "associationism," a violation of the faith's fundamental emphasis on monotheism, born of concern about associating the Prophet Mohammed so fully with God that he appears divine.
28 Allawi (2014).
29 Dodge (2003).
30 Indeed, since the tenth century, Muslim geographers and historians had referred to the lands extending southeast from Mosul to Baghdad to Basra as *al-Iraq*.
31 Khoury and Kostiner (1990) address a range of issues related to tribes and state formation in the region.
32 www.statista.com/statistics/1066952/population-iraq-historical.
33 https://web.archive.org/web/20160303220020/http://www.galeuk.com/iraq/pdfs/Treaty%20of%20alliance%20btw%20GB%20%26%20Iraq%2010%20Oct%201922%20CO%20730%20167%201.pdf.
34 https://web.archive.org/web/20160303220020/http://www.galeuk.com/iraq/pdfs/Treaty%20of%20alliance%20btw%20GB%20%26%20Iraq%2010%20Oct%201922%20CO%20730%20167%201.pdf.
35 Longrigg (1953), 148.
36 Stansfield (2016), 69.
37 The constitution was called the Organic Law in the Anglo–Iraqi Treaty.
38 https://biblio-archive.unog.ch/Dateien/CouncilDocs/C-49-1929-VI_EN.pdf. Senators were appointed by the king for eight-year terms. Bashkin (2009).
39 Khadduri (1960), 19–20. The Second Amendment of 1943 gave the king power to dismiss the prime minister.
40 See "Prerogatives of the Crown," Part II, Article 19. https://biblio-archive.unog.ch/Dateien/CouncilDocs/C-49-1929-VI_EN.pdf.
41 Stansfield (2016), 85.
42 Al-Marashi and Salama (2008), 20–31.
43 Osman (2015) grapples with the place of sectarianism in Iraqi state formation and national identity.
44 Batatu (1978).
45 Tarbush (1982); al-Marashi and Salama (2008), 45.
46 Dawisha (2009), 62.
47 Rapid political turnover accelerated in subsequent years, with an additional three dozen governments by 1958, many led by a returning set of repeat prime ministers.
48 Tripp (2007), 48.
49 Batatu (1978), 25.
50 Longrigg (1953), 221.
51 There is speculation that he died of arsenic poisoning, but no definitive proof.
52 Marr (2017), 15–16.
53 Tripp (2007), 78.
54 Khadduri (1960), 74–76; Dougherty and Ghareeb (2013).
55 Ahali's politics developed over a few years and included democrats, socialists, and Marxists of various stripes, united by their opposition to the government and an evolving doctrine of *sha'biya* ("populism") cultivated by two of its original members, Abd al-Fattah Ibrahim and Muhammad Hadid, who had studied at Columbia University and LSE. See Khadduri (1948), 271–275.

56 For the full text, see Khadduri (1948), 283.
57 Dawisha (2009), 137.
58 Khadduri (1960). Also Khadduri (1948).
59 Tripp (2007), 91.
60 Batatu (1978); al-Marashi and Salama (2008), 54–62.
61 Cole (2012), 206.
62 Dawisha (2009), 100.
63 Cole (2012), 205.
64 In general, see Jackson (2018).
65 Wien (2006) refutes the claim that Iraq was a quasi-fascist state in this period.
66 Longrigg (1953), 288.
67 Tarbush (1982).
68 Khadduri (1960); Tripp (2007), 112.
69 Dawisha (2009), 142.
70 See https://kurdistanmemoryprogramme.com/history-of-the-kurds.
71 Stansfield (2016), 70.
72 Some Kurds found the ICP appealing because of its programmatic emphasis on wealth inequality.
73 McDowall (2004).
74 Batatu (1978), 545–559.
75 Tripp (2007), 122.
76 Bashkin (2012).
77 Calculated from World Bank, "Population estimates and projections," https://databank.worldbank.org/source/population-estimates-and-projections. The Jewish community was nearly 2% of Iraq's population at the time.
78 Tripp (2007), 105–106; Khadduri (1960).
79 Ismael (2008).
80 Batatu (1991), 213.
81 Ismael (2008), 40.
82 Sassoon (2012), 18–19.
83 Dawisha (2009), 113.
84 Hinnebusch (2017), 159–175.
85 http://gjpi.org/wp-content/uploads/iraqiconst19250321.htm.
86 Marr (2017), 49.
87 Khadduri (1960).
88 Tripp (2007), 139.
89 Batatu (1978); Dann (1969).
90 The only survivor was Princess Badiya bint Ali bin al-Hussein, King Faisal II's aunt and the Regent Abd al-Ilah's sister, who was not at the palace that morning and escaped to Cairo, then living in London to the age of 100. Her son, Sharif Ali bin al-Hussein, considers himself heir to the throne and advocates a return to the monarchy. Lessware (2020).
91 Louis (1991), 58.
92 Tripp (2007).
93 From 1921 to 1958, the number of students in secondary, vocational, and university education rose from several hundred to over 130,000. Batatu (1978), 477.
94 Batatu (1978).
95 Fawcett (2019), 72.
96 Marx's aphorism from the *18th Brumaire* is a restatement of the agent–structure problem.

2
FROM REVOLUTION TO DICTATORSHIP, 1958–1988

Thousands of years of Iraqi history culminated in the achievement of an independent, sovereign state with the 1958 revolution. For the first time ever, Iraqis—not various Mesopotamians, Persians, Greeks, Romans, Abbasids, Mongols, Mamluks, Ottomans, Britons, or Hashemites—were fully in charge of the land. It had a capital in Baghdad, mostly settled borders, and no foreign occupier. And while the first Iraqi Republic had countless legacies from its long and celebrated past, it was entering a new era, its reimagined sense of self open to all possibilities. Political life refocused on the home front's many ongoing concerns. These ranged from the completion of state formation and nation-building to the pursuit of power, interplay of identities, and development of institutions in a quickly evolving regional context.

The revolutionary regime had its work cut out for it. Iraq's developmental challenges alone were substantial, with unremitting poverty and deprivation in both urban and rural areas, despite the country's newfound wealth from rising oil revenues. Societal expectations for rapid improvements were high. The political coalition that had supported the revolution was exceptionally broad and varied, but also quite shallow in each group's refusal to support any leader other than its own. Social and political elites were remarkably divided in their visions of Iraq's future. All this occurred in a volatile international environment that weighed heavily on the fledgling Iraqi state by undermining its legitimacy and threatening reversals ranging from military intervention to unwanted unification with neighbors. The great powers remained relatively unconstrained, as norms of nonintervention and sovereignty for postcolonial states were only weakly limiting at this world historical moment.

Successive regimes, starting with that of Abd al-Karim Qasim, pursued agendas of regime survival and stability at a minimum while also undertaking more ambitious if erratic domestic and international initiatives. Individual leaders varied in personal ambition and ideological aspiration, and they had different strengths and

DOI: 10.4324/9781003056447-3

levels of talent for holding power. The initial, postrevolutionary moment under Qasim was especially important because it offered political and ideological fluidity and possibility. It was a classic crisis moment, as structural constraints loosened and the country's revolutionary leadership had a brief opening to act with fewer limitations. While the political opportunity was available to launch major changes during this time of contentious politics, the moment proved ephemeral.[1]

Abd al-Karim Qasim, 1958–1963

Despite the monarchy's fragility and most Iraqis' readiness for change, the revolution arrived faster than expected and displaced the established authority with almost too much ease. As it turned out, the Hashemites were only as durable as the small group of individuals shot in the garden behind the palace on the morning of July 14. And because the July events were little more than a coup d'état and a promise of broader transformation, the erasure of stability and predictability fed a sense of excited possibility, but also considerable uncertainty. For their part, the Free Officers anticipated stiff resistance and feared foreign intervention from Britain or the United States. The Americans actually landed U.S. Marines in Beirut on July 16 as part of the Lebanese crisis in a first demonstration of the Eisenhower Doctrine's anticommunism, while British paratroopers were sent to Jordan to support the Hashemite monarchy there. After taking power, Iraq's revolutionary leadership called immediately for the mobilization of a wide variety of supporters, from those who had been operating underground like the Iraqi Communist Party (ICP) and the Ba'athists to established opposition groups like the National Democratic Party.

As a result, the first few days of the revolution saw a wave of street-level unrest and disorder, with the Free Officers quickly becoming concerned about stability on the ground. While no earthly domestic or foreign power could restore the Hashemites, a Pandora's box of potential upheaval had been opened. Agitated mobs killed a handful of foreign nationals, including three Americans, a Briton, and a German taken from the Hotel Baghdad.[2] The new regime recognized its sudden, immense power and quickly declared martial law and imposed a curfew. Over the next two weeks, it announced an interim constitution and created a combined executive and legislative Council of Ministers and a three-person Council of Sovereignty vested with limited powers. The latter included Sunni, Shi'i, and Kurdish representatives, with the Sunni Lt. General Muhammad Najib al-Ruba'i designated as the president of Iraq, a mostly ceremonial position.

The real power was primarily with Abd al-Karim Qasim and, to a lesser extent, Abd al-Salam Arif, who took control as the leaders of the revolution. While the cabinet they formed was civilian-dominated and had National Democratic Party, pan-Arab, Ba'athist, communist, and Kurdish representatives, they were quick to claim the key positions. Qasim and Arif appointed themselves, respectively, prime minister and deputy prime minister, head of the ministries of defense and interior, and military commander in chief and deputy commander. The two men worked together, but in fact were immediate rivals. Forty-three-year-old Qasim was more established and prominent in reputation, took a measured and disciplined approach to governance, and brought with him an image of moderation, inclusivity, and modesty. The son of a Sunni Arab from Baghdad and a Shi'i (Feyli) Kurd, his vision of an integrated, socially diverse Iraq was relatively egalitarian and balanced. Arif, in contrast, was lower-ranking, a little younger at 37, lesser known in the country, and more strident. He considered himself the actual leader of Iraq's Free Officers and was a staunch devotee of Egypt's Nasser, characterizing Qasim as the Iraqi equivalent of General Mohammed Neguib, the Egyptian revolution's senior figurehead who had been pushed aside by Nasser. In subsequent weeks, after traveling around the country to gin up political support, Arif went so far as to visit the Ba'athist ideologue Michel Aflaq in Damascus and offer up Iraq for immediate integration into the recent Egyptian–Syrian merger, the United Arab Republic.

The tension between Qasim and Arif was more than personal, as it represented an unbridgeable divide between those promoting an Iraq-centric nationalism and the pan-Arabists who were dismissive of Iraq's uniqueness and advocated rapid political unification with other Arab states. Qasim recognized this and moved quickly, dispatching Arif to West Germany as ambassador and then having him arrested after Arif attempted a surreptitious, Egyptian-aided return in late October. Added to the mix and raising social tension, the communist party, as a core supporter and constituency of the July revolution, deployed street-level organizations like the Peace Partisans and the Popular Resistance militia, ostensibly to protect the regime but equally to make its presence known after years of clandestine organizing. Qasim saw the communists as a necessary counterweight to the Arab nationalists and initially gave them great leeway to mobilize, along with delivering a few cabinet and military leadership positions. He appointed his cousin, Colonel Fadhil Abbas al-Mahdawi, an outspoken Soviet sympathizer with no legal training, to preside over the military tribunal responsible for delivering postrevolutionary justice to former regime officers accused of high crimes.

To Iraq's Arab nationalist faction, just as worrisome as Qasim's cultivation of the far left was his resistance to regional integration and his acrimonious relationship with Nasser, who was ascendant in the Arab world in this era and to whom they looked for guidance and, if necessary, deliverance. In a matter of months, the nationalists grew more alienated, resigned en masse from the cabinet in February 1959, and launched a bloody coup attempt in March with support from Nasser. The failed revolt, led by the Mosul garrison commander Abd al-Wahab al-Shawaf, cleared the way for Qasim to act decisively against the nationalists and accompanied a further, if temporary, ascent of the communists, who were emboldened to put hundreds of thousands of supporters on the streets of Baghdad in April 1959, followed by a massive May Day celebration.

The pendulum reversed direction by mid-July, however, when brutal Kurdish and communist attacks on Turkmen in Kirkuk during a parade celebrating the revolution's first anniversary led a horrified Qasim to begin checking the communists and relaxing controls on the Arab nationalists. Qasim's reining in of his erstwhile partners antagonized the Kurds, who were natural allies to the communists, being lower on the socioeconomic ladder, employed as oil workers and laborers in the north, and understandably skeptical about pan-Arabism. All these efforts to balance and counterbalance exacted an inevitable cost. Rather than bringing the country together, the regime exacerbated the most important social cleavages. Ethnic, sectarian, tribal, and class divisions grew more pronounced and acquired political meaning not previously known.

After a year in power, exhausting efforts to play the revolution's largest factions against each other, Abd al-Karim Qasim moved to take full control for himself. He came to be known as the Sole Leader (*al-za'im al-awhad*), an appellation he may have taken to heart. He thus continued the pattern established before the revolution of Iraqi politicians focusing primarily on maintaining their personal power, and only secondarily on achieving gains for the country or developing independent, capable state institutions. Qasim brought this tendency to a new level by cultivating a populist style, enhanced by the state-controlled media, and placing himself at the center of Iraqi political life, without peer or institutional constraint or a permanently committed social base. He did likewise internationally, putting Iraq ahead of the other Arab states by taking a decidedly Iraq-first approach to regional relations, pulling out of the Baghdad Pact, and shifting Iraqi foreign policy to the left. He rejected calls for unification and cultivated a fierce rivalry with Egypt's Nasser, with whom he had more in common than their mutual antipathy suggested.[3]

As a result, Qasim alienated nearly all parties, including the Ba'athists, who attempted to assassinate him on October 7, 1959, with a bomb and machine-gun attack on his car, possibly with Nasser's assistance. Qasim was wounded and deeply shaken by the very close call, which led him to distance himself further from an already dwindling collection of potential supporters and seemed to affect his outlook and approach to governance. A 22-year-old Saddam Hussein participated in the assault, fled to Damascus then Cairo, and began to build his own reputation. The Ba'ath Party first achieved national prominence through this attack, with several dozen Ba'athists put on trial. Despite the failed outcome and strong state countermeasures, the Ba'athists parlayed the attempt into a successful recruitment effort and began regrouping for its next effort.

Progress and Possibility

Despite his growing political isolation, Qasim did launch important reforms in his first two years in power, prioritizing socioeconomic improvements to reflect an ambitious revolutionary mandate that was broader than a simple demand for political change. It started almost immediately with the September 1958 Agrarian Reform Law, which targeted large landowners and sought to limit individual holdings to 1800 acres. While the law proved difficult to implement and enforce, it was the first of several initiatives that eventually benefited hundreds of thousands of landless peasants by redistributing millions of acres of land to them, diminishing the outsized influence of large landowners, and shifting spending away from agriculture and irrigation and toward industry. Qasim also eliminated the separate legal status of tribes, a provision that had been used since the monarchy to elicit the support of the tribal sheikhs by excluding them from taxation. His regime introduced new labor laws to improve work conditions, raise wages, and offer new protections for workers.

In the social domain, his regime promulgated a progressive Personal Status Law No. 188 of 1959, which was instrumental in advancing the position of women by prohibiting underage marriage and polygamy, strengthening women's rights in divorce and inheritance, and giving equal status to women's testimony in court. Qasim appointed Dr. Naziha al-Dulaimi—a feminist pioneer, cofounder of *al-Rabita* (the Iraqi Women's League), and eventual central committee member of the ICP—as Iraq's and the Arab world's first female cabinet member, the minister of municipalities.[4] Finally, Qasim oversaw the construction of hundreds of hospitals and clinics in poorly served areas, along with thousands of housing units in a large new development, *Madinat al-Thawra* (Revolution City), on the eastern outskirts of Baghdad, designed for the poor Shi'i migrants coming up from southern Iraq and facing appalling living conditions.

Iraq's growing oil wealth helped to pay for all this and, as a general matter, was substantially redirected toward developmental improvements and the more immediate benefit of the needy. Qasim took the first meaningful steps to gain control over the country's rapidly expanding oil resources and to reduce the power of foreign-owned corporations like the Iraq Petroleum Company (IPC), the consortium that had controlled Iraqi oil development since the 1920s. Most consequentially for the long term, the regime began serious coordination with other national oil producers, seeking to elicit more advantageous arrangements in a sector still dominated by a small number of multinationals. Qasim hosted delegations from Saudi Arabia, Kuwait, Iran, and Venezuela at a Baghdad conference that established the Organization of the Petroleum Exporting Countries (OPEC) in September 1960.

Early on, Qasim's Iraq also took a few modest steps toward forging an integrated, coherent national identity that could overcome its arbitrary divisions and seeming artificiality. His emphasis on Iraqi uniqueness and social diversity led him, for example, to highlight ancient Mesopotamian symbolism in official representations of the new republic, including the eight-pointed Babylonian star of Ishtar and the golden sun disk of Shamash, which were put on the national flag and emblem as reminders of Iraq's deep and illustrious past.[5] Likewise, the Kurdish position seemed to improve momentarily under Qasim. In September 1958, the famed Kurdish fighter Mullah Mustafa al-Barzani returned from exile to Baghdad and was accommodated in the late Nuri al-Sa'id's former home. The interim constitution included a reference to Kurdish national rights, and a Kurdish representative, Khalid al-Naqshabandi, was appointed to the Sovereignty Council. The regime relaxed educational and linguistic constraints to allow for the teaching of Kurdish languages and culture, permitting the establishment of a Department of Kurdish Studies at the University of Baghdad.

More broadly, despite its close hold on all aspects of Iraqi political life, the regime in its early years demonstrated a preference for at least a measure of social openness and vibrant intellectual exchange. It allowed, for example, the expansion of al-Hikma University in Baghdad, a cosmopolitan educational institution founded in 1956 by the Jesuits and modeled after Baghdad College, an elite secondary school dating to the 1930s. Serving a religiously and ethnically diverse student body that came to include women by 1962, al-Hikma offered a wide range of courses, including business, engineering, and the physical and natural sciences, but also English language and literature, drama, and the arts. It had debate, basketball, and track teams and operated much in the spirit of a small, American-style liberal arts college.[6] The country more generally experienced a brief period of constructive intellectual foment, creative expression, and artistic openness, with a rise in scholarly publication and creative expression via theatrical performances, sculpture, and painting. Books, journals, and newspapers were quick to launch into the public space with less concern about provoking a government response.[7]

Closure and Constraint

While the change and its possibilities were very real, it all proved fleeting, and a turning point or decisive moment may have been reached in 1960. The regime began allowing official political party activity in January 1960, with the country not having held elections since the monarchy's final, contrived parliamentary shake-up in May 1958, just weeks before the revolution. In his public pronouncements, Qasim appeared willing to countenance party organization with an eye toward possible elections. While he was not looking to enhance parliamentary legislative power, much less to launch a democratic transition, he felt sufficiently confident to grant party licenses to a few groups, such as the National Democratic Party (NDP), the Kurdish Democratic Party (KDP), and a new Islamic Party (*al-Hizb al-Islami*) uniting Sunnis and Shi'a.

This seeming opening was illusory, however. The NDP only had a small and elite following that gave it little potential, whether as a mass-based organization or as anything other than an adjutant to those in power. The KDP was divided between Barzani supporters and urban intellectuals, reflecting the fundamentally unfinished nature of the Kurdish national project and its various competing strands. The Islamic Party was licensed by the regime primarily to counterbalance the communists and acknowledge a growing popular skepticism about secularism and atheism. It was shuttered and arrests were made in October 1960 after it voiced criticism of the regime. The Ba'athists were neither allowed to form an official party nor interested, for that matter, in winning free elections or competing openly for popular support. The communist party was not granted an official permit and could do little about it other than continue to organize and shift some activity back underground. By November 1960, the only communist—and female—cabinet minister, Naziha al-Dulaimi, was dismissed, and communist-affiliated organizations like the Peace Partisans and various youth organizations were banned or closed. In the end, parliamentary elections were never held in Qasim's Iraq, or for another two decades. By late 1960, the regime began turning more forcefully to the surveillance and repression of adversaries, who moved more and more toward clandestine operations.

One target of state surveillance was the Shi'i population, which had begun to experience a political reawakening in the 1950s, accelerated by the deposing of the monarchy and the arrival of the new regime. The Qasim government, with its early reliance on the communists for street power and its avowedly left-leaning and secular orientation, became increasingly alarming to the Shi'i clergy. The ideological and social concerns of the clerics combined with threats to the economic interests of Shi'i landowners and merchants to animate the organizing of new political initiatives and organizations. This included the Society of Ulama, comprised of clerics from the holy city of Najaf, and the *Hizb al-Da'wa al-Islamiyya*—also known as *al-Da'wa* (the Call)—which encompassed a younger generation of clerics and laypersons.[8] Founded and led by Mohammad Baqir al-Sadr, the *Da'wa* constituted the first formal, organized Shi'i political movement of the postcolonial era and deployed a cell structure, somewhat ironically, like that of the Ba'athists and the communists they feared. Working to organize and revitalize Shi'i awareness, the *Da'wa* called for the establishment of an Islamic state, an objective entirely at odds with the aspirations of both the regime and all large segments of the population.[9]

The latter two years of the Qasim regime tell the story of a pure military dictatorship endeavoring to maintain control but ultimately coming undone, as opposing forces strengthened their networks and prepared to move. The communist party, accustomed to state repression, reconfigured itself while safeguarding the advances it had made in the regime's initial years. The Ba'athists under Ali Salih al-Sa'di organized clandestine cells in the military, state bureaucracy, professional syndicates, and student groups, determined to achieve a better outcome after its first unsuccessful bid for power. The Kurds shifted from cautious if unsuccessful efforts at extracting durable political concessions to renewed fighting by September 1961, when the army was dispatched to challenge their hold over the mountainous north. It soon became evident that lasting political reforms were unlikely and less important to a leadership determined to stay in power in the face of multiple, inherently incompatible ethnonationalist and political forces, all organizing and mobilizing to achieve their own very different ends.[10]

Assessing the Qasim Regime

The Qasim regime had an opportunity to transform Iraqi politics with the end of the monarchy. Ultimately, it proved disappointing at best and utterly destructive by some measures. The regime was unable to build anything of lasting political value: no new state institutions to channel political initiative, no enhanced national cohesion to unify the young country, no strong regional relationships with friends and allies, and limited but modest progress on developmental challenges. The regime attempted but failed to make social and economic advances in the face of strong headwinds from interested parties. Even more troubling than its failures were its seemingly permanent achievements, especially the extent to which it solidified the role of the military in Iraqi governance, diminished the rule of law via a postrevolutionary Mahdawi kangaroo court, and blocked the possibilities of genuine political representation and party development. All these actions left legacies for the future. Qasim's autocratic strongman approach established a pattern that would be replicated for years to come.

Ultimately, if there were any real promise of a new Iraq born of the revolution, it was undone by both its leaders and the circumstances they faced. Qasim, for his part, proved to be as dedicated to maintaining and cultivating his own power as any prior Iraqi state leader. He became increasingly dictatorial after the March 1959 Mosul revolt, and even more so after the October 1959 assassination attempt. Despite a modest background and outlook, he came to think of himself as the embodiment of the Iraqi nation, encouraging a cult of personality by keeping himself in the public eye, without peers or competitors. He refused to give potential opponents any institutional power that could challenge his dominance. His efforts to play factions against each other left him with few genuine supporters and ratcheted up the political pressure so fully that it induced a further authoritarian response on his part. It remains unclear whether Qasim had a greater personal capacity for political reform than he delivered, though his skills and experience as a military officer did not incline him toward democracy so much as, at best, the potential tolerance of a relatively benign dictator. The tragedy of revolutionary Iraq was not merely one of poor choices but also the inherent limitations of a ruler more skilled at social control than at the creation of an authentic, responsive, capable independent state.

While Qasim was the wrong leader for the moment, he operated under conditions that limited his options in some areas and created apparent opportunities in others. On the one hand, he lacked a skilled and experienced civilian political counterpart, institutionally empowered to manage the country's postcolonial transition. With a military background, no hard limits to his powers, and no one else to manage the politics of competing factions, Qasim assumed all roles. He created a ruling structure that gave him full power, but then had to take responsibility for everything untoward that happened. On the other hand, the country's economic circumstances and financial constraints were less confining than those facing many new leaders in resource-poor postcolonial states. Iraq had agricultural and industrial potential, a growing population, an expanding education system, and evident oil wealth by the late 1950s. Nonetheless, this may have undermined his prospects by creating the illusion of having room to maneuver politically, when in reality he had very little.

Finally, the international context was anything but helpful to Qasim's prospects. Most obviously, at a time before the Arab states were settled in their national borders and accepting of their division into more than a dozen countries, political pressures for integration were unrelenting. Even if some of these pressures were disingenuously applied by political operators not actually interested in unification, Qasim had to respond and justify his reluctance, paying a political price in the process. Cross-border ideological currents—nationalist, liberal, communist, Islamist,

Third Worldist, neutralist—were powerful forces to be reckoned with because they moved people to political action. Great power rivalry, in addition, added a dimension to regional leadership calculations that constrained Iraqi choices. The unsettled nature of regional conflict and rivalry, both Arab–Israeli and also relating to Iran and even, increasingly in the Arab world, between the conservative monarchies and the new republics, did nothing to enhance regional stability or make political life easier for the Qasim regime. To some extent, it is a wonder the regime lasted as long as it did.

The First Ba'athist Coup and Interlude, February–November 1963

The regime's survival became less likely as the Ba'athists and Arab nationalists developed stronger connections to those controlling the levers of power, especially the military. With Qasim's devolution into a pure military dictator, he had come to rely on loyal praetorian elements to keep him on top, showing the classic vulnerability of authoritarian leaders who rule only at the pleasure of those protecting them. Unwilling to share power, his demise reflected the inherent limits of an autocratic governance strategy of balancing rival factions against each other. Eventually, he no longer had strong support from the communists, who had done little more for him than provoke both the nationalists and foreign powers before Qasim himself repressed them. Relations had fully soured with the Kurds, whose aspirations for political autonomy were always at odds with Qasim's vision of a strong Iraqi state under his rule, and who began talks with other regime opponents, offering a ceasefire in exchange for Qasim's removal.[11] The Ba'athists, nationalists, and Kurds grew confident in their capacity to orchestrate a change by 1962. The regime, in the same period, found itself isolated internationally, with no major patrons or partners in the Arab world or beyond to which it could turn for assistance. Relations with the Soviets had cooled, and the United States certainly was no friend, with the distinct possibility that the CIA, at a minimum, had gotten wind that change was in the offing.

Qasim's downfall came in the "Ramadan Revolution," a February 1963 Ba'athist coup d'état. Unlike the July 1958 revolution, which was undertaken by the military alone, this one included a civilian element. The coup was organized by Ali Salih al-Sa'di, a rising Ba'athist leader who had remained in Baghdad after the 1959 assassination attempt and worked clandestinely to recruit new members and develop a capacity to mobilize supporters to the streets. The critical revolutionary alliance was between the Ba'athists and the military, circles that overlapped but were not the same. The first had sufficient ideological coherence to move their members to action, and the second had the organization, firepower, and disciplined structure to carry out a coup. The Ba'ath itself had formed a six-person military bureau in 1962, led by Brigadier General Ahmed Hassan al-Bakr and Lieutenant Colonel Salih Mahdi Ammash. Former July 1958 revolutionary Abd al-Salam Arif had been released from prison and was recruited to the alliance, bringing with him other Arab nationalist military officers.

After several false starts in previous weeks that led to the arrest of various conspirators, on February 8, 1963, the coup was launched with the assassination of Brigadier General Jalal al-Aqwati, commander of the air force and one of the only well-known communists left in the regime. Anti-Qasim forces took the airfield at outlying al-Rashid military base before moving toward central Baghdad, where they faced serious resistance. The government called out the ICP's street cadres, as did the Ba'athist opposition, though Qasim reportedly refused to arm his ICP supporters. Fighting lasted for two days before the Ba'athists and nationalists took control of the Ministry of Defense and captured Qasim, who had taken refuge there and attempted to negotiate his surrender. He was executed on the spot after a quick tribunal, with gruesome photos displayed publicly to counter any claim of his escape.

Power was immediately vested in a civilian-dominated National Council of the Revolutionary Command (NCRC), comprised of a dozen Ba'athists and a handful of Arab nationalist military officers with Nasserist leanings. Some of the Ba'athists were also military officers, and all the military figures tended to be older, more experienced, and politically savvier than their civilian counterparts. A senior officer and non-Ba'athist instigator of the prior 1958 revolution, Abd al-Salam Arif, was designated president, while two leading Ba'athists were installed in prominent positions: Ahmed Hassan al-Bakr as vice president and prime minister, and Ali Salih al-Sa'di as deputy prime minister and minister of interior. The latter two clearly had the upper hand at first and expected Arif, despite his popularity and seniority, to play a mostly ceremonial role. The Ba'ath Party was still small and inexperienced in governance, but it had momentum and had been planning to take charge for months, under the fiercely determined and intemperate al-Sa'di.

The tension between the Ba'athist architects of the coup and its military supporters was evident, but all parties agreed at first to repress the ICP, which suffered thousands of casualties in a months-long campaign of assassination, torture, and imprisonment.[12] To wage the campaign and provide an armed counterweight to the Nasserists in the military, the Ba'athists formed a paramilitary National Guard (*al-Hars al-Qawmi*), commanded by a reliable colonel, Mundhir al-Wandawi. The National Guard was menacing if undisciplined, grew over several months to more than 30,000 men, and engendered resentment from the regular officer corps. The entire leadership of the guard almost perished when communists attempted a revolt in early July by seizing the Rashid military base and trying to liberate nearly 1000 pro-Qasim military officers detained there. The revolt failed and only elicited a more brutal response.

At the same time, fighting resumed with the Kurds, who demanded full political, financial, and security autonomy under the new regime. This was the price of their support for eliminating Qasim months earlier, but it amounted to much more independence than the Ba'athists were willing to give, now that they were in power. While an obvious liability of the Kurdish movement was its awkward geographic position at the intersection of four countries, its strongholds along the mountainous Turkish and Iranian borders did provide an ongoing advantage: Kurdish forces could always retreat to hinterlands that were difficult to control, much less conquer. This allowed them to survive to fight at a later point, preventing the imposition of any political arrangement that did not accommodate at least their minimal wishes as a distinctive group identity.

Kurds and communists aside, the new Ba'athist regime's immediate political troubles included a set of factional, family, and interpersonal rivalries. Using patronage and personal relationships rather than formal institutions to advance interests meant that competing circles of supporters enveloped several senior figures. These figures included the Prime Minister Ahmed Hassan al-Bakr, the Defense Minister Gen. Salih Mahdi Ammash, and the military Chief of Staff Gen. Tahir Yahya. This longstanding tendency toward cliquishness and personalized politics, partly a product of colonial and imperial history, enhanced the significance of individual leader idiosyncrasies and interests. It undercut the regime's capacity to present a united front to both domestic and international audiences.

Such rivalries also intersected, once again, with political and ideological pressures from outside Iraq. Iraqi–Egyptian relations were delicate because Iraq's Ba'athists did not tend to share President Arif's enthusiasm for the Egyptian leader. This became a problem when Iraq's Ba'athist coup in February inspired a Syrian Ba'athist coup in March, which led to Iraqi–Syrian–Egyptian tripartite unity talks in April. Despite a quick agreement, it soon became evident that no genuine unification could be achieved. An inevitable falling-out with Nasser a few months later only weakened Baghdad's legitimacy in the eyes of many. Persistent divisions and bickering among the Ba'athists reflected the movement's emergence into a world of postcolonial states, where national elites had localized interests often incompatible with larger pan-Arab concerns. The slogan "unity, freedom, socialism" could be interpreted in many ways, so even a strong ideological commitment to unification ran afoul of competing leadership claims, different security and economic concerns, and rival visions of how to implement the larger Ba'athist agenda.

As shared ideological aspirations did little to advance any political project, narrower interests, personalities, and factionalism prevailed at the end of the day. Such was the case by the fall of 1963, when Interior Minister and Ba'athist Secretary General Ali Salih al-Sa'di became embroiled in conflict with more conservative Ba'athists. The result was an eventual confrontation and bloodless coup, on 18 November 1963, led by President Arif and aided by disillusioned military Ba'athists. Unlike the brutal ouster of Qasim the previous February, Arif's forces were able to wrestle control from the National Guard with only the threat of violence and an intimidating positioning of forces. The military had had enough.

This first abbreviated period of Ba'athist rule yielded no accomplishments in the domains of state- or nation-building. Other than pandering to social conservatives by repealing Qasim's progressive Personal Status Law, the regime did not make a legislative mark. The regime did reinforce the place of violence in Iraqi politics by targeting the communists and punishing pro-Qasim military officers. Ultimately, military power proved to be the chief determinant of political success in a weakly institutionalized regime with wide acquiescence to the interventionist impulse in the armed forces. It was an eventful, even turbulent, nine-month interlude, marked by rivalry, violence, and intense factionalism. The doors were closing on Iraq's future political possibilities, only five years past the July revolution.

Abd al-Salam Arif, 1963–1966

From Abd al-Salam Arif's perspective, he had launched the original 1958 revolution himself, only to have it hijacked by his senior coconspirator, Abd al-Karim Qasim, and then all but stolen again five years later by his Ba'athist partners. Now 42 years old and having finally outmaneuvered and pushed aside all rivals, he would not make the same mistakes again. Arif positioned himself as president, commander in chief, and chairman of the NCRC, promoting himself to the rank of field marshall.[13] He installed his 47-year-old brother, Abd al-Rahman, as chief of staff and Taher Yahya as prime minister. Having learned to be less brash and impetuous but retaining the levers of power, Arif replaced civilians with military officers in vital roles and initially ruled by decree. While he was less openly dictatorial than Qasim, Arif demanded personal loyalty from all, taking great care with his appointments to assure his own predominance and maintaining political control to the point of limiting press freedoms and expanding the government's propaganda capacity.[14]

Arif did not have Qasim's inclusivist social orientation or see himself as Iraq's national patriarch, nor was he as inclined toward mass-scale brutality as the Ba'athists, or as openly undemocratic as Qasim. He did have both a well-developed sense of personal confidence and a ruthless attachment to Sunni Arab privilege, which shaped his approach to governance and the rights of other ethnic and sectarian groups in the country. Arif's disdain extended equally to both the Shi'a and the Kurds. With the latter, he did not share his predecessor's interest in finding even modest ways to accommodate Kurdish distinctiveness and demands for autonomy. He was willing to explore all manner of unification projects with the Arab world, entirely dismissing Kurdish claims that this would leave them an even smaller minority in the larger entity. As for the Shi'a, Arif displayed a kind of near-open sectarian chauvinism toward the majority population, reinforced by his tendency as an Arab nationalist to associate pan-Arabism with the MENA Sunni majority.

His most important priority was to remain in power. In his first several months in office, he eliminated the Ba'ath from all crucial positions, dissolved the National Guard, and eventually banned the Ba'ath Party entirely. To centralize authority, he combined executive and legislative institutions, essentially subsuming the latter into the former under his direct control. In a move with implications for future regimes, he established the Republican Guard under a kinsman from his own al-Jumaila tribe, Colonel Sa'id Slaibi, who recruited heavily from among extended family in the Ramadi area of Anbar province. He knew the limits of ideological solidarity in assuring his rule and was confident that the military, especially in the hands of close family relations, would be more willing and able to protect him than any civilian actors or institutions. To keep the military loyal, he developed and maintained targeted forms of patronage, using financial leverage to accompany the bonds of kinship and tribal affiliation. This was a shift that would long outlive his regime.

Relatively early on, in a nod to the Nasserists among his supporters, Arif also began creating new state-affiliated bodies and taking economic measures to emulate the Egyptian leader's turn to the left. This was consistent with his own pan-Arabist sensibilities and the spirit of the time. On the sixth anniversary of the Iraqi revolution in July 1964, with an interim constitution giving him extensive powers, he created a one-party political organization, the Arab Socialist Union (ASU), to mirror its eponymous Egyptian counterpart.[15] The ASU replaced all other political organizations with a single-party regime and even took charge of some activity in civil society, with its own newspaper. Arif simultaneously launched a rapid series of socialist reforms paralleling those in Egypt, with hopes of creating structural compatibilities between the two national economies. Accordingly, the July 1964 decrees established a major public sector and nationalization initiative that included steel and cement production, large-scale manufacturing, and essential services like banking and insurance.[16]

These hastily taken measures had rapid negative effects on the economy, however, leading to unemployment, capital flight, and a serious trade imbalance. Following the Egyptian lead came with great costs. While the Ba'athists attempted another coup in September 1964 and actually were repelled with Nasser's help, by mid-1965, Arif recognized the limits of Nasserism and began working to free his regime of Egyptian influence. After all, despite commonalities ranging from storied ancient pasts to British colonial histories and aspirations to regional leadership, Iraq and Egypt were very different countries, not least in that oil was starting to assume a central role in Iraq's economy. Iraq also had relatively unalterable demographic and geographic challenges that precluded fully emulating its more socially homogenous Egyptian counterpart.

In fact, despite the soaring rhetoric and momentous-sounding initial steps, neither Arif nor Nasser were keen on unifying their two countries and sharing sovereignty with what they saw as foreign, if fraternal, powers. Nor did either lead united movements, with interests transcending their national borders. Egypt and Iraq both had their own concerns. Iraqi Nasserists were vocal but nowhere near a mass-based organization capable of gaining power through their numbers. Nasser, for his part, did seek the political benefits of international engagement and encouraged his supporters to maintain pressure on the Iraqi regime, issuing a stinging rebuke when Arif began to turn away from the plan. Arif's distancing from Nasser's Iraqi allies led to a coup attempt by newly appointed prime minister, Brigadier General Arif Abd al-Razzaq, in mid-September 1965, which was repelled by Arif's family-supported Republican Guard under Colonel Slaibi. The failed coup gave Arif cover to move decisively against the Nasserists and establish the regime on his own terms, without undue interference from either internal or external competitors.

To improve his security in the face of Nasserist and other threats, Arif appointed 31-year-old Colonel Abd al-Razzaq al-Nayif, Sa'id Slaibi's cousin and a younger Jumaila kinsman, to a protective role in military intelligence.[17] Iraq's leaders were increasingly learning to keep power all in the family. In seeming contradiction to the cultivation of clan-based rule—but really designed to undercut his military rivals—he also brought in Republican Iraq's first civilian prime minister, Abd al-Rahman al-Bazzaz, in September 1965. Al-Bazzaz was a British-educated reformist politician, dean of Baghdad Law College, and a dedicated pan-Arab nationalist. He had supported Rashid Ali al-Gaylani's coup attempt decades earlier in 1941 and been jailed during the Second World War and again later under Abd el-Karim Qasim. He may have represented a last chance for more open governance in Iraq under the rule of law.

Recognizing the dysfunction of pure military rule, al-Bazzaz sought to professionalize the Iraqi state bureaucracy and free it from military control by returning competent civilians to positions of authority and eliminating the military-dominated NCRC. He also hoped to cut the defense budget and divert Iraqi oil revenues from military spending to national economic development, having served briefly as secretary general of the newly formed Organization of Petroleum Exporting Countries. He was friendlier to the private sector, and his tenure included renewed discussion of the possibilities of democracy, free speech, and a system of governance that was more nationally inclusive and less wedded to the single-party rule of the ASU. Al-Bazzaz even initiated a brief period of improved relations with the Kurds after a resounding Kurdish military victory at the Battle of Mount Handren in May 1966, negotiating a 12-point peace plan with Mustafa Barzani, with whom he had a better relationship than any of his predecessors.

But none of this would last, least of which the slight liberalization. Al-Bazzaz's efforts were stymied by a series of factors. First, and not surprisingly, he encountered resistance from military circles seeking to defend their power and privilege. While Arif had reintroduced Iraq to patrimonialism with an oil-based patronage network of rural sheikhs, urban landowners, small businesses, and religious leaders, the military retained pride of place in the system and would not be displaced easily. Second and more generally, the structural troubles of the Iraqi economy were difficult to address over a short time period, despite al-Bazzaz's halting of the nationalization program and willingness to unleash the private sector. Finally, the prospects for a return to parliamentary elections were limited by the nonexistence of any mass-based political parties willing to play by democratic rules. The two largest political organizations—the Ba'ath and the ICP, both no longer operating legally—were antisystem parties and not prepared to compete for votes or cooperate with a regime that had turned against them. Neither the most active and capable political operators nor the structural conditions of Iraq in the mid-1960s were conducive to liberalization or democratic governance of any real substance.

Abd al-Rahman Arif, 1966–1968

The challenges facing al-Bazzaz and Arif's willingness to entertain political change became irrelevant on April 13, 1966, when President Arif died suddenly in a plane crash. While foul play was not evident, and no single group moved quickly to take advantage, the cause of the crash remains contested.[18] After a few days of uncertainty and maneuvering, with al-Bazzaz serving as acting president and seeking to make his position permanent, Abd al-Salam Arif's older brother, Abd al-Rahman Arif, was installed as president by the National Defense Council and the cabinet. Al-Bazzaz was pushed out of the prime minister's office by August and replaced by a nationalist military officer and cabinet member, Naji Talib, who returned Iraq to the unevenly beneficial status quo ante of a functioning military-dominated regime. The Kurdish agreement, which was achieved after Arif's death, soon came apart, and with a less effective leader in charge, much of political life shifted to underground activities.

Given his family ties to the Jumaila tribe, Abd al-Rahman stepped into the role at least nominally in full command of the patronage system his brother, Abd al-Salam, had developed. It was a network of loyalty, obligation, and reciprocal support that kept the military regime in power and working smoothly. Yet, Abd al-Rahman was nearly five years older than Abd al-Salam and had just turned 50 when he found himself in power. He was widely seen as weaker, less ruthless, and less politically skilled than his late younger brother, lacking personal connections to regime supporters and a capacity to keep the system operating harmoniously. Importantly, he also had a harder time playing the role of populist leader in a political system that had eliminated all middle, mediating institutions since ending the monarchy and combining all authority in a single autocratic figure at the top. Abd al-Rahman could not even pretend to play the part of Qasim the Sole Leader, nor could he be the savvy operator orchestrating a system his brother, Abd al-Salam, had devised.

Abd al-Rahman's shortcomings notwithstanding, the regime was as authoritarian as any in Iraqi history to that point, matching and even exceeding the worst years of both the Qasim era and the monarchy under Nuri al-Sa'id. The latter at least was obligated to offer a semblance of responsiveness to legislative wishes and needed the acquiescence of pivotal social actors, who were able to extract limited concessions and push back in defense of their interests. As a purer dictatorship that embodied the inherent hierarchy of military command, the regime squashed dissent and replaced even the notion of a free press with the paternalism of a Ministry of National Guidance—even when the guide at the top no longer had a good sense of direction. Command economics in a partly nationalized economy contributed to the authoritarianism of decision-making, with national resources allocated by centralized plans more than individual initiative or market mechanisms. A crude normalization of violence had crept into Iraqi politics, traceable partly to the colonial occupation and the harder years of the monarchy and growing exponentially throughout the decade of military rule from Qasim to the Arif brothers. Settling old scores and eliminating rivals permanently became the norm in an emerging era of bare-knuckle politics.

In this period, the regime remained very weakly institutionalized, with clear implications. Significantly, much of Iraqi political life remained underground, or outside the confines of open and transparent political processes. This included the activities of organizations declared illegal, such as the Ba'ath Party and the ICP at various times. As a related tendency, weak state institutionalization enhanced the role of personal relationships as the essential mediators of power. Any effort to regularize and institutionalize political authority met with intense resistance, often channeled in the direction of undermining both the initiator and their immediate efforts. Ideology mattered little in this domain, so commitments to nationalism or socialist reform, for example, were lesser priorities than staying in power.

Perhaps most enduringly, in such an environment, family ties grew in importance for several reasons. First, the traditional social landscape had remained relatively intact, with little change since the earlier years of foreign-dominated, indirect, often indifferent rule. Most Iraqis retained their ties to tribe, clan, and region. These societal realities combined with the absence of strong national-level institutions beyond the military, state bureaucracy, and growing educational system. Especially missing were legal, mass-based political parties, trade and professional unions, and an independent judiciary to resolve disputes under the rule of law. This relative absence gave people few options beyond their local connections when looking to articulate and defend their interests and political preferences. The ASU served primarily as a mechanism for channeling support to the regime and did not serve a popular constituency or aid individual efforts. Finally, the fact that power had passed from one brother to another in the Arif regime, and both brothers had relied on their kinsmen in the Jumaila tribe, reinforced the notion of politics as a family affair. The hereditary monarchy of the Hashemites was long gone, but the power of family connections remained.

Locally oriented dynamics notwithstanding, events beyond Iraqi borders once again did have a catalytic effect on the country's unsteady politics and contributed significantly to the next chapter in national life. The regime drifted through the June 1967 Arab–Israeli War, with domestic critics eviscerating Iraq's lackluster military performance, despite its manifest incapacity to have affected the larger course of events. Change was in the air throughout the Arab world, as Nasserism lost its shine nearly overnight and Nasser's local allies in Iraq and elsewhere began to turn to other partners for alliance. Political Islam became the most salient oppositional political current running throughout the region, though it would take years to weigh in fully. The most dynamic regional force shifted from the European colonial powers of the old world to an emboldened and ascendant Israel, along with—soon enough—superpower adversaries vying for regional influence. Iraq sat on the sidelines through much of the tumultuousness and waited.

The Ba'athist Coup of July 17, 1968

The Ba'ath Party had begun to change after losing power in November 1963. The shrill Marxist Ali Salih al-Sa'di was ousted as secretary general in 1964, while Hassan al-Bakr's Tikrit-centered faction regrouped and asserted its leadership in the organization. Bakr appointed his 31-year-old cousin, Saddam Hussein, secretary of the regional command in the summer of 1964 and charged him with revitalizing the party. An overly hasty Ba'athist coup attempt in the fall of 1964 landed the two of them in prison, though this may have benefited Saddam's reputation on the street and with his party followers. The Ba'athist movement throughout the MENA region had already begun fragmenting along national lines, a process that accelerated when the Syrian and Iraqi branches separated following Syria's faction-driven, leftist military coup in February 1966. Pan-Arabism and state socialism remained powerful currents in the mid-1960s Middle East, but the absence of a strong, centralized political authority and the distinctive interests of individual countries and their leaderships generated powerful centrifugal pressures inhibiting cooperation across borders and even within them.[19]

Regime authorities in Iraq, perhaps thinking the Ba'ath was tamed, released Saddam from prison in 1966, and in short order he rose to the position of deputy secretary general of the party and began building a new militia. In addition to agitating against the Arif regime for its handling of the 1967 war, Bakr and Saddam extended their contacts to create political alliances, strengthen their power on the street, and enhance their intelligence collection capabilities. They reached out to influential figures in military and intelligence circles, whose self-interested and transactional thinking freed them to reconsider their loyalties in a political system that remained weakly institutionalized and strongly incentivizing of individual initiative. As pressure mounted on Abd al-Salam Arif's regime, a few key officials grew disaffected and turned toward the Ba'athists, including Colonel Abd al-Razzaq al-Nayif, the deputy director of Military Intelligence; Colonel Ibrahim Abd al-Rahman al-Dawud, who headed the Republican Guard; and Sa'dun Ghaidan, commander of a Republican Guard tank regiment. The dynamic holding the regime together—a weak military now mostly organized as a strong patronage network—also provided the crucial factor that was the regime's undoing.

On July 17, 1968, just a few days after the tenth anniversary of the July 1958 revolution ending the monarchy, the Ba'athists launched a successful bloodless coup. As in past Iraqi coups d'état, the move sprang from the combined efforts of a few well-placed military and civilian groups. The Ba'athists again led the way, with the main conspirators including Ahmed Hassan al-Bakr, who was joined by two regime insiders responsible for protecting Arif: the aforementioned Abd al-Razzaq al-Nayif and Ibrahim Abd al-Rahman al-Dawud. Given the strength of their positions, the event itself was less violent and dramatic than prior coups. Without much resistance, the plotters and their allies took control of the Ministry of Defense, the Broadcasting Authority, and the Republican Guard headquarters. They arrested Prime Minister Yahya and most of the cabinet, and they sent President Arif out of the country to London.

The coup also was relatively quick and easy because dissatisfaction was widespread among those in positions to oust the regime—or defend it. The coalitional nature of the plot, however, meant there would have to be a further settling of accounts by the plotters themselves in short order. In the meantime, Hassan al-Bakr assumed the presidency, Abd al-Razzaq al-Nayif became prime minister, and Abd al-Rahman al-Dawud was made the defense minister. Other noteworthy appointments included Salih Mahdi Ammash as minister of the interior, Hardan al-Tikriti as chief of staff and commander of the air force, and Sa'dun Ghaidan as commander of the Republican Guard. While the cabinet included some Ba'athists, it comprised mostly non-Ba'athists, including Kurds and members of the Muslim Brotherhood.

Unlike in 1963, when internal Ba'athist squabbling loosened the party's hold after several months in power, Bakr and his closest allies made sure to consolidate their position quickly, not allowing non-Ba'athist military supporters a chance to gain the upper hand. On July 30, knowing the coup was a result of joint action by an unreliably diverse coalition, the Ba'athists solidified their control via an additional "corrective" coup. It was the eighth coup or coup attempt since the end of the monarchy a decade before and the last successful one in contemporary Iraqi history.[20] After dispatching Defense Minister Dawud to Jordan under false diplomatic pretenses, Bakr and his fellow Ba'athists took control of strategic sites in Baghdad with an armored brigade, informing Dawud not to return home. Simultaneously, when Prime Minister Nayif was at the presidential palace with Bakr, Saddam appeared with armed loyalists, seized him, and delivered him to the airport to be put on a plane out of the country. A new cabinet was announced, with Bakr taking over as prime minister. Full Ba'athist rule had arrived, and it would last for decades.

Bakr, Saddam, and Regime Consolidation

The new regime was dominated by the Ba'athists, but not defined by Ba'athism. Several years of operating underground, from prison, or in exile had taught lessons of ruthless pragmatism and, above else, resilience and survival in difficult environments. The star of pan-Arabism was fading with Nasser and Egypt's defeat in the June 1967 war, which lessened the appeal of the most strident forms of Arab nationalism. The Ba'ath Party provided a measure of ideological coherence, an authority structure, a form of factional affiliation, and a mechanism for street mobilization. Yet, Bakr and his core supporters were not dogmatically wedded to Ba'athist ideals. They did not interpret the Ba'athist slogan of "unity, freedom, and socialism" as an absolute obligation to unify immediately with other Arab states, struggle for freedom from colonial interference, or implement rigorous socialist reforms. Even if they had wanted to bet on Ba'athism, actual party membership was limited in this early period, indicating the extent to which the regime was not built on populist foundations or with widespread support.

Bakr and Saddam were most committed to strengthening the Iraqi state and their control of it, before anything else. While Bakr was unquestionably the dominant figure, the two of them worked together effectively, asserting their control over the presidency, a revamped and smaller five-person Revolutionary Command Council (RCC), the cabinet, and the Iraqi Ba'ath Party. There was little conflict between them, and Saddam never challenged Bakr. Their symbiotic, mutually beneficial relationship united a senior military man with a junior civilian partner from the same extended family. Saddam was still too young and disconnected from the military to pose a threat to Bakr, but he worked assiduously to maintain the partnership and complemented his older cousin effectively as an operator and enforcer. If Bakr brought respectability, seniority, military connections, and a reputation for seeming personal piety, Saddam was less softspoken and more adept at confrontation. No one in the regime questioned his power, which exceeded his formal authority and official title, especially initially.

Saddam Hussein Abd al-Majid al-Tikriti was born in late April 1937 in the village of al-Awja, several miles south of Tikrit on the western bank of the Tigris, about 80 miles northwest of Baghdad. His father, Hussein al-Majid, was a peasant farmer who died around the time Saddam was born, and his family was poor and illiterate. His mother, Subha al-Talfah, raised him, helped by his uncles, including Subha's brother, Khairallah Talfah. Saddam had half-brothers Barzan, Sab'awi, and Watban, in addition to cousins that included Ali Hassan al-Majid.[21] His uncle Khairallah was particularly influential if abusive in Saddam's upbringing, acting as a surrogate father and eventual father-in-law, having arranged to have his daughter Sajidah one day marry her cousin Saddam. Khairallah was a former military officer, strident anti-British nationalist, and a participant in Rashid Ali's short-lived revolt in the early 1940s, imprisoned for his efforts. While Khairallah reportedly had a modern outlook, Saddam grew up in an environment where family and clan connections mattered greatly. As a member of the Al-Bejat clan and Al-Bu Nasir tribe, Saddam was raised with Bedouin tribal norms emphasizing the importance of honor, courage, and loyalty to family and clan. The countryside in the Tikrit area had a rough edge, and its inhabitants displayed skepticism verging on hostility to outsiders, along with a willingness to exact vengeance for normative violations. Firearms were ubiquitous.[22]

Saddam had joined the Ba'ath Party in 1957 as a young man. Never particularly ideological, he reportedly was more drawn to nationalism than the active communist movement because his part of north-central Iraq was uniformly poor and did not have prominent social divisions.[23] Politically, he came of age in the ferment of the Iraqi revolution in 1958, with its combination of tumultuousness and open possibility. Early on, he developed a reputation for thuggery, which may explain his involvement as a 22-year-old in the failed assassination attempt against President Abd al-Karim Qasim in 1959. The latter event led to Saddam's flight to Cairo, where he lived from 1959 to 1963, finishing high school, apparently studying law, and certainly maintaining his social and political connections. While he did not obtain a university education or travel widely, by all accounts, Saddam from his early years onward proved highly capable, resilient, detail-oriented, and dynamic, with a talent for organizing and skill as a ruthless political tactician. His conspiratorial, distrustful, and secretive personality may have stemmed in part from his experience beginning at a young age.

After the corrective revolution and regime consolidation, Bakr and Saddam focused in their first few years on protecting their power from potential threats emanating from military and civilian rivals. The military was managed with a combination of positive and negative inducements, from promotions of allies and their implication in a financially lucrative patronage network to purges of adversaries and their removal from positions of authority. As an institution, the military retained its status and privilege, though the regime was careful to maintain sufficient control to prevent military elements from being able to push aside the Ba'athists. Hardan al-Tikriti and Salih Mahdi Ammash, both essential military coconspirators left over from the Arif regime, found themselves elbowed aside soon enough because they were threats to Bakr's dominance, and therefore to Saddam's prospects. Ammash was demoted and sent abroad as ambassador to the Soviet Union, while Hardan, despite his family connections and position as defense minister, was targeted by Saddam, relieved of his various positions in 1970, and assassinated in Kuwait in March 1971. Others were accused of hatching conspiracies and sent to prison or worse.

The operative factor in all these intraregime dynamics was not ideology, party affiliation, or even the civilian–military divide. It was the logic of political competition—essentially power struggles—between leadership rivals and their patronage networks. These networks supported individuals with the best chances of achieving positions that benefited their members. Questions of rank in the political hierarchy were more fluid and contestable than in democracies or more formally institutionalized polities because authority—legitimated power—was not measured by electoral outcome or institutional role. Holding an office or a position was often necessary but not sufficient to benefit the members of a patronage group. Authority flowed from actual access to power and privilege, which itself accrued to those connected to the very top of the regime, provided they could remain in good graces with the leadership. A measure of populism was consistent with the patronage system, especially in the provision of food subsidies and special resources for peasants, who welcomed the attention and benefited from being swept into the larger system. Saddam worked to increase the size of his patronage network, expanding the number of individual and group dependents.

While the official regime policy after the July revolution was to discourage tribalism, an approach that lasted for more than a decade, Saddam's consolidation of his own position demonstrated a keen awareness of the immediate value of close family ties in the regime's first few years. Saddam used family connections and loyal lieutenants like Taha Yasin Ramadan al-Jazrawi and Izzat Ibrahim al-Duri to defend and maintain his place. He relied especially on his kinsmen from the Al-Bu Nasir tribe in the Tikrit area, numbering in the thousands and extending downriver to the next good-sized town to the south, Samarra. Ramadan and Ibrahim were appointed to an expanded RCC in November 1969, just as Saddam was made vice chairman of the RCC, suggesting—though not entirely or formally confirming—that he was the second most powerful individual in the government.

Violence was also at the heart of the new regime's governance strategy. Here is where Saddam's organizational talents served him well in the early stages of creating what would come to be called the *mukhabarat* state, defined by the presence of a powerful, omnipresent police and security apparatus. He began by building highly capable instruments of state coercion and violence, including an expanded Ba'athist militia (*al-Jaysh al-Sha'abi*) in 1970, and renewed security services that functioned as mechanisms for intimidating opponents and presenting the regime as more popular and capable than it actually was. He had at his disposal the Ba'ath Party's special security apparatus (*al-Jihaz al-Khass*), the presidential security service, and the state public security service (*al-Amn al-Amm*) under Nadhim Kazzar. Multiple, redundant security services spied on everyone, including each other. Saddam and the regime also saw to it that promotion through the military ranks became aligned with political loyalty. While previous regimes had paid due deference to the distinctions and niceties of military rank, the Ba'athists this time around had less concern for such norms and were willing to promote their allies almost immediately, elevating them from field officers to generals without much hesitation.

The extent of these developments was unprecedented in Iraq and the greater MENA region, with parallels and precursors only in countries like the Soviet Union under Stalin, whom Saddam reportedly admired.[24] This growth of security capabilities notwithstanding, the rise and consolidation of the power of an individual Iraqi autocrat was not wholly novel and unexpected. In important ways, it was a logical continuation of earlier, enabling historical factors. These included the increasing use of political violence, which was present from the establishment of the Iraqi state by Britain in the 1920s; the expansion of patronage networks, which were implicated in King Faisal's original approach to state-building; the military's politicization, which had roots in young King Ghazi's attachment to nationalist officers in the 1930s; and the manipulation and mobilization of social identities, which can be traced at least to the administrative structures of the Ottoman era. Each of these elements was present in earlier decades, but they were amplified, refined, and extended under Saddam.

After coming to power in July 1968, the Ba'athists were free to take on street-level adversaries, from the Nasserists, communists, and politically organized Shi'a to errant individual politicians and even dissident Ba'ath Party members. Initially, Bakr and the regime engaged the communists, who were deeply divided internally and concerned about their prospects, given the tremendous past animosity between the ICP and the Ba'athists. The communists were offered cabinet-level positions and the possibility of political participation, with the regime contemplating a more serious underlying objective of staying on reasonable terms in order to cultivate ties to the Soviet Union. Not surprisingly, the ICP rejected the overture and suffered the consequences in the form of imprisonment, torture, and assassination. The Nasserists, for their part, were less coherent an opposition, did not have their own political party, and constituted little more than a collection of individuals devoted to a foreign leader. They had been cut loose by the previous regime, but they remained represented in the military, requiring careful management.

The Shi'i opposition presented a more vigorous challenge, since Shi'i identity provided a powerful form of social and political solidarity. The Shi'i leadership's inherent disdain for a secular, kinship-based approach to governance put them at odds with Baghdad. By June 1969, Shi'i activists had taken to the streets in support of the senior Shi'i *marji'*, the 81-year-old Grand Ayatollah Muhsin al-Hakim, who refused government overtures and maintained a traditional, quietist distance from political life that the regime found unhelpful. Protests led to arrests and eventual executions, school closings, the confiscation of *awqaf* property in Najaf, the deportation of thousands of people with family ties to Iran, and even the banning of Qur'an readings on state radio. With al-Hakim's death by natural causes in June 1970, political space opened for the Islamic *Da'wa* party's leading theologian and theorist, Mohammed Baqir al-Sadr, to promote a more activist approach for his followers.[25] This approach mirrored the rising, post-1960s activism in the Sunni world and would accelerate and be inspired by later developments in Iran and the larger region.

While the early regime intensely focused on its internal opposition, it also was mindful of Iraq's external adversaries. Some of the purges and actions by the new Ba'athists had a broader antiwestern tenor, reflecting an ideological register that had been rising since the June 1967 Arab–Israeli War and growing U.S. support for Israel. State actions included a crackdown on western-affiliated educational institutions like the elite secondary school, Baghdad College, and its newer higher education counterpart, al-Hikma University, both established and run by the Jesuits. Al-Hikma was targeted in early September 1968 with a government declaration that it would be "Iraqicized," followed by the expulsion on short notice of 36 Jesuit members of the faculty and administration in October and November. A Ba'athist Iraqi president was imposed, and the Zafarania campus in southern Baghdad was taken over by the state and eventually shuttered, ending Iraq's most promising experiment in liberal higher education.[26] Baghdad College remained open, but lost its cosmopolitanism and worldly orientation, even if its graduates would one day comprise a who's who of prominent Iraqis, including Saddam Hussein's sons.[27] The cultural effervescence and openness that had periodically appeared in Iraq of the 1950s and 1960s diminished substantially as the new regime took hold, asserting a more aggressive, possessive, demanding authoritarianism in its dominance of wider segments of society.

Such actions were accompanied by public drama and, in some cases, the launching of criminal proceedings that included show trials and hangings over alleged plots and foreign espionage. While some of the plots and espionage may have been real, much of the response was designed to intimidate and terrorize regime opponents. The regime's main concern was its own survival through a variety of means, including an unchallengeable public affirmation of its right to rule. It was not inherently antiwestern by firm ideological commitment, despite its strident rhetoric and diplomatic turn to the Soviet Union. It did, however, seek domestic and international targets in order to demonstrate its power against adversaries and aspiring coup plotters. In the aftermath of breaking relations with the United States and Britain in June 1967, the regime was confident that the latter countries had little to offer other than to serve as public foils and scapegoats.

Policy Initiatives: Kurds, Soviets, and Oil Politics

Other than the endless pursuit of regime security and his own longevity, Saddam also took the initiative in several critical policy areas as second-in-command of the

RCC after November 1969. The Iraqi–Kurdish War had continued mostly unabated since 1961, with the Arif–Bazzaz peace plan never implemented in 1966 due to President Arif's sudden death, an embittering disappointment for Kurdish leaders. After initially offering cabinet posts to Kurdish representatives divided between the Barzani and Talabani factions in the KDP, the new regime relaunched a military campaign in the summer of 1969, without much success. Hoping to reduce an ongoing and debilitating source of instability and military disgruntlement, Saddam negotiated in secret for new arrangements with the Kurds, signing an agreement on March 11, 1970. The agreement offered limited administrative and cultural autonomy, called for the integration of Kurdish military forces into the Iraqi military, and included substantial plans for a Kurdish legislature and school curriculum, among other measures. The so-called March Manifesto eased hostilities for a few years, buying time for regime consolidation and shelving one of the thorniest issues of national integration so that Saddam could focus on other concerns.

Yet, the Kurdish issue had moved well beyond simple resolution by half-measures and split-the-difference compromises, especially when undertaken by Arab and Kurdish leaders who saw the matter in zero-sum terms. By May 1971, Saddam made it clear that security, oil, and financial affairs were beyond Kurdish control, also launching initiatives to resettle a substantial number of Arabs in the traditionally Kurdish areas of Kirkuk. KDP leader Barzani himself was skeptical of Baghdad's intentions and kept control of his *Peshmerga* forces. The Naqshabandi sheikh and tribal leader had prior experience with Baghdad's broken promises, especially in the Qasim and Bakr eras. Relations deteriorated by 1974, despite the incorporation of the agreement into the Iraqi constitution, prompting a return to the decades-long pattern of Kurdish national self-assertion followed by Iraqi state repression.

When full-scale fighting resumed in March 1974, Iran supported Barzani's forces as leverage against its neighbor, hoping to force Iraq to renegotiate the border along the *Shatt al-Arab* waterway dividing the two countries at the head of the Persian Gulf. Aided by Iran and covert U.S. and Israeli assistance, Kurdish fighters were sufficiently successful that Iraq ultimately was driven to the negotiating table—with Iran. The two powers signed the Algiers Agreement in March 1975, ending their border dispute, at least temporarily. Iran gained a major Iraqi concession on the border demarcation, with Baghdad accepting a line drawn at the so-called *thalweg*, the midpoint in the waterway. In exchange, Iran abruptly terminated its support for the Kurds and encouraged the United States and Israel to do the same.

The episode once again left the Kurdish movement in disarray, as thousands of *Peshmerga* gave up the fight, accepted amnesty, and returned home. On a leadership level, Barzani went into exile in Iran and Jalal Talabani's faction created its own new group in June 1975, the Patriot Union of Kurdistan (PUK). The Kurdish population found itself further crowded out of its traditional areas, with government relocation programs for Arabs and the removal of hundreds of thousands of Kurds from their villages. The regime devoted new resources to building roads and infrastructure in the north to integrate the territory more fully into the country and to enable the Iraqi military to extend its control. More generally, the calming of the

70 From Revolution to Dictatorship, 1958–1988

Kurdish issue allowed Saddam to distract from his territorial concession to Iran and to focus on his larger ambitions, demonstrating the relative significance of sovereign state power arrayed against minority groups and nonstate actors in the region, who had little recourse if they lacked external patrons.

The regime's early years also included broader political and economic initiatives. President Bakr launched a National Action Charter in November 1971, seeking to bring together all progressive political groups, advance state control of the economy, and build state power. Its associated call for democratic freedoms, liberal reforms, and wider political participation was an indication of the regime's growing confidence, buoyed by its successful efforts to stabilize the country and Iraq's rising economic prospects. The regime did not go so far as to actually implement any significant liberal reforms, preferring the rhetoric of national solidarity and community-building, all while keeping a watchful eye on major opposition groups, from the communists to the Kurds and the Shi'a.

The oil industry was integral to the regime's ambitions, regarding both economic development and its larger geopolitical aspirations. Initially, it proceeded with the same noteworthy caution that prior regimes had displayed in not wanting to put at risk a vital national source of revenue. The Arif regime had attempted to reach an agreement with the IPC in June 1965, requiring it to cooperate with the Iraqi National Oil Company (INOC) formed in February 1964, but giving it generous leeway in setting production levels to suit its business interests. This accommodation was well out of sync with wider popular sentiment and led to nationalist agitation and Nasserist resignations from ministerial positions, effectively scuttling the agreement while maintaining IPC independence. When the Bakr regime arrived a few years later, Iraq appeared to remain trapped between powerful nationalist sentiments and an unyielding and well-entrenched multinational corporation. To manage the dilemma, the regime's first move, despite its socialist leanings, was to enlist international assistance. This included getting help from the Soviet Union in developing the vast Rumaila oilfield in southern Iraq, as well as from the United States in building an offshore oil terminal at Mina al-Bakr in the Persian Gulf.

The regime continued to negotiate with the IPC, seeking better terms and increased output, but eventually it grew frustrated with what it saw as IPC intransigence in refusing to raise production levels to match the growth of Iraq's MENA counterparts. After several months of failed negotiations, the regime finally elected to nationalize the IPC in June 1972. To facilitate the move, aided by its own rising economic power and prominence as a national oil producer, it cultivated additional international partners. Baghdad obtained French and Soviet assistance, including an improved set of pipeline and refinery facilities that culminated in the completion in 1975 of a strategic pipeline running from Haditha in northwest Anbar province to Rumaila near the Kuwait border and onto the Faw peninsula and the Persian Gulf. Iraqi state power prevailed and was growing rapidly, along with its economic prospects.

More generally, the early to mid-1970s marked a few different turning points for Iraq. Saddam negotiated a Treaty of Friendship and Cooperation with the Soviet

Union, heralded by a high-profile visit by Soviet Foreign Minister Kosygin in April 1972. The Soviet–Iraqi agreement reduced pressure on the ICP, though it did not require Iraq to fall fully into the Soviet camp. National oil revenues were sufficiently high to give the regime a new capacity to maintain its independence from external powers. Iraq in fact was soon able to reduce its reliance on Soviet assistance, as it diversified its economic connections to Europe, Japan, and even the United States. It began to procure weapons from new sellers, such as France.

As important as international developments were to Iraq's changing place in the world, the Bakr regime remained focused primarily on consolidating its hold and meeting domestic threats in these early years. Security concerns were very real, given the evolving, no-holds-barred nature of national politics. In June 1973, Nadhim Kazzar, the head of state security, *al-Amn al-Amm*, took his turn at a coup attempt. With an insider's knowledge of the regime's security weaknesses, he devised a plan that entailed killing the entire leadership. The plot failed and he was executed, leaving behind a further incentive and excuse for Saddam to eliminate more of his opponents via dozens of additional arrests and the imprisonment or execution of numerous senior officials, including the head of the Ba'athist Military Bureau. President Bakr himself took control of the Ministry of Defense, while Saddam's half-brother, Barzan al-Tikriti, was put in charge of the General Intelligence Service, the *Mukhabarat al-Amma*. The plot marked a further transition toward relying on extended family and clan members to head the security services and essentially run the country.[28]

This change coincided with the emergence of a fundamental shift in the global economy and Iraq's place in energy markets. That is, the Ba'athist regime's building of an increasingly capable state security apparatus accompanied a massive increase in the financial resources it had available to do so. The Kazzar coup attempt of June 1973 preceded by only a few months the fortuitous and consequential rise in oil prices that accompanied the October 1973 Arab–Israeli War. Thereafter, annual oil revenues rose from several hundred million dollars at the start of the decade to $8 billion by the middle and over $20 billion by the end.[29] The combination of domestic incentives and international opportunities was instrumental in solidifying the regime's capacity to achieve its growing ambitions at home and abroad.

Ba'athism and the Mukhabarat State

The Ba'ath Party by the mid-1970s also started to develop into a more substantial institutional vehicle for the regime to channel and control all Iraqi political activities, as Saddam laid the foundations for a one-party state. Building on years of clandestine or semi-legal political activism, it did not operate like a mainstream, western-style political organization. Aspiring party members, called "friends" or "supporters," were vetted closely for a five- to eight-year probationary period, during which they were observed, indoctrinated, and had to complete small tasks before being granted full membership. Party membership grew from only several hundred in 1968 to several thousand less than a decade later, with much larger numbers of supporters implicated in Baʻathist patronage networks. It took another decade before it grew into a mass movement as the regime transformed from simple authoritarianism into a new and more ominous form.[30]

Mirroring a Marxist–Leninist or revolutionary structure, the party organization itself was complex, multilayered, and more formal than conventional parties, whose members simply were loosely affiliated. The party was divided along multiple levels, starting at the bottom with the *Khaliya* (Cell), which had three to seven members, operated in neighborhoods, discussed party decisions, and implemented them. Above it was the *Firqa* (Division), comprising several cells, which were active in individual urban areas, schools, offices, or factories, primarily serving as mechanisms to collect information for the regime. From two to five divisions constituted a *Shuʻba* (Section), which controlled large urban areas or even larger rural spaces. A *Farʻ* (Branch) typically included more than one section and covered an entire regional province. Finally, the *Qiyadat al-Iqlimiya* (Regional Command) presided over all of Iraq, while at least nominally, the *Qiyadat al-Wataniya* (National Command) oversaw the entire party across state borders and into most other countries in the Arab world.[31] While the state paled in significance compared to the Arab nation in Baʻathist ideology, post-1968 Iraq still witnessed concerted state-building efforts by the new Baʻathist regime.

Accordingly, parallel to the party structure was the increasingly fearsome intelligence and security apparatus that Saddam expanded and oversaw. It was complex and multipronged, with overlapping authorities and intentional redundancy. As in many other countries, Iraq's apparatus included several distinctive bodies. A critical difference, however, is that some of Iraq's agencies were designed to spy on other agencies or perform regime security and political oversight. By the end of the 1970s, the entire apparatus came to include several elements, including the *Amn al-Amm* (Public Security Directorate), which conducted criminal investigations under the Ministry of Interior; the *Mukhabarat al-Amma* (General Intelligence Service), which observed all political activities, both in the Baʻath Party and outside it, domestically and internationally; the *Istakhbarat Askariyya* (Military Intelligence), which monitored foreign militaries in addition to Iraqi officer loyalty; the *Maktab Askari* (Military Bureau), which addressed issues of military security; and the *Maktab al-Amn al-Qawmi* (Bureau of National Security), which oversaw the *Amn al-Amm*, *Mukhabarat al-Amma*, and *Istakhbarat Askariyya*. These were supplemented by intelligence collection capabilities contained within the military services.

As for the military itself, it grew substantially in size but was monitored and controlled by Saddam, who cultivated his contacts in the officer corps, in addition to adding and promoting politically loyal followers. Never having served in the military, in January 1976, Saddam had Bakr make him a general in the rapidly expanding Baʻathist militia, the Popular Army (*al-Jaysh al-Shaʻabi*), which was headed by Saddam loyalist Taha Yasin Ramadan al-Jizrawi and served as a counterbalance to the regular military. In July 1978, the regime outlawed non-Baʻathist political activity by members of the military, both current and former, designating it a capital offense. Since most adult males had mandatory military service, this decree made it difficult to speak out against the regime without potentially incurring the death penalty.[32]

Saddam Claims the Presidency

If the regime's first five years, from 1968 to 1973, saw its consolidation and expansion, the next five witnessed the beginning of Saddam Hussein's ascent from regime insider, Bakr enforcer, and presumptive second-in-command to dominant figure in the country, second to none. Saddam and Bakr still worked well together and did not have major policy disagreements, but the balance of power between them shifted and Bakr began withdrawing from political life in the mid-1970s. Bakr turned 60 in 1974 and may have been in poor health, having reached the average Iraqi life expectancy in that era. Saddam, in contrast, was in his late thirties and finally on the verge of being old enough in traditionalist Iraq to reach for the highest office. Saddam's modest background and limited social standing as the son of a landless peasant no longer mattered as much after several years in power. Even more importantly, by the middle of the decade, Saddam could begin asserting his dominance because he had sufficiently developed patronage networks, military contacts, and control of the security and intelligence apparatus. By 1977, decision-making increasingly flowed through Saddam's office rather than the RCC or President Bakr, though the president continued to perform all formal, ceremonial duties. The state and party bureaucracy recognized this shift and began reporting to Saddam directly rather than to his nominal superior.

Saddam complemented this shift in the authority structure with a more personalistic approach to governance, as power and authority came to focus more on the man himself. Such an approach had been seen in minor ways in the past—under Qasim as "the Sole Leader," for example—though never remotely as fully. Part of this move was institutional, particularly regarding lines of authority. Increasingly, Saddam made decisions that were rubber-stamped by the RCC and the larger Regional Command, both of which he dominated by stacking them with dependable allies. He expanded his contacts, whether directly or through networks of loyalty and obligation, and he found ways to structure decision-making so as to keep himself in command of it all. Saddam perfected mechanisms of surveillance to watch over the system as he built it, including only a small circle of trusted advisers. Even within itself, the regime intimidated and surveilled both horizontally and vertically, with individuals subject to scrutiny both up and down authority structures and from parallel positions staffed by nominal equals. Everyone reported to Saddam.[33]

Along with these institutional innovations, Saddam became more than just the regime's most powerful decision-maker. He began to emerge as Iraq's dominant personality and the central character in the country's national story, the core figure in a cult of personality. Saddam appeared in the media on a daily basis, always active and engaged and moving Iraq forward. People, especially young party acolytes, began to emulate some of his clothing styles and even physical appearance and speech mannerisms. A combination of self-advancement and fear drove a growing cult-like admiration for Saddam, especially in ways that could be demonstrated publicly. His picture was displayed virtually everywhere, including on office walls and countless billboards. Statues proliferated and a crass iconography appeared. Parents even began naming their children after him.[34]

Saddam had sufficient charisma and confidence to pull this off, especially when combined with his other attributes and advantages, both personal and institutional. He had preternatural survival instincts in the political domain, seemingly able to ascertain his associates' loyalties and to discern his rivals' plans in time to thwart them. He reportedly could be charming in conversation, if quietly menacing. His combination of energy, ego, and ruthless political skill made him an effective autocrat. By the same token, his savvy generosity to supporters helped to maintain loyalty, and his organizational skills gave him a capacity to institutionalize the support system needed to put him at the apex of power and stay there relatively securely for a long time.

The point of soliciting cultish adulation for Saddam was not to feed his ego or indulge his vanity. It was to connect supporters, however committed and close or unenthusiastic and distant, to a vast project of national domination, with Saddam at the top. It was to perpetuate a form of patriarchy and clientelism that drew in those participating in his network while cutting off, discarding, and even punishing those on the outside. It shifted allegiances away from rivals and toward his regime, providing privileges and opportunities not otherwise available. This put Saddam at the center of the system, but it also made him indispensable and irreplaceable, since no one else could operate, much less replicate or reconfigure, his institutional networks. All this reassured his closest aides that Saddam could continue to provide the stability, order, and special privileges they enjoyed.

This system would not have been possible without an extended network of supporters to begin with, not all of whom could be vetted personally but who remained connected via patronage and the significant institutional advantages he held. One such advantage was his large family. In this same period in the mid-1970s, the regime became even more family-dominated than before, as Saddam came to rely more fully on his clan and tribe, the Al-Bu Nasir of Tikrit, for a politically loyal and reliable kinship network. While family ties mattered from the beginning of the regime—Saddam and Bakr were cousins, after all—Saddam was now the patriarch at the center. He was aided by concentric circles that, in the innermost ring, included Adnan Khairallah Talfah, who was his brother-in-law, cousin, and the son of Saddam's surrogate father and uncle, Khairallah Talfah. Talfah was elected to the Regional Command and appointed to the RCC before Saddam made him the minister of defense in 1977, with instructions to monitor the military. Saddam also relied on his half-brothers Barzan, Sab'awi, and Watban, all of whom held increasingly important positions in the security apparatus from the mid-1970s onward. Others from the Tikriti clan would rise to prominence in the years to come.

The Regime in Transition

By the late 1970s, several broader elements, both fortuitous and carefully planned, contributed to the impending transition. Iraq's oil wealth had begun to transform its possibilities and empower its leadership to direct resources in ways that benefited both its political prospects and the country's development in general. Oil revenues, controlled since September 1977 by Saddam, were directed with a political eye on regime security and his own centrality as much as anything else. Perennial challengers like the Kurdish national movement were more easily coopted with state largesse and targeted payments to assure the control of potential regime threats. The same held for the Shi'i opposition, though to a lesser extent, since the latter tended to be managed mostly by strict surveillance and repression, as when Shi'i protests in Karbala in February 1977 met with a government crackdown and leadership executions. Yet, Saddam typically was astute enough to deliver carrots with sticks and to deploy cultural resources in a way that made him the cornerstone of the regime. He started using Islamic symbology in mid-1977, for example, to enhance his own leadership status, an approach used to even better effect in other MENA countries like the Saudi, Moroccan, and Jordanian monarchies.

By 1978, it became clear that Saddam would be taking charge, though he did not act until 1979, when confronted with changing international circumstances. Egyptian–Israeli peacemaking was proceeding rapidly after Sadat's historic trip to Jerusalem in November 1977 and the subsequent Camp David Accords of September 1978. The Arab League met in Baghdad in November 1978 to contend with Egypt's peace initiative, with Saddam leading the mainstream opposition and seeking to position himself as the new leader of the Arab world. Public discourse filled with plans to unify Iraq and Syria to help defend the frontline state, but Saddam was leery that a union with Syria would leave him a further step from power, behind both Bakr and Syria's Hafez al-Assad. Some of Saddam's rivals for leadership in Iraq may have promoted closer ties to Syria for just this reason, increasing the pressure on Saddam to act while he could.

Closer to home, neighboring Iran was in full revolutionary turmoil by mid-1978, with the potential to affect Iraq via its majority Shi'i population and the presence of the firebrand exile Ayatollah, Ruhollah Khomeini, who resided in Najaf until Saddam deported him at the Shah's request in October 1978. When the Shah was deposed in January 1979, Iraq recognized the new revolutionary government, but Shi'i underground opposition groups in Iraq like the *Da'wa* were not placated and pressed their own case, making it clear that the turmoil was not temporary and threatening a wave of revolutionary contagion. They were met with severe repression. Even the Kurds were ramping up pressure on the regime, with the KDP launching attacks under a new generation of leadership by Masoud and Idris Barzani after their father, Mulla Mustafa, died in March 1979.

The pervasive sense of crisis in the region and at home prompted Saddam to take full control of matters in the summer of 1979. On July 16, President Bakr announced his retirement from public life for reasons of ill health, in all likelihood pressured by Saddam to resign. Saddam stepped in immediately as Iraq's new president, as well as prime minister, secretary general of the Ba'ath's Regional Command, RCC chair, and commander in chief of the armed forces. In a further reshuffling, Saddam's lieutenant Izzat Ibrahim al-Duri became vice president, RCC deputy, and Ba'ath Party assistant secretary general, while Taha Yasin Ramadan al-Jazrawi was made Iraq's first deputy prime minister. Gathering up all the institutional levers of power—the state bureaucracy, Ba'ath Party, military, and security services—Saddam was unstoppable at this point.

Ironically, this was Iraq's first peaceful transition of power in more than a dozen years, though Saddam's ascent was not entirely without political opposition from a handful of remaining potential rivals and their supporters. To complete his move, he orchestrated an extraordinary, Stalinesque purge the following week by declaring that he had uncovered a plot by the only Shi'i RCC and Regional Command member, the Ba'ath Secretary General Muhyi al-Din Abd al-Hussein. Muhyi al-Din, who had objected to Bakr's replacement by Saddam, was forced to offer a confession on July 22 at a dramatic, televised meeting of hundreds of Ba'ath Party members. The extraordinary gathering took place at the presidential palace in a large, closed hall, with on-the-spot denunciations by other supposed plotters in the terrified audience who were escorted out as their names were called. Nearly two dozen supposed conspirators were executed immediately, including five RCC members, while numerous others were imprisoned or fled the country.[35] Additional purges continued into early August.

Now in full command of the Iraqi state, Saddam was free to abandon a legitimizing pan-Arab unification project begun with Syria some months before.[36] At 42 years of age, he transitioned Iraq from a single-party regime under the Ba'ath to a more personalized authoritarian dictatorship, aided by an extended network of family and personal associates. Saddam quickly added further family support by appointing his cousin, Adnan Khairallah Talfah, deputy commander in chief and installing Barzan al-Tikriti as the head of the *Mukhabarat*. Harnessing family and clan solidarity to his control of state and party institutions produced unprecedented regime security and stability by 1980. No rival individual or group was able to threaten Saddam's hold on power. While the transition from Bakr to Saddam was anything but peaceful in the end, careful planning had precluded any need for open violence or extralegal measures. If only amateurs steal power via military coup, Saddam was a professional conspirator at this point. Without any checks or controls on his authority, he was ready to follow an even more expansive agenda that included targeting threats and pursuing opportunities beyond Iraq's borders.

Saddam in Command, 1979–1988

Saddam had ambitious plans, both for himself and for the country. He pursued power, built state institutions, and shaped identities to suit his purposes. Some of his actions continued earlier initiatives, while others were considerably more aggressive, reflecting his leadership style and perceptions of risk and potential benefit. Central to it all was an abiding, somewhat contradictory wish to dominate both Iraq and the MENA region while remaining secure in his position at the apex of the state. Personal power and regime security were his first priorities, though in seeking these ends he sometimes launched actions that had provocative international dimensions and consequences. He did not play it safe, but he was wholly strategic in deploying a wide range of resources, whether at home or in neighboring countries.

One such early initiative in June 1980 was to hold Iraq's first national elections since the end of the monarchy in 1958. Several million Iraqis chose representatives for a 250-member national assembly (*al-Majlis al-Watani*), with regime dominance assured by the careful vetting of candidates conducted by an RCC-appointed commission. The result was that 75% of the election winners were from the Ba'ath Party, including members of the RCC and Saddam's own cabinet ministers; 40% were Shi'a; and 12% were Kurds.[37] The assembly was created ostensibly to give voice to popular concerns and to provide opportunities for people to participate more fully in political life. In reality, holding what were touted as democratic elections was at best a safety valve mechanism for the regime to permit the controlled expression of opinions.

Iraq's closed political system had become more opaque and disconnected from ordinary Iraqis since Saddam's rise to the top. The assembly did not help in this regard, though it did serve as a forum for Saddam and his acolytes to address the nation in grand fashion and to promote a favorable image of his leadership, vision, strength, and paternal oversight of the Iraqi people. Ultimately, it was not an arena for debate or serious legislative action, or a means of channeling popular wishes in democratic fashion, so much as a venue for pontification, obsequiousness, and loyalty pledges. It had more in common with totalitarian approaches to governance, since it sought to shape and mobilize political opinion around the leader more than limiting and demobilizing popular impulses. The people had to do more than tolerate Saddam's rule. They had to love him and willingly say so.

Another long-running Saddam project to strengthen the regime involved tapping into and deploying Iraq's extraordinary history as one of the cradles of civilization. This effort had begun with the Ba'athist return to power in the late 1960s and had been attempted in more limited form under Abd al-Karim Qasim's revolutionary regime a decade before that. Once fully in power in the late 1970s, Saddam accelerated efforts to reconfigure Iraqi identity around the country's unique past, all while maintaining claims to the mantle of contemporary Arab leadership. The regime launched archeological restoration programs at Babylon and Nineveh, changed town and regional names, established new museums, and promoted theatrical performances celebrating past Mesopotamian civilizations in Sumer, Assyria, the Akkadian empire, and Babylonia. It constructed a false but appealing narrative of political and historical continuity from ancient times to contemporary Iraq. It invoked renowned leaders like King Nebuchadnezzar and managed to integrate Saddam into the pantheon of historically significant leaders.[38]

In general, the regime encouraged a much longer timeline in discussing Iraqi history, attempting to draw a straight-line connection between the distant past and the present. The idea was to find a cultural commonality that could elevate Iraq and unify the country's various ethnic and sectarian divisions.[39] The move bore some resemblance to the persistent efforts of modern Israeli state- and nation-builders to construct a unified national identity rooted in the Jewish past using biblical-era symbolism and aesthetics in areas ranging from the name of the national currency to faux-ancient calligraphy in street and shop signage to an architectural preference for antiquity-invoking building materials like stone. Likewise, contemporary Egyptian leaders, especially Anwar Sadat and Hosni Mubarak, did much the same, though Egypt has not had the same unity and demographic challenges facing Israel and Iraq, and the ubiquity of antiquity in Egypt has made referring to the past easier and more natural.

In the hands of the Iraqi state under Saddam, this ploy was not especially successful, though its long-term influence on Iraqi national identity was more ambiguous. The initiative never gained significant traction with the Kurdish ethnic minority, which had its own connections to antiquity. The Shi'i majority, for its part, appeared to find Iraq's ancient, pre-Islamic cultural origins less than compelling, even as many Shi'a were skeptical about their fit within Iraq's Sunni-affiliated Arab nationalist movement. Since Iraq's founding in 1921, the most salient political identities have been associated with the family, clan, tribe, ethnicity, region, and sect, making it difficult for a would-be nation-builder to form a coherent, national sense of self rooted in ancient Iraq. This is not to say that all Iraqis reject their ancient cultural heritage. Not unlike those contemporary Egyptians who take pride in their long civilizational past, some Iraqis express a sense of awe and wonder at the continued existence of several thousand years of settled existence in their land. But Iraqi national identity itself has only been formed over the past century, and it remains to be seen where the legacies of its past will fit into the country's nation-building efforts moving forward.

Iran and the Shi'i Challenge

Nonetheless, identity-related challenges were central to Iraqi actions under Saddam, typically connected to regime security and his leadership tenure. One of the most significant such initiatives was Iraq's invasion of Iran in September 1980, only a year or so after Saddam consolidated his political dominance and ousted the former President Bakr. While the military and diplomatic dimensions of the Iran–Iraq War will be examined further in Chapter 4, the war's origins lie mostly at the intersection of Saddam's personal idiosyncrasies, geostrategic ambition, and the perceived threat of revolutionary contagion from the new Islamic Republic. The latter threat was seen as acute because of the potential for Iraq's Shi'i majority to be moved by calls to action emanating from its neighbor.

The Iraqi *Da'wa* had expanded its political activism in the previous few years under a new generation of leadership, leaving behind the traditional quiescence of past Shi'i organizations. An affiliated group, the Islamic Action Organization (*Munazzamat al-'Amal al-Islami*), tried to assassinate Deputy Prime Minister Tariq

Aziz in a hand-grenade attack in central Baghdad in April 1980. The assassination attempt, in its larger context, elicited a furious state response that included the arrest of one of Da'wa's founders, the Ayatollah Mohammed Baqir al-Sadr, and his outspoken sister, Bint al-Huda. Within days he became the regime's first prominent execution of a high-level Shi'i cleric. Others were detained or put under house arrest, such as the relatively apolitical chief *mujtahid*, Abu al-Qasim al-Khoei.

Just as consequentially, the regime began to expel from the country tens of thousands of so-called Iranian Shi'a, people with Iranian-origin names and backgrounds. The idea was to eliminate, one way or another, Shi'i leaders and segments of the population who could not be intimidated, coopted, or drawn into accommodation and patronage networks in the state. It was launched at a time of seeming opportunity in Iran's strategic instability and weakness after the large-scale purging of the Iranian officer corps in 1979 and 1980 and the loss of U.S. patronage and arms supply. Saddam's decision to invade, therefore, had both offensive and defensive aspects, as he sought advantage while protecting his own regime. All that the move really accomplished was heightening the tension between Baghdad and Tehran.

Not surprisingly, much of the 1980s was consumed by Baghdad's efforts to prosecute and then merely survive a war it had started with its neighbor and to consolidate its hold on Iraqi society. As in other areas of statecraft, Saddam practiced a form of cold realpolitik in pursuing material objectives while remaining acutely sensitive to the dilemmas created by Iraq's malleable and evolving identity. He was aware of the state's multidimensional capacity to dominate its adversaries, but also to shape and even construct shared senses of national self. The media and cultural apparatuses of the Iraqi state, which oversaw its writers, journalists, artists, and filmmakers, were deployed to influence popular views of the regime's leadership. Early in the war with Iran, for example, Iraqi state media began referring to the conflict as "Saddam's *Qadisiyya*," invoking the well-known seventh-century military victory of Arab Muslim forces over the Sasanian Empire of Persia. Saddam sought in general to frame the war in civilizational terms, with his regime at the forefront of an epic battle against a longstanding rival. This was part of Ba'athist Iraq's governance and legitimation strategy, taking care to attend to and cultivate a reliable population that remained supportive.[40]

The regime had to tread carefully with the majority population. It succeeded partly by cultivating Shi'i differences, particularly between those living in the cities and those in the countryside, who varied in socioeconomic position, ideological inclination, and orientation toward the faith. Rural Shi'a were more traditional, conservative, and followed conventional norms relating to family and clan. In an appeal to this large segment of society, the regime in the 1980s pivoted occasionally to emphasize traditional tribal values in place of larger Arab identity, which it normally leaned into when confronting Iran. The urban Shi'a, in contrast, tended to be either better-educated professionals or part of the clerical establishment, or they resided in poor districts like Baghdad's Revolution City (*Madinat al-Thawra*), renamed Saddam City (*Madinat Saddam*) in 1982. They were subjected to a wide range of approaches that included both positive inducements and the harshest measures of the security services. It is not entirely clear what worked best: fear of Baghdad, loyalty to Iraq, aversion to Iran, or whether regime efforts had any decisive influence on Iraqi Shi'a views of Iran.

Yet, throughout the war, most Shi'a acted no differently toward Iran than their Sunni counterparts or the Kurdish population, with the latter having slightly higher desertion rates in the military. Small numbers of Shi'a did advance upward in the military ranks, promoted largely on the basis of loyalty to Saddam's regime. Others did form new opposition groups that stemmed directly or indirectly from the war. With the *Da'wa* under pressure from Saddam's regime, the Supreme Council for the Islamic Revolution in Iraq (SCIRI) was established in November 1982 by Iraqis deported by Baghdad to Iran for disloyalty. SCIRI was led by the Ayatollah Mohamed Baqir al-Hakim, whose political vision mirrored the Iranian Ayatollah Khomeini's doctrine of *velayat-e faqih*, and who was fully supported by Iran's revolutionary government. Hakim also created a military wing, the Badr Brigades, which was led by Iranian officers and included Iraqi prisoners of war, exiles, and defectors.

The War's Domestic Impact

The Iraqi state of the 1980s grew in capacity, especially in areas related to the war effort, which required extraordinary expenditure and drained the state of the substantial hard currency reserves it had acquired in the previous decade. The political apparatus supporting Ba'athist dominance also expanded. From the mid-1970s to the mid-1980s, the Ba'ath grew into a mass movement, with its combined membership and supporters rising exponentially from tens of thousands to well over a million people.[41] By the logic of an emerging, near-totalitarian state, Ba'ath Party membership became mandatory to hold any noteworthy professional position. The party's importance affirmed its institutional centrality in Iraq itself, but did not extend to a stronger political emphasis on Arab nationalism. The latter was deployed just as much on a regional or international level, especially regarding the war with Iran.

The war's domestic impact varied with Iraq's battlefield successes and, just as often, failures. During a year of initial advances in 1980 and 1981, the war had little negative effect on national life, as its costs were cushioned by extraordinary growth in the country's oil revenues and the expectation of a relatively quick victory. Iran began to rebound and counterattack in 1982, staking its revolution's credibility on repelling the assault, and it met with some success. Iraqi losses, costs, and casualties soon became a serious challenge, both militarily and for Saddam's rule. State coffers emptied, oil revenues plummeted due to a world oil glut and damaged pipeline and export infrastructure, foreign debt grew rapidly, and tens of thousands of Iraqis were captured and became POWs. Soon enough, Saddam's strategic and even political judgment came into question, most dangerously by his inner circle. He was able to survive via a series of calculated cabinet and RCC shuffles and other initiatives to keep his critics off balance, possibly including the murder of his own minister of health for suggesting he step down.[42]

By the second half of the 1980s, the conflict became a brutal war of attrition, with both countries demonstrating a capacity to inflict harm on the other, but neither able to prevail. The Iraqi military, for its part, was able to obtain and keep relative operational autonomy, and it benefited from increased expenditures and fuller control over strategic decision-making. No individual leader in the military or the upper echelon of the regime, however, could rise to a level of authority that would allow a challenge to Saddam's rule. The stalemate fed and justified the creation of even closer surveillance mechanisms to keep the population as a whole in check, with the Ba'ath Party exploiting wartime conditions to extend its control.[43] The regime's wartime rhetoric shifted toward traditional tribal values like courage, honor, and sacrifice, while its domestic social policy moved in a regressive direction via, for example, the return to legalized honor killings.[44] With tight control over potential opponents and popular sentiment, a conservative social policy, patronage networks maintaining large numbers of supporters, and continued efforts to find a way to win the war, Saddam's regime managed to hold on.

Beginning in 1987, the war's impact on Kurdistan became more tragic and unprecedented. As the military stalemate in the south led to more battlefield engagements and initiative in the north, the Kurds were drawn further into the fighting. The Iraqi regime turned to using chemical weapons against Iranian troops, a tactic that initially had more psychological than strategic effects. Kurdish forces under both the KDP and the PUK became involved in the fighting and were targeted by the regime with particular intensity. Saddam sent his cousin, Ali Hasan al-Majid, to oversee efforts in Kurdistan. "Chemical Ali," as he came to be known, was the former head of state security and a member of the Ba'ath Regional Command for Iraq. He initiated *al-Anfal* (Spoils of War), a genocidal terror campaign against the Kurdish population that started in 1987 and included the destruction of entire villages, large-scale executions, agricultural ruin, and population transfers. The brutality eventually entailed the use of chemical weapons against civilians, with one of the most devastating attacks occurring in March 1988 in the northeastern town of Halabja, about ten miles from the Iranian border. The attack took an estimated 5000 lives, and all told, the Kurdish genocide killed approximately 100,000 people.[45]

Life for most Iraqis in the rest of country in this same period was anything but peaceful, stable, and safe. Wartime deprivations grew, as did the constraints on national development possibilities limited by full-scale military mobilization and the redirecting of shrinking resources. As a result, tens to hundreds of thousands of educated, middle-class professionals began to emigrate from the country, fleeing two perils. On the one hand, they were excluded from economic, social, and political opportunities by being shut out of a closed patronage system that rewarded only loyalists, party members, and people connected by tribe or kinship to the regime. Economic conditions worsened, with little immediate relief in sight. On the other hand, they faced the growth of the state's expanding surveillance and repression apparatus, as the country transitioned from longstanding, tough-minded authoritarianism toward more invasive, all-encompassing forms of oppression. The combination of exclusion and repression left them with little choice but to leave if they could.

The war ended in a stalemate when Iran accepted a ceasefire under UN Security Council Resolution 598 in August 1988, almost eight years after the start of hostilities. Iraq's geostrategic advantages and economic resources helped it to survive, though the war achieved nothing. It was not, however, without conspicuous domestic impact. Most obviously, it came at astounding human and material expense, leaving the country weakened and its people battered. Iraq's developmental prospects were delayed substantially, given the loss of nearly a decade and a financial cost in the hundreds of billions of dollars. More subtly and indirectly, the war paved the way for further—and somehow more costly—troubles in the years to come. It contributed to developing a set of governing institutions that verged on totalitarian. Its genocidal attacks on the Kurdish population all but ended the possibilities of national reconciliation and the forging of an inclusive Iraqi national identity, even if it shored up and confirmed the loyalty of the Shi'a. It left Saddam in power, defiant and vulnerable and exuding a sense of bitter entitlement in the Arab world for having fought Iran for so many years, with nothing to show for it but death, destruction, and debt.

Notes

1 Tarrow (1998); McAdam et al. (2001).
2 "Telegram from the Embassy in Iraq to the Department of State," at history.state.gov/historicaldocuments/frus1958-60v12/d112.
3 Dann (1969).
4 Dougherty and Ghareeb (2013), 185.
5 Baram (1991). The Kingdom of Iraq's coat of arms included the Star of Ishtar and the Lion of Babylon, so Qasim's move was not entirely novel. Ishtar was the goddess of love, desire, beauty, and war; her twin brother Shamash was the god of the sun, justice, truth, and morality.
6 MacDonnell (1994); on Baghdad College, see Shadid (2011). The "Iraq Mission" began in 1932 and was staffed by Jesuits from eight American universities, including Boston College and Georgetown University, led by Edmund A. Walsh, S.J., after whom Georgetown's School of Foreign Service eventually was named. See RG 11.1, Missions Offices Records, Series—New England Jesuit Foreign Missions—Iraq," at http://jesuitarchives.org/wp-content/uploads/2016/03/RG-11.1-Missions-Offices-Records-Series_-New-England-Jesuit-For.pdf
7 Tripp (2007), 155.
8 Marr (2017), 81.
9 Nakash (2003), 135.
10 Dann (1969), 311.
11 Rubin (2007).
12 Ismael (2008), 106–113.
13 Al-Marashi and Salama (2008), 93.
14 Khadduri (1969).

15 https://law.stanford.edu/wp-content/uploads/2018/04/ILEI-Constitutional-Law-2013.pdf.
16 www.nytimes.com/1964/07/15/archives/iraqis-nationalize-some-businesses-but-oil-is-spared.html,
17 Not to be confused with Arif Abd al-Razzaq, the five-time coup-plotting former prime minister.
18 Charles Tripp holds that it was likely an accident because no group took immediate advantage. Tripp (2007), 178.
19 On inter-Arab politics, see Kerr's classic (1971).
20 Al-Marashi and Salama (2008), 232–234, provide a list of two dozen Iraqi coup attempts between 1936 and 1995.
21 Coughlin (2002), x–xi, has a useful family tree.
22 On Saddam, see Aburish (2000); Coughlin (2002); Sassoon (2016); Karsh and Rautsi (1991).
23 Cockburn (2002), 70.
24 Egypt and Syria also developed formidable state security organizations. Kandil (2012), 194, quantifies the growth of Egypt's services as well as the shift from military to civilian dominance under the ministry of interior.
25 Tripp (2007), 195–196.
26 MacDonnell (1994), 235–258.
27 Graduates included Uday and Qusay Hussein, Ahmad Chalabi, Ayad Allawi, and Kanan Makiya.
28 Farouk-Sluglett and Sluglett (2001).
29 Tripp (2007), 206; Rivlin (2009), 134.
30 Sassoon (2012) is the most comprehensive study.
31 Marr (2017), 117; Sassoon (2012), 37.
32 RCC Decree 884, Human Right Watch, at www.hrw.org/legacy/backgrounder/mena/iraq031103.htm#_ftn13.
33 Tripp (2007), 216.
34 See Makiya (2004).
35 Marr (2017), 140.
36 Mufti (1996), 217.
37 Dawisha (2009), 229.
38 For a study of Iraq's deployment of historical memory, see Davis (2005).
39 Baram (1991).
40 On the strategic use of language, see Bengio (1998).
41 Makiya (2004), 39; Helms (1984), 87.
42 Murray and Woods (2014); Razoux (2015).
43 Khoury (2013).
44 Dawisha (2009), 235.
45 Hiltermann (2007); McDowall (2004).

3
FROM DICTATORSHIP TO TROUBLED DEMOCRACY, 1988–2022

Over the course of three decades, from the Iraqi revolution in 1958 to the end of the Iran–Iraq War in 1988, the country traveled a great distance but, in some ways, did not get very far. Iraq began its independence with revolutionary fervor, though this sentiment devolved quickly into an authoritarian impulse that grew stronger with each successive regime, from Abd al-Karim Qasim to the Arif brothers to Saddam Hussein. Saddam represented a new level of authoritarianism, verging on totalitarianism in its mass mobilizing tendencies and the cultish centrality of its leader. His ambitions and miscalculations led Iraq into a dismally violent and disastrous, if transformative, period. This eventuated in surprising and noteworthy movement toward democratic governance, albeit as shallowly rooted as it was deeply flawed. The question remained whether the country would advance toward a more just, stable, secure future, or loop back toward the tendencies it manifested at the beginning of its independence. There were reasons for optimism, mostly because the alternative was so unpalatable.

The Late 1980s Interlude

Iraq did have a momentary opportunity after its war with Iran, when it could have worked to take stock, repair the damage, and look to the future. It did not follow this path. Despite the war's military failure, Saddam sought to parlay it into a political success, for his very survival depended on it. This disconnect between military and political outcomes followed a pattern evident in other MENA states in previous years, including Gamal Abdel Nasser's rocketing regional influence and domestic popularity after losing the 1956 Suez War, and Anwar Sadat's strategic realignment with the United States after being defeated in the 1973 Arab–Israeli War. In Iraq's case, Saddam wanted to succeed both at home and in the larger Middle East. At home, he had ambitious development plans that he hoped would

DOI: 10.4324/9781003056447-4

permit a revitalization of the regime and a reassertion of his hold on the country. Regionally, Saddam sought to cultivate his leadership of the Arab world, particularly vis-à-vis Iran and Israel. He believed the Gulf states, at the very least, owed him their full support. The interplay of these domestic and international factors, combined with Saddam's personal idiosyncrasies, led to a startling outcome that created even greater vulnerabilities for the country in the subsequent decade.

Saddam's initial postwar focus was necessarily on the home front. Iraq had emerged from the war a regional giant, albeit one with a battered infrastructure, massive external debt, and a weary, troubled population. While "Saddam's *Qadisiyya*" had exacted a terrible price in human and material terms, he was careful to characterize it as a great victory, and monuments to the war and its single hero proliferated rapidly.[1] The end of the war offered some hope of a return to normalcy for most Iraqis as demobilization brought home tens of thousands of soldiers, antiaircraft guns disappeared from the streets of Baghdad, and the tremendous task of reconstruction began. Soon thereafter, plans for port expansion were drawn up, along with the rebuilding of Basra and hard-hit border areas, and the restoration of services began. Travel restrictions lessened, and even hints were made as to the possibility of democratic reform.[2]

For the first time in years, the country had the opportunity to focus on an increasing number of domestic problems, though the challenges were formidable, starting with several constraints in the economy. With the end of the war, over 250,000 demobilized Iraqi soldiers returned home to find Egyptian expatriates in the workforce. Unemployment rose to nearly 25%, much of it among the urban Shi'i underclass that had formed the bulk of the infantry and suffered directly through much of the fighting.[3] Low oil prices from the lingering world oil glut of the 1980s continued to deprive the regime of desperately needed revenues for reconstruction. Negotiations with Iran for control of the *Shatt al-Arab* remained as much at an impasse as the ordinance- and shipwreck-filled waterway itself. A tangible malaise soon gripped Baghdad as rising inflation diminished buying power, in spite of the steady stream of consumer imports that worsened balance-of-payments problems. No peace dividend seemed to be on the horizon for a population mollified during the war by imports but anticipating postwar improvements.

Not surprisingly, the regime continued to use repressive measures to control all elements of the state and society, having already turned northward to crush the perennial if faltering Kurdish movement. The officer corps was a particular regime concern, since it had fought a devastating war for several years, forged an important degree of institutional and interpersonal solidarity in the process, and risked being sidelined while the political apparatus of the Ba'ath pushed forward plans for strengthening the economy. While the military had grown immensely and become more diverse in political leanings, sectarian representation, and even ethnic identity, individual leaders also had carved out positions of authority and respect that gave them platforms from which to potentially challenge the regime. To respond, Saddam had at his disposal a full repertoire of carrots and sticks: patronage, promotion, and financial rewards for some, or demotion, retirement, and imprisonment for others. The regime moved against coup plotters in 1988 and 1989. Fearing another plot, Saddam temporarily arrested General Maher Abd al-Rashid, who was a friend, a fellow member of the Al-Bu Nasir tribe, his son Qusay's father-in-law, and a prominent and highly regarded military leader during the war. Even more darkly, General Adnan Khairallah Tulfah, the high-profile minister of defense and Saddam's brother-in-law and cousin, died in a suspicious helicopter accident in May 1989.

Acutely aware of the country's troubles, throughout 1989, while the world's attention was drawn to the dramatic changes sweeping through the Soviet Union and eastern bloc, the regime busied itself with plans to improve matters. By December 28, Deputy Premier and RCC member Saadoun Hammadi outlined Iraq's primary economic aims for 1990, which included fighting inflation, accelerating development, securing the supply of essential consumer goods, maintaining the combat quality of the armed forces, and reducing foreign debt.[4] These objectives, and the five-year plan for 1991–1996, reflected Iraq's attentiveness to military strength, reconstruction, revitalizing the economy, and placating a war-weary public.[5] With government projects that included the recommissioning of several vast petrochemical, iron and steel, and phosphate complexes in the region, the crucial linchpin to all these efforts was the rebuilding of infrastructure and export facilities in southeastern Iraq.[6] This would prove frustratingly difficult.

The war had forced Iraq to reroute its shipping from Basra and Fao at the head of the Persian Gulf to the Kuwaiti ports of Shuaiba and Shuwaikh, Dammam in eastern Saudi Arabia, Aqaba in Jordan, and various ports in Turkey—at a cost averaging $600 million per year.[7] Yet, the August ceasefire brought little relief because Basra and Fao were damaged and access to the *Shatt* was blocked by the physical remnants of the war and the tenuousness of the peace. Even with Iranian cooperation, the cost of clearing the *Shatt* of some 75 sunken ships, tons of ordinance, and tremendous silting loomed in the billions and would take a year.[8] For this reason, the regime moved to expand the Iraqi ports of Umm Qasr and Khor al-Zubair, which had been closed to commercial traffic during the war but were reopened in August 1988. While the Khor Abdullah channel linking Umm Qasr to Khor al-Zubair and the Gulf had been secretly cleared before the ceasefire, complete access was still blocked by narrow navigation channels and millions of tons of silt. Vast clearing and expansion projects were commenced, including plans to double the berths at the ports, increase their size limits to accommodate liquified petroleum gas carriers, and rebuild the offshore oil platforms of Mina al-Bakr and Khor al-Amaya.[9] But all in all, the nearly billion-dollar price tag on the project and the physical limitations inherent in their location proved all but insurmountable.[10] Even if a rebuilt Umm Qasr could have expanded Iraq's export capacity for manufactured goods, physical constraints limited its prospects as an oil-exporting facility, because large crude carriers could never pass through the channel or dock there. Iraqi economic recovery and its political independence were hemmed in.

More broadly, severe financial constraints limited the regime's postwar domestic plans to a degree unknown since the Ba'athist rise to power two decades earlier. Over the course of the war, Iraq went from having over $35 billion in hard currency and gold reserves to being nearly $80 billion in debt.[11] Most of this debt was to Saudi Arabia and Kuwait, which had provided approximately $1 billion per month in cash from 1980 to 1982, and billions more in the ensuing years in oil export revenues from the Kuwait–Saudi Divided Zone.[12] The pressure created by Iraq's non-Arab debt was equally significant. By 1987, Iraq had accumulated over $20 billion in debt to Japanese, French, Italian, German, and British creditors, largely in the form of high-interest, short-term loans that generated debt service obligations at precisely the moment when the regime needed fresh capital. Its indebtedness made acquiring additional loans more difficult, forcing the regime to roll over the accumulated debt and restricting the availability of new credit. While the state's revenue and credit crises were short-term in nature, the regime interpreted them as existential threats.

As important as these financial pressures were, the story of Iraq's invasion of Kuwait, detailed further in Chapter 4, reflects more than domestic economic drivers. A range of factors at various levels of analysis—individual decision-making, Iraqi domestic politics, and the broader international system—all conspired to lead to the events of August 2, 1990. Saddam's choices certainly reflected his personal calculations and interests, as he weighed his own prospects and made moves consistent with his determination to survive and even thrive as the leader of Iraq and, he hoped, of the greater MENA region. State-level domestic factors were vital in many ways, mostly centered on the powerful incentives generated by the country's short-term debt, revenue shortfall, credit crisis, reconstruction needs, industrial expansion plans, high unemployment, and inflation. International and regional dynamics most certainly also contributed in unexpected ways, particularly through the actions and choices of Iraq's wary and skeptical Arab allies, such as Saudi Arabia and, even more so, Kuwait. The August invasion represented a second bold but calamitous external foray by the regime in a decade, with dire consequences lasting for years to come.

Regime Survival and the Long Stalemate, 1991–2001

By May 1991, after the invasion and international response—and once it became less likely that Saddam would be overthrown by foreign military forces or domestic rivals—Iraq entered a long, difficult period marked by a variety of grinding struggles. The regime itself did everything it could to remain in control, while Saddam endeavored to stay on top, and his various supporters and acolytes worked to keep on good terms with him. To some extent, Saddam's regime was purpose-built and fully tested for the particular postwar challenges it faced, having already survived long periods of international opprobrium, violent conflict with foreign enemies, a floundering economy, insider betrayal, and deeply flawed national unity. For their part, Iraqis throughout the country were accustomed to hardship, though they faced new daily challenges from stepped-up state violence, stalled reconstruction, externally imposed sanctions, and a virtual economic blockade. In general, conditions went from bad in the 1980s to worse in the 1990s, even if the immediacy of the wartime crisis faded. These several years of postwar struggle, stalemate, and retrenchment were punctuated by occasional crises, both foreign and domestic in origin.

The regime's key supporters in this period, referred to as *Umana' Saddam* (Saddam's Faithful), numbered as many as 500,000, including their families, and were shielded from the worst effects of the sanctions put in place under U.N. Security Council auspices.[13] Mostly from Anbar in the Sunni-dominated Arab northwest, these people served to connect the regime to a larger portion of Iraqi society. They competed with each other for privilege, attention from the leader, and positional advantages that might benefit their particular subgroup. Supporters included select non-Sunnis, such as Shi'i and Kurdish tribal leaders willing to work closely with the regime in exchange for otherwise unavailable privileges. It was a classic Iraqi strategy of coopting potential threats and dangers to the regime by tapping into existing tribal hierarchies to bring amenable, cooperative sheikhs—and all those under their authority—into the fold. The *Umana' Saddam* and the sheikhs together had a measure of power in that Saddam had to placate and provide for them to win their support, as no authoritarian regime can survive without the backing or acquiescence of important social groups. Yet, Saddam retained the upper hand because he always had the option to drop individuals or groups from the mix of his supporters.

Not concerned with perceptions of hypocrisy, the regime used all forms of influence at its disposal, including noncoercive efforts to enhance its legitimacy in the eyes of key constituencies. For example, it deployed religious symbolism and posturing to garner political support and burnish its image. Some of this had begun during the runup to the war in January 1991, when the regime added the *takbir* (the phrase "*Allahu Akbar*/God is Great") to the Iraqi national flag, in a transparent bid for support in the Islamic world.[14] Long after losing the war, it promulgated new laws in 1992 restricting alcohol consumption and shuttering more than half of Baghdad's 40 nightclubs.[15] RCC Vice Chair and long-time, top-level Saddam stalwart Izzat Ibrahim al-Douri led a full-blown "faith campaign" (*al-hamla al-imaniya*) starting in 1993, promoting Islamic values. The regime eventually banned alcohol except at private parties or at home, curtailed women's freedoms, enhanced religious programming in the media, and authorized the use of hand amputation for theft. These actions were consistent with a turn toward Islamism and paralleled its promotion of traditional tribal values to win the support of conservative groups in Iraqi society. The campaign appeared to succeed at least very modestly in garnering some support among the more conservative Sunni tribes.

The Kurdish territories in this period suffered ongoing difficulties and achieved mixed and mostly unsatisfactory results. An internationally imposed no-fly zone in the north protected the Kurdish cities of Erbil and Dohuk, but did not include Sulaimaniyya or Kirkuk, just south of the 36th parallel, leading to further clashes there with the Iraqi army. Once the army withdrew in October 1991 to the regional boundary drawn in the 1970s, the Kurds had sufficient autonomy regionwide to establish self-governing political institutions. This permitted elections in May 1992 for a new Kurdish assembly that convened in June in Erbil, with the KDP dominating the northernmost territories and the PUK prevailing in the south around Sulaimaniyya. While a more capable Kurdish regional government was formed in July 1992, KDP and PUK leaders Masoud Barzani and Jalal Talabani did not throw all their support behind it by participating personally, undermining the government's legitimacy and leading to eventual deadly conflict between the two major factions.

Worse yet, with continued internal divisions and complicated external relations, both the KDP and PUK engaged and sometimes cooperated with the regimes in Baghdad and Tehran, eliciting their support against factional rivals or other Kurdish groups like the Kurdistan Workers' Party (PKK). Relations between the two factions deteriorated to the point of open warfare by 1994, with thousands of casualties as additional Kurdish fighters were drawn in from Turkey and Iran and the PUK took control of Erbil. The result was more years of costly conflict and disunity in Kurdistan, mitigated eventually by international diplomatic intervention. While the Kurds gained a significant degree of de facto autonomy in the 1990s, they remained in a state of limbo and contradiction. On the one hand, they were politically divided, geographically isolated, disconnected from the rest of Iraq, and deprived of trade ties or salaries and government assistance from Baghdad. On the other hand, they remained part of the MENA region and largely dependent on external actors, whether from neighboring states offering aid but seeking influence or from international forces with their own complex geopolitical agendas. By the latter part of the 1990s, they had patched up some of their internal differences and made progress toward better governance, but they remained vulnerable and, given a long history of betrayal and tragedy, were aware of the continued precariousness of their position.[16]

Throughout this period in the 1990s, the Shi'i majority was no better off. The Shi'a in the south, in particular, were subjected to ongoing Iraqi military operations even after the army crushed the month-long uprising of March 1991, following Iraq's expulsion from Kuwait. More than a year of such operations led the United States, Britain, and France to impose a southern no-fly zone in August 1992, though this simply shifted Iraqi military activities toward indiscriminate artillery attacks. In tandem with this, the regime launched initiatives to drain much of the southern marshlands, or *Ahwar*. The *Ahwar* had served as a base and a refuge, initially for relatively small numbers of Shi'i conscripts deserting during the Iran–Iraq War a few years earlier, and then for thousands of civilians and insurgents fleeing post-uprising state repression.

Among the regime's efforts to dominate the *Ahwar* was the so-called Third River Project. Conceived as a desalination and farmland irrigation scheme some four decades earlier under the monarchy, the project made little progress until the 1980s and acquired a wholly different purpose. The new version targeted the marsh Arabs, a 5000-year-old, mostly Shi'i Indigenous population of about 250,000 people, who descended from the ancient Sumerians. It advanced the regime's political effort to quell all opposition and its development agenda of tapping into a new, southern zone of likely oil deposits and building industrial infrastructure closer to the head of the Gulf.[17] Over time, the regime did almost irreversible damage to both the population and the marshland ecosystem, even if efforts to repair some of the damages were undertaken years later.[18]

An embittered, post-1991 Shi'i opposition was active in the form of underground political groups like the *Da'wa*, as well as via a changing clerical establishment that was becoming more politically engaged. Recognizing the threat posed by clerics leading a mobilized population, the regime continued its repression of the organized opposition while targeting noncompliant clerics. It succeeded in further fragmenting the establishment by the gradual, methodical arrest or assassination of several prominent figures. Actions began with the house arrest of the relatively apolitical chief *mujtahid* Abu al-Qasim al-Khoei in 1991 along with his student, the Ayatollah Ali al-Sistani. This was followed by the killing of al-Khoei's son, Mohammed Taqi al-Khoei, in 1994 while he was driving from Najaf to Karbala, in addition to the killing of other Ayatollahs like the Iranian-born Murtadha Ali Mohammed Ibrahim Borujerdi in Najaf in April 1998. Finally, the prominent *marja'* Mirza Ali al-Gharawi al-Tabrizi was murdered in June 1998, as well as Mohammed Sadiq al-Sadr and two of his sons in February 1999. In some cases, the regime arrested individuals who it claimed had committed these murders, though its own responsibility typically was evident.

Along with sectarian and ethnic political struggles, one other noteworthy trend occurred in this era relating to class dynamics. The emigration of middle-class professionals from Iraq, which had started in the 1980s during the Iran–Iraq War, accelerated substantially in the 1990s. By the end of the decade, Iraq began to experience a great hollowing out, as a growing number of people chose to leave rather than remain behind in suffering. Iraq lost doctors, engineers, teachers, writers, and other professionals. This exodus applied only to those with the means and the incentives to go elsewhere. The poor and popular classes had few exit options, since depressed oil prices and geopolitical tensions precluded large numbers of Iraqi workers from leaving to find jobs in the Gulf. Likewise, the rich and well-connected had little reason to depart and managed to find ways to survive, with a limited number actually thriving. Those in the small segment between rich and poor—Iraq's middle class—left in disproportionate numbers, taking with them much of the training, talent, and initiative needed to improve Iraq's economy and potentially make strides in its political life. They largely ended up in Europe and North America.

The bureaucracy and what had been a growing array of state institutions also shrank in this period, with far fewer resources and jobs and a less central role to play in regulating social interaction. Iraq was not alone in its diminishing state capacity, since the pattern had been common throughout the MENA region since the 1980s.[19] But it was especially pronounced in 1990s Iraq, a country that had not previously witnessed state-level institutional deficits experienced by other regional actors like Lebanon, Libya, and Yemen. In Iraq after 1991, state sovereignty was limited by international intervention, not only in the security domain but also in having only limited control of imports and exports. Shrinking state resources meant that even the official development agenda had to be put on hold. The state no longer held sway in breakaway Kurdistan, nor was it heavily active in the south except in its security and policing functions. Even in the security sector, Saddam's invasive, mobilizing totalitarian state yielded to a basic, crude authoritarianism designed to limit all political activity more than to cultivate any active participation in national life.

Despite the weakness of Iraq's formal state structures, its informal institutions were sufficient to keep the regime in power, given the strength of family, tribal, personal, and regional connections between the leader and his various constituencies. In fact, Saddam's grip on the country seemed to grow stronger in this period compared to the influence of the organized opposition. In this sense, the decade from 1991 to 2001 was lost for domestic challengers, who remained as divided as ever, despite attempts to forge a consensus around the goal of removing Saddam from power. Unsurprisingly but unhelpfully for collective action, opposition groups reflected Iraq's rich diversity. They encompassed ethnic and sectarian differences as well as the full ideological spectrum, ranging from a fragmented communist movement on the far left to a host of liberals, nationalists, dissident military officers, and former Ba'athists.

The most potentially powerful domestic groups were easily held in check by the security services, while a weak array of exiled dissidents tried to organize and unify overseas under various auspices. The United States led an aggressive charge on international weapons inspections and sanctions in this era, but the Americans under the Clinton administration were only half-heartedly concerned with Iraqi domestic affairs. The Iraqi National Congress (INC), a U.S.-sponsored collection of personalities and factions more than an organically coherent expression of opposition, convened in Vienna in June 1992 but got caught up in internecine Kurdish politics and a disastrously failed coup attempt in 1995. Eventually it resurfaced via its connections to the United States, especially the White House and Pentagon under a new administration. The United States got much more serious about the nature of Saddam's regime only after dramatic events on its own soil.[20]

Iraq on the Brink, 2001–2003

Saddam's Iraq had no involvement in the attacks of September 11, 2001, nor any association whatsoever with Osama bin Laden's al-Qa'ida organization. By 2001, it no longer had any ongoing and viable WMD programs, having dismantled them over the course of a decade of intrusive international inspections that it attempted to thwart but failed.[21] Yet, the consequences of 9/11 for Iraq were as profound and transformative as they were for the United States or any other country.

The American response focused momentarily on invading Afghanistan to oust the Taliban and pursue al-Qa'ida, but it pivoted quickly toward planning a war to remove Saddam from power. To justify the case for war, the Bush administration conjured up a fictitious regime connection to bin Laden—seemingly a product of wishful thinking—and pounced on the real fact of ambiguous, grudging Iraqi compliance with U.N. Security Council resolutions. Saddam himself made doing so easy with the brutality of his rule and the inscrutability of his intentions. No one other than Saddam and, at most, a few top aides knew the full truth about the country's military programs and strategic planning. Fearful of seeming weak and vulnerable to regional adversaries like Iran, he allowed himself to look more dangerous and noncompliant than he was, and this proved to be his undoing. While Chapter 4 will detail the international dimensions of this episode, Iraq's domestic political context during the 18 months between 9/11 and the U.S.-led invasion had features worth noting.

First, in the early 2000s, a general sentiment prevailed in Iraq that it had survived the worst of the 1990s-era deprivations. While the country remained widely impoverished, the sanctions regime was fraying in the face of a gradual, nearly worldwide realization of the futility and perhaps injustice of aggressive economic sanctions isolating Iraq. By 2001, most observers had cooled to the idea of subjecting the entire population to severe constraints that seemed broadly damaging but utterly ineffective in dislodging the regime itself from power. The U.N.-sponsored Oil-for-Food Program had improved general conditions, particularly for the more privileged segments of the population, even if it was marred by corruption and manipulation by the regime. French, Chinese, and Russian companies, among others, were increasingly active in evading international constraints on trade, and more consumer goods were available to the public. Oil prices had started to rebound from earlier declines. Life was anything but rosy, but it had been considerably worse, and the new millennium held the promise of a better future.

Second, the regime itself was effectively as secure as ever and generally confident of its continued survival. Somewhat surprisingly, it had managed to use the conditions imposed at the end of the 1991 war to off-load responsibility for some of Iraq's most intractable problems of national unity and identity. As far as Baghdad was concerned, Kurdistan's newly achieved relative autonomy created an opportunity for the central government to put aside the challenges of national integration and minority demands. It could allow the Kurds to govern themselves—and engage in internecine warfare—intervening occasionally in KDP/PUK fighting to maintain its influence and demonstrate its inescapable relevance.[22] Just as importantly, the regime evaded culpability for the country's ongoing economic problems by trumpeting the punitive nature of the collective punishment meted out by the international community and eliciting an unlikely degree of sympathy. By late 2001, when the United States began ramping up pressure on Iraq regarding its alleged connections to al-Qaʻida, it was easy for the regime to fit that claim into a general narrative that the Americans simply had it in for Iraq. While the regime's compartmentalized information flows prevented most Iraqi officials from knowing the extent of illicit government activities, Saddam knew Iraq had not been involved in 9/11. He expected to avoid a full-blown U.S. invasion.[23]

Third, throughout this period, Saddam's informal institutions stood in effectively for the state, but only in protecting the regime from internal enemies. Saddam had mastered Iraq's long-established system of patronage, loyalty, and political favoritism.

His informal network operated outside state authority channels. It complemented and overlapped with the direct and explicit authority of the bureaucracy, Ba'ath Party, state ministries, and even the military. It was marked by opaque decision-making and ambiguous relationships, with individual authority a function of the whims of the leader. It served a single, precise purpose: keeping Saddam Hussein in power. While it was effective at doing so and keeping his rivals off balance, Iraq's informal governance structures could not protect him from his own errant decision-making, which had led to two disastrous foreign adventures and now precipitated a third national trauma in three decades. Being unable and, to some extent, unwilling to convince the world of his compliance with U.N. resolutions regarding its possession of WMD, Saddam's Iraq invited invasion, destruction, state failure, and ultimate transformation.

War and Regime Change, 2003

The United States invaded Iraq in March 2003, intent on deposing Saddam and ending Ba'athist rule. Toppling the regime and winning the conventional war was easy and only required about six weeks. Taking control of Iraq and transforming the political order proved much more difficult, came at enormous human and material cost, and took years. Indeed, it remained an unfinished project long afterward. While Chapter 4 digs deeper into the international dimensions of the war and subsequent troubled efforts by the United States to bring stability and democracy to the country, the domestic aspects of what amounted to externally imposed regime change were fundamentally important. While the events on the ground were shaped by foreign powers, especially the United States, they had their own dynamics worth understanding.

The war and its aftermath had wide-ranging consequences for Iraq and, in fact, changed the entire MENA region, given its follow-on effects over the years. In short, it eliminated Saddam's regime with ease, destroyed his informal political networks, undermined already weakened state institutions, and reenergized social identities to give them new political relevance. With no organized authority taking power or restoring a minimally functioning state, Iraqis resorted to alternative forms of governance and political mobilization, some favored by external patrons like the United States but most rooted in sectarian, kinship, and ethnic identities. As a result, all the troubles associated with externally imposed regime change and eventual state failure became the key features of Iraqi political life for the next several years: a multiheaded insurgency, continued economic deprivation, heightened sectarian and ethnic polarization, unrelenting terrorism, and an eventual low-grade civil war, as various parties vied for control of the state.[24]

Pushing aside the regime immediately was easy because it had become so deeply personalized. With Saddam and his sons, Uday and Qusay, on the run, there was no one at the top of the decision-making hierarchy to direct government activities. Uday and Qusay were killed in a firefight when trapped in a building by coalition troops in Mosul, late in July 2003. The following December, Saddam himself was captured hiding in a small "spider hole" at a farm near al-Dawr, south of Tikrit. He had eluded coalition forces for months but was caught, ironically, not far from where he had escaped across the Tigris River in 1959 after attempting to assassinate Abd al-Karim Qasim. He would be executed by hanging three years later in December 2006. Other high-ranking regime officials took a few different paths. Some, such as Deputy Prime Minister Tareq Aziz, surrendered immediately in late April during the war itself. Many others were captured by coalition or Kurdish forces between April and August, including Saddam's half-brother and Interior Minister Watban Ibrahim, Vice President Taha Yassin Ramadan, presidential secretary Lt. General Abid al-Hamid Mahmud al-Tikriti, the notorious "Chemical Ali" Hasan al-Majid, and Ba'ath Party head Aziz Saleh al-Numan. A handful of top officials, such as Saddam's half-brother and secret police head Sabawi Ibrahim al-Tikriti and Vice President Izzat Ibrahim al-Douri, managed to evade immediate capture, in al-Douri's case continuing on to help organize the subsequent Iraqi insurgency.[25]

Importantly, it was not just the displacement and elimination of these formally empowered state leaders that ended the regime and transformed Iraqi political life. Just as significant was the undermining of the informal political networks they oversaw. Saddam was at the top of both the institutions of the state and the networks that animated all political activity. The nominal heads of the various ministries and state bodies were only as powerful as the strength of their connections to Saddam and his inner circle. Individuals and groups fell in and out of Saddam's favor and were kept perpetually off balance in a fluid, changing array of loyalties and favors. Saddam maintained this array in his head, taking care to prevent any individual or faction from coming or remaining close to the center for long or building a rival power base. Eliminating Saddam meant disrupting the delicately balanced patronage relationships at the heart of Iraqi politics in this era.[26]

The related story of Iraq's war-induced state failure is well known and fundamentally important. Not only did the invasion displace the Baghdad regime, it went a step further in undermining the entire state apparatus governing Iraq. In going to war, the United States leaned hard on the regime and brought down the state in the process, not as a core political objective so much as a byproduct of the strategy informing its entire approach to the matter, a function of the particular ideas dominating Bush administration's thinking at the time.[27] In this sense, the war was not just a "war of choice," but a war of bad choices, informed by troubled ideas. State failure resulted specifically from a series of decisions by the war's planners and implementers that weakened an already-fragile set of institutions atrophied by the pressures of a decade of sanctions. The most prominent two sets of decisions related to the state's administrative capacity and its security services.

Regarding administration, the war's initial assault on Baghdad included attacks on nearly every government ministry, as American forces attacked a wide range of public facilities and infrastructure, including roads, bridges, electrical transformers, and communications. By its conclusion, the coalition had damaged most government facilities and devastated the institutional apparatus of state decision-making.

While the Ministry of Oil complex in northeast Baghdad's Mustansiriya neighborhood was famously spared, few other physical or bureaucratic manifestations of the Iraqi state escaped the opening phases of the war. In fact, American occupation authorities were fairly systematic in ridding Iraq of state administrative authority and transforming its institutional landscape. Most prominently, Paul Bremer's Coalition Provisional Authority (CPA) eliminated or acquiesced to the removal of the entire upper tier of the state bureaucracy. With Order No. 1 of May 16, 2003, the CPA expelled all Ba'ath Party members from government service, firing approximately 30,000 people working in various state ministries, including a majority of its most experienced functionaries, even if it left in place mid-range and street-level bureaucrats.[28]

In July 2003, the CPA established a 25-member Iraqi Governing Council (IGC), with limited legal and budgetary authority, but membership—13 Shi'i and 5 Sunni Arabs, 5 Kurds, 1 Turkmen, and 1 Assyrian—was based on purely ethnic and sectarian identities and included a large number of returning exiles. This decision reflected the American notion of how to govern Iraq and was a recipe for future ethnosectarian mobilization and conflict.[29] In addition, the CPA subsequently overturned the state's lawmaking apparatus, substituted over 100 administrative decrees, and created a Transitional Administrative Law (TAL) in 2004, which was replaced by a new constitution in 2005. Not confining itself to the political domain, the CPA sought to liberalize the economy by slashing subsidies on food and energy, promoting foreign direct investment, and introducing international banking. Its Office of Private Sector Development prepared to privatize or close most of the country's 189 state-owned enterprises, targeting over 100,000 Iraqi employees for firing or forced retirement. Given the larger context of the invasion and the unraveling of organized authority, these measures opened to contestation the most basic questions of political life, all but collapsing the Iraqi state as an organization and undermining the Iraqi nation as a community.

As for state failure in the security domain, the most obvious effect of the war was the persistence and subsequent growth of domestic political violence in its chaotic aftermath. Iraq did not have even momentary peace after the end of the initial war. This can be traced partly to the CPA's "dissolution" of the military and security forces under Order No. 2 of May 23, 2003, which dismissed over 350,000 trained soldiers. Any officer at the rank of colonel or above was declared ineligible for a pension and could not work for a future Iraqi military or government. Additional elements of the state apparatus eliminated by this order included the Ministry of Information, the Ministry of State for Military Affairs, the Iraqi Intelligence Service, and all subsidiary military, paramilitary, and intelligence organizations. The order also included the Revolutionary Command Council, the national assembly, and the revolutionary, special, and national security courts.[30]

Accordingly, this eliminated Iraq's state coercive apparatus without replacing it with either U.S. occupation forces, a comparable international contingent, or revamped and repurposed Iraqi forces. Without a capable mechanism to provide security, rein in the most implacable militants, oust foreign agitators, and assure the rule of law, little could be done to prevent an almost immediate deterioration after the regime's collapse in late April 2003. Large numbers of individuals from the various state institutions shifted from potential supporters to determined opponents of a post-Saddam Iraq, forming the heart of an insurgency and launching a civil war that developed in subsequent months. American forces proved unable to stem the violence, though they too suffered some of the consequences.

In this sense, the decapitation of the regime was consequential because the Iraqi state could not function effectively without its top decision-maker and his formal and informal political apparatus. This would have been the case even if a temporary leader or ruling body had been substituted in Saddam's place immediately. No individual or small group could have reconstructed the lines of authority and obligation in Iraq's "shadow state," as Charles Tripp calls it, which held political life together.[31] Saddam had constructed the regime precisely to make himself irreplaceable. Cutting off the regime at its head was a surefire invitation to anarchy, or at least violence among the disparate Iraqi groups contending for dominance in a post-Saddam Iraq. With three vice presidents, several major security and intelligence bodies, a rival political apparatus in the Ba'ath Party, and a powerful if damaged military establishment, no single entity could have grasped the reins and managed a stable, peaceful transition after Saddam's ouster. Norms of political violence, which had accrued for decades, did not disappear with the regime. And no bottom-up democracy could be created in short order, despite the administration's ideological assumptions about its naturalness or inevitability.

This reality had enormous consequences beyond matters of security, including in social relations. Social identity in Iraq already had been persistently significant from the Ottoman era onward, at the very least. It became even more important in a contested, fractured political environment with a weakly developed national identity. In the absence of state authority and facing chaotic conditions, Iraqis turned to the most reliable social networks available: family, kinsmen, coethnics, or fellow Sunnis and Shi'a. In an existentially threatening security environment, with no alternative mechanism for self-defense and survival, people leaned on the basic connections available to help them, whether for purposes of survival or the pursuit of larger ambitions. It was on this basis that the Iraqi insurgency and civil war began.

Insurgency and Democratic Development, 2003–2006

Starting in the summer of 2003 and accelerating in the fall, the prospects for a peaceful postwar transition fell apart. All types of domestic groups began waging asymmetric warfare and employing guerrilla-style tactics against coalition troops. They were joined in short order by foreign fighters able to penetrate the country's porous borders. An insurgency took hold, as indiscriminate violence was directed against civilians in public spaces like markets, mosques, and government buildings. Suicide and car bombings proliferated and began to take their toll. One early, politically devastating attack was the August 19, 2003, truck bombing of the U.N. headquarters in Baghdad, killing the United Nations' special representative for Iraq,

Sergio Vieira de Mello, a dedicated diplomat and international public servant. The bombing led the United Nations to remove its entire international staff for nearly five years. This was followed ten days later by a massive car bombing of the Imam Ali Shrine in Najaf, killing the Shi'i cleric Mohammad Baqir al-Hakim, who led the Supreme Council for the Islamic Revolution in Iraq (SCIRI). He had just returned from two decades of exile in Iran and had cooperated with the United States.

Both attacks, in addition to the bombing of the Jordanian embassy in Baghdad early that month, were perpetrated by Abu Musab al-Zarqawi, a Jordanian-born Sunni Islamist militant. Zarqawi at that moment was the head of an aspiring al-Qa'ida affiliate, called al-Qa'ida in Iraq (AQI), which eventually broke with bin Laden's al-Qa'ida and became the organizational predecessor to the Islamic State.[32] Such attacks transformed security conditions in Baghdad and were the first indications of great impending upheaval, which would last for many years and have wide-ranging further consequences in the MENA region and for the world.

Importantly, the insurgency that developed in subsequent months was not one but several. It was not a coherent, unified struggle by a single group with a common purpose, but a set of overlapping efforts by many groups, united only in their hostility to the occupying forces and their willingness to use violence against noncombatants for political ends. Attacks were initiated by nonstate actors ranging from former members of the Iraqi security services and military to sectarian militias and a growing number of foreign fighters drawn to the country by the absence of organized authority. Some insurgents were locally or nationally oriented, while others were more international in origin and objectives. Some were secular, and others were Islamists of various stripes, mostly Sunni until later stages in the upheaval. Some were motivated by narrow political ends, others by broader ideological considerations or sectarian antipathy. Eventually a criminal element found its way into the fray. Insurgents who were ex-Ba'athist officials and army officers retained access to unsecured weapon depots and caches. Others had technical and material assistance from interested foreign powers like Iran. Most had a high degree of local knowledge and, in some cases, sympathetic popular support or fear-driven acquiescence.

The initial invasion and war of 2003 had damaged Iraqi infrastructure, including public buildings, roads, bridges, water systems, sewerage treatment, the electricity grid, health services, and even educational opportunities by way of school closures. All of this was compounded by the exceptional amount of unhindered looting done by Iraqis themselves, having suffered materially for years under harsh international sanctions and an even harsher ruling order. When the physical destruction and governance failures were not remedied, this made postwar everyday life more difficult, exacerbated economic hardship, and fed conflict by incentivizing recruitment to militant groups. It was apparent to all that effectively no one was in charge and nothing would be fixed quickly. A quasi-anarchic, self-help system emerged from the absence of any capable, legitimate authority to regulate social, political, and economic relationships.

The effort to reassert organized political authority and rebuild Iraqi institutions was marked by a series of advances and, more often, setbacks. Deteriorating security had prompted the CPA to move its headquarters to a 10-square-kilometer protected area or "Green Zone" on the long, curving western bank of the Tigris, centered on a former presidential palace in the middle of Baghdad.[33] Despite its isolation and the inexperience of its ill-prepared staff, the CPA indicated it would move forward quickly and end its control of Iraq within a year. It launched efforts to draft a new constitution, establish a transitional government, and hold democratic elections for a national assembly. The Law of Administration for the State of Iraq for the Transitional Period (TAL)—essentially an interim constitution—was approved by the CPA and the IGC in March 2004.[34] Very limited powers were given to an interim government under Shi'i secularist Prime Minister Ayad Allawi in June, with the departure of the CPA, the dissolving of the IGC, and the ostensible return of sovereignty to Iraqi authorities. Regardless of the apparent progress in rebuilding Iraqi institutions on a more democratic basis, no dominant, sovereign, legitimate power governed Iraq, more than a year after the previous regime had been displaced.

Several months later, in January 2005, Iraq held its first postwar elections for a 275-member Transitional National Assembly. A Shi'i coalition—the United Iraqi Alliance (UIA), combining SCIRI and Da'wa—won almost half the seats, but the vote was marred by threats of violence and very little participation from the Sunni minority, which largely boycotted. After three months of heated discussions, the new parliament named PUK leader Jalal Talabani to the mostly ceremonial presidency in late April, and Talabani declared Da'wa leader Ibrahim Ja'afari the prime minister. Ja'afari's caretaker government was not sworn in until May 20, four months after the original election. Worse still, the cabinet was dysfunctionally large, having 32 members plus an additional 6 ministers without portfolio to satisfy all major stakeholders. It also was heavy in exile representation, only weakly empowered, and divided along ethnosectarian lines under a *muhasasa ta'ifiya* (quota or apportionment) system, with an 18-minister Shi'i majority compared to 6 Sunnis and 8 Kurdish ministers. The new power-sharing arrangement was so fragmented that each ministry operated almost independently, with an exceptional lack of accountability to a central authority. In a sense, it adopted a leaderless version of the Saddam-era patronage system, exacerbated by further corruption and nepotism.

The Ja'afari government's main charge was to oversee the drafting of a permanent constitution and hold a general election to establish a regular government. It managed to win approval by referendum of the new constitution in October 2005, though just barely.[35] This allowed it to hold Iraq's first fully democratic election for a constitutionally mandated Council of Representatives (*Majlis al-Nuwwab*) on December 15, 2005. The council, often referred to as the Iraqi parliament, was a 325-seat body, later expanded to 329, and part of a unicameral legislature with representatives holding four-year terms.[36] The parliament was empowered to pass laws, ratify treaties, and oversee the government formed by the prime minister on the basis of a majority, whether outright or via a coalition of parties. The prime minister himself was selected by the president, who in turn was not directly elected but chosen by the parliament. The prime minister created a Council of Ministers (*Majlis al-Wuzara'*), or cabinet, typically with individuals from all the major parties in the coalition supporting the government.[37]

In the December 2005 election itself, voter turnout was high overall, but the final results were not announced for weeks, amid protests, violence, and claims of fraud. In the end, the UIA won 128 seats, a slight decline from the previous January's transitional vote, while Sunni Arab candidates improved their performance by participating actively and winning 55 seats. The narrower UIA electoral margin required the formation of a coalition government, which presented great difficulty and took until May because the Shi'i-preferred candidate—caretaker Prime Minister Ja'afari himself—was rejected by the Sunni, Kurdish, and secular parties. On May 21, 2006, the Council of Representatives finally approved long-time *Da'wa* Party stalwart Nouri al-Maliki. He was the first regular prime minister of a democratically elected, constitutionally empowered government since the departure of Saddam Hussein more than three years earlier. All the while, there had been little to no stability in governance. In fact, Iraq already had begun to descend into an even grimmer struggle for control of the state.

The Civil War, 2006–2007

Iraq's multiple insurgencies became more sectarian over time and contributed to the outbreak of a low-grade sectarian civil war by February 2006. The slide into larger-scale violence was accelerated that month by AQI's bombing and destruction of the tenth-century *al-Askari* shrine in Samarra, one of the most important Shi'i shrines in the world. This attack, along with extrajudicial killings by Shi'i militias, triggered extraordinary violence in the Baghdad area especially. With weak governing institutions and a paralyzed political process still undecided on a new prime minister, few if any mechanisms were available to stop the intense ethnic and sectarian mobilization and reprisal attacks. Thousands of Iraqis died in the spring, summer, and fall of 2006.[38] More than a million Iraqis became internally displaced and had to seek shelter beyond their homes by the end of the year. Once-cosmopolitan Baghdad's social diversity declined, as people fled indiscriminate attacks and sought refuge in closed, walled-in communities free of their ethnic and sectarian counterparts.[39]

The Iraq of 2006 and 2007 was a maelstrom of violence and sectarian mobilization, much of it a byproduct of the absence of an organized, legitimate, capable state authority to manage and regulate political life. State institutional weakness gave nationalist insurgents and foreign antisystem groups like AQI an outsized capacity to do harm and exacerbate social tension. The United States, while the seemingly authoritative power, could do relatively little to stop the mayhem. It was present but absent, an occupying force without the will or capacity to govern an unruly, divided, traumatized society that it did not understand well. It could not even control the conditions of Saddam Hussein's execution in late December 2006, after his conviction by a special Iraqi tribunal. The United States did locate and assassinate AQI leader Abu Musab al-Zarqawi in June 2006, but he was replaced by Abu Ayyub al-Masri and Abu Omar al-Baghdadi, who renamed the organization the Islamic State in Iraq (ISI) and continued to wreak havoc.

The Surge, Sunni Awakening, and U.S. Withdrawal, 2007–2011

In January 2007, President Bush announced the deployment of nearly 30,000 additional U.S. troops, mostly to Baghdad, in an effort to tamp down violence in the capital and Anbar province to the west. The Surge, as it came to be known, repositioned troops to combat outposts and joint security stations close to residential neighborhoods while expanding operations against both ISI and Shi'i militias. It allowed for a better application of the new American counterinsurgency doctrine developed in 2006 by the U.S. military. Adding to the 130,000 U.S. troops already in the country was not without risk or cost. The initial result of the Surge in the first half of 2007 was the highest U.S. casualty rate of the insurgency, rising to 127 U.S. service member deaths in May before declining for the rest of the year.[40] Even more grimly, the number of Iraqi civilian casualties approached 100 per day in much of 2006 and 2007, though the tide began to turn part way through 2007.[41] While the Surge alone was not responsible for ending the horrific violence, it did have a discernable impact by late 2007 and into 2008, largely in conjunction with more locally originated actions by Iraqis themselves.

Well over a year before the Surge, starting in 2005, Sunni tribesmen from Anbar province had become disillusioned and turned against Abu Musab al-Zarqawi's AQI in what would be called, among other names, the Anbar Awakening (*al-Sahwa Anbar*).[42] Initially in Ramadi and led by tribal leaders like Sheikh Abd al-Sattar al-Rishawi, organized into Awakening Councils, the rebellion was motivated as much by local political and economic grievances as discomfort with AQI's brutal methods or strict Islamic practices. The U.S. invasion and ensuing arrival of foreign militant groups had dislodged certain tribes from their relatively privileged positions and disrupted previously beneficial trade, smuggling, and patronage networks.[43] AQI's internationalist aspirations also were at odds with the Iraq-first nationalism of many of the tribes, some of whom saw the Islamists as yet another foreign power. The United States took advantage of the discontent and built on the Anbar Awakening by coopting tens of thousands of tribesmen—including some former insurgents—to create networks of "Iraqi security volunteers." It coordinated with the Awakening Councils, put their fighters on the U.S. payroll, provided some weapons, and trained these groups to keep the peace. This action flipped many former American adversaries from enemies to at least temporary allies and leveraged their significant local knowledge.[44] It ramped up the level of conflict between Iraqis themselves in Anbar, but contributed to the eventual improvement of security in the province, as Iraqis took back control of the territory.

The Maliki government formed in mid-2006 was never comfortable having an organized force of Sunni fighters on the payroll. It viewed many of the *Sahwa* groups—not entirely without reason—as little more than unreconstructed Ba'athists and insurgents. When the United States handed over control of the program to Baghdad in October 2008, the Iraqi government disbanded it and even arrested some of its leaders, refusing to pay them or to integrate the Sunni forces into Iraq's security apparatus. More broadly, it pursued an unapologetic sectarian path, as it sought to build a new, post-Saddam Iraq in which the Shi'i majority dominated. Maliki moved tentatively at first, but he was able to become more assertive in 2008 after the successful paring down of ISI, which eventually lost much of its leadership in the fighting and was driven out of Anbar and Diyala provinces to a few strongholds like Mosul in the north. Latent support for Sunni militancy remained in the tribal areas, however, fed by resentment and fear of Shi'i domination.

This is not to say that the Maliki government followed purely sectarian policies or failed to challenge Shi'i groups and leaders operating independently. One of Maliki's most threatening political rivals was Muqtada al-Sadr, the fourth son of assassinated Saddam critic and *marja'* Mohammed Sadiq al-Sadr, as well as the nephew and son-in-law of executed Saddam opponent and *Da'wa* founder Mohammed Baqir al-Sadr. Al-Sadr's prominent family and street appeal in the Shi'i districts of eastern Baghdad—renamed Sadr City after his father—allowed him to create the Mahdi Army (*Jaysh al-Mahdi*) after the American invasion, first attacking American forces as early as April 2004. Considered Iran's closest ally, he emerged as an influential leader and gained strength in the years of the occupation and transition back to Iraqi rule. Once Maliki's government was in a position to take on Sadr's Mahdi Army, it sent Iraqi forces to Basra to drive out the militia and reassert control in the Charge of the Knights campaign in March 2008. This was the first major operation planned and launched by the Iraqi military after being reconstituted by the United States. While it resulted in hundreds of casualties, required considerable coalition air support, and was somewhat inconclusive, the end result was a limited reassertion of government authority in an important region and a successful assertion of political will. It sidelined the Sadrists for the time being and allowed Maliki to move forward with his plans, enhancing his credibility as an Iraqi nationalist unbeholden to foreign powers.[45]

Maliki's focus was not limited to challenging ISI or Muqtada al-Sadr. Like past Iraqi leaders, he had grown convinced of the necessity of his rule, in the process acquiring more adversaries determined to end his time in office. This issue came to the fore in the Council of Representatives election of March 2010, which was expected to be a first demonstration of political turnover, with the government changing after four years in power. Democracy, after all, is a political system in which parties lose elections.[46] Iraq was at a critical juncture as a country, having suffered the trauma of invasion, insurgency, and civil war, but also having transitioned to a new political era of—potentially—competitive multiparty democracy and the rule of law. The Maliki government had negotiated an agreement with the Bush administration in late 2008, insisting on an end to the American troop presence by 2011 that would allow Iraq to return to a fully sovereign existence and to chart its own path forward. The Obama administration entered office determined to exit Iraq and was not going to renege on the agreement.

But before the U.S. withdrawal, a critical parliamentary election had to be held. The March 2010 election was conventional in some ways, with campaigning and all the hallmarks of democracy, though it was accompanied by a fair amount of violence and the exclusion of several hundred former Ba'athists seeking office. In the end, Maliki's State of Law (SOL) party did in fact lose the election to the secular, pragmatic Iraqi National List, aka *Iraqiyya*, led by former interim Prime Minister Ayad Allawi, whose bloc eked out a seeming victory with 91 seats (28% of the vote). *Iraqiyya* was a new nationalist grouping that included Sunni parties supported by ex-Ba'athists who had realized it was better to compete than to boycott and be shut out. Its winning, nonsectarian approach was a sign that a substantial segment of the Iraqi public had tired of divisions. Maliki's SOL, by splitting the Shi'i Islamist vote in a personal bid to remain in power, won only 89 seats (27.4%), with its rival Shi'i grouping, the Iraqi National Alliance (INA), taking a disappointing 70 seats (21.6%), while the Kurdish bloc secured 57 seats (22.2%) and smaller Sunni parties won 10 seats (5.3%).[47] No single party or bloc had anything approaching a majority, producing results that mirrored Iraq's social divisions and doing little to enhance the country's public confidence in the power of democracy to manage political pluralism.

If the vote outcome itself was problematic, Maliki focused less on Iraq's fragmented politics and more on taking advantage of the situation to remain in power. Given the close results and the combined strength of the two Shi'i sectarian blocs, he was able to use the authority of his office to prevent Ayad Allawi and *Iraqiyya* from forming a new government immediately. He pressured the Supreme Court to rule that under the constitution, the largest bloc—his own if joined by others—should be allowed to take charge. This tactic delayed the political process for months, with the prime minister presiding as caretaker while offering blandishments to smaller parties to induce their participation in a new government under his leadership. After eight months of negotiations, Maliki finally brought the Sadrists of the INA and then the KDP and PUK Kurdish parties into an agreement approved by the Council of Representatives in December 2010. The result was a seeming government of national unity that included a vague mechanism to elicit the participation of Ayad Allawi and others from *Iraqiyya*. Its inclusiveness proved debilitating, as the prime minister's deeply divided, 45-person cabinet was as unwieldy and ineffective as any. Maliki's authoritarian streak was given further license, just as problems of corruption and inefficiency were becoming particularly acute. Given what was unfolding elsewhere in the MENA region that December, Iraq needed stable, capable, legitimate governance as much as ever.

From the Arab Spring to the Islamic State, January 2011– December 2014

Events elsewhere in the MENA region shifted international attention in early 2011, as the Arab Spring swept through Tunisia, Egypt, Yemen, and Libya, among other countries, reaching neighboring Syria in March. Iraq itself experienced relatively minor protests, not remotely comparable to what was experienced by a few of its neighbors. Syria's descent into a deeper conflict by July 2011, however, provided a metastasizing environment for regional Islamist militants, including some hailing from Iraq when ISI leader Abu Bakr al-Baghdadi sent operatives to open a branch across the border. This decision gave new life to his organization once certain events occurred at home in Iraq, starting with the final American military withdrawal from the country in late December 2011. Most Iraqis welcomed the departure, but this left the United States without much leverage vis-à-vis Nouri al-Maliki. The newly reupped prime minister wasted no time in issuing an arrest warrant for one of his vice presidents, Tareq al-Hashemi, lodging terrorism charges against the Sunni leader and former Ba'athist military officer from Fallujah the day after the American departure. Doing so had extraordinary consequences.

In response to this and general Sunni perceptions of the Maliki government's sectarian bias, 2012 saw rising protests and disillusionment, the bombing of Shi'i pilgrims, and *Iraqiyya* suspending its participation in the Council of Representatives. ISI launched a 12-month "Breaking the Walls" campaign, attacking prisons in Tikrit, Abu Ghraib, and elsewhere to free hundreds of hardened militants. A heavy-handed government response to protests in Hawija, west of Kirkuk, killed dozens, alienating Sunnis further and leading tribal leaders to acquiesce to a renewed ISI presence in Anbar, Ninawa, and Diyala provinces. A full-blown Sunni insurgency emerged and intensified, as leader Abu Bakr al-Baghdadi rebranded the rejuvenated ISI as the Islamic State in Iraq and Syria (ISIS) in April 2013 after his expansion across the border provided new resources. In July 2013, ISIS started a second 12-month campaign, "A Soldier's Harvest," which entailed targeting Iraqi security forces for intimidation and assassination, bombing Erbil, and beginning to conquer territory. By the end of 2013, two years after the American exit, ISIS held Fallujah, much of Ramadi, and had an expanding presence throughout Anbar province.[48]

The Maliki government struggled to respond to the ongoing crisis and had to face an election in April 2014 prompted by a crumbling coalition. In his second term, Maliki had presided over a weakening state apparatus and resentful political partners, with accusations not just of sectarianism but also of corruption, authoritarianism, and incompetence. In the April vote, his SOL party nonetheless won 92 seats and was surprisingly unaffected by the dire security situation. The Sadrists and the ISCI came in second and third, winning 34 and 29 seats, while Ayad Allawi's party scored 21 seats and the Kurdish parties—KDP, PUK, and the reform-oriented Gorran—won 25, 21, and 9 seats.[49] Two Sunni parties led by Usama al-Najaifi and Saleh al-Mutlaq obtained 23 and 10 seats. Parties had not formed preelection coalitional blocs because the 2010 Supreme Court decision affirming Maliki's constitutional interpretation eliminated any incentive to join one before the vote. This meant another extended period of uncertainty and difficulty in obtaining the 165-seat majority needed to form a government.

Ultimately, Nouri al-Maliki could not cobble together a coalition to gain support for a third term as prime minister because outside events—caused partly by his own actions—called his leadership into question. In June 2014, just weeks after the parliamentary election, ISIS captured Iraq's second largest city, Mosul, and declared invalid the Sykes–Picot border established in 1916 between Iraq and Syria. By the numbers, it was the worst month in decades for Iraqi civilians, with over 4000 dead.[50] In Mosul and throughout the northern Tigris River valley, the Iraqi military melted away, mostly refusing to engage ISIS forces, which by then had passive support from some of the Sunni population and included former Ba'athists and army officers. Late in the month, ISIS announced the reestablishment of the Islamic Caliphate and renamed itself the Islamic State (IS). Abu Bakr al-Baghdadi made his first public appearance, leading prayer from al-Nuri Mosque in Mosul and declaring himself Caliph Ibrahim.[51]

It was a radicalizing and transformative moment for the IS, as its rising power and military gains translated into increased ambition that could be fully realized only by the destruction of an already-fragile order in Iraq. In early August 2014, IS took the northwestern Iraqi Yazidi towns of Sinjar and Zumar, committing further atrocities while also capturing Mosul Dam, which controlled the Tigris flow and supplied electricity to over a million people. Other than Kurdish forces, which moved into Kirkuk and began taking defensive actions when Iraqi security forces departed, Iraq's national military was powerless. The Obama administration responded by launching air strikes to defend the Yazidis trapped in Sinjar and to hold back IS. The IS, in turn, released a video in mid-August showing the beheading of American journalist James Foley and threatening another kidnapped journalist if the United States did not end all operations in Iraq.

Throughout these events in the summer of 2014, the Iraqi government was in limbo. A wide range of influential political figures, from Grand Ayatollah Sistani to the governments of both Iran and the United States, called on Maliki to step down in favor of Haidar Abadi, a conciliatory, western-educated engineer and long-time exile now part of the *Da'wa* party. Maliki finally relented in mid-August, having both contributed to the reconstitution of an independent Iraq and exacerbated several extraordinary problems in the period between 2008 and 2014. As a result, the new Prime Minister Abadi found himself presiding over an epic crisis when he took office in September. He had a weakened and badly managed military, a deeply aggrieved Sunni minority, damaged relations with the Kurds, widespread corruption, an economic crisis, and a partly homegrown nonstate actor taking possession of large swathes of the country. These troubles were beyond Baghdad's capacity to manage, but the same forces that made them so serious and threatening—the rising power of the IS, as it erased borders and sought to remake the Middle East—called forth an international reaction that would change the equation over time.

The IS Goes Global, 2014–2017

As much as the Obama administration wanted to avoid being drawn into a new conflict in the MENA region, it could not ignore events on the ground in Iraq and Syria. In response to the spreading violence, the United States organized a major international coalition in September 2014, "The Global Coalition to Defeat ISIS," including the European NATO powers, several Gulf states, and eventually dozens of other countries in lesser roles. Using mostly air power and special forces, this new coalition began to augment Iraqi efforts to restore its territorial integrity, launching thousands of airstrikes and funneling money, weapons, and intelligence to forces on the ground. It also pursued IS targets in Syria while generally avoiding direct confrontation with the Assad regime, which was both in the fight against IS and the object of U.S. efforts to support its removal by the Syrian opposition. The international coalition came to have minor Russian military support and Chinese acquiescence, though coalition politics grew complicated due to Russian backing for Syria's Assad. Regardless, no state party supported IS's bid to establish itself by force in the heart of the region.

This is how IS found itself fighting not just the Iraqi and Syrian militaries but also the United States, Britain, France, Australia, Canada, and the Netherlands, along with Iran (one of the first states to send ground forces to Iraq), Turkey, Jordan, Egypt, Saudi Arabia, and even distant Morocco. One could add to the list a variety of Syrian opposition groups, Lebanon's Hezbollah, and the indispensable Kurdish forces not always under Iraqi government control. The only reason the extraordinary mismatch did not produce faster results was the unwillingness of coalition participants to commit large numbers of ground troops to what would have been a costly and difficult venture. In Iraq, the ground war was left principally to a gradually reconstituted military, Kurdish *Peshmerga*, a few thousand American advisors, occasionally intervening Turkish forces, and sporadically involved Iranian Revolutionary Guards. Just as important were the Popular Mobilization Forces (PMF; *al-Hashd al-Sha'abi*), a large and diverse collection of Shi'i militia that began to form in early 2014, expanding considerably after the Ayatollah Ali al-Sistani issued a *fatwa* on June 13, 2014, calling on Shi'i fighters to resist the IS encroachment and protect Baghdad.

The IS responded to the mounting pressure of the global coalition with the same horrific acts of violence that had made it infamous since its earlier incarnations as AQI or ISIS. It combined conventional tactics with relentless terror attacks and guerrilla warfare. Given the international nature of the coalition, IS soon began to choose targets in Europe, aided by affiliates and radicalized fellow travelers. In early 2015, gunmen attacked the Parisian newspaper *Charlie Hebdo* and, months later, a Paris stadium and nightclub, killing over a hundred people. The year 2016 saw a bombing in Brussels and vicious truck attacks in Nice and Berlin. Europeans were targeted in Istanbul, at a Tunisian beach, and at the Bardo museum in Tunis. That same year, IS-inspired homegrown attacks in San Bernardino, California, and St. Cloud, Minnesota, made clear the possibility of the IS extending its reach to the United States. Attacks in 2017 on Westminster Bridge near Parliament, at London Bridge, and at Manchester Arena demonstrated British vulnerability. IS militants used a similar approach in Barcelona in 2017, when a van assault on a prominent pedestrian area killed and injured dozens. IS explicitly threatened Vladimir Putin's Russia; and beyond Europe, this period saw IS-inspired or -affiliated attacks in such far-flung places as Bangladesh and Indonesia.

The main conflict zone, however, remained closer to home in Iraq, Syria, nearby Libya and Yemen, and on Egypt's Sinai Peninsula, where the IS had established affiliates. As in Europe, IS violence often was designed for maximum provocation and had a staged theatricality. It revealed discursive objectives, such as persuading enemies and followers alike of the group's deadly seriousness and willingness to break all international humanitarian norms in pursuing its objectives. A Jordanian pilot, for example, was immolated in a cage after being downed and captured; Egyptian Christians were beheaded wearing the orange jumpsuits made infamous at Guantanamo Bay in Cuba and Abu Ghraib prison in Iraq. A Russian airliner exploded after taking off from the Sinai. IS militants also launched hundreds of conventional terror attacks, directing violence at noncombatants as part of a psychological strategy in pursuit of political ends. There were large numbers of vehicle-borne suicide attacks in Egypt, Syria, Yemen, and Iraq itself.

The IS took control of nearly 40% of Iraqi territory at its peak in 2015, and the fight to free the country was arduous and painful. The Shi'i PMF militia, a partly reconstituted Iraqi national military, and Kurdish *Peshmerga* did almost all the work on the ground, with foreign air support and advisors playing a significant role. The IS had tremendous momentum at the start of the year and took Ramadi by May 2015, keeping it until late December. By April 2016, the Iraqi military had reclaimed Hit, a town along the Euphrates held by IS for nearly two years, and then the even more central Fallujah by the end of June. IS responded with bombings in Baghdad killing over 100 in mid-May and over 200 in early July during Ramadan. The subsequent struggle for Mosul ensued over an eight-month period between October 2016 and June 2017. After that, it took another six months to eliminate IS from smaller outlying locales like Tal Afar in the northwest in late August, Hawija in the north-center of the country in October, and al-Qa'im and Rawa along the western Euphrates in November 2017. Prime Minister Abadi did not declare victory until the end of December 2017, even as IS cadres remained hiding in Iraq and in the crumbling remains of Syria. IS leader Abu Bakr al-Baghdadi was finally tracked down in northwest Syria in late October 2018 and blew himself up when cornered by U.S. special forces. While the struggle was not over, the country was whole.

Protest and Stalemate, 2017–Present

With the IS threat diminishing, domestic political challenges returned to center-stage, foremost initially regarding the status of Kurdistan. The Kurdistan regional government held a long-sought independence referendum on September 25, 2017, having postponed it from 2014 due to the IS incursion. The referendum won the support of nearly 93% of Kurdish voters. While the result was not surprising, given Kurdish aspirations and the nonbinding polling of previous years, the outcome and the political momentum it generated alarmed the Abadi government. The Kurdish position under KRG president Barzani no longer was to negotiate for fuller autonomy so much as to make a bid for complete independence in a fully sovereign Republic of Kurdistan.⁵² The Kurds were divided on many issues, but not on the question of national rights. And the embittering, recurring experience of Baghdad's failure to defend Kurdistan, this time from the IS's initial entry into the region, seemed to be the last straw. The Kurds also knew they remained an integral part of the larger international fight against IS in Syria and had won new support for their actions in the region and the world. Hopes were high.

The view from Baghdad, not surprisingly, was different. Seeing the referendum as a fundamental threat to Iraqi territorial integrity, the Abadi government moved quickly to block travel to Kurdistan by closing the international airports at Erbil and Sulaimaniyya and positioning additional troops at border crossings with Iran. Iraqi troops retook oil-rich Kirkuk—abandoned early in the fight against IS—along with much the rest of the expanded territory claimed by *Peshmerga* in previous years. With stronger military capacity than it had in 2014 and support from the PMF militia, Baghdad asserted control and rejected any implementation of the referendum results. Iraq had broad international backing that included Iran and Turkey, with the United States and most of the world taking a studied neutral position upholding international law but maintaining the status quo, which favored Iraqi territorial unity. The *Peshmerga* stood down to avoid what likely would have been an ugly and pointless defeat, given the larger balance of forces. KRG president Masoud Barzani resigned from office, and Kurdish hopes were dashed once again.

With the country intact, Abadi still had a host of other governance challenges to manage. On May 12, 2018, several months after shelving the Kurdish issue and dislodging IS from its remaining strongholds, Iraq held its fourth set of elections for the Council of Representatives. Voter turnout was remarkably low at just over 44%, and the results were challenged by credible allegations of electronic fraud. Worse still, before a scheduled recount could occur, a warehouse in Baghdad containing nearly half the cast paper ballots burned to the ground, calling the entire process into question. When the final results were announced in early August, the winners included three new or restructured parties: the Alliance toward Reforms, aka *Saairun*, a coalition that included Muqtada al-Sadr's party (54 seats); Hadi al-Amiri's *Fatah* Alliance (48 seats); and Haidar al-Abadi's Victory Alliance (42 seats); in addition to Ayad Allawi's National Coalition, aka *Wataniya* (21 seats). Nouri al-Maliki's SOL dropped precipitously in the polls, but still won 25 seats, while the KDP and PUK won 28 and 18 seats, respectively.⁵³ These and the nearly 30 other smaller parties that had won seats tried to form a government by aggregating into larger blocs, but without success given the similar size of the two main groupings, both claiming to have majorities. By early September 2018, a political stalemate emerged from an election that had weak participation and questionable integrity.

At the same time, substantial protests erupted and turned deadly in Basra and elsewhere in the south, not directly over the parliamentary imbroglio so much as a polluted water supply that had poisoned thousands. This fed ongoing anger over public service failures, crippling electricity shortages, and perceived Iranian political interference. Further protests and the widespread burning of government buildings and ruling *Da'wa* Party headquarters ratcheted up the political pressure to break the national stalemate and led Prime Minister Abadi to abandon his pursuit of a second term in a new government. Importantly, what followed was not a resolution of the structural deadlock between antagonistic forces but an agreement between elite leaders to continue with a reshuffled power-sharing arrangement. Iraqi society would remain divided along ethnic and sectarian lines, but the management of that divide would entail elites from all major parties retaining positions of privilege.

Accordingly, after more delay, the new parliament agreed on a speaker and then chose a president, Barham Salih, in early October 2018. Salih in turn nominated the veteran independent Shi'i politician Adil Abdul-Mahdi to become Iraq's new prime minister and form a government. Abdul-Mahdi won the support of both major electoral blocs by dividing the spoils of government service, mostly in the form of cabinet positions, and assuring that the most influential individuals were placated. He had considerable and varied experience as a French-educated economist, one-time communist, past SCIRI member, and former vice president and oil minister. He nonetheless needed several months to win parliamentary approval of his full cabinet, with critical posts unfilled by June 2019. He was poorly positioned to manage Iraq's ongoing governance crisis, facing diminished public confidence in the country's increasingly entrenched but dysfunctional political order.

Iraq's crisis entered a more acute phase in October 2019, when major protests erupted in Baghdad's *Tahrir* (Liberation) Square, Nasiriyya's Habboubi Square, and other cities in the south. The protesters of what would be called the *Tishreen* (October) movement voiced their dismay with the entire political system of ethnosectarian party competition and elite collaboration. The *muhasasa* power-sharing system had persisted throughout the post-Saddam era, originally imposed by the American occupation authorities out of deference to Iraq's communal diversity, which it reified and highlighted in attempting to assure that no single group dominated the others. The resulting governance failures of the system had contributed to extraordinary corruption, youth unemployment, and poor public provision of basics like clean water, electricity, and health care. Governments formed by oversized and divided cabinets cultivated a disjointed, ineffective power structure that meant each portfolio and associated ministry operated like a personal political fiefdom dominated by its patronage-providing minister.

By the fall of 2019, Iraqi political life also renormalized a significant amount of violence in what was supposed to be a postauthoritarian era, as seen in the state's heavy-handed response to the *Tishreen* protests. This violence included several hundred deaths and tens of thousands of injuries in the state's handling of the protests over a period of weeks. State arrests, disappearances, and torture of protesters were commonplace. Not all the violence was directly attributable to the state, as armed groups and militias associated with political parties assassinated activists and civil society leaders. Nonstate or quasi-state actors like the *Fatah* faction of the PMF operated with impunity in perpetrating some of the violence. Foreign actors like Iran supported *Fatah* and sought to maintain the political positions of their client groups, even at the cost of Iraqi lives.[54] This caused some significant reputational damage to Iran's image with the Iraqi public as a whole.

When protests continued to be met with an unrestrained response, killing hundreds by late November, top Shiʻi cleric Grand Ayatollah Ali Sistani called on parliament to reconsider its support for the government. Prime Minister Abdul-Mahdi offered his resignation immediately. Parliament accepted it in December 2019, but kept him in a caretaker role and quickly passed new legislation changing the electoral system to prepare for a new election. The new electoral law eliminated the political party or list-based proportional representation (PR) system in favor of a single, nontransferable vote (SNTV). As a de facto first-past-the-post system, it promised to enhance transparency and credibility by simply awarding seats to individual candidates with the most votes in each district.[55] The law also increased the number of constituencies by subdividing each governorate into electoral districts for representation. Together the changes favored candidates over their parties and were designed to allow locally oriented leaders and small parties to flourish. The hope was that this would improve the integration of organized opposition groups, institutionalizing their political action rather than leaving them incentivized to take to the streets as their only means of expression and participation.

The rapid December 2019 electoral reforms notwithstanding, it still took six months and two failed attempts by other prime minister designates to replace Abdul-Mahdi, who remained in office until February 2020. President Barham Salih's nominee, Mustafa al-Kadhimi, finally succeeded in forming a government in early May 2020. Kadhimi, a pragmatic former journalist, intelligence official, and dual UK–Iraqi citizen, became independent Iraq's sixth prime minister. He faced the same raft of challenges plaguing his predecessors, in addition to a new COVID-19 pandemic and unresolved tensions from the January 2020 U.S. assassination of Iranian general Qassem Soleimani, along with PMF deputy commander Abu Mahdi al-Muhandis. He promised early elections, Iraq's fifth under the 2005 constitution, which he did deliver.

Voter turnout in the October 2021 election was 36%, a record low, with participation continuing a downward trend because so many Iraqis had grown exasperated with a system widely seen as rotating corrupt elites. The Sadrist-dominated *Saairun* bloc took advantage of general voter apathy and disillusionment, increasing its seats to 73 from the 54 it won in 2018. It easily outperformed its main competitor, PMF-aligned *Fatah*, which dropped to 17 seats from 48—a surprise, because *Fatah* and *Saairun* received a similar number of total votes.[56] In fact, the outcome was not a result of fraud so much as a savvy strategy on the part of *Saairun*. The new SNTV electoral system produced noteworthy vote "wastage" for *Fatah* when, under the new law, the excess support for individual winning candidates could not be redirected to secondary candidates. The law eliminated the complex, opaque vote allocation mechanisms of the prior system in favor of a simpler, more transparent system that required a shift in party strategy. Ideally, this would include nominating the correct number of candidates, anticipating support levels in each constituency, and convincing voters to spread their votes appropriately. *Saairun* seemed to have considered these factors carefully and was rewarded with a disproportionate number of seats compared to its actual voter support. Surely, *Fatah* took note after the fact and was not pleased.⁵⁷

Hope and Prospects

There were indications, nonetheless, that certain aspects of the 2019 electoral reforms might have had their intended effect in encouraging smaller parties to run and making it possible for them to win. *Harakat Imtidad* (Reach Movement), an anticorruption party that emerged from the *Tishreen* protests, won a surprising nine seats. The party was run by Alaa al-Rikabi, a 47-year-old doctor from Nasiriyya in southern Dhi Qar province, who favored an end to the ethnosectarian quota system and the direct election of the president and prime minister. Potentially in alliance with small parties like *Ishraqa Kanoon* (six seats) and the Kurdish New Generation Movement (nine seats), Rikabi hoped to make a difference by challenging the government from the inside and creating an opposition bloc of protest parties. He was not alone in his views, though his advocacy of such a position was personally risky and it remained very difficult for individual activists to make transformative structural changes in political life. The *muhasasa* system reflected the Iraqi elite's longstanding role as identity-based power brokers in each community, whether sectarian, ethnic, or tribal. No such leaders supported ending their privileged positions in the power structure.

The new SNTV electoral system did not address this underlying issue and may even have exacerbated the challenges Iraqi parliamentarians faced in forming governing coalitions in a fragmented political context, with 18 parties in competition.⁵⁸ By reducing the number of seats that each party is likely to win, coalition governments are likely to be larger, more diverse, and therefore more unwieldy. Worse still, if the recent past is any guide, powerful groups that fare poorly in national elections are still likely to be accommodated in the formation of a government coalition. Weak institutionalization, the absence of legal precedent or normative consensus, and the presence of credible threats to forcibly disrupt the political system give parties with large popular bases and armed militias a capacity to insist on inclusion in the cabinet. To exclude them would be foolish. For example, *Fatah's* October 2021 electoral setback did not stop it from demanding a place in the government formed in the weeks afterward. It was no coincidence that Prime Minister al-Kadhimi was threatened with assassination on November 7, 2021, when unknown attackers—possibly a militia cadre unhappy with *Fatah's* poor showing—directed multiple bomb-carrying drones at his residence. This might have been an unsubtle way of demanding political accommodation despite the electoral outcome.

By 2022, Iraq's democratic and developmental prospects remained in peril. A rancorous stalemate had emerged, stemming from the difficulty in forming a government after the October 2021 election. This led to a July 31 storming of parliament by populist cleric Muqtada al-Sadr's followers and countermoves by his rivals, including the former Prime Minister Nouri al-Maliki. The issue was, as in the past, an ongoing struggle between influential leaders determined to obtain privileged positions for themselves and their followers. It was not a sectarian struggle, nor an ideological battle, or a conflict over foreign allegiances. It was about power in an institutional environment that has yet to gain traction over those seeking it at the expense of other leaders, factions, and interests.

Yet, Iraqi democracy is not wholly beyond redemption. Electoral reforms and increasing campaign sophistication might help keep many parties engaged in regular, institutionalized political competition. Voter turnout might be improved if people believe something meaningful is at stake. The alternatives of disengagement or extralegal activities are certainly worse for the country as a whole. If all major parties continue to play by well-defined rules, even if they bend them on occasion, they might find themselves drawn into the system and constructively constrained in their actions. The uncertainty of potential political outcomes is a crucial feature of the system in this case, not a liability. If parties calculate that participating might conceivably produce a better outcome than abandoning the formal political process, this can lead to an ongoing willingness to engage. Ultimately, Iraqi popular political preferences must find expression, first, in achievable electoral outcomes and, secondly, in improved government responsiveness, accountability, and beneficial public policies. This might take years to occur, though it does offer hope for the Iraqi future.

Notes

1 Makiya (2004).
2 This section draws on Flibbert (December 1990).
3 *Middle East Economic Digest (MEED)* (December 29, 1989), 8.
4 *MEED* (January 12, 1990), 26.
5 This plan, as set forth by Industry and Military Industrialization Minister Hussein Kamel, called for industrial diversification and a reduced dependence on oil revenues. *MEED* (May 19, 1989), 2.
6 *MEED* (May 5, 1989), 7.
7 Mofid (1990), 52.
8 *MEED* (May 5, 1989), 11.
9 *MEED* (March 30, 1990), 17.
10 The Transport and Communications Ministry had been dredging the Khor Abdullah channel and the shipping canal linking Khor al-Zubair to the Gulf, aiming to remove millions of cubic meters of silt and clear the channels to enable small tankers to load to capacity. *MEED* (July 28, 1989), xiv.
11 The war's approximate cost to Iraq, including lost oil revenues and infrastructure damage, was $453 billion, exceeding the oil revenues of both Iran and Iraq in the twentieth century. Mofid (1990), 53.
12 Mofid (1990), 54.
13 Tripp (2007), 260.
14 See Baram (2014).
15 Dawisha (2009), 237.
16 For an extended timeline, see the Council on Foreign Relations, "The Kurds' Quest for Independence, 1920–2021," at www.cfr.org/timeline/kurds-quest-independence.

17 "The Iraqi Government Assault on the Marsh Arabs," Human Rights Watch Briefing Paper, January 2003.
18 The *Ahwar* itself eventually was declared a UNESCO World Heritage Site.
19 Migdal (1988); Kamrava (2018); Ayubi (1995).
20 Blaydes (2018).
21 See the various bipartisan Senate Select Committee on Intelligence reports, including "Postwar Findings about Iraq's WMD Programs and Links to Terrorism and How They Compare with Prewar Assessments," September 8, 2006.
22 Gunter (1996).
23 Woods et al. (2006) address regime perspectives based on captured Iraqi documents.
24 Allawi (2007).
25 Watban Ibrahim died in prison in 2015. Barzan Ibrahim was captured in 2003 and executed in 2007. Sabawi Ibrahim was captured in 2005, sentenced to death, and died in prison in 2013.
26 See also Sassoon (2012) and Sassoon (2016).
27 Flibbert (2006).
28 Flibbert (2013).
29 Dawisha (2009), 245.
30 Pfiffner (2010), 76–85.
31 Tripp (2007), 259.
32 Warrick (2015); Malkasian (2017).
33 Chandrasekaran (2006).
34 The document was not called an interim constitution because Iraq had suffered under too many such arrangements since the 1958 revolution. Al-Istrabadi (2005).
35 See www.constituteproject.org/constitution/Iraq_2005.pdf?lang=en.
36 A nominal upper house, the Council of Union (*Majlis al-Ittihad*), was supposed to reflect Iraq's federal structure but is not fully defined in the 2005 constitution and has yet to be established by the Council of Representatives, which may see it as a potential institutional rival.
37 That is, the Iraqi people elect a parliament, which choses a president, who in turn selects a prime minister to form a cabinet and govern.
38 The Iraq Body Count database lists July 2006 as the peak of civilian monthly deaths (3298), with nearly 56,000 civilian deaths in 2006–2007. www.iraqbodycount.org/database/
39 The Gulf/2000 Project, SIPA, Columbia University, at https://gulf2000.columbia.edu/maps.shtml.
40 Iraq Coalition Casualty Count, at http://icasualties.org.
41 Iraq Body Count, at www.iraqbodycount.org/database.
42 Its names included the Sons of Iraq (*Abna al-Iraq*), Concerned Local Citizens, and Salvation Brigades.
43 Malkasian (2017).
44 Smith and MacFarland (2008).
45 Dodge (2012).
46 Przeworski (1991), 10.
47 All figures are from the Independent High Electoral Commission (IHEC) and have been widely reported in the media. See https://ihec.iq.
48 Hashim (2018) covers IS from its origins in 2003 to mid-2017.
49 ISCI was the Islamic Supreme Council of Iraq, which changed its name from the Supreme Council for the Islamic Revolution in Iraq (SCIRI) in May 2007 after becoming more orthodox and Iraq-centered and less revolutionary.

50 Iraq Body Count, at www.iraqbodycount.org/database.
51 Hashim (2018); Warrick (2015); McCants (2015).
52 See Barzani (2017).
53 IHEC (2022).
54 EPIC (2021).
55 Stewart-Jolley (2021).
56 IHEC (2022).
57 Mansour and Stewart-Jolley (October 2021).
58 See the graphic at IHEC (2022).

4
INTERNATIONAL RELATIONS

Iraq has been closely connected to the world for millennia. From its ancient past to its modern creation by colonial authorities in the 1920s and contemporary geopolitical centrality in the Middle East, it has never existed in isolation. In recent years, its connections and interactions with the world have become even stronger, but caused many challenges for the country and its neighbors. Iraqi leaders have deployed state power in pursuit of their ambitions and defied dominant countries like the United States. Baghdad has run afoul of international institutions like the United Nations and thumbed its nose at international norms. The transnational identity politics of Arab nationalism and Islamism have created solidarity and antipathy for Iraq across MENA regional borders. Iraq has launched more than one major war and been subject to invasion, incursion, or subversion by parties as varied as the United States, Israel, Turkey, Iran, and the Islamic State (IS). Iraqi refugees and migrant populations are now dispersed to at least two dozen countries and are caught up in European political rivalries. The legacies of Iraq's post-2003 upheaval are active drivers of change in the MENA region and beyond.

This chapter examines the central issues and events in contemporary Iraqi international relations, highlighting the explanatory role of power, institutions, and identities. Just as these three factors are important in Iraqi domestic life, they have shaped the country's interactions with other states and political actors across its borders. They serve as the analytical keys to explaining and understanding Iraq's experiences in war and peace, foreign policy, global economy, and MENA regional dynamics. The chapter begins with a very brief discussion of the theoretical basis for this approach. It then addresses the period from Iraq's establishment as a mandate in 1921 through the Second World War to the 1958 revolution. The rest of the chapter is devoted to the postrevolutionary decades, especially after Saddam Hussein's rise to dominance and including more recent developments in Iraqi foreign relations. It builds on Chapters 2 and 3 in particular, which provide a foundational discussion

DOI: 10.4324/9781003056447-5

of events that are richly important on both the domestic and international levels of analysis.

Understanding Iraq in World Politics

In a world of immense complexity, understanding Iraqi international relations requires knowing what to pay attention to—what matters most in shaping and driving political outcomes. Despite the temptation to be all-inclusive in exploring the country's international actions, analysts still need guidance as to what precise variables to consider. Otherwise, it would be hard to know where to begin and easy to deploy underexamined, even implicit senses of what makes the world go 'round. To remedy this problem, international relations theory provides generalized accounts of the larger patterns and tendencies in world politics, painting pictures in broad strokes that explain why countries typically act as they do. As noted in the Introduction, such theories are like maps: stylized simplifications constructed to make certain aspects of political reality more legible and navigable. They do not explain everything. While the leading paradigms of international relations are valuable as general frameworks, they are limited by the need to set aside the richness of specific cases and countries. It is useful and even necessary, therefore, to draw on insights from a variety of theories when exploring individual cases.[1]

The realist, liberal institutionalist, and constructivist theoretical approaches provide just such guidance, supplemented by a few other perspectives. On the one hand, the tendency of states to pursue power in an "anarchic" system—politics in the absence of legitimate, capable government authority—has long been emphasized by the realist tradition in international relations.[2] This approach sheds light on at least some Iraqi actions in the past several decades, especially in matters of war and foreign policy, where the pressures of anarchy can generate surprising outcomes not wanted by any individual leader. On the other hand, the significance of international institutions as fundamental regulatory bodies, constraining and enabling conflict and cooperation in the world, is the central focus of liberal institutionalism. Both the Middle Eastern and the broader international institutional landscapes, no doubt, have affected Iraqi actions and merit close consideration. For example, the absence of even a modest security-enhancing multilateral institution in the MENA region has incentivized aggressive action and inhibited conflict resolution. It has deprived states of a neutral third-party mechanism to manage their inevitable disputes and obligated them to turn to self-interested great powers, larger and unreliable international institutions, or their own devices to defend their interests.[3]

These two traditions of realism and liberalism occupy the most space in mainstream accounts of international relations. Their strength lies in their clear, measurable focus on the tangible, material world, as well as their simplicity and parsimony, which are great virtues in theory, the main purpose of which is to illuminate social outcomes that otherwise are endlessly complex and incomprehensible. While one can tell a simple story of Iraqi international relations as the pursuit of state power in a weakly institutionalized environment, the downside to this simplicity is that it misses critically decisive factors in this particular set of cases. Iraq's history as a colonial construct with incomplete state formation and contested national identity makes it preferable to include intangible, nonmaterial social factors, along with domestic-level political processes and leadership idiosyncrasies in the analysis of its international outcomes. One could not understand important aspects of Iraqi foreign policy in the 1980s and 1990s, for example, without taking into account Saddam Hussein's choices and domestic political calculations.

For this reason, three other theoretical domains are relevant: the social world emphasized by constructivism, the influence of domestic politics, and the particular characteristics of individual decision-makers. First, so-called social facts like norms, ideas, and identities—shared standards of behavior or senses of self—are at the heart of the constructivist approach, which highlights the nonmaterial forces animating political action and sometimes moving people to make otherwise inexplicable choices. Iraqi international behavior, for example, has been subject to cross-national ideological pressures, including powerful currents of Arabism and Islamism, making it essential to take into account such ideational factors. Second, a longstanding, intuitively sensible school of thought emphasizes that state actions in the world often emanate from domestic political developments. In short, the internal drives the external. This perspective is especially plausible for non-European, late developing countries like Iraq that have powerful social forces and weakened, unfinished states. Finally, the idiosyncrasies of leaders like Nuri al-Sa'id, Abd al-Karim Qasim, or Saddam Hussein are hard to ignore, as they pursue their own interests and make choices that sometimes defy conventional political logic. This is not to say that they are irrational, but only that their perceptions and choices are relevant to the analysis.

Together, these five analytical maps—realism, liberal institutionalism, constructivism, domestic politics, and individual decision-making—provide the guidance necessary to understand Iraqi international relations over the past century. Some of their insights seem minor but are revealing, such as the liberal institutionalist suggestion to keep an eye on regional security institutions, or the realist claim that states sometimes get caught in security dilemmas that lead to seemingly foolish, destabilizing choices in foreign policy. The kinds of arguments they support and the evidence they consider are distributed across all levels of analysis, as well as the material versus ideational divide, with constructivism paying special attention to the latter. Despite their substantial diversity as schools of thought, they allow us to remain focused empirically on Iraqi power, institutions, and identities. These metatheoretical concepts have been around for a long time, though we will start only a century ago, with the founding of the modern Iraqi state.

British Legacies

While Iraq was established as a monarchy in 1921 and gained nominal independence in 1932, its early years did not afford it much room to move in international relations. Britain was militarily dominant in the country, and in Iraq's first decade, London had full legal authority under the League of Nations–sanctioned arrangement to regulate Baghdad's interactions with the world. King Faisal's cosmopolitan orientation—he was not born in Iraq, after all—gave him an interest in world affairs, though his focus was principally on Iraqi national problems and he had more than enough to manage without extending his vision over the horizon. Even after Iraqi independence, Britain maintained military control and unfettered access to Iraq, having secured in 1930 an updated version of its earlier Anglo–Iraqi Treaty of Alliance, which included provisions permitting British troop transit, weapons transport, and war materiel storage.[4] Faisal's death in 1933, and the passing of the crown to his less-than-capable son, Ghazi, assured that Iraq would not soon develop an independent foreign policy under a skilled, charismatic leader. While Ghazi favored young nationalists in the officer corps, his weak political instincts and inexperience undermined the monarchy's institutional centrality and allowed other state actors to grow in influence. Britain remained able to orchestrate policies that advanced imperial interests.

While most Iraqis in the era were focused on narrow, everyday issues rather than national or international affairs, a few internationally oriented ideas and ideologies did circulate among people from all walks of life. In fact, Iraq's earliest and most significant foreign policy preoccupation related to Britain itself, with nationalists pressing for greater independence and a loosening of the constraints on Iraqi sovereignty imposed by the Anglo–Iraqi Treaty. The anti-British impulse was a powerful animating force, driven by years if not centuries of foreign rule, and the Iraqi military was imbued with it early on. The 1934 conscription law expanded troop numbers and the military's political influence, though Shi'i, Kurdish, and Yazidi rebellions triggered by the same law kept the army oriented toward internal rather than external affairs, normalizing such a focus and all it entailed. The Sidqi military coup of 1936 and his assassination in 1937 by Arab nationalist officers then set the stage for a more direct confrontation with Britain in 1941, when a pro-Nazi cabal led by Rashid Ali staged yet another coup. The action prompted the Anglo–Iraqi War and a British reoccupation of Iraq until 1947. Anticolonial sentiment could not overcome direct and determined British war-time opposition, even if London was growing weary and less able to assert itself regarding peripheral concerns like Iraq.

Aside from strident anticolonialism, the other current of thought that affected Iraqi relations with the world was the rising appeal of Arab nationalism in all its forms. Anticolonialism and Arab nationalism were distinctive perspectives, though one became conjoined with the other. The first related to pushing Britain out and asserting Iraqi sovereignty and independence. The second was about uniting the Arab states, or at least acknowledging a sense of historical and cultural commonality. They were closely connected in that Arab nationalists held the colonial powers responsible for dividing the Arab nation in the first place and subsequently blocking unification efforts. A slight tension existed between them, nonetheless, verging on contradiction in the Iraqi case, because one emphasized Iraqi state sovereignty above all else, and the other sought unity among Arab peoples and even integration among the states.[5]

The anticolonial view prevailed ultimately with Britain's eventual withdrawal from most of the region. Arab nationalist ideology became a powerful force, though its boldest aspiration for the political integration of all Arab states went unrealized. As MENA states formed separate, sovereign entities, in the process acquiring their own national interests, state leaders became reluctant to implement full unification plans, even if they paid lip service to the objective. Self-interested elites did not want to give up their power and positions for the sake of a larger imagined entity. The Arab League, created in Cairo by Egypt, Iraq, Lebanon, Saudi Arabia, Syria, and Transjordan in March 1945, institutionalized the separateness of individual, sovereign Arab states. Under its Charter, the League constituted itself as an intergovernmental organization devoted to coordinating inter-Arab policies rather than cultivating intra-Arab political unification. Four of the six Arab League founding states were monarchies, and no monarch was prepared to relinquish his crown. This ratio would be turned on its head in the decade to come, as Arab ethnonationalism swept through the region. But a common identity alone could not transform the MENA space by erasing the state borders and associated interests established by the colonial powers.

All the mandate-era borders created after the First World War in the Middle East survived intact through the end of the Second World War. This included Iraq, by then nominally independent, as well as Palestine, increasingly the site of a bitter nationalist rivalry between the minority Zionist movement and the majority Palestinian Arab population. In the postwar era, exhausted British authorities essentially threw up their hands and prepared for departure by handing the mandate over to the newest major international institution, the United Nations, which replaced the League of Nations. Despite a common ethnicity and emerging currents of nationalist solidarity, Palestinian Arabs faced very different circumstances compared to Iraqis and other Arabs in the region. After all, Zionist successes in settling the territory and transforming its political identity spelled an end to any Palestinian opportunity for gradual, autonomous national development. Its identity and institutions would have to emerge in relation to a growing and powerful rival. The ethnic connection among Arabs was sufficiently important, however, that changes in Palestine had widespread and profound consequences for the entire MENA region, most immediately in the form of the 1948 Arab–Israeli War and associated Palestinian *nakba* (or "catastrophe"), which saw the displacement of hundreds of thousands and took a heavy toll on Palestinian society.

While Iraq initially sent a limited force of a few thousand troops to fight in May 1948, it eventually committed several thousand more and suffered a clear defeat at the hands of the better-trained, better-equipped, eventually more numerous, and more highly motivated forces of the new Jewish state of Israel. When Prime Minister Nuri al-Sa'id was able to withdraw the last Iraqi troops in 1949, Iraq still found itself embittered and tumultuous over a combination of continuing domestic economic troubles, political repression, and residual anger at Britain for its actions at home and in Palestine. The 1948 war and Israel's creation also had follow-on social implications for Iraq and other MENA states when their longstanding Jewish populations, numbering perhaps 100,000 in Iraq alone, emigrated to the new state, in many cases driven out by discriminatory laws and practices if also drawn by the promise of a better, more secure, more fulfilling national life.

Iraq was not a frontline state in the Arab–Israeli conflict, directly adjacent to Israel like Egypt, Jordan, Syria, and Lebanon. Still, Israel's founding was a seminal event in modern Iraqi politics because the Arab and Muslim aspects of Iraqi national identity were inextricably linked to the Palestinians and to cities like Jerusalem. The conflict could not be ignored, at a minimum due to its genuine resonance in the streets and in nationalist circles among political and military elites. This was the case even if opportunistic nationalist leaders used the Palestinian issue instrumentally and disingenuously to promote their own interests. Changing social identities in the nineteenth- and twentieth-century Middle East, with incomplete state formation and transformative nation-building, guaranteed that events in Jerusalem, Haifa, and Jaffa would echo in Baghdad, Basra, and Mosul. As long as Israeli–Palestinian nationalist contention remained unresolved, with two peoples seeking self-determination in the same land, the issue would be an active current in Iraqi domestic life and international relations.

Postwar Initiatives and Retrenchment

International change in the MENA region required either a constellation of structural forces coming together over time, as in the Arab–Israeli conflict, or well-positioned change agents, who often took the form of soldiers, clerics, or determined civilian politicians. One individual politician, Nuri al-Saʿid, had an outsized impact on Iraqi international relations under the monarchy throughout this era. He was one of the most important Iraqi political figures in the twentieth century, and the only Iraqi present at both the Paris Peace Conference as part of the Emir Faisal's delegation in 1919 and the Iraqi revolution in 1958. Fundamentally conservative in orientation, he served as prime minister eight times starting in 1930 and was tenacious in his support for the monarchy, his advocacy of close Iraqi ties to Britain, and his authoritarian approach to domestic critics and opponents.

Especially after the Second World War, Nuri was active in foreign policy in an era of increasingly complex and high-stakes regional dynamics. He had his own vision of an Iraq-dominated, oil-funded Hashemite Arab federation, even if he was often caught up in day-to-day political struggles and failed to implement his views, which cut against the grain of what younger generations of Iraqis wanted. While he was an Iraqi patriot in a narrow sense and a long-time Arab nationalist, he evolved into a pragmatist and a realist regarding pan-Arabism. Given Iraq's uniquely exposed geography and fractured demographics compared to the rest of the Arab world, he believed that Arab integration would antagonize Iraq's non-Arab neighbors and exacerbate its internal ethnic divisions. He made considerable efforts in the 1930s and 1940s toward Arab unity, but he also sought better relations with neighboring Iran and Turkey, and his foreign policy preferences rarely wavered from supporting continued association with Britain.[6]

Nuri also was strongly anticommunist in the emerging Cold War contest. He was the architect, as prime minister, of the February 1955 Baghdad Pact, a security alliance designed to limit Soviet influence in the MENA region, even if most Iraqis were unconcerned about a Soviet threat. It started as an Iraqi agreement with Turkey, soon joined by Britain, Pakistan, and Iran—with the unofficial participation of the United States.[7] Nuri favored it as a solution to Iraqi problems more than as part of a global Cold War strategy. Its supporters saw it as beneficial to Iraq in that it would end the 1930 Anglo–Iraqi Treaty and return the Habbaniyya and Shu'aiba air bases without creating a new Portsmouth Agreement, the secret arrangement with Britain that had sparked the *Wathbah* uprising in Baghdad in 1948. The Baghdad Pact was not popular with the military or on the street, and it reinforced Nuri's long-time association with colonial-era Britain, all but dooming his other initiatives. This was especially the case given his penchant for heavy-handed police tactics and close political control, which alienated most Iraqis in the final years of the Hashemite monarchy.

Suez and the End of the Monarchy

By the mid-1950s, growing polarization in world politics began to affect the Middle East significantly. This polarization had multiple axes, from the Cold War competition between the United States and the Soviet Union to the Arab–Israeli conflict to the emerging radical-versus-conservative regional rivalries that began with the Egyptian revolution in 1952 and evolved into an Arab Cold War. The Suez crisis of October–November 1956 combined all three lines of contention, amounting to a late colonial conspiracy by Britain, France, and Israel. It had wider origins in the abrupt refusal by the United States and Britain to finance Egypt's construction of the Aswan High Dam due to Egyptian President Nasser's growing ties to the Soviet Union. This refusal prompted Nasser to nationalize the Suez Canal Company, which was still British- and French-owned and controlled. Nasser noted that Egyptian labor had built the canal in the 1860s and its transit fees could pay for the dam project, which was critical to Egypt's economic modernization plans.

Over American objections, Britain and France began military planning, in league with a junior partner, Israel. Each country had its own objective. Britain sought to assert itself against what it saw as an upstart revolutionary regime that had deposed a friendly monarchy. France wanted to punish a state offering arms and sanctuary to its nemesis in Algeria, the National Liberation Front (FLN). Israel, for its part, sought shipping access to the Straits of Tiran and hoped to eliminate the border incursions by Palestinian *fedayeen* operating out of the Egyptian-controlled Gaza Strip. Dubbed the Tripartite Aggression in the Arab world, Israel invaded Egypt from the northeast through Sinai down to the Suez Canal on its western side in late October 1956. Shortly thereafter, under the pretext of protecting the Suez Canal, Britain and France sent in their own forces. Together they won the battle easily, but in important ways, they lost the war.

While Iraq was not directly involved in the Suez fighting, the crisis had complex consequences that echoed for decades and altered the course of regional and even world events. Most immediately, rather than putting Egypt's Nasser in his place and securing a vital strategic interest, the Suez crisis heightened the stature of the same radical political forces that Britain, France, and Israel sought to thwart. The attack elevated Nasser's national and regional profile and energized other MENA revolutionaries, not least in Iraq, where he had well-placed admirers throughout the military. It also caused the deployment of a U.N. emergency force, setting the stage for a subsequent and more consequential Arab–Israeli War a decade or so later. When the United States under President Eisenhower called on the invaders to withdraw from the canal zone by the end of 1956, the crisis humiliated Britain in particular, ended Prime Minister Anthony Eden's career, and demonstrated Britain's difficulty adjusting its postwar foreign policy to the reality that its time as a dominant power had passed. It also showed U.S. willingness to put broad geostrategic concerns ahead of narrow alliance interests, representing a rare example of the United States tipping the scales against its closest allies. In Eisenhower's estimation, Britain and France had lost sight of the greater threat in the form of Soviet influence and were engaged in a ham-fisted military intervention.

Suez also made the close Iraqi–British relationship too hot to handle for Nuri al-Sa'id, who felt trapped between pit and pendulum and was compelled to put a little distance between Iraq and Britain, though he could not bring himself to break diplomatic relations. It was too late, however, because the crisis ramped up anti-British sentiment in the country, already high, carrying it to Nuri and the monarchy itself. The domestic impact of the crisis was evident in November 1956, when saboteurs blew up the Iraq Petroleum Company pipeline through Syria, cutting Iraqi oil revenues greatly for several months. Even more forebodingly, opposition groups formed the underground United National Front in February 1957, joining together political parties as diverse as the National Democrats, *Istiqlal*, communists, and Ba'ath. Members of the front had close connections to the Iraqi Free Officers, who had been organizing since Nasser's rise a few years before and had selected a senior figure, Brigadier General Abd al-Karim Qasim, to chair their leadership committee. Less than a year-and-a-half later, Qasim and his Nasserist partner, Colonel Abd al-Salam Arif, launched the July revolution.

The Iraqi Revolution and the World

The Iraqi revolution ended the Hashemite monarchy definitively, changing Iraq's place in the Middle East and the world. Some of this change took time, and its impact on foreign affairs did not operate through the conventional drivers of transformation in international relations. Iraqi power did not rise in the short term, even as its oil revenues continued to grow. The revolution did not lead to Iraq joining a new network of international institutions or relationships, though the country did tilt to the left in realigning with the Soviet Union over its erstwhile imperial partner, Great Britain. Despite much back-and-forth about Iraqi national identity, the country's shared sense of self did not shift dramatically in July 1958. On an international level at least, Iraqi power, institutions, and identity showed a fair degree of continuity throughout this period.

Iraq nonetheless entered a new era, driven by similar factors—the pursuit of power, cultivation of institutions, and manipulation of identities—on other levels of analysis. While the political regime in Iraq remained authoritarian, before and after the revolution, its governance started to become more personalized and autocratic. Before the revolution, the power-wielding national leadership had been a narrow set of elites, including Nuri al-Sa'id, the king and crown prince, feudal sheikhs, and key military figures. Afterward, however, leadership fell to an even more limited number of individuals. As the top of the hierarchy became smaller, individual idiosyncrasies and predilections weighed more heavily than ever on decision-making. These individuals were connected in crucial ways to state institutions, informal patronage networks, and key social groups, but their personal preferences and actions mattered as much as anything to shaping Iraq's fate. In the next five decades, only a handful of critically important leaders ruled Iraq: Abd al-Karim Qasim, Abd al-Salam Arif, his brother Abd al-Rahman, Ahmed Hassan al-Bakr, and Saddam Hussein. In steering Iraqi international relations, they protected and augmented their power as leaders, built and destroyed state institutions, and cultivated identities for their own purposes.

Qasim's Republic

Ironically, the same nationalist figures and forces that drove the Iraqi revolution and helped propel Qasim to power quickly became formidable obstacles to his success in governing. Within weeks of taking the helm, Qasim was challenged by his second-in-command, Abd al-Salam Arif, a strident Nasserist who saw himself as the true leader of the revolution. Arif sought to join Iraq with Nasser's Egypt, which already had united with Syria to form the United Arab Republic (UAR) several months before in February 1958. Given Qasim's Iraq-first approach and the political support he had from the Shi'a and the Kurds—both groups fundamentally opposed to integration with the UAR—Qasim was not interested. He agreed with the late Nuri al-Sa'id's view that the UAR was a danger to Iraqi independence and sidelined Arif by dispatching him abroad as ambassador, then arresting him upon his attempt at a surreptitious return.

Not surprisingly, Iraqi-Egyptian relations under Qasim and Nasser got off to a poor start, with the tension overdetermined by factors at all levels of analysis. For one, Qasim had his own ideas about Iraq's place in the region, channeling a view that saw Iraq as distinct from the rest of the Arab world and seeking to preserve Iraqi uniqueness and independence. This perspective was widespread enough to have traction with a number of political groups not taken by other ideologies like pan-Arabism. A second if related factor was that the political coalition supporting Qasim's regime, especially the Kurds and the Shi'i majority, was bound to prefer policies at odds with what Cairo wanted. Unification could only happen against the wishes of a clear majority of Iraqis. An additional element was the personal rivalry between Qasim and Nasser, two military men with strong personalities and expansive egos who preferred to remain in paramount leadership positions. Nasser could not tolerate a rival like Qasim, whom he called "The Divider of Iraq" (*Qassim al-Iraq*), playing on the Iraqi leader's name. Qasim responded by calling Nasser "The Pharaoh of the Nile."[8] Nasser, in turn, supported a March 1959 coup attempt, led by Mosul garrison chief Abd al-Wahab al-Shawaf, and gave safe haven in Cairo to a young Ba'athist, Saddam Hussein, after he attempted to assassinate Qasim in October 1959.

As if this were not enough, a final and more basic driver of the enmity in Egyptian–Iraqi relations was structural. Established powers like Egypt typically resist rising powers like Iraq in the perennial interstate competition of international relations. This is usually so, regardless of the internal social and political characteristics of each country, including when they have similar authoritarian regimes and the same dominant ethnicity. As the two most potentially powerful Arab states in the region at the time, Iraq and Egypt were bound to conflict, and the tension had started even before the Iraqi revolution, when Nasser identified Nuri al-Sa'id as a rival and sometimes an impediment in his efforts to unify the Arab nation. In the end, strain in the relationship was only mitigated by having no common border and enough physical distance between them to preclude a direct clash. It also was beneficial to have common adversaries like the United States, the United Kingdom, and Israel, as well as a shared ally in the USSR.

Qasim knew his country would never be as important to Moscow as Egypt was becoming, and he might have preferred to carve out a middle path in foreign policy and maintain Iraq's neutrality. Yet almost immediately, both his closest domestic supporters and the geopolitics of the era required a shifting of external alliances away from the western powers and toward the Soviet Union. Like his rival Nasser, Qasim was by no means a doctrinaire communist or even a committed socialist, but he increasingly turned to the Soviets, starting with a comprehensive bilateral agreement in March 1959. The agreement had economic, cultural, and military dimensions. It offered technical assistance with oil exploration, agrarian reform, and railroad development, as well as capital equipment for heavy industry. The cultural dimension was wide-ranging and included educational opportunities, cultural exchanges, film, and tourism. The military aspect was substantial and included advanced weaponry like the MiG-21 jet fighter, helicopters, and tanks, allowing Iraq to switch from British and American arms to Soviet and Warsaw Pact support.[9]

These developments were met with some alarm on the part of U.S. and British officials, though their responses reflected their distinctive perspectives and experiences in the region. Britain understood Iraq better, given its more than four decades of close involvement there. It knew that Qasim's brand of nationalism differed from Nasser's, and it had a better sense for the challenges Qasim would encounter in the months and years ahead. The United States, on the other hand, interpreted everything through a Cold War lens and had trouble—or perhaps could not bother—distinguishing between Qasim and Nasser. It viewed Iraq's seeming embrace of the Soviet Union as evidence of Baghdad's fealty to America's most dangerous peer competitor. The Anglo–American alliance had its tensions, as seen at Suez, though both sides remained generally aligned regarding the MENA region. London by the late 1950s was beginning to accept Washington as a credible and reliable replacement for the MENA regional stewardship role it no longer could play. Washington would play that role but only on its own terms.

Americans and Britons were not the only ones concerned about Iraq under Qasim. In March 1959, in the same month that Iraq inked its agreement with the Soviet Union, it also withdrew from its regional security arrangement, the Baghdad Pact. This move, necessitated by its realignment with the Soviets and turn to the Iraqi Communist Party for support, was dismaying to neighboring Turkey and Iran. The alliance was renamed the Central Treaty Organization, and its headquarters was relocated from Baghdad to Ankara. Turkey, as a NATO member bordering the USSR, had a strong interest in avoiding being flanked by hostile powers, and it had enjoyed the Iraqi *ancien regime*'s cultivation of closer ties under Nuri al-Sa'id. Despite his Iraq-first orientation, Qasim did not have Nuri's enthusiasm for close relations with non-Arab Turkey. When it came to international relations, he had a narrower field of vision than his more worldly civilian predecessors, discounting the benefits of staying on good terms with his large northern neighbor. Qasim did little to signal a willingness to explore the possibilities of regional cooperation between Baghdad and Ankara.

Iraqi–Iranian relations were even more complicated, and the rising tension on that front put in motion other regional and transnational problems, from Kurdish nationalism to border and territorial disputes. Iran at the time was a U.S.- and British-friendly monarchy under the Pahlavi dynasty. The regime in Tehran had become more autocratic of late, having benefited from an Anglo–American, CIA-sponsored, antidemocratic coup against the nationalist Mosaddeq government in 1953. In general, Iran had an acrimonious, centuries-long history with the land that became Iraq in the twentieth century. It had dominated the region for long periods under various Persian empires, often at odds with Ottoman power in more recent centuries. Its larger size and geographic position, including a vastly longer coastline on the Persian Gulf, gave it clear advantages over its bottled-up neighbor to the west. Iran's substantial Arab population in the southwestern province of Khuzestan, and its even larger Kurdish population further north, sometimes created political liabilities for Tehran, just as Iraq's majority Shi'i population, with historical and communal ties to Iran, posed challenges to minority Sunni rulers in Baghdad.

Iran had deep and immediate concerns about Qasim's new, left-leaning regime and its emerging relationship with the Soviets. The withdrawal of Iraq from the Baghdad Pact was a step backward for Iranian security, because Iran shared a border of more than a thousand miles with three Soviet republics. Unlike Iraq, Iran had experienced protracted Russian intervention in the past, most recently when the Soviets under Joseph Stalin had joined the British in occupying the country for nearly five years during and after the Second World War. The Soviets delayed their postwar departure in 1946, prompting the new U.N. Security Council's first crisis, and Stalin only backed down and exited when subjected to intense American pressure in an early expression of the Truman Doctrine. Iran under the Shah was not keen to have a Soviet client state to its immediate west and soon found ways to express its skepticism about Qasim's regime. This included voicing its discontent with the 1937 treaty delimiting the Iraq–Iran border in the *Shatt al-Arab* confluence of the Tigris and Euphrates Rivers. With a few exceptions to accommodate Iranian port cities, the treaty accepted Iraqi sovereignty claims over most of the *Shatt al-Arab*, but Qasim still responded by demanding a reconsideration of the boundary.[10] The dispute led to shelling in the border area and a temporary closure of the *Shatt al-Arab* to both parties, persisting as an irritant in bilateral relations for more than a decade.

More broadly, Iraqi foreign policy under Qasim was especially sensitive to issues of geostrategic constraint. This is a perennial concern for all states, especially those seeking regional leadership roles or facing acute security threats in weakly institutionalized regional environments, where states need to take a go-it-alone approach. Because Qasim, as a leader of the revolution, was so adamant about asserting Iraq's newly achieved independence, a function of his Iraq-first orientation and the country's long history of being subject to external domination, he was bound to look for ways to break free. Geostrategic and commercial constraints were particularly evident to the southeast with Iran and the *Shatt al-Arab*. Iraqi access to the open waters of the upper Gulf was limited by the country's virtually landlocked location and the capacity of its nemesis, Iran, to surveil and control its one outlet. This made Iraqi oil exports, which were rapidly growing in volume and economic significance, vulnerable to the whims of several other countries controlling export pipelines and waterways. Unable to remedy its constraints by pressure on Iran or moves to the west or north against Turkey or Syria, Iraq under Qasim turned south to Kuwait, which was in the process of becoming fully independent.

Iraq had contended that Kuwait should be part of its territory as far back as the 1930s and Kuwait's discovery of oil. Iraq's claims had no real legal merit, though the upper Gulf's imperial, state-building, and border demarcation history was complex and contested. Kuwait was established as a small sheikhdom in the mid-eighteenth century, with de facto independence despite occasional obligations to pay tribute to larger powers. Eventually, it came under, at best, nominal Ottoman control via the Basra province. Seeking to maintain Kuwaiti autonomy and distinctiveness, local ruler Sheikh Mubarak al-Sabah rejected Ottoman authority and signed a secret treaty with Britain in 1899, giving the United Kingdom control over Kuwaiti foreign affairs in exchange for protection from internal and external adversaries. Britain subsequently came to an agreement with the Ottomans in 1913 as to Kuwait's status, but the First World War threw all arrangements into disarray. From the interwar period onward, Kuwait saw continued upheaval and a series of tentative settlements overseen by Britain, starting with the Emir Abdulaziz al-Saud's attempt, in 1919, to annex Kuwait to a fledgling version of what became Saudi

Arabia. Depression-era economic distress was relieved by the discovery of oil in 1938, leading to tremendous growth and state-building success in the postwar era.

Formalizing its status as a sovereign state was close to inevitable with the postwar decline of colonial-style governance by the European powers. On June 19, 1961, Kuwait declared its independence following an exchange of diplomatic notes with Great Britain terminating the Anglo–Kuwaiti Treaty of 1899. Less than a week later, on June 25, Abd al-Karim Qasim voiced his opposition to Kuwaiti independence and restated Iraq's claim to the territory, contending that the Emirate had been unjustly separated from the Ottoman Empire and was rightfully part of Iraq. Kuwait immediately called for British military assistance under Section 4 of its recent independence agreement, and Britain obliged by dispatching a strong deterrent force that included air assets and a naval taskforce with the aircraft carrier HMS *Victorious*. Qasim had little choice but to back down. The Arab League, for its part, supported Kuwaiti independence and sent forces to replace the British in the fall of 1961, showing the extent to which it was fundamentally an intergovernmental organization favoring the discreet interests and sovereignty of its constituent states. The crisis never became an armed confrontation, though it would be repeated with a very different outcome some three decades later.

In the end, the entire episode was instructive, as it was driven by factors on all levels of analysis. A brief glance at the map (Fig 1) shows that Iraq had a geostrategic problem demanding a solution: it was a large state blocked from access to the sea by a small, inconveniently situated southern neighbor and an even larger, long-time eastern adversary. A structural view of interstate relations would hold that conflict was inevitable, with no remedy—except having cordial relations with its neighbors, institutionalized through legal arrangements favoring the free movement of goods and services. Not inconsistent with this approach, Qasim's claims to Kuwait also can be seen as an expression of historical regret or even political resentment that local, regional, and imperial powers all made choices that favored eventual Kuwaiti independence but damaged Iraqi interests. While Iraqi historical claims were disingenuous, they reflected its leader's grievances and geostrategic concerns. Iraq's position was easily characterized as unfair, and more to the point, it was politically useful to do so under the circumstances.

This final factor was both personal and political in that Qasim himself in this period was put upon from all sides. To some extent, the Kuwait gambit was an effort to break out of his own isolation, which was becoming more substantial by the beginning of the 1960s. In turning increasingly to repressive measures to maintain power, he had lost or discarded most of his domestic allies, finding himself as cut off from support as his country was physically confined in the world. The Kuwaiti crisis also served to distract attention from troubles like the outbreak of hostilities in the north, where relations with the Kurds had deteriorated considerably. Renewed fighting in Kurdistan angered elements in the military, who knew how costly it could be and were growing skeptical about "the Sole Leader." It would not be long before a plot to eliminate Qasim was hatched, featuring a short-lived alliance between the Ba'athists and his old partner—and adversary—Abd al-Salam Arif.

The Arif Brothers

The February 1963 coup and Qasim's execution was a brutal and destabilizing event that, like the 1958 revolution, included a coalition of plotters and enablers. Ba'ath Party operatives joined with key military elements, all in league with a handful of disgruntled regime officials. Once again, regional events in Egypt and Syria also impacted Iraq, as some of the coup instigators were Nasserists, while others decidedly were not. It took several months for the results to shake out and for Abd al-Salam Arif to remove his Ba'athist coconspirators and consolidate his position at the top. Having suffered the indignity and near-fatal danger of a failed bid for regime dominance in 1958, Arif stepped in decisively when the Ba'athists began squabbling among themselves in the fall of 1963. He took charge via a secondary coup in November 1963 and then installed loyalists in every upper-level position, implicating them carefully in his rule.

Iraq found itself in the Arif era confronting many of the same international problems that its leaders in earlier periods had faced: the geographic vulnerability of an odd location incompatible with a world of national states, looming foreign powers who had demonstrated a repeated willingness to intervene, capricious allies who were not always reliable, and hard adversaries bent on maximizing their own interests. It also faced transnational ideological threats that could affect street-level political mobilization, a fast-changing regional economic environment, and its own domestic problems spilling over borders and provoking other states. It was a state not yet fully formed, in a sea of also-incomplete competitor states, with the corresponding challenge of an unfixed, evolving national identity. It was closely connected to the rest of the Arab world, but sometimes too close for its own stability because problems in one corner echoed across the region to others, as with Palestine and the larger Arab–Israeli conflict. Like so many postcolonial states, it did not have the luxury of unconstrained space and time to develop autonomously and organically.

Abd al-Salam Arif's new regime was put together a little differently from what it replaced, being slightly less individually autocratic and more purely military-dominated. Arif himself had matured and grown savvier as a leader in the previous five years, a period that included his arrest, near execution, and removal from any position of authority. This brought at least the possibility of improved governance and more subtle, careful diplomacy. His first international moves were toward stability and an effort at normalizing Iraqi foreign relations with both regional and international powers. He attempted to dial down the sense of urgency and crisis that had gripped the country in the previous few years under Qasim. This included calming relations with the Soviet Union, thrown off-kilter by the prior repression of the Iraqi Communist Party, while placating the military and building international clout by purchasing advanced Soviet weaponry and a nuclear reactor in 1964. Arif was careful, at the same time, not to alarm the major western powers, who remained leery and watchful but were open to Iraq having a new and more pragmatic figure in charge.

Yet, there was no real calming of the political mood in or outside Iraq. The environment in inter-Arab politics in this era saw the remaining conservative monarchies of the region, primarily Saudi Arabia and Jordan, aligned against the radical, revolutionary republics led by Egypt, Iraq, and Syria.[11] Indeed, Arif initially moved to align Iraq more fully with Egypt, establishing a joint military command in May 1964 and bringing in several thousand Egyptian troops by September.[12] As Egypt and Saudi Arabia settled into what amounted to a proxy war in Yemen, however, Arif was reluctant to take things too far or too quickly, despite the enthusiasm of his regime's most vociferous Nasserists. This reluctance eventually raised tensions with Egypt, which manifested in a Nasserist coup attempt in September 1965. It also stoked disunity among the Arab states. Close ideological affinity and comparable regime types never eliminated the rivalries generated, almost automatically, by the region's division into separate sovereign states with individual leaders and associated national interests and personal preferences. While the republics challenged the legitimacy and leadership aspirations of the monarchies, they also battled each other in subtler ways.[13]

In this sense, inter-Arab politics in the 1960s was much more complex than a stark confrontation between two neatly divided warring camps. In fact, Iraq and the MENA states balanced threats to their interests without great deference to ideological considerations, as changing military and economic capabilities created dynamism in political relations.[14] They also engaged in "defensive unionism" when agreeing to new, institutionalized forms of interstate cooperation. These ventures were not sincere efforts at political unification so much as politically obligatory gestures, paying lip service to ideals without sacrificing national autonomy or hard-won independence.[15] Likewise, the impetus to some of Iraq's foreign policy in the mid-1960s was its complicated domestic politics, from challenges to Iran over the Kurdish issue to support for Palestine to placate public sentiment.

The sudden accidental death of Abd al-Salam Arif in April 1966, and his replacement by his older brother, Abd al-Rahman, did not change Iraqi foreign policy dramatically. It may have contributed to Iraq's tentativeness in the spring of 1967, as the Arab states lined up against what they perceived to be a weaker, even temporary power in Israel. In an important sense, the ensuing catastrophic events of the 1967 war were a direct result of this widespread strategic inattention and misperception. Posturing and rivalry got the better of leaders engaging each other through the radio airwaves and news media while trying simultaneously to confront a more single-minded Israel. Unlike Iraq, Israel only had to defend its borders or expand them outward if it could, with the simplicity and urgency of national survival driving decisions in foreign policy. The contradictions and inconsistencies of Zionism disappeared in the face of what appeared to be a menacing set of adversaries, much larger in size and poised to destroy the country.

In the war itself, Iraq dispatched only a token force that was too small and arrived too late to make a difference to the stunning, rapid outcome. Iraq was not central to the Arab–Israeli conflict in this period, because it was not a frontline state. With an overmatched air force, several years before the regional deployment of ballistic missiles like the Scud, it could not project much power across the 250 miles of Jordanian or Syrian territory between it and Israel or the West Bank. Nor did it have direct historical or territorial claims, or a population with immediate family ties to the land, or aspirations to expand its borders all the way to the Mediterranean. Not unimportantly, however, the abiding, regionwide sense of Arab national identity was sufficiently strong and resonant in this period to preclude Iraqi leaders from ignoring the establishment of a non-Arab state in Palestine. And given the weight of a long colonial and imperial history, some leaders were genuinely taken by the issue, as was a sizable portion of the general public who both followed their lead and pushed from below for resistance.

In the end, 1967 was an earthquake throughout the region, with its impact and related aftershocks felt for many years. Egypt's Nasser offered his resignation and had as much culpability as anyone for his mishandling of a crisis that his adversaries could steer to their full advantage. While he remained in power for three more years before dying suddenly of a heart ailment in September 1970, the Arab nationalist movement never recovered. Even though the war was not fully Iraq's to wage, such a rapid and conclusive loss did foster discontent with the military-dominated Arif regime. A general sense of malaise prevailed, aiding in the events of 1968. Changing ideological currents in the region provided an opportunity for a new, intensely focused Iraqi regime to assert itself, first at home and later much more widely and with consequences for all.

The Ba'athist Return

The July 17, 1968, coup was led by Ba'athist veteran Ahmed Hassan al-Bakr and a pair of confederate regime insiders. The two insiders were shoved aside by an additional "corrective" coup on July 30, when one was sent on a fake diplomatic mission to Jordan and the other was escorted to the airport at gunpoint by Bakr's younger cousin, Saddam Hussein. The new regime had advantages over the old with regard to the emerging international conditions it faced, which were both more dire and more generative of political opportunities. The world was on the cusp of a revolution in energy markets, which would transform Iraq's economic prospects and regime resources. In time, this shifted the regional balance of power toward Iraq and the Gulf states and away from Egypt and Syria. Just as significantly, the dimming of Nasserism brought by the 1967 war permitted Bakr to focus intently on Iraqi development without the distraction of transnational ideological threats from popular rivals. The other forms of transnationalism that supplanted Nasserism—especially political Islam—took years to develop enough potency to threaten the regional order. In the meantime, Iraq restyled itself on its own terms as a leading Arab state and the modern manifestation of a venerable civilization with roots in the ancient world.

The Ba'athist regime's first five years were a departure in that it took a more strident, aggressive approach to international relations than its predecessor. The impetus to this was not ideological so much as a concern about regime security and more dangerous international conditions. The regime used strong rhetoric against both a newly dominant Israel and its increasingly supportive American arms supplier and patron, having broken relations with the United States in June 1967. Likewise, it continued to view the Shah's Iran as a major geostrategic adversary and obstacle. Relations with Iran deteriorated in 1969 after Iran unilaterally abrogated the 1937 *Shatt al-Arab* agreement. They grew even more strained after 1970, when the Shah began a major defense-spending initiative, induced by the Nixon Doctrine's commitment to arm states willing to counter regional threats. Parallel U.S. military support to Saudi Arabia and the newly independent Gulf states of the UAE, Qatar, and Bahrain combined with a rising American naval presence to feed Iraq's sense of geographic constraint. It clashed with Kuwait in March 1973 over the Gulf islands of Warba and Bubiyan, prompting Saudi Arabia and the Arab League to intervene on behalf of the small sheikhdom.

Not all of its actions were openly aggressive, with the regime leadership's junior partner, Saddam Hussein, pursuing several important agreements in these early years. To stabilize domestic as well as regional affairs, he negotiated with the Kurds, giving them a measure of cultural and administrative autonomy in March 1970. This seeming accommodation turned out to be temporary and disingenuous, but it gave Baghdad time to better integrate Kurdistan into Iraqi territory by building infrastructure and resettling some of the population. On the economic front, Saddam planned and implemented the nationalization of the Iraq Petroleum Company in 1972. This facilitated the tremendous growth of state revenues after the 1973 Arab–Israeli War, which led to a quadrupling of international oil prices and a permanent transformation of global energy markets. In the security domain, he negotiated a new Treaty of Friendship and Cooperation with the Soviet Union in 1972. This did not require much from Iraq and soon was accompanied by additional improvements in relations with western countries eager to do business and secure oil supplies. He also made a secret deal with France in November 1975 for a new nuclear research reactor, ostensibly for the research and development of a civilian nuclear industry. The reactor was given the name Osirak, had potential military applications, and was sabotaged in France when almost complete in 1979. Its replacement was bombed by Israel when nearly installed in 1981.

By the mid-1970s, with control of the regime in hand, Iraq began to alter and even moderate certain aspects of its foreign policy, first by negotiating the 1975 Algiers Accord with Iran. This agreement secured an end to Iranian support for the Kurds in return for a significant territorial concession: accepting the midpoint or *thalweg* in the *Shatt al-Arab* as the territorial border. More broadly, Iraq's dramatically rising oil wealth enhanced its appeal as a trade partner and arms purchaser, leading it to drift from the Soviet orbit and forge closer ties with a wide range of European countries, in addition to Japan and even the United States. The regime also improved its MENA regional relations and asserted its leadership ambitions, particularly after Anwar Sadat's trip to Jerusalem in November 1977, which paved the way for the Camp David Accords in September 1978 and the Egyptian–Israeli peace treaty in March 1979. Iraq led the charge to expel Egypt from the Arab League and staked a claim as the new defender of the Arab world, patching up relations with Jordan and Syria in the process. In Arab politics, Iraq no longer called for political unification so much as regional interstate cooperation, with Saddam at the fore. This approach reduced the tension between Iraq's domestically divided, mixed-ethnicity polity and Saddam's seeming wish to retrace Nasser's early footsteps as the preeminent leader of the Arab world, struggling against the region's enemies.

Saddam Takes Charge, and Invades Iran

By the end of the decade, Saddam Hussein was ascendant at home and considering his next moves abroad, especially vis-à-vis his state rivals to the east and west. As part of Iraq's longstanding nuclear program, the United States had helped in founding the Iraqi Atomic Energy Commission (IAEC) in 1956, and the Soviet Union had furthered the mission with the provision of a research reactor, which became active at the Tuwaitha nuclear complex on the southern outskirts of Baghdad in 1968. Serving as head of the IAEC, Saddam had taken new and tangible steps toward developing nuclear weapons capabilities, including the French nuclear deal in 1975. After sending Hassan al-Bakr into retirement and assuming the presidency in July 1979, Saddam reportedly initiated additional and immediate efforts in the nuclear realm, recruiting scientists to pursue what had become a full-fledged weapons program.[16] By then, he was well aware of Israel's growing arsenal, along with other potential threats that would have incentivized any Iraqi leader to consider pursuing WMD. Iraq faced a powerful security dilemma, a structural condition that can bring about self-destructive choices, and it had both an aggressive new president and domestic conditions suitable to risky foreign behavior.[17]

In this same period, Iran's Islamic revolution was in full swing over the eastern border, with significant political and social consequences in Iraq. The revolution posed too great a challenge and created too much of an opportunity for Saddam to ignore. He launched an invasion of Iran on September 22, 1980. As noted in Chapter 2, the war's fundamental causes were a combination of factors, all filtered through the prism of Saddam's calculation of personal political interest. Some of these larger factors had not changed much over several decades. The geostrategic antagonism between Iraq and Iran was longstanding and effectively unresolvable, at least via unilateral measures. Iran's decades-long involvement with Iraqi Kurdish and Shi'i populations also could not be eliminated and only lent itself to careful management. The Iranian revolution nonetheless changed the Iraqi leader's cost/benefit calculation. The threat posed by the Ayatollah Khomeini's call to Iraqi Shi'a to overthrow Saddam's regime was too grave to ignore, as was Khomeini's novel political-theological doctrine and his willingness to export it beyond Iran. This combined with Iraqi assumptions about the impact of revolutionary upheaval on a purged Iranian officer corps, as well as Iran's loss of U.S. arms supply and political support. Together, all these factors brought about one of the most devastating regional wars of the twentieth century.[18]

The war itself began with an airstrike and brief Iraqi advances into oil-rich Khuzestan in southwestern Iran, followed months later by a sharp reversal and realization that the war would not be short and easy. In fact, it lasted nearly eight years and became massive in scale and scope. The war included several phases and military theaters, and much of it was fought like the First World War, with large-scale ground offensives, the brutal use of basic technology like the machine gun, martyred Iranian human waves, and devastating Iraqi chemical attacks on both the battlefield and Kurdish civilians. It also involved air campaigns, Scud missile warfare against Iranian cities, a tanker war, and eventually an international naval dimension when the United States, Britain, and France got involved in protecting Kuwaiti oil tankers from Iranian attack.[19]

Initially, Saddam put himself in charge of strategy, with poor results that led to a successful Iranian counteroffensive, driving back Iraqi forces and nearly endangering his rule. Iraqi battlefield setbacks prompted the United States to reconsider its approach and begin a significant "tilt" toward Iraq in 1982, ending its studied ambivalence toward the war out of a concern that Iran might win. It dropped Iraq from its list of state sponsors of terrorism, conducted a formal policy review, and held diplomatic discussions that included a visit from presidential envoy Donald Rumsfeld. The United States soon began providing various kinds of support to Baghdad, from agricultural credits and Export–Import Bank financing to military intelligence regarding Iranian forces.[20] Formal relations were restored in late 1984. By the mid-1980s, Iraq had the support of the United States, the Soviets, most Arab states, and much of Europe, including substantial arms sales from France, among other countries. This was enough to produce a damaging, stalemated war of attrition and an eventual realization by Iran's Khomeini that he would have to accept U.N. Resolution 598 calling for a ceasefire, a return to prewar borders, and a prisoner exchange.

The war ended in a pointless draw in August 1988, though the leadership of both sides claimed victory, as Saddam declared that he had successfully defended the Arab world from an Iranian onslaught, invoking the Arab Muslim victory over the Persian Sasanians at Qadisiyya in 636. Yet, there were no real gains for either country and tremendous human and material losses. Over 100,000 Iraqi soldiers died and hundreds of thousands were wounded or captured, with similar if slightly larger numbers on the Iranian side. Civilian casualties were substantial from air and missile attacks, as well as from Iraq's war-related genocidal campaign against the Kurds, which killed many thousands. The economic toll was in the hundreds of billions of dollars for both countries in direct war expenditures, foregone oil exports, diminished economic productivity, and damaged infrastructure. Exhausted public sentiment was evident, though the war did allow both regimes to consolidate themselves and reinforce a sense of national unity and purpose. It also contributed to other major regional changes, such as the reintegration of post–Camp David Egypt into the Arab fold, though it is hard to determine, counterfactually, what trajectory Iraq and the larger MENA region would have taken without the war.

Iraq emerged from the fight a battered giant, with a much larger military capacity than before and a strong measure of entitlement for its sacrifices. As noted in Chapter 3, it had a brief postwar opportunity to reassess, rebuild, and move to a better future, but it did not do so. Saddam's strategic judgment in initiating the war and overseeing its early conduct had been called into question by the Revolutionary Command Council and military leadership alike. Internal regime plots to replace him abounded in the period from 1988 to 1990. The world itself was also in transition. The year 1989 was a historic moment of rapid international change, gripped by political and economic transformation in the eastern bloc and jolted by *glasnost* and *perestroika* in the final years of the Soviet Union. The new decade brought a sense of possibility, progress, and even—to some—the arrival of a new era. It is no surprise therefore that the historical moment that produced the end of the Cold War and a contemplation of the "end of history" did not foresee what would happen next in a region seemingly left behind.

Invasion of Kuwait, Defeat, and Uprising, 1990–1991

Neither the Iraqi public nor regime insiders in 1990 could have anticipated all that would befall the country after Saddam sent Republican Guard units over the Kuwaiti border in the earliest morning hours of August 2. The consensus in Baghdad and beyond was that Iraq was at the end, not the beginning, of an especially difficult episode in its contemporary history. Iraq's media and information environment remained relatively closed on a popular level in this era, allowing the regime to manage popular perceptions of what was transpiring, to some extent. State-controlled television, newspapers, and radio fed the public stories of Kuwaiti treachery, U.S. perfidy, and Saddam's heroic resistance to the entire world, even as the American media conveyed somewhat underexamined opposite claims in classic, rally-'round-the-flag style. In the end, U.S. power prevailed in a changing world. And while Saddam miscalculated badly in the summer and fall of 1990, it is not clear that a full appreciation of the U.S. willingness to go to war would have changed his actions once he committed forces to Kuwait.

The world's reaction to Iraq's invasion was swift, uncharacteristically unified, and impactful. The immediate response included vigorous defensive action by the United States to protect against a possible follow-on invasion of neighboring Saudi Arabia, dubbed Operation Desert Shield. This segued into five months of methodical diplomatic and military preparation, laying the groundwork for a war the George H. W. Bush administration thought wholly necessary. The U.S.-led multinational coalition then commenced a coordinated attack on Iraqi forces occupying Kuwait, called Operation Desert Storm. It started with a long air campaign in mid-January 1991 and ended with a ferocious 100-hour ground attack before a quick ceasefire in late February. The Gulf War, as the entire episode came to be called, was a stunning victory for the coalition, with its own military casualties limited to the hundreds and an extraordinary demonstration of new technologies of war. The coalition's rapid and decisive military success, legitimized by U.N. Security Council

Resolution 678 authorizing the action, made it politically difficult and seemingly unnecessary to mount a full-scale invasion and occupation of Iraq. The success led many to conclude that Saddam and his regime, which suffered tens of thousands of losses and a near-fatal humiliation, would not be long for this world. Iraqis themselves would finish the job.

The widely held assumption about regime weakness inspired Iraqis to rise up in much of the country in early March, just as the ceasefire took hold. This was the case especially in the heavily Shi'i-populated south and in Kurdistan to the north. Encouraged by U.S. President Bush's public calls to eliminate the regime and secure their own freedom, rural Shi'a in Basra, Nasiriyya, Amara, Najaf, and Karbala were the first to rebel, joined by a limited number of Iraqi military units. Acting spontaneously and without organized leadership, the uprising in the south mostly entailed targeting local Ba'athists, regime supporters, and sympathizers, with mobs killing hundreds of Iraqi officials and taking over government offices. Islamist groups like the *Da'wa* participated, as did a fair number of Shi'i soldiers, who deserted and joined the rebellion. For their part, the Kurds to the north ramped up their own efforts with somewhat greater organization and success, coordinated by the KDP and the PUK, winning control of Kirkuk and other major cities by mid-March.

With its back to the wall and facing both a powerful multinational adversary and unprecedented domestic upheaval, the regime responded with exceptional viciousness to suppress both uprisings. It deployed the Republican Guard units left intact by the war and was unconstrained in its use of helicopter gunships, which were permitted to fly under the terms of the February ceasefire. It conducted offensives against both the southern and northern uprisings, killing tens of thousands of civilians indiscriminately. The uprisings probably aided Saddam's effort to stay in power because he could focus his security services on regime survival and claim that without him they all would be swept away. Iraqi forces prevailed by early April, triggering a massive, nearly 2-million-person refugee exodus, particularly among the Kurds, who fled to the mountainous north and to Turkey and Iran. The U.N. Security Council, under Resolution 688, created a no-fly zone north of Erbil and Mosul on the 36th parallel to begin stabilizing the crisis, while the Kurds established an autonomous self-government zone. Iraqi government operations against the Shi'a in the south were relatively quick, forceful, and successful, and they continued after the reassertion of state authority. For many Iraqis, these events proved more destructive and transformative than the short, sharp stroke of violence that befell the overmatched Iraqi army occupying Kuwait.

The Gulf War and its aftermath represented a second major blow to Iraq in a decade, this one only slightly lower in casualty numbers but with consequences more evenly distributed across society. It harmed the Shi'i and Kurdish civilian populations and impacted the Sunni minority on a popular if not elite level. The Shi'a of southern Iraq were especially affected. The southern uprising was quelled first, but state repression lasted longer in the south, targeting rural areas for the next three years until 1994. The Kurdish north suffered the largest population displacement and was still reeling from harm done in the Iran–Iraq War, though it gained a measure of autonomy for a time via the protection offered by the establishment of the no-fly zone. The Sunni population was not unscathed and suffered under the uncertainty of what seemed to be the end of an era of Sunni dominance, even if conditions would become much worse in the years to come.

Saddam himself survived by relying on the formal state institutions he had built—the security services, loyal military units, Ba'athist cadres—and his equally important informal patronage network of intricately connected regime supporters. The latter overlapped with the former in that his supporters occupied the upper echelons of all critical state institutions, especially in the security domain. At the apex of the entire system, Saddam displayed an exceptional capacity to balance, manipulate, or eliminate those in his clique, shrinking somewhat the size of his immediate ruling group. This allowed him to circle the wagons, reduce pretenses to populism, and narrow his support base to include only those most indispensable to regime survival. Closing ranks required relying even more heavily on extended family, tribal kinsmen, and close associates, who were running the security apparatus, including the Republican Guard. Saddam also made symbolic and conciliatory moves, such as stepping down as prime minister and appointing in his place Sa'dun Hammadi, the first Shi'a to hold the office in the Ba'athist era, though this only lasted from March to mid-September 1991.

Sympathy for the Devil, 1991–2003

All these strategies kept Saddam in power in the postwar era, though the country as a whole was still under great duress from a variety of sources. The primary external pressure came from the international community's insistence, led by the United States, on maintaining all sanctions in accordance with the war-related U.N. Security Council Resolutions of 1990–1991. This included introducing a weapons inspection regime under U.N. auspices. The Iraqi government would have to give up its WMD before the Iraqi people would have any relief. The U.N. resolutions had begun with Resolution 660 on August 2 condemning Iraq's invasion of Kuwait and calling for its withdrawal, followed by Resolution 661 on August 6 establishing international sanctions and banning all imports, exports, and financial transactions with Iraq, other than humanitarian aid. An additional ten resolutions were passed by late November 1990, culminating in Resolution 678, which authorized member-states to use "all necessary means" to eject Iraqi forces from Kuwait if Iraq failed to comply with the entire set of international demands.[21] Iraq's noncompliance—Saddam's defiant refusal to withdraw from Kuwait—provided the legal basis for the war in mid-January 1991.[22]

The coalition military victory was followed by U.N. Security Council Resolution 687 of April 3, 1991, which encompassed and reaffirmed all 13 prior resolutions and, most critically, called for Iraq to disarm itself of a particular class of weapons that included "all chemical and biological weapons and all stocks of agents and all related subsystems and components and all research, development, support and manufacturing facilities related thereto."[23] It also forbid Iraq from having any ballistic missile with a capability over 190 miles. Noting "the threat that all weapons of mass destruction pose to peace and security in the area and of the need to work toward the establishment in the Middle East of a zone free of such weapons," it also insisted that Iraq reaffirm its commitments under the nuclear Non-Proliferation Treaty (NPT) to forgo the pursuit of nuclear weapons and submit to inspections from a newly established Special Commission on Iraq (UNSCOM). Together, these and several other provisions relating to borders, recognition, and reparations to Kuwait established the international political foundations for 12 subsequent years of conflict between Saddam's regime and the international community. It had a dramatic, enduring impact on the country.

As a consequence, Iraqi domestic political life in this period was heavily intertwined with regional and international relations. External forces acted as both intrusions on Iraqi sovereignty and exclusions from full engagement with the rest of the world. They affected many aspects of national life, almost as much as the choices and policies made by the regime. The level of pressure on everyday Iraqis took many forms and came from all sides. The humanitarian impact of international sanctions was deeply unfortunate.[24] In addition to the obvious problem of sanctions limiting access to all manner of imported goods and services, the regime itself manipulated the sanctions and the fact of international pressure to justify its actions. It demanded relief and excoriated the United States and the international community for their seeming indifference to human suffering. Their claims were not without merit. The regime even made sure the sanctions did damage especially to the large swathes of the Shi'i population containing its domestic adversaries, whose targeting would be in the regime's interest. Ironically, the sanctions, inspections, and international pressure may have helped to keep Saddam in power by allowing him to channel the pain, blame other parties for the country's travails, and hold out rewards in the form of relief for his supporters.[25]

Iraq's relationship with the Arab world in the 1990s evolved considerably over the decade, beginning with animosity and ending with ambivalence. The regime jettisoned its preinvasion Arab nationalist rhetoric and even the pretense of regional leadership, having been at war in 1991 with a coalition that included troops from Saudi Arabia, Egypt, Syria, Morocco, Kuwait, Oman, the UAE, Qatar, and Bahrain. With no possibility of a rapprochement between Saddam and the heads of state he had variously challenged, betrayed, or attempted to depose, some analysts predicted an end to Arab nationalism, forgetting that authoritarian Iraq had acted on the orders of its paramount leader, who was not representative of sentiment throughout the country, let alone the region. There also remained ethnic, tribal, family, and communal connections between Iraq and its neighbors that were disassociated from the conflict between the Ba'athist leadership and an American-dominated international community increasingly perceived to be vindictive and overreaching.

As Saddam's regime withdrew into itself to survive, international sympathy for the many Iraqis suffering under a deeply punitive sanctions regime grew stronger.

The Oil-for-Food Program was adopted under U.N. Security Council Resolution 986 of April 1995 but not implemented until after Iraq, ostensibly concerned about the impingement on its sovereignty, acquiesced in May 1996. The program provided an escrow mechanism to allow the regime to import more food and medicine paid for by oil exports. This stabilized food prices, increased caloric intake, and doubled the country's GDP from 1997 to 2000, improving the economy overall and alleviating social pressure.[26] As an unintended consequence, it led to an increase in Saddam's popularity among his supporters. It was plagued, moreover, by corruption and the misuse of some funding, and the country remained mired in inflation and unemployment.

More generally, Saddam's Iraq in the 1990s was widely seen as trapped in a bygone era of authoritarianism. Partial democratic transitions were sweeping through other parts of the world, including the post-Soviet space and sub-Saharan Africa, while the MENA region was marked by a puzzling authoritarian persistence. American diplomatic attention focused on the Oslo Accords of 1993 and 1995, which were expected to end Israeli–Palestinian enmity via a two-state solution and to contribute to a broader resolution of the Arab–Israeli conflict. Much to the surprised dismay of U.S. policymakers, Israeli and Palestinian hardliners together began undermining the peace process in several ways, including via the assassination of Israeli Prime Minister Yitzhak Rabin in November 1995 by an Israeli nationalist, a series of devastating Hamas and Palestinian Islamic Jihad suicide attacks over a three-year period, the election in May 1996 of a right-leaning Israeli government that was unenthusiastic about a two-state solution, and a Palestinian leadership better suited to rebellion and survival than negotiation. As the peace process collapsed by the latter part of the decade, a distracted United States under the Clinton administration lost much of its credibility in the MENA region and came to be seen as perpetually favoring the Israeli position, just as it was perceived as callous and even bullying with regard to Iraq.

In this same period, especially during Clinton's first term, the initial strategic consensus in the United States was that Iraq was to be kept in a box, along with Iran, via a policy of "dual containment," while higher-priority problems like the genocidal ethnic conflicts in Bosnia and Rwanda were managed if not actually addressed.[27] The United States supported modest covert attempts to depose Saddam, usually through either of the major Iraqi exile groups, Ahmed Chalabi's Iraqi National Congress (INC) or Ayad Allawi's Iraqi National Accord (INA). It maintained steady pressure on Saddam's regime, not openly calling for his removal but hoping that the combination of international sanctions and the inspections regime would bring about this result. Over time, the inspections ran into continued resistance, the sanctions began to fray, and covert efforts failed miserably, as Saddam typically got wind of them and acted accordingly.[28] The administration had no real interest in deeper U.S. involvement in what it saw as the intractable side of MENA regional politics, but it was increasingly difficult to maintain the inspections and sanctions, punish Baghdad's misdeeds via an occasional airstrike or missile attack, and leave it at that.

Neoconservative activists, on the other hand, began raising the volume on their demand for a more aggressive American foreign policy during Clinton's second term after 1996, tapping into a longstanding set of claims about the need to demonstrate U.S. power and exercise a benevolent American hegemony.[29] In league with democratic hawks and even liberal interventionists, they raised the pressure for a more aggressive move against Saddam's regime. Accordingly, a Republican-controlled U.S. Congress passed the Iraq Liberation Act of 1998 (ILA) in October of that year "to support a transition to democracy in Iraq."[30] The Act was a nonbinding resolution and partisan political theater as much as anything, not signaling a policy change and with no one seriously expecting Iraq to make a democratic transition as a result. The Clinton administration had serious reservations about it, but found it difficult to oppose. The ILA did signal, however, shifting thinking about the efficacy of the current approach to Iraq.

In mid-December 1998, the Clinton administration conducted a four-day bombing campaign against Iraq, called Operation Desert Fox. Desert Fox was ostensibly a stern consequence of Iraq's noncompliance with UNSCOM inspections requirements. Iraq indeed was resisting inspections, though by then most of its WMD and missile arsenal had been eliminated. Saddam, in fact, did not kick out UNSCOM inspectors; the United States itself withdrew them just before the campaign, contending that Iraq was not cooperating sufficiently. The operation was not motivated by a determination to oust Saddam so much as to seize the political initiative in the face of an array of domestic and international pressures. Some observers claim it was partly intended to distract attention from a domestic scandal, as the U.S. House Judiciary Committee a few days earlier had approved a fourth article of impeachment for President Clinton, who was impeached in the House on the last day of the bombing campaign. The president's various troubles aside, the general view across the political spectrum was that U.S. policy toward Iraq was coming apart, even if there was no consensus as to what should be done differently.[31]

Saddam used the occasion of Desert Fox to discontinue all further cooperation and end the weapons inspections that had been carried out under UNSCOM auspices since 1991. Though strong evidence of his thinking is unattainable, he may have done so for at least three reasons, with the action directed at internal and external audiences. First, terminating the inspections allowed him to claim he was defying the great powers, as indeed he was. This benefited him politically with domestic allies and adversaries alike by demonstrating his resolve in the face of clearly superior forces. He had played "cheat and retreat" games with the inspections for years, but now he could end the games on a defiant note that conveyed confidence. This was unusually important in a national context of long-time sensitivity, given Iraq's colonial and imperial history, to foreign powers impinging on Iraqi sovereignty. After all, the "freedom" in the Ba'ath's slogan of "unity, freedom, and socialism" refers to freedom from external interference. Other than the Kurds, most Iraqis had grown weary of UNSCOM operating in the country, even with U.N. permission, as well as the United States, Britain, and France controlling the skies above much of Iraq in no-fly zones that did not have specific legal authorization.[32]

More importantly, Saddam's actions were perfectly rational from a perspective that prioritized his own power and regime survival over all else. Saddam surely was convinced that the United States would continue to try to end his rule no matter what he did. After all, the ILA, while created for largely domestic political purposes by a Republican-held congress, said as much, and Saddam very likely would have taken it at face value. Whether he regretted his early-1990s, grudging, minimalist compliance with UNSCOM inspections is not knowable, but after several years and successful efforts on his part to strengthen his regime and shift international public opinion in his favor, the Desert Fox campaign made it easy for him to end all compliance. After all, as Foreign Minister Tareq Aziz later claimed, probably accurately, if the regime had known how relatively little damage Desert Fox would do, it would have terminated the inspections years sooner.[33]

Finally, and less obviously, Saddam's abrupt ending of the inspections reinforced the assumption that Iraq still had WMD that had yet to be uncovered. Why else would he do so, observers asked, if he had nothing to hide? But maintaining ambiguity and the possibility of a hidden WMD arsenal benefited Saddam with external foes like Israel and Iran, whom he still sought to deter. From Baghdad's perspective, this was not irrational, given the regime's threat perception. It also was not unprecedented in the region. Israel's nuclear posture, after all, had long been one of strategic ambiguity and opacity, or *amimut*, regarding the country's possession of a nuclear arsenal, even if there was little uncertainty regarding whether Israel had undeclared nuclear weapons.[34] More generally, as deterrence theorists have long posited, it is the mere possibility of nuclear retaliation that establishes deterrent power with rivals. It is not the iron-clad certainty of an arsenal's existence so much as the uncertainty of its possible existence and use that motivates minimally rational decision-makers to tread lightly.[35] Saddam very much wanted to be able to deter Iran, in particular, from taking advantage of his weakness. Allowing himself to appear stripped of all such fearsome weapons was unacceptable to a leader bent on staying in power.

As eventually it became evident, UNSCOM had discovered, destroyed, or otherwise eliminated nearly all of Saddam's WMD and missile programs over the course of several years in the 1990s.[36] Saddam acquiesced to the dismantling of weapons programs that the record shows he had prioritized for some two decades, beginning in the 1970s. He did not do so willingly, have a change of heart, act transparently, or accept the legitimacy of international inspections. He was extraordinarily uncooperative and attempted to thwart inspector access throughout the years. His foot-dragging turned out to be no match for a dedicated if abrasive and intrusive set of inspectors following a rigorous inspections process. He does appear to have bowed to the threats and pressures of the process. The process itself was politicized by its very nature in seeking to deny powerful weapons, even with justification, to a sovereign state deemed unsuitable to possess them. The international community had reached that conclusion, though the conclusion itself was not politically neutral, nor was the inspections process, which was compromised by its likely penetration by U.S. intelligence. The great and tragic irony is that while the inspections process succeeded, at least enough to avoid more dramatic international action, widespread perceptions of its failure—furthered by Saddam's cagey seeming noncompliance—established the conditions for the next episode in Iraq's long and difficult national path.

9/11 and the Road to Baghdad

In this context, the 9/11 attack occurred as a wholly separate set of events. That is, it bears emphasis that Iraq had nothing to do with the al-Qa'ida attacks of September 11, 2001. Saddam did not trust and had not assisted bin Laden, and he had rejected prior al-Qa'ida requests for aid and operational support.[37] Contrary to public claims made by President Bush, Vice President Cheney, Defense Secretary Rumsfeld, and National Security Adviser Rice, no close working relationship between Iraq and al-Qa'ida existed.[38] The U.S. intelligence community concluded that the Iraqi Intelligence Service (IIS) was not in regular contact with al-Qa'ida and had not met 9/11 operatives in Prague or elsewhere, as previously claimed. Ba'athist Iraq was a sworn enemy of jihadist groups like al-Qa'ida and had persecuted relentlessly their own, somewhat milder Islamist opposition. Saddam may not have been lying when he told his FBI interrogators after his capture that if he had wanted to ally with a U.S. enemy, he would have chosen North Korea or China.[39] While Saddam leaned more heavily into Iraq's Islamic identity in the 1990s as part of a regime legitimization and survival strategy, he did not embrace any of the fundamental objectives held by the likes of bin Laden.

The one commonality Saddam and bin Laden did share was that they were both Sunni Arabs by faith and ethnicity. In addition, Iraq's geographic location in the Middle East made it easily associated with Islam as the birthplace and spiritual center of the faith. This pair of associations is likely to have loomed large in the minds of some Americans, with or without their awareness. It may have shaped both the Bush administration's preferences in devising a response to 9/11, starting with Defense Secretary Rumsfeld's well-known September 12 exhortation to include Iraq in the plan. It may also have affected American popular and political receptiveness to such claims associating Saddam and bin Laden. Many other factors aside from ignorance, bias, and guilt by association operated in driving the United States to war in Iraq. In the end, the war was driven by an unfortunate conspiring of unfortunate ideas and complex interests, with nothing much to stop those animated by them.

While the attack proved to be transformative in American politics and had global repercussions, it was only the most dramatic example of militant violence emanating from fringe Islamist opposition groups since the 1970s. Al-Qa'ida was founded by Osama bin Laden in 1988 and remained for years a small collection of international jihadists with mostly Saudi, Egyptian, Sudanese, and Pakistani members. Bin Laden himself was Saudi-born and from a prominent wealthy family in the construction business. He had joined the anti-Soviet jihad in Afghanistan in the 1980s, before turning his ire to his home country in 1990, ironically, for accepting U.S. troops to counter Iraq's invasion of Kuwait and rebuffing his offer to defend the Saudi kingdom from Iraqi threats. Bin Laden was not a serious thinker, religious scholar, or innovator, though he had wealth and some apparent leadership skills. His organization already had struck U.S. embassy targets in Kenya and Tanzania in 1998, followed by an attack two years later on the USS Cole in the port of Aden, Yemen, in 2000. The "principal architect" of the 9/11 plot was Kuwaiti-born Khalid Sheikh Mohammed, who planned the operation in Hamburg, Germany, and recruited over a dozen men, mostly young Saudis, to participate in what turned out to be the most spectacular and devastating terror attack in history.[40]

The Bush administration responded to 9/11 with nearly immediate covert and then overt military action in Afghanistan. The objective was simple at first: to oust the Taliban regime, which had harbored al-Qa'ida, and to pursue and destroy bin Laden's organization, beginning in October 2001. Simultaneous discussion and then planning for a possible attack on Iraq also started right away, when Defense Secretary Rumsfeld suggested striking Saddam Hussein as part of a larger U.S. response to the 9/11 attack.[41] In late November 2001, President Bush formally directed CENTCOM Combatant Commander Tommy Franks to begin updating the Pentagon's operational war plans for Iraq, OPLAN 1003-98.[42] In his January 2002 State of the Union address, Bush deployed a new phrase, the "axis of evil," to focus attention on a purported dangerous alliance between countries like Iraq (along with Iran and North Korea) and groups like al-Qa'ida. Iraq was to be a central front in the emerging "war on terror."

The 18-month period between 9/11 and the Iraq War bore little resemblance to the previous crisis of 1990–1991, when Iraq had invaded Kuwait and the international community reacted firmly and was united in opposition. While the global response to 9/11 was sympathetic to the United States, few outside the United States understood or supported the Bush administration's rapid shift in focus toward Iraq. Al-Qa'ida's attack on the United States provided no obvious rationale for a U.S.-led war in Iraq, though by June 2002 at the latest it became clear that one was in the offing. The United States that month commenced Operation Southern Focus to degrade Iraqi air defenses, flying over 20,000 air sorties over southern Iraq, attacking over 300 targets, and infiltrating special forces into Iraqi territory, and CIA officers into northern Iraq.[43] The Bush administration entertained ongoing public and private discussions of the options with Iraq, but soon enough began to mobilize its forces, prepare its case, rally the U.S. public, and seek international backing.

Into the fall of 2002, an invasion still did not have direct and explicit authorization from the U.N. Security Council, where support for the American hard line on Iraq typically was limited to the United Kingdom under the Blair government. With clear opposition from France, Russia, and China, the United States maintained that with Iraq in material breach of all Security Council resolutions, military intervention was justified. Weeks of intensive negotiation at the Security Council led to Resolution 1441 of November 8, 2002, which was a final multilateral effort to induce full Iraqi compliance but also, to skeptics and critics of the

United States on the Council, a restraint on impending U.S. unilateral action. It passed unanimously, giving Iraq a "final opportunity to comply with its disarmament obligations under relevant resolutions of the Council."[44] Iraq soon acquiesced to a return of international inspectors.

Inspections this time were to be under the auspices of two entities: the United Nations Monitoring, Verification, and Inspections Commission (UNMOVIC), created in 1999 to replace and relegitimize UNSCOM and headed by Swedish diplomat Hans Blix, along with the longstanding nuclear watchdog, the International Atomic Energy Agency (IAEA) under Egyptian diplomat Mohamed ElBaradei. These bodies moved to secure full Iraqi compliance in the face of yet another round of obfuscation and delay by Iraqi authorities. Baghdad produced an expansive declaration about its prior programs that UNMOVIC and IAEA inspectors contended did not contain any new information. Part of the difficulty was the inherent ambiguity of a process designed to establish beyond doubt the nonexistence or elimination of weapons programs, and to do so without wholehearted regime cooperation. Saddam in late 2002 and early 2003 still seemed unconvinced that noncompliance would lead to war, or perhaps he believed that if war came, it would not bring about his removal from power. His first priority remained his own rule, and this shaped all his interactions with adversaries like the United States and extended to institutions like the United Nations, which he saw as typically doing American bidding.

The year 2003 brought a growing inevitability that the United States would make good on its promises, but not before further drama at the U.N. Security Council. In early February, U.S. Secretary of State Colin Powell, flanked by CIA Director George Tenet, appeared before the world and made the American case for the danger Iraq posed and the imperative of forceful international action. Powell had been a restraint on the drive to war, cognizant of its uncertainties and sensitive to the obligations associated with his Pottery Barn rule: "If you break it, you buy it." Regardless of his prior caution, he and much of the U.S. political class appeared confident of the necessity of a military campaign to disarm Iraq under the circumstances, never particularly questioning the underlying idea that Iraqi noncompliance should be met with a full-blown invasion. The United States was simultaneously waging a larger "war on terror" in far-flung locations worldwide, having put itself on a war footing at home. This made it easier to cast the Iraq War as one front in the war on terror, as the dominant ideas in American domestic politics took hold and moved a majority toward actions far from home.

Inevitably, the situation in Iraq precipitated a significant crisis in relations between the United States and continental Europe, especially what Defense Secretary Rumsfeld called "Old Europe"—France and Germany. The European countries had their own perspectives on how to manage security concerns, along with differing calculations of risk and uncertainty in world politics. They also had their own interests at stake, given Iraq's geostrategic centrality, oil resources, and business opportunities. France, for its part, was attentive to the longstanding prospect of arms sales and oil purchases, as well as leftover unpaid Iraqi debts. Both France and Germany—then serving on the U.N. Security Council—had very different senses of the efficacy of military force and the likelihood that the United States could successfully invade Iraq, remove Saddam, stabilize the country, and install a democracy. Beyond Europe, China's leadership was anticipating a tremendous increase in its need for oil and gas to feed its rapidly growing economy and, with Russia, was not one to follow the U.S. lead at multilateral institutions. Russia itself was resistant to a rush to war and consistently oppositional at the Security Council without getting ahead of other war skeptics like France and China.

In late February 2003, the United States, Britain, and Spain attempted to cosponsor a final resolution condemning Iraq's failure to comply and authorizing force under Security Council auspices. The measure was not adopted when France and Russia responded with a memorandum opposing the use of force. After the failure in early March of one last diplomatic effort to obtain a resolution authorizing force, the United States declared Iraq's violation of prior resolutions to be sufficient justification for military action, even as a majority on the Security Council contended otherwise. On March 17, President Bush gave Saddam and his sons 48 hours to leave the country to avoid war. International inspectors withdrew the next day, and the U.S. launched the invasion shortly thereafter.

The world could do nothing to stop the United States, given America's unmatched military and economic power, along with its peerless political capacity to marshal support for its larger initiatives, or at least nonopposition, from smaller countries worldwide. It had linked Iraq rhetorically to its war on terror, stating that all countries had to choose sides and were either with or against the U.S. effort. The limits of global governance became obvious, with no institutional mechanism, power, or alliance of states to restrain determined U.S. action or prevent it from taking the path it chose, despite widespread regional and international opposition. American veto power on the Security Council precluded substantial international reaction or constraint of any kind. All that its members could do was to claim individually that, according to their own interpretations of prior U.N. Security Council resolutions, the measures adopted did not constitute an authorization of the war. The United States could disagree while lobbying individual countries to participate in its effort to rein in Saddam. With no multilateral security institution to defend it, Iraq could not call upon collective efforts to ensure its protection in the face of a hostile power bent on war.

In the MENA region, Saudi Arabia stood very publicly against an invasion, concerned about potential destabilizing effects and alarmed by the Bush administration's rhetoric about democracy, whether in Iraq, which under a majoritarian system could mean Shi'i rule, or at home. Syria was adamantly opposed, leery about the United States targeting regional powers for weapons programs. Egypt under Mubarak refused U.S. requests to participate as it had in 1991, aware that Egyptian public opinion had shifted substantially since then. Jordan's King Abdullah attempted to promote a diplomatic solution and walked a fine line, though the kingdom reportedly provided quiet support for U.S. efforts. Turkey was skeptical about the potential consequences of a war in a neighboring state, and at the last moment, its national assembly refused a U.S. request for troop passage through the southwest. Iran was more ambivalent, with long-time antipathy toward Iraq but genuine unease about the prospect of U.S. troops on its doorstep. Israel was in a delicate position again, agreeing quietly to not favor or oppose the war publicly for fear of affecting other state positions. Kuwait, still reeling from the 1990 invasion, was the only Arab country to openly and actively support the United States. The Arab League as an institution opposed the war, though with little consequence because it did not constitute a regional security pact and could not oblige its members to do anything in Iraq's defense.

The U.S. Invasion and Occupation

The U.S. invasion arrived from the air, starting with an effort to "decapitate" Saddam's regime. In the early morning of March 20, 2003, with short notice based on intelligence intercepts, the United States launched a stealth airstrike on the Iraqi leader, who reportedly was hiding at Dora Farms, south of Baghdad. The attack hit the facility but missed its actual target because Saddam had not been there since 1995, and he succeeded in remaining hidden for several more months.[45] It nonetheless marked the opening salvo of a six-week conventional war that was a classic mismatch, with the Iraqi army either overwhelmed when confronting superior forces or, just as often, melting away to avoid certain destruction. As Operation Iraqi Freedom proceeded, Baghdad fell in three weeks, on April 9, and the rest of the country was in the hands of the U.S.-led military coalition by early May. From the deck of the USS *Abraham Lincoln* on May 1, American President George W. Bush declared, "Mission Accomplished" and an end to major combat operations.

Unlike Operation Desert Storm in 1991, the initial invasion was largely a unilateral U.S. endeavor. The United States deployed a relatively small force of about 150,000 troops, albeit with major advantages in technology, airpower, and operational capabilities. Only a few countries—the United Kingdom, Australia, Poland, and Denmark—joined at the very outset, though some 37 states eventually participated in what the Bush administration called a "coalition of the willing."[46] The international community was torn between a desire to assist Iraq and cultivate post-Saddam ties in what would be a new era, and a reluctance to support what many viewed as the wayward and even illegal actions of a powerful member. It was not until mid-October 2003, five months into the war and occupation, that the Security Council passed Resolution 1511 authorizing the formation of a multilateral security force. While U.S. military forces remained the dominant presence, the international coalition made significant contributions in a wide range of forms, from aid delivery, humanitarian assistance, and civilian medical care to bomb disposal, intelligence collection, combat troops, and special forces. What began unilaterally became more multilateral over time and lasted until all non-U.S. foreign forces left Iraq in late July 2009. The most significant international opponents to the war—France, Russia, China—never joined the coalition.[47]

The international political disagreement over the resort to war was apparent, but a more fundamental question lingered unanswered: Why exactly did the United

States insist on invading Iraq, when most indications were that it would be a costly and prolonged endeavor, with an uncertain and potentially unwinnable outcome. Analysts offered several distinctive accounts to explain the Bush decision to go to war. Most explanations centered on a handful of purported policy objectives, claiming it was a war for security from WMD, democracy and human rights, regional transformation, oil and business interests, presidential vendetta, or domestic political considerations. Others contended that the war simply resulted from an intelligence failure that overstated the Iraqi threat and underappreciated the gains made on Iraqi disarmament. All these explanations had at least some supporting evidence, a fact that highlighted the complex and multifaceted origins of the drive to war.[48]

Still other accounts were less focused on U.S. goals—what the war was for—and more on why the pursuit of such objectives made sense, resonated, or seemed appropriate to decision-makers in the Bush administration.[49] Such accounts included some of the same causal elements noted above, in addition to ideational factors—socially shared ideas, opinions, and perspectives—whether policymakers were aware of them or not. They had analytical space for powerful ideational currents in American decision-making circles at the time. These currents, or dominant ideas, included a belief in the efficacy of military force to solve problems; faith in the benevolence of American hegemonic power in the world; a Manichean, or black and white, understanding of international relations; and a sense that regime type—whether a country is democratic or not—determines its foreign policy and international behavior.[50] They also could accommodate underexamined social assumptions, such as the common if flawed supposition that Iraqis and al-Qa'ida terrorists must have been in league because of their ethnic and religious commonalities. Without these foundational ideas and understandings, the Iraq War was unlikely.

Regardless of the war's origins and rationale, the United States found itself occupying Iraq by late spring of 2003, with full international legal responsibility for governing a country it had conquered. It had won the conventional war easily but had to contend with its aftermath. Hoping for a quick exit and a return to Iraqi rule, the White House initially gave the task to retired army Lt. Gen. Jay Garner's Office of Reconstruction and Humanitarian Assistance (ORHA), which operated for only three weeks in April and May 2003. Realizing, somewhat belatedly, the enormity of the governance and transition challenge, President Bush then appointed a State Department official, L. Paul Bremer, to lead a temporary American governing body, the Coalition Provisional Authority (CPA). As detailed in Chapter 3, Bremer took charge and issued the CPA's first and second official orders of May 2003, removing all upper-tier Ba'ath Party members from government service and dissolving the Iraqi military and security services.

This had a predictable double effect. First, it motivated large numbers of trained soldiers, security officers, and former state officials to launch an insurgency in the summer of 2003. These individuals had military skills and access to weapons, safehouses, and war materiel, as well as organizational experience from being part of a highly bureaucratized political entity. Second, the orders undercut the state's institutional capacity to contend with postwar security and reconstruction challenges and to manage and participate in the transition to a new Iraqi government. When tens of thousands of people switch from building to breaking the political order, the consequences are inevitably extraordinary. Bremer's CPA and American occupation forces insisted on retaining full authority to run the country but were unprepared to play the role of surrogate state in the subsequent 12 months of CPA rule. As a result, Iraq all but fell apart.

Security was the first casualty of weak governance. In August 2003, a terror attack on the U.N. headquarters in Baghdad by Jordanian terrorist Abu Musab Zarqawi's al-Qa'ida in Iraq (AQI) destroyed the United Nation's multilateral capacity to contribute to Iraqi reconstruction. His and other foreign groups entered the fray to exacerbate conditions for their own purposes. Consequently, the insurgency morphed into multiple forms of insurrection and political violence. In short order, Iraqi ethnic and sectarian groups mobilized to both defend their constituencies and take advantage of the lawlessness. With that came a low-level civil war and near state collapse by early 2006, which eventually prompted stepped-up U.S. intervention in the form of a troop surge in 2007, along with a political realignment and anti-insurgent rebellion by Sunni tribes in Anbar province. The Iraqi government finally was reconstituted after an extended political process that included forming an interim government, writing a new constitution, and holding parliamentary elections in 2005 and 2010.

The Bush administration remained popular at home, even as it became increasingly clear that Iraq no longer possessed prohibited WMD or active WMD programs. The failure of U.S. forces to find WMD required a rhetorical shift in the war rationale from a search for such weapons in accordance with the American view of Security Council resolutions to the ousting of a dictator and establishment of democracy. The latter objectives were only implicit in some interpretations of the Security Council resolutions, though they were easy to promote and defend. Implementing them was another matter. Saddam's removal had been accomplished, but achieving a full democratic transition was not a simple undertaking. It became even less so as security conditions deteriorated and the insurgency gained momentum between 2003 and 2006, finally falling into the abyss of civil war. While the fundamental, if reconfigured, American objective remained one of establishing democratic institutions in a free Iraq, the security situation demanded a more immediate shift toward stabilizing the country and establishing public order.

Part of what this demanded, as a result, was U.S. acquiescence to the electoral and broader political power of Shi'i leaders like Nouri al-Maliki. Maliki's political self-assertion, which grew notably stronger in 2008, was both concerning and a relief to the United States. On the one hand, he was not the secular, prowestern figure that the Bush administration envisioned governing Iraq in the post-Ba'athist era. His strong sectarian leanings and policies alienated many in Iraq and undercut the country's support in most of its neighbors in the region. As a long-time *Da'wa* Party activist, he was at the center of oppositional Shi'i politics and presumed to be pro-Iranian, fueling speculation that the United States had delivered Iraq into Iranian hands and now would have renewed geopolitical trouble. On the other hand, Maliki was a capable and determined leader in a chaotic and uncertain political and security environment. After several years of intensive if costly and frustrating involvement in Iraq, the United States was looking for a path forward—and eventually out of a central role in governing the country. Maliki offered that possibility.

The Bush administration negotiated a bilateral Status of Forces Agreement (SOFA) and a Strategic Framework Agreement (SFA) with Maliki and the Iraqi government over several months in 2008, signing them in December at the end of Bush's second term in office. The SOFA was heavily debated and needed the approval of the Iraqi parliament and the three-person Presidency Council. In the final version accepted by all parties, the SOFA required a complete U.S. military withdrawal, with no lingering American security presence, military base rights, or legal immunity for nondiplomatic personnel like military contractors. Ambiguities in its wording and residual suspicion led to some uncertainty about its implementation, which was left to the incoming Obama administration. President Obama had campaigned partly on a promise to get the United States out of Iraq, giving him little reason to renege on the SOFA or renegotiate its provisions. He followed through on his promises and abided by the SOFA commitment, removing all U.S. combat troops from Iraqi cities by the end of June 2009, transitioning to a military "advise and assist" role by September 2010, and withdrawing the remainder of forces from the country on December 16, 2011, ending the eight-and-a-half-year U.S. military presence.

Iraqi reaction to the American military departure—the U.S. diplomatic presence remained—ranged from mild concern by some in the Kurdish north to relief and even delight by most others. It had been a decade since the Americans first spoke publicly of going into Iraq on a mission to disarm it, dislodge its leader, and change its government. While Saddam's regime was gone and much of the institutional landscape was transformed, the country was anything but on a stable path to a better future. The U.S. withdrawal did have dire security consequences in short order, when militant Islamists from a rejuvenated ISIS began a bombing campaign in early 2012 and then started taking Iraqi territory in 2013. But Iraq's fate was again more fully in its own hands.

Foreign Relations after Saddam

Iraq was able to restore diplomatic activities and reset its foreign policy after the Ba'athist regime's removal and the eventual return of Iraqi independence as a sovereign state. This could not happen quickly because the United States had disassembled not just the upper reaches of the regime but also much of the state apparatus. The Foreign Ministry no longer had accredited diplomats or senior officials directing foreign policy. Foreign Minister Naji Sabri had fled to Damascus and then to Cairo during the initial invasion, though he reportedly had worked for the Americans before the war.[51] Other externally oriented state institutions in the security and defense domains no longer existed. Iraq needed new leaders in new institutions to develop and pursue new policies. This would take years and would not entirely reflect a coherent, nationally oriented, and unified political process.[52]

With the U.S.-led occupation force authorized under U.N. Security Council Resolution 1483 of May 2003, the CPA governed the country and had responsibility for all of Iraq's domestic and foreign affairs.[53] In September 2003, the CPA-appointed Iraqi Governing Council selected one of its own members, Kurdish-born KDP central committee member Hoshyar Zebari, to serve as foreign minister, a role he would play for the next decade. A well-educated former *Peshmerga*, dual Iraqi–UK citizen, and uncle to KDP leader Masoud Barzani, Zebari had extensive international experience and was an executive committee member of the INC. After the end of CPA authority in June 2004, Zebari and the new government of interim Prime Minister Ayad Allawi began dispatching representatives, reconstituting the Ministry of Foreign Affairs, and reaching out to their counterparts worldwide. The process accelerated after Iraq's January 2005 parliamentary elections led to the appointment of the Ja'afari's caretaker government in May 2005, with its 32-member cabinet and its many ministries operating semi-autonomously and expanding.

Iraq's prior cultural and political connections to other MENA states allowed it to start reconnecting with most of its neighbors, albeit slowly and with significant difficulty in some cases. The process was complicated by several factors, beginning with widespread uncertainty about the prospects for the U.S. occupation and America's willingness and capacity to rebuild an Iraqi state it had contributed to dismantling. While Saddam was not missed in most MENA capitals, many state leaders were skeptical or downright fearful of the U.S. presence in itself. For some of the Arab states, an even worse problem was the likelihood of Iranian influence in Iraq via the Shi'i-based sectarian political parties and militant groups. This concern only grew stronger when Prime Minister Maliki began to assert himself in 2008, despite his initiatives to establish his independence as an Iraqi leader, not beholden to Teheran. Some states like Turkey were also worried about the potential for Iraqi Kurdish political parties and leaders to reshape regional politics, either via an independent Kurdistan or an autonomous entity in a weak Iraqi state. Identity politics on a regional level, especially the weakening of Arabism and the strengthening of Islamism or various forms of sectarianism, tended to undercut interstate cooperation and solidarity in the post-Saddam Middle East and North Africa.

Just as fundamentally, and regardless of opposition to the U.S.-led invasion, lingering resentment about all the distress Iraq had brought to the neighborhood shaped regional perceptions of cooperative possibilities. For some, Iraq's very existence in the heart of the region came with risks, no matter who ruled in Baghdad. For such states, which included Iraq's six immediate neighbors in addition to nearby countries like Egypt and Israel, it was not easy or beneficial to have a large, potentially powerful but unsettled state close by. Iraq's past troublemaking and present distress created a preference for keeping it weak and dampened enthusiasm for renewed ties. Without the glue of Arabism or the material incentives of economic integration or military cooperation, there was no basis for welcoming Iraq back to the fold. The decline of solidarity among the Arab states in particular, accelerated by Iraq itself and its invasion of Kuwait in 1990, was particularly damaging in this regard.

With the final American withdrawal a few months earlier, Baghdad did host an Arab League summit in Baghdad in March 2012, only the third such meeting to be held in Iraq over several decades. The agenda largely centered on the deteriorating situation in Syria, as well as Iraq's need for development and reintegration after years of isolation, sanctions, war, and foreign occupation. To enhance its prospects for success and to eliminate potential obstacles, the Maliki government launched a regional charm offensive several months beforehand. A terrible wave of bombings by the IS in Iraq in January and February threatened to derail the entire event, which already had been postponed by a year due to Iraqi volatility and the pressures of the Arab Spring. To prepare, the Maliki government locked down the capital and spent a reported $500 million sprucing up the city, repaving major roads, and renovating hotels and the Republican Palace.[54] The summit was a mixed success in that, at the very least, it was convened and had 20 national representatives in attendance. But for such a grand gathering that in the past had welcomed Arab kings, presidents, and prime ministers, the summit included few heads of state and did not produce substantial new benefits for Iraq. It was a bellwether of the reality that post-Saddam and post–American-occupied Iraq was on the cusp of yet another round of domestic turmoil that threatened the state's viability and potentially its continued existence.

Relations with the Arab States

These larger patterns and pressures notwithstanding, Iraqi foreign policy after Saddam was dependent on multiple factors and varied from country to country. Relations with Egypt improved relatively quickly, aided by a common interest in the possibility of renewed trade and security cooperation. Despite their longstanding rivalry for leadership in the Arab world, both countries had curbed their regional ambitions in the face of internal challenges, diminishing a source of potential friction between them. The military power and political influence of non-Arab regional states like Iran, Turkey, and Israel provided an additional incentive spurring Egyptian–Iraqi cooperation, as was the case during the Iran–Iraq War in the 1980s. In intra-Arab world dynamics, Saudi Arabia's increasing size, deep pockets, regional influence, and continued wariness about Iraq also turned Baghdad toward Cairo, as it once had with the Arab Cooperation Council (ACC), a short-lived regional institution formed in 1989 to hedge against the Saudi-dominated Gulf Cooperation Council (GCC).

Egyptian concerns about Shiʻi sectarianism limited Cairo's enthusiasm initially, but the Mubarak government soon became guardedly optimistic about cooperative ventures with Baghdad. While Egypt was the first Arab state to dispatch an ambassador to the new Jaʻafari government in 2005, Ambassador Ihab el-Sherif was abducted and killed by the AQI only a month after he arrived at the beginning of June. Threats and intimidation succeeded for a time, and it was a few years before Egypt returned an ambassador or other countries followed suit. With prompting from the United States in April 2008, several countries stepped up their engagement with Iraq, and Egyptian Foreign Minister Ahmed Abul Gheit traveled to Baghdad for the first such visit since 1990, seeking to strengthen Egyptian–Iraqi cooperation in areas ranging from reconstruction and agriculture to security.[55]

Unlike the relationship with Egypt, ties between Saudi Arabia and Iraq took much longer to mend. Formal relations, tense since the end of the Iran–Iraq War and shattered by the invasion of Kuwait in 1990, were not restored until 2015. A summer 2006 meeting between new Iraqi Prime Minister Nouri al-Maliki and Saudi King Abdullah only increased Saudi distrust of a Shi'i-led Iraq, precipitating several years of ill-will between the two leaders and cold nonengagement between their countries. This missed opportunity in 2006 both undermined Iraq's reintegration into the region and left Saudi Arabia without a potential partner to help manage its difficult relationship with Iran. Iraq was left burning in this period, with hapless American efforts at reconstruction and no support from regional Arab leaders, some of whose own days were numbered. Even after the Arab League summit of 2012 in Baghdad, no significant regional cooperative improvements were achieved, and internal pressures from Iraq's post-American upheaval threatened to poison progress in its recultivation of ties.[56]

Abdullah's passing in 2015 and his replacement by King Salman and Crown Prince Muhammad bin Salman created new possibilities, aided by shifting pressures in the region from the Arab Spring, which had started in late 2010 and swept across most of the region, leaving few states unaffected. The Saudi kingdom was able to use targeted financial incentives, along with very modest domestic political reforms, to manage its own wave of protests from 2011 to 2012. An awareness of Riyadh's vulnerability eventually translated into a slight foreign policy adjustment in its openness to stronger relations with Baghdad, with a resumption of diplomatic relations in December 2015. The two countries held a series of high-level political visits that included Saudi Foreign Minister Adel al-Jubeir traveling to Baghdad in February 2017. This facilitated the creation of a Saudi–Iraqi Coordination Council (*Majlis al-Tanseeq al-Sa'udi al-Iraqi*) in August 2017, the establishment of a Saudi consulate in Baghdad in April 2019, and the opening of the Arar border crossing in northern Saudi Arabia in November 2020, allowing direct passage between the two countries for the first time in 30 years.[57] The Iraqi prime minister followed up with another long-time first, visiting Riyadh in March 2021. While the relationship still faced challenges over issues like Iran's role in the region and in Iraq, the activism of Saudi nationals in militant Sunni Islamist groups, and regional oil politics, there were multiple bases for potential cooperation and mutual gains.

Syrian–Iraqi relations after 2003 were as unsettled and complex as their own changing domestic landscapes. Damascus was a traditional rival to Baghdad, but a fraternal one, given their historical ties and shared Arab identities. Ba'athism took different, antagonistic forms in each country under separate and increasingly alienated leaderships that had split years before in the mid-1960s. Syrian President Bashar al-Assad inherited his job in 2000 from his late father, the long-time ruler and master political operator Hafez al-Assad. He was at odds with Saddam Hussein and had strategically friendly relations with Iran. Nonetheless, he opposed the American-led invasion for its obvious potential implications for his own rule, and Syrian–Iraqi relations improved considerably under the new, Shi'i-majority Iraqi governments that formed after elections in 2005 and 2010. Syria accepted large numbers of Iraqi refugees, hosting as many as 1.5 million people during Iraq's civil war in 2007.[58] The Maliki government generally supported the Assad regime in its battle against outside forces, unlike much the rest of the Arab League, which suspended Syrian membership and called for the Assad regime's removal after Syria's descent into civil war in 2011 and 2012.

Syria's deep troubles were fed by external actors and events, from the original antiauthoritarian inspiration coming out of Tunisia and Egypt in late 2010 and early 2011 to the rolling turmoil next door in Iraq. More directly, Iraq's IS leader Abu Bakr al-Baghdadi had dispatched operatives to open a Syrian branch in 2011, leading eventually to an IS bid to obliterate the entire regional political order. As a consequence, all the major MENA powers, including Turkey, Iran, and Saudi Arabia, were drawn into a complex struggle in Syria that combined elements of insurgency, multilateral civil war, and international intervention. Great powers like the United States and Russia became engaged, with on-and-off American support for democratic, antiregime forces, and Russia siding with its closest regional ally, Bashar al-Assad. For a limited time, the most dynamic and successful force was the militant Islamist group that cohered into the IS, as it attempted to erase the colonial-era boundaries and conquer enough of Syria and Iraq to hold a territory the size of Britain. It succeeded until the weight of the opposition it provoked—including most of the great and regional powers—led to its collapse back on itself, even if some of its opponents were also arrayed against each other. Syria retained active IS elements, though IS leader Abu Ibrahim al-Hashimi al-Qurayshi was killed in a U.S. raid in northwest Syria near the Turkish border in February 2022.

Iraqi relations with the smaller Arab states were generally quicker to improve in the post-Saddam era, though ties were limited by the absence of shared economic interests or capable security institutions binding them together. The Iraqi relationship with Kuwait moved in a surprisingly positive direction, given its difficult history and Iraq's obligation under U.N. Security Council Resolution 687 of 1991 to pay what eventually totaled $52.4 billion in compensation for the 1990 invasion.[59] By the time of the American departure in late 2011, a number of bilateral issues with Kuwait had been resolved, mostly by Iraqi acceptance of the border, financial, and sovereignty provisions in the Security Council resolutions of the previous decade. New—but old—problems did arise relating to border concerns and Persian Gulf access, though progress was made in advance of the Arab League summit in Baghdad in 2012, which Kuwaiti Amir Sabah al-Ahmad al-Jaber al-Sabah attended.[60] The amir was known as the "Dean of Arab diplomacy," having served previously as foreign minister for 40 years, from 1963 to 2003.[61] He promoted a normalization of relations with the larger power, and Kuwait soon was at the forefront of states providing financial support to rebuild Iraq, even supporting an Iraqi bid to join the GCC. For its part, Iraq completed reparations payments to Kuwait in January 2022.[62]

Aside from Kuwait, Iraqi relations with the more distant Gulf states of Bahrain, the UAE, Qatar, and Oman generally were slow to return to normalcy. They had a tentative, ad hoc quality stemming from ongoing Iraqi instability and serious misgivings about Iraqi Prime Minister Nouri al-Maliki's sectarian approach to governance during his tenure between 2006 and 2014. Gulf rulers also showed a degree of indifference and even complacency, given the extent to which the United States had committed itself to assuring that Iraq would no longer threaten its neighbors. Leaders tended to blame the United States for most Iraqi problems, from its state weakness to the strength of Iranian influence via paramilitary groups. Iraq's difficulty defending itself from IS incursions in 2014 did intensify Gulf concerns and a willingness to engage Baghdad directly. In addition, the particular geopolitical positions and concerns of each country also affected their relationship with Iraq.

The small island kingdom of Bahrain joined several other Arab states in late August 2008, naming Salah Ali al-Maliki its first ambassador to Iraq since Saddam's downfall in 2003. He served there until he was recalled in June 2019 after Iranian-backed protesters stormed the embassy over Bahrain's hosting of U.S.-led peace discussions with Israel.[63] Bahrain's Sunni minority rulers were in an awkward position vis-à-vis Iraq, but its emerging post-oil economy competed only minimally with Iraq's oil sector, and the two countries found common purpose in resisting pressures from more militant parties in the region. The UAE posted an ambassador, Abdullah Ibrahim al-Shehhi, shortly thereafter in September 2008, having previously been dissuaded from doing so by Sunni militant attacks, which were designed to isolate the new Iraqi government and included a kidnapping in 2006. The Emirates cultivated economic ties more than close political relations, focusing on business ventures rather than political initiatives likely to get ensnared in regional rivalries. A little-known Iraqi militant group's drone attack on facilities in Abu Dhabi years later in 2022 highlighted such risks, along with the way Iraq's complex social mix could have an impact beyond the country's borders.[64]

Extending into the Persian Gulf from the Arabian Peninsula, Qatar did not restore full diplomatic relations with Iraq, broken in 1990, until after a 2015 meeting between Iraqi President Fu'ad Masum and Qatari Emir Sheikh Tamim bin Hamad Al Thani. Qatar had alienated Baghdad somewhat by its steady support for Sunni Iraqi leaders and its reported engagement with regional Sunni Islamists like the Muslim Brotherhood.[65] After being the target of a Saudi-led blockade from 2017 to 2021 for attempting to punch above its diplomatic weight, Qatar reached out more widely and cultivated connections to both Iraq and Iran as hedges against its larger Saudi rival. Oman, on the eastern edge of the Peninsula and playing a perennial intermediary role, also had shuttered its embassy in August 1990 and restored ties in 2003 for a short time. Iraq's severe instability forced a reversal, and Oman was among the last Arab states to reopen a permanent embassy in May 2019, a month after Saudi Arabia finally established a consulate.

Iraqi–Jordanian relations showed greater resilience and were less transactional than Iraq's relations with the Gulf because they were more deeply rooted and multifaceted. They oscillated over the years but moved in a positive direction in the post-2003 era, despite Jordan's immensely delicate position in the region. The countries were historically close, both carved out of the Ottoman Empire by Britain and governed originally by two Hashemite sons of Hussein bin Ali: Abdullah as Emir of Transjordan and Faisal as King of Iraq. Younger brother Faisal's line did not survive the July 1958 revolution, and Iraq's connection to what had become the Hashemite Kingdom of Jordan in 1946 was deeply strained between 1958 and the late 1970s, when Saddam Hussein assumed full power in Iraq.

Beginning at an Arab League summit in Baghdad in 1978, Saddam moved to strengthen ties to Jordan to improve his strategic position in the region. This paid off during the Iran–Iraq War in the 1980s, when Jordan provided diplomatic support and a vital transportation outlet to minimize the constraints of Iraq's limited access to the Persian Gulf and its loss of an oil pipeline route through Syria. For its troubles, Jordan received heavily discounted oil, a booming cross-border trade going in both directions and extending to the port of Aqaba, the development of its transportation sector, and grants-in-aid from Baghdad.[66] Political and economic ties, along with Saddam's popularity in Jordan, were strong enough that when Iraq invaded Kuwait in 1990, Amman took a neutral stance toward Baghdad's transgression and did not join Egypt, Syria, or the Gulf states in the international coalition. It was a costly but necessary position for the monarchy, as it struggled to balance competing pressures from domestic and international allies and adversaries.

Relations with Iraq weakened after Jordan made peace with Israel in 1994 and shifted more fully into the U.S. orbit, with enhanced security cooperation, debt forgiveness, billions of dollars in economic assistance, and an eventual soft democratic opening that mostly made the monarchy more vulnerable. Jordan also hosted a large Sunni Iraqi exile community and provided refuge to many high-level Iraqi oppositionists. Still, throughout the 1990s, cross-border trade—both illicit and U.N.-approved under the Oil-for-Food Program—flourished, and many Jordanians maintained a sympathetic view of their neighbor. Jordan publicly opposed the U.S. invasion of Iraq in 2003 and had to contend with the results, including the destabilizing activities of Islamist militants like the Jordanian-born Abu Musab al-Zarqawi, who destroyed the Jordanian embassy in Baghdad in 2003. While Amman sometimes found itself at odds with Baghdad's new rulers, who seemed uncomfortably close to revolutionary Iran, in August 2008, King Abdullah II was the first Arab head of state to visit Iraq after the war. He was able to partner with both the United States and the new Iraqi government in attempting to rebuild the regional order. Both Jordan and Iraq had strong incentives to make the relationship work, including economic ties, opposition to the forces unleashed by Syria's collapse, a growing threat from the IS, and a shared interest in promoting renewed MENA stability and development.

Iraq pursued improved relations with more distant Arab states like Lebanon, though their relationship was not historically warm, and the small Mediterranean country was more attuned to managing its interactions with closer Levantine neighbors, especially Israel, Syria, and the Palestinians. Lebanon and Iraq nonetheless had commonalities in their sectarian divides, episodic civil upheaval, relatively large Shi'i populations, governments structured to reflect communal representation, and ancient roots—with Lebanese Maronite nationalists claiming a Phoenician past. While they had very different regional aspirations and orientations in that Lebanon had never thrown its weight around or sought the mantle of Arab leadership, both countries had suffered lengthy external interventions and had heavy Iranian involvement via their Shi'i populations. After the departure of the Syrian military in 2005, Lebanon was freer to chart its own foreign policy, even if it remained buffeted by the intrusions of larger MENA countries. Lebanon's prime minister visited Baghdad in August 2008 as part of a flurry of Arab leaders reconnecting with an increasingly independent postwar Iraq under Nouri al-Maliki.

On the other side of the Mediterranean, the Maghreb states of Morocco, Algeria, Tunisia, and Libya generally were less engaged with the drama surrounding Iraq further east. None had Iraq's Arab leadership aspirations or capacity to play a central role in regional politics, though historically some of their leaders—Libya's Muammar el-Qaddafi, Morocco's King Hassan II, Tunisia's Habib Bourguiba, Algeria's Houari Boumediene—had gained prominence or notoriety on the world stage. They did share a few commonalities, with a Berber indigenous identity that grew stronger when traveling from east to west along the Mediterranean. Two Maghreb countries—Algeria and Libya—were major oil and gas exporters, if not quite on Iraq's level. Libya also was a former monarchy, with King Idris deposed in 1969 in a military coup by the idiosyncratic Colonel Qaddafi. Algeria, like Iraq, had suffered through two terrible periods of civil upheaval, the first from 1954 to 1960 in its war of independence from France, and the second in the 1990s after a failed democratic transition. These various connections were enough to keep Iraq in dialogue with the Maghreb.

Iran, Israel, Palestine, and Turkey

Beyond the Arab world in the MENA region, Iran presented a complex case in the new era. Iran and Iraq have a centuries-long historical connection spanning all aspects of their relationship. They have strong Shi'i cultural affinities and historical ties for a majority of their populations, yet noteworthy political differences stemmed from many factors, including civilizational rivalries. These differences inhibited but did not entirely eliminate what some outsiders feared: a close alliance between Iran and Iraq against the Sunni Arab states. The cultural connections and common sectarian identity did translate into a political opportunity for Iran to present itself as a natural ally to Iraq, affirmed by decades of genuine Iranian support for Shi'i opposition groups facing severe repression in Iraq. From a broader perspective, however, the simple fact of having distinctive state entities with their own national interests reduced the possibility of seamless cooperation that could threaten other regional actors. Such cooperation could not be sustained by a shared sectarian identity, which was only one aspect of most Iraqis' lives. The Maliki government and those that followed charted relatively independent paths vis-à-vis Iran.

This is not to say there was no effort at finding areas of common purpose, along with clear and recurring successes for Iran in using its connections to powerful Iraqi domestic actors to increase its influence in the country. Teheran's efforts reflected a pragmatic outlook and a concern about external adversaries more than any ideologically rooted vision. It regarded Iraq as a potential threat, though also a candidate for strategic cooperation with a lesser partner, and it hoped to cultivate relations in order to hedge against all possibilities. Recent years have seen a diminishing of Iranian influence, starting with the departure of the Maliki government but including the Iraqi public's negative reaction to Iranian-backed militia crackdowns on the massive popular protests of 2019–2020. The January 2020 U.S. assassination of Quds Force commander General Qassem Soleimani further weakened Iran's control over various pro-Iranian factions in Iraqi politics seeking influence. It remains to be seen, but Iran's capacity to operate independently and in support of its own interests in Iraq may be diminishing.

Looking westward, nothing about post-Ba'athist Iraq suggested a warming of relations with Israel, which remained, from the perspective of most Iraqis, a major threat. Bilateral conflict long predated Saddam's regime and had origins in the 1941 pogrom against Baghdad's Jewish community and the 1948 Arab–Israeli War. An additional complicating factor was the immigration to Israel of over 100,000 members of Iraq's large Jewish community in 1951 and 1952, some forced out of the country and dispossessed of their land and property. In recent years, with no resolution to the Palestinian–Israeli conflict, Iraq refused to normalize relations or establish diplomatic engagement of any kind, and it continued to support an economic boycott of its longstanding adversary. Israel, for its part, had been an intermittent backer of Kurdish nationalists, had taken direct action against Iraqi nuclear programs in the 1970s and 1980s, and had quietly supported U.S. efforts to remove Saddam, including the 2003 war. Its right-leaning governments in the past decade were especially concerned about potential cooperation between Iraq and Israel's most powerful and worrisome regional nemesis, Iran. That said, individual Iraqis like President Jalal Talabani reportedly met with Israeli officials outside the region.

The Iraqi–Palestinian relationship had multiple layers, including popular sentiment as well as more official relations between the representatives of both peoples. Iraqi Arab nationalists looked to support Palestinians, as fellow Arabs, as far back as the 1920s, and Iraq dispatched military forces to Palestine in the original Arab–Israeli War of 1948, only to achieve disappointing results. The large-scale movement of Iraqi Jews to the new State of Israel in the early 1950s created additional complications. Arabs from distant Iraq took their place in a new country, but the country did not accommodate their culturally connected, physically displaced fellow Arabs born in the immediate vicinity. Thousands of Iraqi Arabs became

Israeli citizens, as the Arabs of Mandate Palestine found themselves excluded from citizenship in the land of their birth.

All modern Iraqi leaders, from the Hashemite monarchs to Abd al-Karim Qasim, the Arif Brothers, Hassan al-Bakr, and Saddam Hussein, at least nominally supported Palestinian national rights, though their actions often reflected mixed motives and even the cynical manipulation of the issue for their own purposes. Palestinians tended to support those Iraqi leaders who were most strident in favoring the Palestinian cause. This explains the otherwise odd, politically disastrous level of Palestinian support for Saddam Hussein's invasion of Kuwait, where many Palestinian residents resented their wealthy, privileged hosts. In an example of the region's interconnected politics, Iraq's invasion led to a defeat for Iraq and political pressure on the Palestinian leadership to accede to the U.S.-led Madrid peace conference in 1991, the failure of which prompted the behind-the-scenes Oslo peace process.

Turkish–Iraqi relations have been moved by a small number of thorny issues for decades, especially the Kurdish population straddling their borders, and the Tigris and Euphrates Rivers, which originate in Anatolia and are important to Turkey but essential to Iraq. To promote economic development and undercut support for Kurdish militants, Turkey in the 1970s and 1980s started building the Southeastern Anatolia Project (*Güneydoğu Anadolu Projesi*, GAP), a massive series of hydroelectric dams and water control systems in the Tigris and Euphrates basins. The GAP threatened to reduce the water flow to downstream riparian states, most notably Iraq. Water-related tensions were on the bilateral agenda in the summer of 1990 and constituted a secondary impetus to Iraq's invasion of Kuwait by contributing to Baghdad's sense of vulnerability and encirclement. Turkey's strategy was somewhat effective, though it did not eliminate all support for Kurdish national aspirations. The quasi-autonomous status enjoyed by Iraqi Kurds after 1991 and into the post-2003 era did little to allay Turkish fears. Concerned about rising Kurdistan Workers Party (PKK) attacks on Turkey from strongholds in northern Iraq, in July 2008, Prime Minister Tayyip Erdogan was the first Turkish leader to visit Baghdad in nearly 20 years.

France, Britain, and European Relations

In its relations with Europe, Iraq was free to pursue the full range of opportunities denied by the sanctions-era Security Council resolutions, most of which were lifted by the passing of Resolution 1483 in May 2003.[67] Iraq's approach varied from country to country, though it generally saw the Europeans as viable supplemental partners or, in some cases, as alternatives to the American sources of economic aid, political support, security assistance, and business opportunities. French–Iraqi relations had complex roots and a hot-and-cold history, with both countries at times looking to the other in the economic and strategic domains. France sought a measure of continued political engagement in the MENA region, and business ties were especially important, as France had cultivated commercial ventures and promoted military sales over many years in the past. France was increasingly concerned about Chinese economic competition in traditionally French markets in Africa and Asia, especially after 2010, and was motivated and well positioned to press Iraq for business. French oil and gas multinational TotalEnergies, for example, signed a multibillion-dollar deal to build gas recovery and photovoltaic installations to fuel electricity generation in the Basra region.[68] France also bought a fair amount of Iraqi crude oil.

Britain, in contrast, had an even more complicated relationship with Iraq, given its colonial involvement in creating the Iraqi state and dominating its first few decades, as well as its partnership with the United States in the 2003 war. It also had the largest Iraqi immigrant population in Europe, along with a substantial number of more recent refugees. Britain participated in postwar reconstruction efforts after 2003, especially in Basra to the south, and provided bilateral foreign aid.[69] British businesses were less active and successful in Iraq than France's, and Britain was not a major direct purchaser of Iraqi oil. The primary British concern remained security-related, especially after the emergence of the IS as an international threat in 2014.

Like Britain and France, other European countries had Iraq-related interests that manifested in their foreign and domestic policies. In some cases, these interests centered on their economies and Iraqi oil exports, postwar reconstruction, and industrial development, but in others they were tied to immigration and refugee populations in Europe itself, an increasingly vital issue. Large states like Germany and Italy joined in the rebuilding of Iraq's manufacturing and consumer bases, diminished by years of war and sanctions. Germany bought a significant amount of Iraqi oil while exporting heavy machinery, chemicals, industrial inputs, automobiles, and electronics.[70] It also had a sizable and diverse Iraqi immigrant population numbering in the hundreds of thousands, second in Europe to Great Britain and including Kurdish, Turkmen, and Yazidi minorities. Two decades after the original upheaval of the 2003 invasion, smaller but consequential numbers of Iraqis lived throughout Europe, notably present in the Nordic countries of Norway, Finland, and Sweden, with the latter having well over 100,000 Iraqi-born people, comprising the second largest minority group in the country. These populations created new societal dynamics and affected European foreign policies toward Iraq and the larger MENA region, as Iraq joined Syria, Afghanistan, and many other places where internal turmoil—created partly by external actors—echoed back to the rest of world.

China and Russia

The Europeans and Americans were not the only major international actors involved with Iraq. China and Iraq found areas of potential political cooperation and shared economic interest, as the rising Asian power extended its engagement with the MENA region and as Iraq sought to balance external threats and reduce its dependence on western countries like the United States. China was very active in Iraq's petroleum sector, making lasting commitments to become Iraq's largest purchaser of oil by a wide margin. The state-owned China National Petroleum Corporation (CNPC), for example, bought over $21 billion of crude and refined oil in 2019 alone.[71] The CNPC, as one of the largest companies in the world, was able to sign fixed, long-term contracts that were untenable for other multinationals. In addition to the oil trade, China sold light manufactured goods to Iraq, including armed drones in 2015 during the battle against the IS.[72] As part of an Iraqi–Chinese economic cooperation forum in 2019, Prime Minister Adil Abdul-Mahdi traveled to Beijing to strengthen the relationship further, signing several major agreements related to finance and infrastructure development, as well as cultural and educational exchange.[73]

Iraqi–Russian relations were less driven by direct economic interests, since the two countries were partial competitors in world oil markets, and neither manufactured much of interest to the other nor had shared investment commitments. Russia, however, did seek to continue extending its political influence in the MENA region, resurgent since its intensive deployment of air power in the Syrian civil war in 2015. It sought a seat at the table in all major regional matters, and its Iraq policy played a secondary but important role in its effort to wield influence in a geostrategically vital part of the world.[74] Iraq, from its perspective, saw in Russia an occasional source of political support in international forums, a potential military supplier, an oil and gas giant with useful technical expertise, and a diplomatic counterbalance to the other major powers. The relationship was more coldly transactional than fraternal or ideological, but it produced gains for both parties.

Iraq in a World of National States

Some countries seem incompatible with a world of national states. In 1921, as one of the first such creations in the Middle East and North Africa, Iraq was formed out of an artificial, though not arbitrary, collection of peoples. It had a measure of coherence and ancient roots, but transforming it into a rigidly defined political entity, constructed along the lines of a European-style state with fixed borders and a definitive sense of national belonging, was an extraordinary challenge. Doing this quickly, in a difficult regional environment, proved to be essentially unmanageable. Its talented, determined founding king was foreign to Iraq itself, had precious little actual power, and died at age 48 before he could establish or consolidate Iraqi state institutions and national community. His 21-year-old son inherited the throne, but did not share his father's better attributes and died in a drunken car crash several years later. Iraqi political life deteriorated rapidly from then on. State formation without the structural benefits of historical time—like state-building without a capable and deeply committed leadership—was likely to fall short if not fail outright.

Iraq did remain whole and survived for over a hundred years. Yet, it fostered dictatorship, launched invasions, suffered war, and incurred repeated internal rebellions. Some of its worst offenses were international, while others involved the targeting of ethnic, sectarian, and political adversaries outside the ruling circle. It contributed more than its share to regional upheaval, provoking and bullying its neighbors without end. This was especially the case with the Iran and Kuwait invasions of 1980 and 1990, though it also had complicated and sometimes distressed relationships with Saudi Arabia, Jordan, Syria, and Turkey, not to mention Israel over the horizon and much of the world on occasion. No doubt, some of this stemmed from the nature of Iraqi state formation and the extent to which it was too rapid, too artificial, too uneven in its emphasis on coercion over social welfare, and too vulnerable to political and ideological pressures from the other MENA Arab states to which it was connected.

Some of Iraq's troubles also, however, may have been structural in a more basic sense beyond remedy. As a general matter, the larger and more powerful the state, the larger the problems they can create when their development goes awry. Economic resources like an oil windfall can enhance state power by giving it the wherewithal to do what otherwise it might not do, for better or worse. Iraq has a middle-state dilemma in that it is large and powerful enough to disrupt all adjacent countries, though not so big as to maintain an orderly hegemonic dominance. With better domestic governance, leadership, and regional institutions in the future, it is possible that Iraqi aspirations will be directed toward a constructive regional role matched to its size and capacity. It is equally plausible, however, that Iraq will remain embroiled in conflict, because as it recovers from past traumas and rebuilds its strength, its ambitions may return. In such a case, the best outcome would see a reasonable regional balance achieved in hopes of building a better future.

Notes

1 Different theories sometimes have mutually inconsistent assumptions about international life, but the objective here is not to test or elaborate an existing theory so much as to use the varied insights of a few major approaches to understand a single case.
2 Realism sees anarchy as a technical term describing the key structural feature of world politics: there being no higher power beyond the individual state. The seminal neorealist work is Waltz (1979).
3 Overviews of international relations theory include Dunne et al. (2021).
4 See the full text at the Qatar Digital Library, www.qdl.qa/en/archive/81055/vdc_10000 0000602.0x0001a7.
5 Arabic expression has used two different words for the idea of nationalism: *Qawmiyya* (from the root *Qawm*, a broad, nonterritorialized community); and *Wataniyya* (from the root *Watan*, a geographically limited, state-centered patriotism associated with a particular territory). Modern-day nationalists prefer *Qawmiyya* and see *Wataniyya* as more limited and parochial. For a clear discussion, see Brand (2014).
6 His several fertile crescent unity schemes, for example, all ran into resistance and failed to materialize.
7 To avoid the commitments of a full treaty, the United States did not join the Baghdad Pact officially but cooperated closely via Embassy Baghdad. Niel M. Johnson, "Oral History Interview with Nicholas G. Thacher, 1st Secretary American Embassy," May 28, 1992, at www.trumanlibrary.gov/library/oral-histories/thachern.
8 Marr (2017), 86.

9 Khadduri (1969), 156–160.
10 Cusimano (1992).
11 Kerr (1971).
12 Marr (2017), 98.
13 This is Kerr's most underappreciated contribution. See Lawson (2015).
14 Walt (1987).
15 Mufti (1996), 191.
16 Cockburn (2002), 86.
17 Flibbert (2003).
18 Razoux (2015); Ramazani (1988).
19 Murray and Woods (2014).
20 Battle (2003).
21 https://documents-dds-ny.un.org/doc/RESOLUTION/GEN/NR0/575/28/PDF/NR057528.pdf?OpenElement.
22 For all resolutions, see www.un.org/securitycouncil/content/resolutions.
23 https://peacemaker.un.org/sites/peacemaker.un.org/files/IQ%20KW_910403_SCR687%281991%29_0.pdf.
24 Gordon (2012).
25 Mazaheri (2010); Graham-Brown (1999).
26 Blaydes (2018), 120–123.
27 Gause (1994).
28 Baer (2002); Blaydes (2018), 293–302.
29 Project for the New American Century, "An Open Letter to President Clinton: 'Remove Saddam from Power,'" January 26, 1998, reprinted in Sifry and Cerf (2003), 199–201; Ahmad (2014).
30 The Iraq Liberation Act of 1998, Public Law 105-338, at www.govinfo.gov.
31 Stieb (2021) argues that a consensus favoring regime change did emerge in the 1990s.
32 The United States claimed authorization under UNSCR 678, 687, and 688.
33 Duelfer (February 2012); Duelfer (2009).
34 Cohen (1999).
35 Sagan and Waltz (2002).
36 Duelfer (2005).
37 Conclusion 1, "Iraqi Links to al-Qa'ida," U.S. Senate (2006), 105.
38 Bush's 2003 State of the Union declared, for example, "Saddam Hussein aids and protects terrorists, including members of al-Qa'ida." January 28, 2003.
39 U.S. Senate (2006), 67.
40 *9/11 Commission Report* (2004).
41 Martin, in Sifry and Cerf (2003), 213.
42 Franks (2004), 329; Woodward (2004), 30.
43 Gordon (2003), A1.
44 www.un.org/Depts/unmovic/documents/1441.pdf.
45 Woods et al. (2006), 126.
46 The Coalition Forces Land Component Command (CFLCC) conducted the initial invasion and was replaced in June 2003 by Combined Joint Task Force 7 (CJTF-7), which was replaced in May 2004 by Multinational Force-Iraq (MNF-I), also known as the Coalition forces for several years thereafter. See Carney (2011), vii.
47 Bozo (2016).
48 The best book-length accounts include MacDonald (2014), Stieb (2021), Mazarr (2019), Draper (2020). For a range of perspectives, see Cramer and Thrall (2011).

49 On the "logic of appropriateness," see March and Olsen (1998).
50 For an elaboration, see Flibbert (2006).
51 Sabri may have provided information to French and American intelligence services about Iraq's WMD programs, revealing that Iraq had nuclear ambitions but no active nuclear program or biological weapons stockpile, and only limited chemical munitions in the hands of loyal tribes. Pincus (2006).
52 Chatham House (2012).
53 https://documents-dds-ny.un.org/doc/UNDOC/GEN/N03/368/53/PDF/N0336 853.pdf?OpenElement.
54 Sly (March 2012).
55 "Egyptian Foreign Minister in Landmark Iraq Visit," France24, October 6, 2008.
56 Sly (April 2012).
57 Saudi Ministry of Commerce (2017); *Asharq al-Awsat*, "Saudi Arabia Opens Consulate in Baghdad," April 4, 2019; Reidel and Harvey (December 2020).
58 Al-Khalidi et al. (2007).
59 In 2005, the United Nations Compensation Commission (UNCC) finished processing 2.7 million claims from 1.5 million Kuwaiti individuals, businesses, organizations, and government entities. https://uncc.ch/home.
60 Fordham (March 2021).
61 www.thediplomaticaffairs.com/2020/09/29/the-dean-of-arab-diplomacy-dies-in-91.
62 "United Nations Compensation Commission Pays Out Final Compensation Award," Press Release, 13 January 2022.
63 Abdul-Zahra and Mroue (June 2019).
64 Ibrahim (February 2022).
65 Younis (May 2021), 9.
66 Ryan (Summer 2000), 40–42.
67 The exceptions included prohibited arms and ongoing reparations payments to Kuwait. https://documents-dds-ny.un.org/doc/UNDOC/GEN/N03/368/53/PDF/N0336 853.pdf?OpenElement.
68 TotalEnergies, Press Release (September 2021).
69 Matsunaga (2019).
70 https://oec.world/en/profile/bilateral-country/irq/partner/deu.
71 https://oec.world/en/profile/bilateral-country/irq/partner/chn.
72 Marcus (October 2015).
73 Calabrese (October 2019).
74 Trenin (2018).

5
POLITICAL ECONOMY

Iraq has nearly 10% of all the proven oil reserves in the world. This tremendous asset has brought extraordinary benefits to the country, as well as some unusual costs. Its overall effects are surprisingly hard to calculate over several decades of dramatic political and economic change. Oil has transformed Iraq's historical trajectory and affected every aspect of Iraqi national life, from the economy and industrial development to state political institutions, informal patronage networks, social dynamics, and leadership calculations. It has created political and economic opportunities otherwise unavailable to the country and facilitated state actions at home and across borders, some highly beneficial and others deeply destructive. Oil is what differentiates Iraq from a great many developing countries throughout Asia, Africa, and Latin America. It has put Iraq on the geopolitical map, attracting international attention and leading to impressive gains and no small amount of trouble.

None of this has occurred automatically or inevitably. Oil is a naturally occurring substance, devoid of agency, or a capacity to act independently. All decisions about who controls it, how or even whether to develop it, and for what purposes are subject to human initiative and the choices of state and business leaders. Merely having it in the ground does not come with instructions for these leaders, whose decisions have their own personal and political dynamics. The possession of oil neither compels particular industrial actions nor guarantees economic growth, national prosperity, or social development, though it does expand the options of countries having it in great abundance. Oil creates developmental possibilities and enhances the potential power of decision-makers, subject to the constraints of the institutions surrounding its ownership, extraction, production, and export, as well as a wide range of international geopolitical and market conditions.

This chapter explores Iraq's economy, giving particular attention to the role of oil and the contemporary state of the country's national economic development and resource use. It does so through the lens of political economy, a broad-gauged analytical approach in the social sciences. Unlike the earlier, historically organized chapters, it is limited in scope in order to offer a closely structured review of only the most relevant and enduring contemporary concerns. After a brief elaboration of a conceptual framework, the first half of the chapter summarizes the basic features of the economy and resource profile, along with several core demographic factors, both overall and in relation to other MENA countries. The remainder then examines Iraqi oil, external rents, industrial development, water resources and agriculture, international trade, labor migration, earnings remittances, and foreign assistance. Throughout the chapter, comparisons to a wider set of countries provide context and permit a fuller understanding of how Iraq relates to other states in the region and beyond.

What Is Political Economy?

Political economy is a social scientific discipline that comes in many varieties, mostly centered on the relationship between politics and economics. That relationship is best understood as reciprocal in that political and economic factors influence each other in fundamental ways that cannot be ignored.[1] For this reason, according to most political economists, both kinds of variables must be included in any account of domestic and international life. An approach from political economy, it bears emphasis, does not simply entail studying politics and economics at the same time. It entails teasing apart these two domains to see how they shape each other to bring about the outcomes under study. The separation between them is analytical more than empirical, since in the real world, no such distinction exists. Political and economic life are wholly intertwined in Iraq, as everywhere, but this approach takes seriously the need to separate the two areas of our thinking in order to explain and understand the larger patterns and processes of Iraqi life.

How does one do this, or how do the political and economic domains, or sides, affect each other? On the politics side, political activity—the pursuit and use of legitimate power, or authority—establishes the legal and institutional framework in which all economic activity occurs. Politically dominant individuals and groups in the state and society shape the economy to benefit themselves in accordance with their subjective senses of what is advantageous and appropriate. Political power has profound consequences for what economic activities occur and for who wins and who loses overall. Iraqi leaders and state authorities, by this logic, have made crucial investment choices and funneled resources in directions that privilege well-connected, favored groups and activities over others. A range of decisions made in Baghdad, from the establishment of state-owned enterprises to the nationalization of the oil sector, have clear political origins with profound impact on the Iraqi economy.

On the economic side, for its part, economic activity itself typically leads to the emergence and strengthening, or dissipation and weakening, of politically powerful individuals and groups. Economic resources, or their absence, influence political choices in any form of government, whether democratic or authoritarian. Economic processes change environments, sometimes proving to be deeply transformative over time. Successes and failures can help or hurt political actors, empowering them or limiting their options sharply. The economy is by no means more fundamental than the polity, because no economic activity on any scale can exist free of political choices and structures. But material factors shape and shove political actors significantly enough to demand consideration in virtually any analysis. Iraqi resources like oil have the potential to give state leaders much wider options in all areas, from the social domain to military development and regional political relations. And the orientation of Iraq's contemporary economy around oil exports has had political consequences requiring exploration.

The academic disciplines of political science and economics typically evaluate factors in the political and economic domains differently. The first emphasizes the power of political forces like the state to shape all else, and the second—especially its mainstream liberal version—is devoted to economic variables like the market, often seeing politics as a kind of irrational distortion of what otherwise would be sound economic decision-making. In contrast, a political economist holds that neither domain is universally more influential, rational, or foundational. They both have their logics and are in constant, ongoing dialogue. To understand Iraqi political economy requires examining that dialogue as a reciprocal relationship between the twin domains of politics and economics. Empirically or factually, this is seen in the everyday interaction of state and market forces in Iraq.

Iraqi leaders generally have followed a state-led rather than a market-oriented approach to development and economic growth over the past several decades. This approach had indirect origins in the efforts of the early Hashemite government to contend with the social and political upheaval of its day. It tended to respond less through careful economic policymaking and more via the army, which began to intervene heavily in domestic affairs as early as the 1930s. A subsequent and more direct marker of the Iraqi state's approach to the economy was the set of agrarian reforms undertaken after the 1958 revolution. These reforms were a product of Abd al-Karim Qasim's revolutionary ambition and his wish to deliver widely sought changes in the distribution of land ownership. A pronounced state role in the economy was further aided by the country's exceptional resource abundance, which became evident by mid-century. By the 1970s, Iraqi oil had changed everything, widening the range of economic possibilities, though some of the doors it opened led to military adventurism, oppressive governance, and a cascade of negative consequences. All these issues require elaboration after a general overview of the state of Iraq's economy and a set of relevant demographic and social factors.[2]

An Economic Overview

Iraq today has a midsized economy, with a total gross domestic product (GDP) that reached $208 billion recently (2021) and a per capita gross national income (GNI) of $9400 (2020).[3] Its GDP is still smaller than that of Finland, Ireland, or Greece, for example, though its population is nearly double that of all the latter three combined.

While Iraq is typically categorized as an upper-middle-income country, it has many of the attributes of a lower-income economy, including low productivity, a high poverty rate, serious youth unemployment, and poor female labor force participation.[4] The contemporary economy also suffers from myriad other structural deficiencies, from a bloated public sector and civil service to endemic corruption and ongoing electricity and water shortages. Its growth rate has been notably uneven over the years, with more dramatic ups and downs than most other MENA states. These oscillations have included brief periods of double-digit negative growth in the 1980s, 1990s, and 2000s caused by political upheaval and, in 2020, the global pandemic.[5] State enterprises remain significantly present in all leading sectors, and the state by law continues to own all underground natural resources like oil, gas, and mineral deposits.

Given its exceptional dependence on oil exports, its economy is strongly linked to global energy markets and therefore subject to significant variation in demand. Higher oil prices, a function of multiple factors, have lifted Iraq's prospects most recently, along with the signing of long-term oil export contracts with major state purchasers such as China. China replaced the United States as Iraq's most important energy trade partner in 2013, with India also serving as a major growth market for Iraqi energy exports. Iraq's continued reliance on oil is evident in the fact that oil has accounted for nearly 97% of the country's total exports in recent years, providing the lion's share of state revenue and the only significant source of hard-currency earnings.[6] Iraq is more oil-dependent than most other oil-producing countries in the world, with only a few coming close in terms of the percentage of export earnings derived from oil: Algeria and Libya (93%), Kuwait (86%), Qatar (85%), and Saudi Arabia (73%).[7] This is largely a consequence of having such a weakly diversified economy that, in recent years, has lost much of its productive capacity beyond the energy sector.[8]

Iraq does nonetheless retain great potential to diversify, at a minimum, its commodity exports. In addition to oil, it has substantial reserves of natural gas, phosphates,

TABLE 5.1 GDP—Iraq ($ billions)

1950	—	1985	48.4
1955	1.1*	1990	180.4
1960	1.5*	1995	12.9
1962	2.0	2000	48.4
1964	2.3	2005	50.0
1965	2.5*	2010	138.5
1970	3.3	2015	166.8
1975	13.5	2019	235.1
1980	52.6	2020	167.2

Source: World Bank, DataBank, at https://data.worldbank.org/indicator/NY.GDP.MKTP.CD?end=2020&locations=IQstart=1960.

Note:
*Calculated from Penrose and Penrose (1978), 496.

and sulfur. It ranks 12th in the world in proven gas reserves, totaling 5% of all global holdings, though this constitutes only a fraction of what top producing countries like Russia, Iran, and Qatar possess. Most Iraqi gas remains untapped or inefficiently utilized, despite recent government efforts to contract with foreign multinationals like France's TotalEnergies to develop this sector further.[9] Natural gas markets were upended by Russia's 2022 invasion of Ukraine and the resulting economic and geopolitical turmoil, but this also created an opportunity for additional producers to leverage their resources more effectively and reach new consumers.

Regarding phosphate rock, a critical element in fertilizer production, Iraq has the second largest reserves in the world, after the gigantic deposits in Morocco. Spread across several sites first identified in the 1960s but not developed for export until the 1980s, most of it is in the western desert of Anbar province.[10] Iraqi production consequently has been relatively small and intermittent, with the state preferring to lean into other sectors. As for sulfur, an environmentally destructive but industrially vital element, the state-owned al-Mishraq company, south of Mosul, was established in 1972 and sits next to reportedly the largest natural sulfur deposit in the world.[11] Al-Mishraq, however, was set on fire in 2003 during the Iraq War, and again in 2016 by Islamic State militants, with its plume visible in space.[12] Iraqi authorities have been unsuccessful in attracting new private investment to rehabilitate the facility, as native sulfur mined directly from the earth is now being replaced worldwide by the recovered byproducts of petroleum refining and natural gas production.

In general, the larger pattern is one of an abundance of certain natural resources, but a failure to translate that abundance into successful economic development, often due to political factors. Even in the oil and gas sector, Iraq's energy infrastructure is outdated and battered, requiring major new investments in production, processing, and export facilities like pipelines and port facilities to achieve its potential. Given substantial and rising global energy demands, public and private resources together are likely to be available to address some of these needs, though only if political, legal, and institutional conditions are conducive. This remains an open question. While the eventual energy transition toward greener, renewable sources is not likely to occur so rapidly as to leave the country without growth potential, governance and infrastructure challenges have to be met and managed in the next decade for Iraq's economy to recover from years of stagnation.

A related general challenge is that Iraq's resources are unevenly distributed across the country and subject to unresolved political conflict. As a result, Iraq is a land of exceptional contradictions and extremes. It is endowed with immense oil reserves, but mostly located in the north and south of the country. It has some of the world's most highly productive land, but it has experienced grievous food insecurity in the northern and southern provinces, induced by years of corruption and political conflict.[13] It benefits from two great rivers that combine into one of the world's oldest settled river valleys, but most of their headwaters originate across state borders and are controlled by geopolitical rivals. The Iraqi people have made impressive educational advances to become well-trained, capable workers, yet ethnic and sectarian divisions, cultivated by political figures of various stripes, have undermined a

Political Economy 167

unified and well-functioning society. Iraq's location on the map puts it at the crossroads of three continents, but it is so fully central that it is essentially surrounded on all sides and therefore vulnerable to the demands of others.

Iraq in the MENA Region

Seeing Iraq in its larger geographic context clarifies its position and prospects. Compared to the rest of the Arab states in the MENA region, Iraq has distinctive economic advantages and enormous potential. As Tables 5.2 to 5.5 note, when combining four factors—population, geographic size, oil reserves, and GDP—no other Arab state quite matches it. It has more potential than others because it is endowed more generously with a combination of key factors of production—land, labor, and capital—as well as important social elements like educational levels and management expertise. The one evident caveat is that Iraq's larger population creates developmental needs that at times have outstripped its immediately accessible resources, though this may be a function of political factors more than genuine, fundamental economic constraints.

While Egypt, for example, has more than double the population of Iraq, equal if better-developed industrial capacity, and a major river-based agricultural system, its population is highly concentrated geographically and it lacks Iraqi oil resources, which potentially could provide tremendous amounts of capital for state expenditure and investment. Saudi Arabia has nearly twice as much oil, but a smaller

TABLE 5.2 MENA country populations (millions, 2021)

Egypt	104.26	Yemen	30.49	Lebanon	6.77
Turkey	85.04	Syria	18.28	Oman	5.22
Iran	85.03	Tunisia	11.94	West Bank and Gaza	4.92
Algeria	44.62	Jordan	10.27	Kuwait	4.33
Iraq	41.18	UAE	9.99	Qatar	2.93
Morocco	37.34	Israel	9.36	Bahrain	1.75
Saudi Arabia	35.34	Libya	6.96		

Source: World Bank, DataBank, at https://databank.worldbank.org/reports.aspx?source=world-development-indicators.

TABLE 5.3 MENA country areas (1000 sq. km)

Algeria	2381.7	Yemen	528.0	Israel	21.9
Saudi Arabia	2149.7	Iraq	438.3	Kuwait	17.8
Libya	1759.5	Oman	309.5	Qatar	11.6
Iran	1648.2	Syria	187.4	Lebanon	10.4
Egypt	1001.5	Tunisia	163.6	West Bank	5.9
Turkey	783.6	Jordan	89.3	Bahrain	.8
Morocco	716.6	UAE	83.6	Gaza Strip	.4

Source: CIA World Factbook.

TABLE 5.4 MENA oil reserves (billion barrels, Jan. 1, 2018)

Saudi Arabia	266.20	Yemen	3.000
Iran	157.20	Syria	2.500
Iraq	148.80	Tunisia	0.425
Kuwait	101.50	Turkey	0.342
UAE	97.80	Bahrain	0.125
Libya	48.40	Israel	0.013
Qatar	25.20	Jordan	0.001
Algeria	12.20	Morocco	0.0008
Oman	5.40	Lebanon	0
Egypt	4.40	West Bank and Gaza	0

Source: CIA World Factbook.

TABLE 5.5 MENA GDP ($ billions, 2021)

Saudi Arabia	833.5	Morocco	132.7
Turkey	815.3	Oman	85.9
Israel	481.6	Libya	69.3*
UAE	417.2*	Lebanon	51.6*
Egypt	404.1	Tunisia	46.8
Iran	291.3*	Jordan	45.2
Iraq	207.9	Bahrain	38.9
Qatar	179.6	Syria	21.4**
Algeria	168.0	Yemen	21.1
Kuwait	136.2*	West Bank and Gaza	18.0

Source: World Bank, DataBank, at https://databank.worldbank.org/reports.aspx?source=world-development-indicators.

Notes:
*In 2019.
**In 2018.

population, less cultivatable agricultural land (there are no permanent rivers or lakes in the country), a lesser developed industrial base, and a longstanding political compact with conservative social groups that may limit Saudi economic choices and potential.[14] Algeria is a comparably large Arab country with strong industrial capacity and other advantages, but only one-twelfth of Iraq's oil reserves, along with its own legacies of political division and trauma.

Some of the region's smaller states, especially Kuwait, Qatar, Bahrain, and the UAE, have achieved high standards of living for their citizens on the strength of oil and gas exports. Both Bahrain and the UAE, for very different reasons, envision transitioning to post-oil economies, reimagining themselves as financial or technological hubs in a globalizing world. The broader and long-term economic potential of most Gulf states may be constrained by their dependence on foreign labor, a trend that is not declining.[15] Their small sizes and populations also may limit their political influence and enhance their vulnerability to powerful, sometimes predatory neighbors. Larger countries like Iraq, Saudi Arabia, and Iran have all the oil-related advantages of their smaller neighbors, along with more capacity to maintain themselves into the future, even if each faces distinctive challenges of their own.

While Iraq's potential may be relatively high among the Arab states, other nearby non-Arab powers have just as much or more, which they have translated into greater development. Iran has more than double the population of Iraq, triple its land area, slightly more oil, vastly superior access to ocean routes, and better-developed industrial capacity. But for the dislocations of the 1979 revolution, war with Iraq, and difficult relations with the United States, Iran might be even more regionally dominant. Both Turkey and Israel also exceed Iraq in many areas relevant to their economies. On the one hand, Israel has only one-twentieth the land area of Iraq, a quarter of its population, and a dearth of natural resources, with very little oil, not enough water, limited agricultural potential, and unresolved political conflict with its Palestinian national counterpart. But these constraints have been offset by its technological sophistication, new Mediterranean natural gas findings, vibrant political and social institutions, national cohesion, military power, and years of political, economic, and military assistance from the United States. Turkey shares a border with Iraq, but has double its population and an economy several times larger, surpassing Iraq in most measures of potential and productive capacity other than natural resources.

All the foregoing points to the reality of Iraq's many contradictions and dilemmas as a moderately large, striving, and well-endowed state, nearly encircled by other countries, some of which outmatch it in important ways. On the one hand, it is positioned for success and a natural leader in the Arab world, with several of the elements needed to build a strong and stable national economy and political community. Other than the structural dilemma of a confined geographic space

TABLE 5.6 MENA GNI, per capita ($, 2021), by Atlas method

Qatar	57,120	Jordan	4480
Israel	49,560	West Bank and Gaza	4220
UAE	39,410★	Algeria	3660
Kuwait	36,200★★	Tunisia	3630
Saudi Arabia	22,270★	Egypt	3510
Bahrain	19,930★	Lebanon	3450
Oman	15,030★	Iran	3370★
Turkey	9830	Morocco	3350
Libya	8430	Syria	930★★★
Iraq	5040	Yemen	670★

Source: World Bank, DataBank, at https://databank.worldbank.org/reports.aspx?source=world-development-indicators.

Notes:
★In 2020.
★★In 2019.
★★★In 2018.

and persistently problematic social divisions, Iraq has few inherent limits beyond remedy. On the other hand, it faces a host of challenges and pressures, from within and without, which threaten to undermine its political success, economic viability, and social cohesion. Iraq's reach often has exceeded its grasp, and Iraqi leaders have not managed its challenges well, let alone found solutions to these problems in the past century. Some of these challenges are demographic.

A Demographic and Communal Profile

Iraq's changing demography and its social composition have been the subject of critical commentary over the years, sometimes but not always with analytical merit. The presence of significant ethnic and sectarian divides has been of particular interest and has affected Iraqi and international assessments of the country's problems and prospects. A general description of the country's key demographic and communal features reveals important trends worth noting, particularly those focused on population growth, age distribution, gender balance, and identity issues associated with religious faith and ethnicity. Equally evident is a cautionary note about reading too much into these basic facts. As important as they can be, more fundamental political and economic forces tend to drive national life, with changes in many social features following in their wake.

The country's total population has grown at a relatively high annual rate, at least 2.5% in most years since 1960.[16] In 2022, Iraq's population of 42 million was much larger than what it was when the United States invaded in 2003 (25.6 million), over double what it was during the weapons inspection confrontations in 1996 (20.8 million), and more than triple what it was when Saddam Hussein assumed full power as president in 1979 (13.3 million).[17] This means that very soon a majority of Iraqis will have no memory of life in the Saddam era.

A high growth rate also translates into an exceptionally youthful population. The median age in Iraq in 2022 is 21. It was considerably higher in a number of prominent countries worldwide and in the MENA region, as noted in Table 5.8.

TABLE 5.7 Population growth—Iraq (millions)

1950	5.7	1990	17.4
1955	6.5	1995	20.1
1960	7.3	2000	23.5
1965	8.4	2005	26.9
1970	9.9	2010	29.7
1975	11.7	2015	35.6
1980	13.7	2020	40.2
1985	15.6	2025	45.2

Source: World Bank, DataBank, "Population Estimates and Projections," at https://databank.worldbank.org/source/population-estimates-and-projections; and United Nations, Department of Economic and Social Affairs, Population Division (2019), "World Population Prospects 2019," at https://population.un.org/wpp/DataQuery.

TABLE 5.8 Median age in select countries (2022)

Japan	49	India	29
Germany	46	Libya	26
France	43	Oman	26
United Kingdom	41	Egypt	24
Russia	40	Syria	24
United States	39	Jordan	24
China	38	West Bank	22
Lebanon	34	Iraq	21
Turkey	32	Yemen	20
Iran	32	Afghanistan	20
Saudi Arabia	31	Sudan	18
Israel	30	Gaza Strip	18

Source: *CIA World Factbook*.

More than a third of the MENA countries fit in this category of median-under-30 youthfulness: Libya, Oman, Egypt, Syria, Jordan, the West Bank, Yemen, Sudan, and the Gaza Strip, along with nearby Afghanistan. Iraq itself is one of the most youthful countries in the region, comparable to the few dozen other fastest-growing countries in the world, mostly in Africa and Asia.

Iraq's high growth rate is double-edged in that it provides more labor, talent, and energy to serve national needs while also generating specific demands. In material terms alone, youthful populations need education, financial support before they are old enough to work, housing once they set out on their own, and eventual stable employment. More than half of all Iraqis today (58%) are aged 24 or under, and these 20 million people are currently or soon to be entering the workforce and seeking a place in larger society.[18] They are sufficiently tech-savvy and interconnected with the world to know what it has to offer and make their own demands. This is enough to put grave stress on the Iraqi economy, which in turn will be a major concern of the country's national leaders, whether democratically elected or not. Young people without economic opportunities can be highly motivated change agents, available for mobilization in multiple ways, whether channeled in the direction of electoral participation or toward less constructive political activities.

Several other demographic trends affect Iraqi political and economic dynamics and are worth noting. It is evident if unsurprising that Iraq is becoming increasingly urbanized, with a shift in urbanization levels from 43% in 1960 to 73% in 2020.[19] This shift reflects both technological change and the movement away from subsistence agriculture toward industry and services, as new work opportunities have been created more quickly in urban than rural areas. Baghdad is Iraq's largest city, with 7.5 million people in 2022, substantially overshadowing other Iraqi cities like Mosul (1.7 million), Basra (1.4 million), and Kirkuk (1.0 million). It is the second largest city in the Arab world and larger than any Gulf or Levantine urban area, though it is smaller than its Iranian and Turkish counterparts in the MENA region,

Tehran (9.4 million) and Istanbul (15.6 million). While Baghdad does not approach the size of a megacity like Greater Cairo (22 million), it does have comparable historical significance. Cairo is the only other major city in the MENA region that rivals it, along with Jerusalem and Istanbul, as long-time and noteworthy centers of political and social gravity.[20]

One distinction that the Iraqi population does not have is a strong numerical gender imbalance—many more men than women—as is the case in the MENA Gulf states of Qatar, the UAE, Oman, Bahrain, Kuwait, and Saudi Arabia. Men comprise 58–75% of the population in the latter countries, due to the presence of large expatriate and migrant worker populations, as well as societal norms favoring males, which can affect infant mortality and other variables.[21] Iraq's relatively large population has precluded the need for foreign labor, except during the Iran–Iraq War in the 1980s, though these workers—mostly Egyptians and Yemenis—were not numerous enough to affect the demographic balance. Iraq's overall infant mortality rates have been declining steadily for decades, having been particularly high in the mid-twentieth century. Nearly one in three Iraqi children did not live past age five in 1950, down to one in 12 by 1975, and one in 40 by 2020.[22] Average life expectancy has also risen dramatically in this same period, from a dismal average of 38 years in 1950 to a more internationally typical age of 71 in 2020.[23]

Despite benefiting from long-term health improvements and maintaining a gender balance, Iraq today does have a pronounced social problem of gender inequality. When measured in terms of economic opportunity, political participation, health care, and educational opportunity, Iraq in fact has one of the largest gender-based disparities in the world, ranking 152 out of 153 countries in a recent analysis, far behind the top-ranking Nordic countries.[24] In the MENA region, Yemen and Syria also score particularly poorly in this same study, suggesting that the inequality originates not only in societal norms but also in harsh war-time conditions and political influences, which have had a disproportionately damaging impact on less powerful groups in society. Decades ago, in the mid-twentieth century, Iraq's secular monarchy and its subsequent postrevolutionary leadership both permitted a wider range of advances for women. Since then, political pressures have grown stronger from the rising power of conservative social forces and, when combined with war-induced upheaval of all kinds, pushed women disproportionately out of the workforce, political life, and school. A remedy would require broad social, political, and economic changes to reverse these complex and interconnected trends.

Two final and related social issues are Iraq's sectarian and ethnic tensions. Sectarian affiliation and ethnicity are group identities that, particularly in the Iraqi historical context, have been highly consequential at times throughout the past century. In simple numerical terms, Iraq is well known for having a Shi'i majority of roughly 60% and for being the largest Shi'i-majority country in the Arab world.[25] The Shi'i population is more substantially but not exclusively located in the country's south. The sectarian violence of the mid-2000s did leave traditionally mixed cities like Baghdad more divided by neighborhood along sectarian lines, even leading to reported population movements and transfers, as people looked to sectarian communal solidarity in the absence of government protection. Nonetheless, Iraq has never been strictly divided into a Kurdish north, Sunni center, and Shi'i south. The sectarian mix is more complicated and diverse. People of various faiths live throughout the country, and many extended families have both Sunni and Shi'i members and branches, with intermarriage common in urban areas.

This is not to say that the division is without importance. Historically, the distinction between Sunni and Shi'i Islam originated in Iraq. It started as a narrow but serious political dispute over succession in the early Muslim community of the seventh century, evolving over the centuries into doctrinal and communal differences that reflect all the complexity of an expanding and diversely practiced faith.[26] A key moment in the divide was the famous Battle of Karbala, which took place in October 680 CE on an open desert plain, where the Prophet Mohammed's grandson and aspiring leader of the Muslim community, Hussein ibn Ali, was martyred. Karbala today is a city of several hundred thousand people in central Iraq, 100 km south of Baghdad, and Shi'i Muslims consider it holy ground, essentially on par with Mecca, Medina, Najaf, and Jerusalem. Iraq itself also has several notable Shi'i mosques and shrines, such as the Imam Ali Shrine in Najaf, the Imam Hussein Shrine in Karbala, the Kadhimiya Mosque in Baghdad, and the Askari Shrine in Samarra to the north, which together attract millions of adherents and pilgrims each year. Iraq, along with Iran, is therefore a vital center of the faith, and this significance gives sectarian issues greater weight and potential political consequence.

The city of Najaf, south of Baghdad, is one of Shi'i Islam's spiritual capitals and a center of Shi'i political power. It also is a seat of learning, where Shi'i scholars gather to study. The Shi'i religious establishment is relatively structured and hierarchical, with scholars of Islamic thought and jurisprudence, or *'ulama*, working under the guidance of more senior figures, who acquire reputations and attract followers. This gives them potential mobilizing power, which they can wield in relation to secular authorities, though carefully and sometimes at great cost to themselves. The theological innovations of Iran's Ayatollah Khomeini, particularly his late 1970s doctrine of the rule or "guardianship of the jurisprudent" (*velayat-e faqih* in Farsi; *wilayat al-faqih* in Arabic), gave additional impetus to Iraqi Shi'i political activism. Traditionally, the community had been disengaged or "quietist" in its avoidance of participation in the secular, political domain. Khomeini's doctrine elevated the status of Shi'i scholars and legitimized their pursuit of power, making possible some of the political initiatives launched by groups like the *Da'wa*, as described in earlier chapters.

For several decades, because both the Hashemite monarchy and post-1958 revolutionary regimes were dominated by Sunnis, regime-opposition dynamics tended to include Sunni–Shi'i contestation, even if cross-cutting political cleavages also were present. This same dynamic continued after 2003 and was exacerbated by the civil conflict of 2006–2007, made intentionally worse by external actors like the Sunni militant group AQI's Abu Musab al-Zarqawi. The United States, via the Coalition Provisional Authority, may not have helped matters by organizing the Iraqi Governing Council along sectarian and ethnic lines immediately upon taking charge of the country in the summer of 2003. In the subsequent postoccupation era, Shi'i political actors and parties became dominant due largely to their greater numbers and a capacity to win national parliamentary elections. Sunni groups of various kinds, displaced after decades in power, took to the opposition, whether in militant form as insurgents or as supporters of the Sunni-dominated Islamic State, or as participants in smaller political parties.[27] The Sunni–Shi'a divide today remains highly salient in Iraqi politics, though its core and most active feature is not doctrinal so much as communal.

The most consequential ethnic distinction in Iraq is its famous divide between Arabs and Kurds, with the Arabic-speaking population constituting a roughly 78% majority and the Kurds being at least a 16% minority, along with several smaller ethnicities.[28] The Kurds are the largest ethnonationalist identity group in the Middle East without their own state. Unlike the region's large Arab population, which is divided among nearly two dozen countries—artificially, according to nationalists—the Kurds are also divided, but lack majority status in any national context. They are clear majorities in a large, arcing swath of fairly contiguous territory, but at the intersection of four MENA countries. Their distribution across much of southeastern Turkey, northern Iraq, western Iran, and northwestern Syria has left them vulnerable to the actions of the central governments in each of these countries, with tragic if varied results in most cases.

Iraq's Kurds in recent years have carved out a relatively autonomous region in northern Iraq, overseen by the Kurdistan Regional Government (KRG). The Kurdistan Region operates with a degree of autonomy from Baghdad and has its own parliament, armed forces (the *Peshmerga*), educational system, and at least some of the trappings of a sovereign state. Iraqi Kurdistan does not declare itself to be a separate country, knowing that such a declaration would elicit a forceful response from all the interested regional parties, as happened after a successful proindependence referendum in 2017 prompted Baghdad to invalidate it. Aside from a range of social and political areas of contention between the Iraqi central government and Kurdish authorities, a core unresolved problem is that of determining ownership rights and revenues from the large oil reserves in northern Iraq, much of it in Kurdistan. Ongoing negotiations have sought to formalize an arrangement, which has yet to be achieved.

Iraqi Kurds themselves are divided in various ways, some more politically consequential than others. In terms of religious faith, the Kurds are mostly Sunni but do have a small Shi'i minority of perhaps 2%—the Feyli Kurds of the eastern provinces, primarily along the border with Iran. There also is substantial linguistic variability across the region in the form of three different major Kurdish dialects: the most widely spoken regional dialect, Kurmanji (in the north and well into Turkey), Sorani (in central Iraq and Iran), and Başûrî or Xwarig (in southern Iraqi Kurdistan and into Iran). A few additional subdialects and variations complicate the picture further and reflect Iraq's ethnolinguistic diversity. These linguistic differences are noticeable but do not render the various dialects mutually unintelligible to Kurdish speakers, who in some cases can also speak Arabic, which historically was emphasized in Iraqi schools. Some of this has changed since the formation of the KRG and the establishment of more than a dozen public and private universities in the Kurdish north.

The linguistic differences across the territory do reflect the fact that Kurdistan has never been a fully united and politically independent territory. They are mirrored by other equally important divides, including between those living in the more mountainous northern and eastern regions of Kurdistan and those closer to cities like Kirkuk and Sulaimaniyya, along with class and other distinctions stemming from the varied economic positions held by people throughout the region. Perhaps most consequentially in terms of divisions, Kurdish politics have also witnessed a longstanding rivalry between political parties and their leaders, particularly the Kurdish Democratic Party (KDP) and the somewhat newer Patriotic Union of Kurdistan (PUK), in addition to the complicating presence and activity—some of it across international borders—of the more militant Kurdish Workers Party (PKK), which is oriented toward Turkey. Iraqi national electoral politics also have several small, new Kurdish parties that have contested elections in recent years with some success, as described in Chapter 3.

An important caveat to any consideration of demographics comes from political economy and the way in which it prioritizes explanatory variables. Social identity can be enormously powerful in shaping actions and leading individuals and groups to be treated in particular ways. Yet, the complex and multifaceted nature of social identity reduces the likelihood that a single facet of a person's identity causes specific political or economic actions. In large group settings like a national state, the challenge is not the presence of diverse identities, or something inherent in a particular social identity. It is the way in which political actors use identities, whether sectarian, ethnic, or any other, to advance their political objectives. Muslim sectarian identity varies worldwide in its social and political significance. It has been deployed by political actors in a wide range of ways, with this variability changing over time.[29] From the standpoint of political economy, there is nothing inherent in a given identity that obligates one political or economic position over others. Political and economic variables tend to have great—and causally prior—influence on the salience of identity markers and can be more fundamental and varied drivers of outcomes.

Ethnic and sectarian divides sometimes matter profoundly, and sometimes not as much. Throughout the world, identities are constructed in a variety of ways, and functioning institutions are able to channel political and economic activity constructively in some places, at least some of the time. Countries as varied as India, the United States, Brazil, and South Africa have divided societies, but have achieved modest success—or at least show variability among them and over time—in managing social differences. This supports the likelihood that Iraqi domestic political conflict is not a direct and simple consequence of demographic heterogeneity in the state and nation so much as other factors in political and economic life. It is essential to look to these factors to learn more about the country's prospects.

Oil

Iraq began the twentieth century with a mostly agricultural economy, having no substantial industry or hydrocarbon extraction until the first commercial discovery of oil in the north, near Kirkuk, in 1927.[30] State revenues from oil exploration, extraction, and production for export rose throughout the twentieth century, with two major growth periods. The first was an early expansion from 1946 to 1955, which included the discovery of large new oilfields in Zubair in 1949 and Rumaila in 1953, both in the south. This brought a 37-fold increase in state revenues and led the regime to become dependent on oil for most of its resources. Several years after the founding of OPEC in Baghdad in September 1960, the second period was one of even more substantial growth, from 1968 to 1979. It stemmed from market and geopolitical factors, entailing a nearly 44-fold increase in state revenues and ushering in the modern era of Iraq as a major oil-producing country.[31] Put differently, in unadjusted dollar terms, Iraqi state oil revenues rose from $6 million (1945) to $105 million (1951) to $244 million (1958) to $488 million (1968) to $21.4 billion (1978).[32] The full nationalization of the Iraq Petroleum Company in 1972 and the quadrupling of oil prices following the October 1973 Arab–Israeli War secured these astonishing gains.

Over the years, the growth of state revenues reflected both increases in oil prices and rising production levels. Both prices and production levels themselves were strongly related to significant political events involving major producing countries. Iraq was subject to this dynamic from the beginning of the oil era, starting with Britain's conquering of Ottoman Mesopotamia during the First World War and continuing through its ousting of independent Iraq's anti-British, Rashid Ali regime in May 1941 during the Second World War. The postwar period witnessed a MENA producer-related price spike and oil shock during the Suez Crisis in the summer and fall of 1956, and again most dramatically during and after the Arab–Israeli War of October 1973. Prices peaked after the Iranian revolution in 1979 and then dropped precipitously for most of the 1980s and 1990s.[33]

Iraq's invasion of Kuwait in August 1990 had only a minor and temporary impact on global markets, but major consequences for its own production levels until the implementation of the Oil-for-Food Program in 1996. Prices rose in response to the U.S. invasion of Iraq in 2003, which took Iraqi production and export offline for a short time, in addition to generating uncertainty that contributed to price hikes. The return of a degree of stability in Iraq in 2008 allowed for a steady increase in Iraqi production for more than a decade, not particularly affected by the turmoil surrounding the Islamic State's invasion and curtailed only by the global pandemic in 2020.[34] Russia's invasion of Ukraine in February 2022 drove international prices skyward, but Iraq's capacity to increase its production in response was limited by the ongoing internal constraints of continued underinvestment.

Due to these constraints, Iraq has an especially large reserves-to-production ratio. That is, compared to other states, it possesses relatively more oil than it can extract from the ground and sell to buyers. This is not a matter of political will, though politics do shape the national investment climate, which in turn affects the production capacity. Other countries have smaller reserves but produce much more oil because political and institutional factors allow—even require—them to do so. The United States in 2018, for example, had 61 billion barrels of proven reserves, compared to Iraq's 147 billion, but produced over 15 million barrels per day that year, compared to Iraq's 4.6 million per day in the same period.[35] High American production levels, facilitated by the shale revolution in the first decade of the 2000s, are driven partly by political and ideological factors favoring the energy industry and the pursuit of "energy independence."[36]

In fact, many of Iraq's proven reserve sites are either under development or producing at least some amount of oil. Even more hopefully, Iraqi oil is relatively easy and cost-effective to produce. Unlike the oil reserves of many other countries, Iraqi oil is not located offshore in the ocean, found in a harsh climate, locked underground in permafrost, inaccessible due to complicated geology, or situated in heavily populated areas. Much of it is in "supergiant" oilfields on flat desert terrain, relatively close to export terminals.[37] In purely economic terms, its development is a more efficient use of capital than the extraction and transport to market, for example, of North Slope Alaska crude from the Prudhoe Bay oilfield near the Arctic Circle. The latter is the largest oilfield in North America but situated in the frozen tundra, 800 miles from export terminals and adjacent to the Alaskan National Wildlife Refuge, a rare and pristine area of natural beauty and unique wildlife targeted for petroleum drilling for decades.

As this demonstrates, production levels are a function not only of technical capacity or resource availability but also of the surrounding political, institutional, and even environmental context. This context is especially important in the energy sector, which typically has exceptional strategic importance to many countries. The uniqueness of Saudi Arabia as a "swing producer," for example, is not simply its immense reserves. Another country—Venezuela—has larger proven oil reserves, and two others—the United States and Russia—have produced at higher rates. But Saudi Arabia is unique because its monarchy has direct and absolute control over production levels and can respond to geopolitical or economic turmoil by raising or lowering production virtually at will. It has few constraints other than its agreements with other OPEC producers, its calculation of the Saudi national interest, and its obligation to maintain a sociopolitical pact that includes the disbursal of general payments to citizens from state oil revenues.

This distinguishes the Saudi kingdom from Iraq, where the state also owns all subsoil resources like fossil fuels but presides over a more fragmented mix of public and private sector companies operating through a more indirect contract and licensing system that gives the latter companies more leeway. In this sense, Baghdad does not have as much political and economic control over its primary national resource as Riyadh and other regional oil exporters do. Iraq differs further still from the United States, where political and property rights institutions allow the private sector to dominate resource ownership and control production levels.

U.S. production is shaped more gradually and indirectly by market forces, the federal government's issuance of drilling and pipeline transit permits on public lands, and occasional environmental constraints channeled through electoral competition. Iraq's future may witness a renegotiation of political arrangements assuring a better distribution of the benefits of oil largesse while also working to diversify the economy so as to not be fully reliant on one national source of revenue.

External Rents

Iraq and other major oil producers are the focus of a longstanding set of analytical claims centered on the concepts of "rent" and the "rentier state." Rent, as a general matter, is income or state revenue derived from the ownership of an asset. It is not directly productive in that it does not entail manufacturing goods, providing services, or growing agricultural products. It might instead involve the direct sale of subsoil or underground natural resources like petroleum, which can be extracted and sold in crude form without adding value to it via a transformative industrial process. When rent is paid by a party outside a given country, it is referred to as "external" rent. A rentier state is one that derives most of its national revenue, or the resources supporting government expenditure, from rents rather than from traditional sources like the taxation of income or business activity, consumer taxes on goods and services, or tariffs on international trade.

It is worth emphasizing that rent accrues from the simple ownership of territory rather than a commodity attribute. Non-oil forms of rent include positional or strategic rents gained by possessing unique or geostrategically important territory. For example, the ownership of international shipping canals, overland pipelines, and natural or man-made tourist sites can generate rent for their owners. Rent also can include revenue from the multiyear leasing of land rich in any kind of resource to a multinational corporation (MNC) for exploration and possible development. In such cases, the state retains nominal ownership but sells private actors the right to control and extract resources. Such deals have terms that vary greatly and depend on the relative negotiating power of the state owner and the private actors it faces. Multinational bargaining power, historically backed by the country from which the multinational originates, can be sufficient to assure favorable terms for companies facing only weak resistance from states needing investment capital, technology, or foreign market access.

Many of the MENA oil producers have been referred to as rentier states because so much of their revenue comes from oil rents. A few MENA countries attract rent in multiple forms. Egypt earns rent from modest amounts of oil and gas, ownership of the Suez Canal, U.S. foreign aid attracted by its geostrategic position, and possession of globally popular tourist sites like the Pyramids of Giza and resorts along the Red Sea and Mediterranean coasts. With a large amount of tourism and foreign assistance flowing into the country as crucial non-oil forms of rent, Egypt may have a full-blown rentier economy because so much of its economic activity takes the form of external rents. Other MENA oil producers, particularly in the

Gulf, have sought to shift their economies away from oil and toward other sectors, such as financial services. Such services are more traditional economic activities, but they share with rent-seeking the quality of not being a form of industrial or agricultural production.

Iraq's rentier attributes remain focused on oil, supplemented by the additional rents it accrues from its geostrategic location, which has helped it to attract international attention but also comes with distinct geographic and demographic challenges. Iraqi oil exports are vulnerable to disruption by foreign powers and threats from domestic groups at odds with the government in Baghdad. Many of the country's largest oilfields are located either in the Kirkuk area to the north, which is heavily Kurdish, or in the vicinity of Basra to the southeast, which is largely Shi'i, with relatively little oil in the Sunni-dominated geographic center of the country. Regardless of where it originates, most exported Iraqi oil has to be delivered either by overland pipelines through Syria, Turkey, and Saudi Arabia or via export terminals off the Faw peninsula to tankers in the Persian Gulf. A relatively small amount has been shipped by tanker truck to Jordan and Iran or is subject to smuggling via overland routes.

Industrial Development

Iraqi state leaders committed relatively early to building a national industrial capacity. Unlike the more sparsely populated, oil-rich Gulf monarchies, the country had all the necessary elements to support the establishment of industry by the beginning of the 1950s. Given its astoundingly long agrarian history, most early state investment targeted the agricultural sector by improving water management through flood control and irrigation measures. With rising state revenues, however, a fair amount of public investment eventually went to transportation infrastructure: roads, bridges, railways, port facilities, and airports. This allowed nonpetroleum manufacturing to grow sharply with rising demand in the postwar era, though it paused briefly when the dislocation and uncertainty of the 1958 revolution discouraged private investment. The state took fuller control of industrial production in July 1964, when the Arif regime expanded the public sector via the nationalization of over two dozen large private firms. It became responsible for 60% of all manufacturing output and half the jobs in the country.[38] This approach yielded somewhat disappointing results and growth slowed.

Global development models favored active state engagement and import substitution industrialization (ISI) from the postwar period in the 1950s until the late 1960s, with state planners seeking to replace foreign imports with domestic production shielded by high tariffs on imports. At the same time, several developing countries in Asia and Latin America began shifting to an export-led growth (ELG) model, based on comparative advantage and the optimal use of available resources.[39] Such an approach was consistent with the larger, American-led movement toward a more liberal, open trading order furthered by the ongoing negotiations of the General Agreement on Tariffs and Trade (GATT) framework. In Iraq of the 1960s, several factors precluded participation in such a shift in economic orthodoxy or the development model. These included pervasive political uncertainty, an entrenched patronage system dominated by the military, political affinity with state-socialist approaches to economic governance, and rising oil revenues. Iraq was not part of the GATT negotiations or subject to its dynamics. Pressure for reform, whether domestic or international, was low as long as external rents from oil remained high and were getting even higher.

The return of the Ba'athists in 1968 only accelerated the movement toward enhanced central planning and state industrial investment. Increased revenues were directed partly toward national development projects in the coming decade, as the regime further transformed the public sector by establishing 10 state organizations, each devoted to a particular industrial subsector, from chemical manufacturing and engineering to textiles.[40] More countries were growing skeptical of the benefits of state-owned enterprises and a statist orientation to the economy, and Iraqi industry remained inefficient. The enhanced state role in Iraq's case, however, was not animated by economic logic so much as an abiding concern with political control. Iraqi state authorities in the 1970s finally had wrestled the oil sector from private actors and foreign powers. In the economic domain, as in the political sphere, they wanted to be in charge. They had little need to follow a development strategy organized around manufactured exports, since oil was in high demand as an export commodity and had been artificially underpriced for some time as it was. Political impulses shaped the economy very strongly as a result.

In conjunction with the energy market transformations of the era, the state invested much of the country's newfound surplus wealth in capital- and material-intensive heavy industries that included iron, steel, and petrochemicals. These state-owned enterprises succeeded for a time, along with medium-sized factories producing textiles and food commodities, though only as long as the state was willing and able to devote extraordinary resources to supporting them. This support diminished in the 1980s under the twin pressures of massively increased war expenditure and globally declining oil prices. Economic imperatives began to push back at political choices, conditions, and preferences. The Iran–Iraq War of 1980–1988 and Kuwait-related events in the 1990s diverted or diminished the state's spending possibilities greatly. From the early 1990s onward, Iraqi industrial capacity was limited by extended international conflict and resource deprivation, which led to two decades of underinvestment and poor maintenance of manufacturing facilities and infrastructure.

In balancing the deployment of state and market forces, Iraq leaned heavily on the state, but even the more state-oriented Ba'athists were not entirely averse to using the private sector to attract and allocate resources, particularly in response to an acute need. The regime launched a somewhat successful privatization effort in the late 1980s when the Iran–Iraq War had done such damage to industry, export capacity, the labor force, and state revenues that the government was compelled to seek private investment.[41] This initiative only fell apart when Saddam's invasion of Kuwait a few years later led to sanctions that made it impossible to privatize further or attract new foreign investment. Industrial output dropped precipitously in the early 1990s, shrinking to a fraction of what it had been more than a decade before.[42] By the beginning of the 2000s, the state still owned several dozen large enterprises, though it employed fewer than half of all workers, and a solid majority of Iraqis worked either in the government bureaucracy or for small, private businesses and activities.

The year 2003 marked another, still more challenging turning point for Iraqi industry. The American invasion damaged factories and critical supporting infrastructure, from electricity generation and sanitation to communications equipment, water provision, and the entire national network of roads, bridges, and airports. As has been well documented, the government ministries associated with the economy, other than the oil ministry, were not secured by the invading forces in the war's immediate aftermath. In some cases, the lack of a security presence, policing, or legal accountability led to wanton destruction, looting, and theft perpetrated on an ad hoc basis by roving bands of individuals and groups, freed of all constraining authority. In other cases, the damage was done by insiders from the former regime who had arranged for the methodical dismantling of entire industrial facilities like the massive state-owned repair works for automobile imports.[43] The overall impact on industry was dramatic and compounded by years of prior neglect and upheaval.[44]

Iraq thereafter could not manufacture much of anything without a restoration of its basic physical and institutional infrastructure, as well as a return of fundamental public goods like a stable currency, clear property rights, the rule of law, and a modicum of stability and social equilibrium. This could not happen piecemeal in that these interconnecting elements of a functioning polity, economy, and society all required standing up at approximately the same time. As a perspective from political economy tells us, the political framework establishes the context and conditions for economic activity, while the pursuit, possession, and generation of wealth shapes the fortunes of all political actors. In Iraq's case, the linchpin holding the country together was a reconstitution of organized political authority. Without a minimally functioning state, or a legitimate occupying authority willing and able to play a surrogate state role, economic activity would be limited to whatever locally oriented, small-scale, informal actors could produce.[45]

A large amount of American and international economic assistance did arrive with the U.S.-led coalition. Significant financial and technical resources were available, at least eventually, to rebuild much of what had been destroyed on the material side. The Coalition Provisional Authority did set out initially to privatize Iraqi industry and followed a neoliberal blueprint to restructure Iraq's economy and reintegrate it into world markets. But the postwar insurgency began relatively quickly in the summer of 2003, and a good deal of that early spending was either lost to corruption and patronage or wasted. Numerous reconstruction projects, large and small, were completed, only to be destroyed in successive waves of violence or intentional destruction when the insurgency morphed into a more full-blown civil war.[46] The missing piece remained the reconstitution of legitimate political authority, which took much too long to arrive.

Eventually, new Iraqi political institutions were established, and state authorities began to come to terms with the needs of the economy, including industrial development. After 2008, the Maliki government was able to assert itself, and industry began to return as a viable source of economic growth, diversification, and employment. With a relatively large skilled labor force, state planners and private entrepreneurs started to rebuild industries around petroleum products, chemicals, fertilizer, construction materials, textiles, leather goods, processed foods, and metalworks. Some of these enterprises were relatively small in scale and locally oriented. With state support, the petroleum sector was given higher priority than all others and made faster headway in getting Iraqi oil back onto the market, its output growing steadily after 2008, along with other industrial derivatives.

Industry overall, particularly in the north, suffered one last major setback from 2012 to 2017, when the Islamic State (IS) took advantage of the 2011 American military withdrawal and persistent Iraqi state weakness, overrunning large parts of northern and western Iraq. IS took control of nearly 40% of Iraqi territory, including some oilfields and vital infrastructure. The latter included the Mosul Dam, Iraq's largest, 25 miles upstream of the city and deemed "the world's most dangerous dam" by the U.S. Army Corps of Engineers because it was constructed on soluble rock foundations that required constant maintenance to avoid a catastrophic breach that likely would kill hundreds of thousands.[47] The retaking of the dam and all of IS-occupied Iraq, including a lengthy and devastating battle for Mosul, proved costly and destructive, as both coalition forces and IS militants destroyed bridges, large numbers of buildings, and the international airport.

Iraqi industry improved in subsequent years, as a measure of relative calm returned to the country. Its prospects nonetheless remained tied to the rest of the country's political and economic fortunes. It received financial assistance from the International Monetary Fund and other multilateral international lenders, who required structural adjustment programs like the reduction of state spending on subsidies and the curtailing of public sector employment, along with deregulation and privatization initiatives. The implementation of the latter discounted the short-term needs and interests of enough Iraqis to make them politically challenging. They came at a time when an extended period of stability and reasonably effective governance was required to rebuild the country's manufacturing capacity, extend it into new areas, and reinvigorate defunct efforts at heavy industry. Only with significant further injections of capital from international public lenders, multinational investors, or the central government could Iraqi industrial capacity rebound in subsequent years.

Water Resources and Agriculture

For thousands of years, Iraq's great rivers have given rise to agricultural productivity and settled communities throughout the region, beginning with some of the first in human existence. The Tigris and Euphrates Rivers have provided both irrigation and exceptionally arable, nutrient-rich soil in the fertile lowlands along their paths.

The river system's headwaters originate in the Taurus mountains of southeastern Turkey, only about 50 miles from each other. The 1900-km Tigris and 2700-km Euphrates comprise nearly half the Fertile Crescent and extend diagonally through Iraqi territory from the northwest to the southeast for over 1600 km. They once took entirely separate paths to the sea, but today are joined at al-Qurna in the south to form the 200-km *Shatt al-Arab* waterway and flow through Basra and into the Persian Gulf together.

Until the mid-twentieth century, the Tigris and Euphrates served as a major transportation route, connecting a string of towns and cities, as well as the hinterlands on either side of them. From north to south, the cities of Mosul, Tikrit, Samarra, Baghdad, and Kut are on the Tigris. Hit, Ramadi, Falluja, Karbala, Najaf, and Nasiriyya are directly on or within 2 km of the Euphrates. A sixteenth-century deviation in the course of the Euphrates left Najaf dry for nearly 200 years and all but wiped out the city, which reemerged as a Shi'i center of learning and eventually regained the flow of the Euphrates when Ottoman engineers diverted it back. Only the major Kurdish and Turkmen cities of Erbil, Kirkuk, and Sulaimaniyya are beyond either river's immediate proximity. If Egypt is "the gift of the Nile," as the ancient Greek historian Herodotus once famously wrote, Iraq also would not exist without these twin rivers and the associated communities they have made possible.

Both rivers have long been integrated into an extensive network of canals and dams for irrigation, flood control, and, in more recent decades, hydroelectric power. Their waters feed and maintain the wetland ecosystem of the southern Iraqi Marshes, a UNESCO World Heritage Site and once the largest of its kind in the region. Of the two rivers, the more easterly Tigris has a stronger flow, fed by several permanent tributaries like the Greater and Lesser Zab and the Diyala, making Iraq's entire river system much wider than Egypt's Nile River valley. With 100% of the Euphrates and nearly 70% of the Tigris waterflows originating outside the country, mainly in Turkey but also in Iran and Syria, water management has been an increasingly delicate national and regional issue throughout the contemporary era. Iraq today faces very serious intermittent water shortages stemming from global climate change and substantially increased upstream usage, particularly in Turkey.[48] Pollution from agricultural production and industrial processes has added to the difficulty.

Despite the challenges, successful river system management over the millennia has permitted substantial agricultural output. The world's oldest cultivated fruit tree—the date palm—has yielded dates on these same lands for thousands of years. Iraq's contemporary agricultural production has included grains like wheat and barley in the north in wintertime, rice and maize in central and southern Iraq in the summer, and fruits and vegetables like dates, tomatoes, grapes, potatoes, and watermelons in much of the country throughout the year.[49] Most crops in recent years have been cultivated for domestic consumption, with relatively limited regional export of dates and a low volume of cross-border trade in local produce. Rainwater helps to sustain northern crops, but the south is almost entirely river-fed and therefore has been most at risk of severe water shortages.[50]

Government intervention and political upheaval have caused agricultural production to diminish measurably in recent decades, dropping from over 18% of the country's total economic output in 1995 during a period of limited oil production to only 2% in 2019.[51] While Iraq used to be the world's largest date producer and was responsible for three-quarters of the world's supply in 1950, its global market share was reduced to 5% in 2021 in the face of competition from Iran and Saudi Arabia.[52] Agriculture has been implicated in black market trading, prompted in the 1990s by international sanctions and state efforts to control markets and offer farmers lower prices for food commodities than they could get on their own. The country's exceptionally fast-growing population and rising food needs are a particular concern, given the dearth of recent investment in modern agricultural equipment. New technology may alleviate some shortfalls, though institutionalized political cooperation is needed on national, regional, and even international levels to allow Iraqis to continue feeding themselves.

International Trade

Iraq has been a part of long-distance trade for millennia. As far back as 2100 BCE, the late Sumerian city-state of Ur was at the center of a major trading network extending from Egypt and the eastern Mediterranean to Anatolia, Armenia, and India. With a unified river system joining distant locales, Iraq's geographic position was deeply advantageous well into the modern era, even if—or perhaps because— Baghdad, Mosul, and Basra were oriented in different directions along the Tigris. Mesopotamia, as the hub of a great trading wheel, attracted high-value goods, such as gold, silver, gems, wood, ivory, and semiprecious stones like lapis lazuli. Typically, these were traded for surplus grains that could be conveyed on riverways in all directions. Some degree of river-borne trade persisted for several thousand years.

The twentieth-century division of the MENA region into separate national states brought the trade disadvantages of stricter international border delimitation and control, tariffs and nontariff barriers (NTBs), currency exchange requirements, arbitrary geography, and bitter political rivalry. More positively, it also prompted Iraqi state-building efforts that included major infrastructure improvements from the 1950s to the 1980s, which greatly enhanced national import and export capacity. Tariffs and NTBs like government regulation typically remained low in independent Iraq until the Ba'athist regime in 1968 expanded the use of import licenses and deployed institutional mechanisms like state trading organizations and retail outlets to control more of the trading system. State officials did not use tariffs for revenue purposes, though they did seek to increase state ownership and political control over major tradable goods.

The growth of the oil industry gave Iraq a lucrative export commodity that incentivized and eventually paid for further integration into the global economy, albeit with a single commodity. Single-commodity trade integration in the contemporary era provided modest if unevenly available improvements to the Iraqi standard of living, even if the gains from trade were sufficient to create developmental possibilities previously unimagined. Iraq's trade balance nonetheless tended to run positive, as the total value of imports was much lower than exports, almost entirely on the strength of the energy sector. Non-oil trade throughout the Ba'athist era focused on strategic commodities like military hardware, as well as food, light manufactures, and consumer imports to placate a war-weary middle class. In the steadiest economic times, Iraqi consumers enjoyed more luxury imports than some of their counterparts in other regional states, deployed strategically by government authorities to soften domestic political dissent.

The international sanctions era left the country fairly isolated for most of the 1990s, even if smuggling and black market trading persisted via overland connections to all six of its neighbors. The isolation ended in 2003, though Iraq's trade reintegration was limited not only by the persistent civil strife but also by hard-currency constraints and a dearth of available exports other than petroleum products. Iran emerged as Iraq's strongest trade partner in the early postinvasion years, with several billion dollars in annual trade in construction material, food, and light industry.[53] Iranian–Iraqi trade was facilitated by growing political ties, close physical proximity, and the existence of established transportation routes, as Iran sought to break free of its own sanctions constraints. More recently, Iraq has developed an expanding set of trade partners, including the UAE, Turkey, China, India, and South Korea, which have provided a modest range of imported goods, ranging from refined petroleum for domestic use to automobiles, agricultural products, and light manufactures.[54]

Iraq today is not yet a member of the World Trade Organization (WTO), established in 1995 to institutionalize the postwar liberal trade regime and currently including 164 member states and 98% of world trade.[55] Encouraged by a market-oriented U.S. occupation authority in 2003, Iraq started the process of joining in 2004 but faced delay due to renewed domestic troubles and only restarted the necessary steps toward fulfilling accession requirements in 2017. Never having participated in past trade talks associated with the GATT, it has not had enough time as a stable, sovereign, sanctions-free country governed by the rule of law to implement the reforms necessary to join. It also has displayed some ambivalence about joining a liberal trade regime, given its history of state-led growth and its ongoing dependence on a single export commodity. A path to entry remains available, and in recent years, even the most illiberal governments worldwide have chosen to become part of the rules-based global economic order, with China joining the WTO in 2001, followed by Saudi Arabia in 2005, Russia in 2012, and Afghanistan in 2016. Several other MENA countries currently are also in the process of joining, including Algeria, Iran, Lebanon, Libya, Sudan, and Syria. Iraq's success in this area will depend on the political question of who governs in the future and what their supporters and constituents want by way of global engagement.

The answers to such questions, and the Iraqi government's willingness to launch deeper legal and regulatory reforms to encourage private investment, are affected significantly by energy markets. Higher energy prices improve the state's short- and medium-term revenues while undermining its leaders' willingness to reform, diversify, and promote the efficiencies essential to longer-term success. Lower oil prices enhance the state's reliance on international financial institutions, which demand politically unpalatable reforms. This inverse relationship—oil-induced financial abundance undercutting the political will to change economic approaches—creates yet another Iraqi dilemma. By sacrificing the opportunity to create a more broad-based economy, less dependent on a single revenue stream from a nonrenewable resource, state leaders jeopardize Iraq's long-term prospects and increase its vulnerability to market volatility. Movement toward more competitive, quasi-democratic governance since 2003 has not mitigated this dilemma, because elected leaders face persuasive short-term pressures to deliver for their constituents. Whether economic reform–minded political parties can win enough support to gain power is an open question.

Labor Migration and Earnings Remittances

Labor migration within and to the Arab world has been a noteworthy factor in the MENA political economy since the 1970s. The Gulf Arab states of Saudi Arabia, Kuwait, Oman, the UAE, and Bahrain have hosted millions of expatriate workers from Asia, particularly in low-wage sectors with unmet labor needs, including construction, energy sector, and domestic services. Iraq generally has not needed to do so, given its larger population, though it has had needs at particular periods worth noting. In general, the demographic and resource asymmetries of the Arab states have led workers to travel from high-population countries to neighbors facing labor shortages, typically for limited periods of time. Cultural commonalities among the Arab states, particularly regarding faith and language, have facilitated this integrative process, along with an occasional political impetus from integration-minded state leaders. Migrant laborers in the region have sent these remittances home to their families while living temporarily away from home.

At certain moments in contemporary Iraqi history, workers from Egypt, Yemen, Jordan, and Palestine have played important roles in the Iraqi economy. The extent of Iraq's integration into regional labor markets has varied and been heavily dependent on both market forces and political relationships. The extensive presence of migrant labor from elsewhere in the Arab world helped and, on occasion, harmed its regional relationships. In the 1980s, for example, hundreds of thousands of Egyptians went to work in Iraq to fill vacancies left by young Iraqi workers conscripted to fight in the war with Iran. The presence of these workers caused political and economic problems for Baghdad when the war ended in 1988 and the Iraqi military demobilized, sending some 100,000 Iraqis back home in search of new jobs. Poor treatment of Egyptian workers remaining in Iraq was one factor in Cairo's calculation in 1990, when the Mubarak regime decided to join the military coalition ousting Iraq from Kuwait.

Foreign Assistance

Iraq's geostrategic significance and extensive international engagement has enhanced its capacity to garner a fair amount of foreign assistance over the years. As a general matter, foreign assistance is a prominent non-oil form of external rent, subject to some of the same dynamics. It takes many forms, from direct financial payments, subsidized loans, and agricultural credits to preferred trade relations, military aid, security cooperation, and technical training. Official foreign assistance to Iraq has been delivered both bilaterally and multilaterally, whether from large countries like the United States or, in a former era, the Soviet Union, or from regional powers like Egypt, Iran, Saudi Arabia, and Turkey. Regional organizations like the Arab League have also been conduits of foreign aid to Iraq, along with a host of other international organizations like the European Union and the Organization of the Islamic Conference. Finally, Iraq also has received assistance over the years from multilateral public international institutions like the World Bank and the International Monetary Fund.

The United States has been the largest aid donor to Iraq since invading the country in 2003. U.S. foreign aid is not simple charity in that it has always been designed to promote American interests in many forms, ranging from supporting strategic partners to preventing vulnerable countries from political or economic deterioration that might benefit U.S. adversaries. A humanitarian aspect is sometimes present but always in tandem with a geostrategic rationale, even loosely in the form of allowing the United States to play a global leadership role. American planners and political leaders have seen Iraq as an important regional actor and have sought to prevent Iraqi actions deemed detrimental to the United States, support its contributions to regional security, and assure its continued functioning in the global economy as a major energy provider. While the Bush-era aspiration to have Iraq serve as a model for regional democracy has given way to more modest ambitions, American economic assistance remains supportive of a cooperative and mutually beneficial relationship with Iraq.

Prospects

One finding evident in this chapter and inherent in its approach is the extent to which Iraqi political and economic life are bound together in all their complexity, even if this is not unique to the country. On the one hand, political choices have driven everything from developmental priorities to state revenue use and Iraq's involvement in international energy markets. Iraqi political leaders have made critical decisions shaping the economy, sometimes benefiting large numbers of citizens through land reform, infrastructure development, and educational opportunities, and at other times yielding disastrous outcomes in the form of political violence and its devastating impact on economic life. Britain and the United States, for their parts, had outsized political influence over economic choices during their dominating moments under the monarchy and again briefly after 2003. In all cases, politics shaped economics profoundly, if unsurprisingly, in its capacity to reach into society to shape how people lived. Political masters always have been present, but rarely have they obtained exactly what they have wanted from their economies.

On the other side of the ledger, as one would expect from the standpoint of political economy, Iraqi economic factors themselves have been deeply influential in the country's political life, both nationally and internationally. Not only has oil in particular mattered in its own right as a commodity, but Iraq's rich human and natural endowments have contributed to shaping its national and international political aspirations and engagements, for better or worse. If it were a more modestly endowed country with a smaller population and a differently oriented economy, its leaders' political choices and actions on all fronts would not be the same. Iraq's economy has fueled everything from its early domestic advances in education and social welfare to its authoritarianism, regional leadership aspirations, and bellicosity toward its neighbors. Iraqi economic dynamics are likely to assume an even fuller significance in the years ahead, as the country's population grows larger and, eventually, it begins to feel the potential effects of the energy transition away from fossil fuels.

The reality of complex, dynamic, and reciprocal interaction between political and economic life is affirmed by Iraq's experience in the past century. What this tells us, moreover, is that for Iraq to move forward and make progress as a country requires an integrated approach in multiple domains. Such progress demands both political reform and economic adjustment, along with all the vital elements of social development to support multiple transitions toward a better polity, economy, and society. The Iraqi economy and the needs of the Iraqi people cannot be met without a more stable, responsive, accountable political environment, such as one that might be possible in a healthy democracy of some kind. Iraqi leaders need resources to move the economy toward a better position for the country, equitably distributed and sustainable over time. All of this is a tall order, but Iraq's prospects are bound up in the larger endeavor.

Notes

1 Gilpin (1987), 4.
2 Cammett et al. (2015) offer the best contemporary account of MENA political economy.
3 World Bank (2021, 2020).
4 World Bank (2020).
5 World Bank, at https://data.worldbank.org/?locations=IQ-1A&name_desc=false.
6 This figure is for 2019; see the UN Conference on Trade and Development (UNCTAD), at https://unctad.org/system/files/information-document/SCD_IQ.pdf. More broadly, see UNCTAD, *State of Commodity Dependence 2021*.
7 UNCTAD, "Map of the State of Commodity Dependence."
8 World Economic Forum, "Which Economies Are Most Reliant on Oil," at www.weforum.org/agenda/2016/05/which-economies-are-most-reliant-on-oil/; and UNCTAD, "World Commodity Export Dependence, 2018–2019," at https://unctad.org/system/files/information-document/SCD_IQ.pdf.
9 *BP Statistical Review of World Energy*, 68th edition, 2019. On natural gas, see the press release, "Iraq: TotalEnergies Signs Major Agreements for the Sustainable Development of the Basra Region," September 6, 2021, at https://totalenergies.com/media/news/press-releases/iraq-totalenergies-signs-major-agreements-sustainable-development-basra.
10 Blair (September 2011).
11 Barker et al. (1979).

12 Ober (2002); NASA, "Sulfur Dioxide Spreads over Iraq," Earth Observatory, October 26, 2016, at https://earthobservatory.nasa.gov/images/88994/sulfur-dioxide-spreads-over-iraq.
13 Bernadaux (June 2021); "Iraq: Food Insecurity and Poverty by District as of 2005," UN Office for the Coordination of Humanitarian Affairs, February 2008.
14 For political reasons in the 1980s, Saudi Arabia began to grow wheat in Qassim province by tapping subterranean aquifers and using center-pivot irrigation, creating crop circles in the desert. State subsidies ended in the mid-2000s.
15 Kamrava and Babar (2011), 1.
16 World Bank, at https://databank.worldbank.org/source/population-estimates-and-projections.
17 World Bank, at https://databank.worldbank.org/source/population-estimates-and-projections.
18 Population Pyramid, at www.populationpyramid.net/iraq/2019.
19 Worldometer, at www.worldometers.info/world-population/iraq-population, based on UN Department of Economic and Social Affairs, *World Population Prospects 2019*.
20 United Nations, Department of Economic and Social Affairs, Population Division (2018), "World Urbanization Prospects: The 2018 Revision," at https://population.un.org/wup/DataQuery.
21 United Nations, Department of Economic and Social Affairs, Population Division (2019). "World Population Prospects 2019."
22 Calculated from www.worldometers.info/demographics/iraq-demographics.
23 Calculated from www.worldometers.info/demographics/iraq-demographics.
24 World Economic Forum, *Global Gender Gap Report 2020*, p. 191.
25 No recent, fully reliable census exists, though a Pew Foundation report from 2012 finds that 62% of Iraqis are Shi'i, and the *CIA World Factbook* estimates the Shi'i population to be 61–64%.
26 On Islam's political variability, see Ayoob and Lussier (2020). To appreciate the artificiality of the Sunni–Shi'a divide, see McHugo (2017) and Wehrey (2017). See also Haddad (2011) and Osman (2015).
27 See Amos (2010).
28 Pew Research Center (August 2012). The *CIA World Factbook* estimates a 75–80% Arab majority versus 15–20% Kurdish minority, but based on a decades-old government survey.
29 In a 2012 global survey, 25% of respondents self-identified as "just a Muslim," not Sunni or Shi'i. This percentage was especially large for Indonesia (56%), the country with the largest Muslim population in the world. See Pew Research Center (August 2012), 28.
30 Alnasrawi (1994).
31 Mufti (1996), 200.
32 Rivlin (2009), 134; Stansfield (2016), 98.
33 Hamilton (2013), 239–265.
34 See "Crude Oil Prices, 1861–2018," in *BP Statistical Review of World Energy*, 68th edition, 2019, 24.
35 "Crude Oil Prices, 1861–2018," in *BP Statistical Review of World Energy*, 68th edition, 2019, 16.
36 Notions of "energy independence" are rooted in realist geostrategic thinking about the imperative of state autonomy versus the neoliberal emphasis on the benefits of interdependence.

37 U.S. Energy Information Administration, *Background Reference: Iraq*, March 29, 2021, at www.eia.gov/international/content/analysis/countries_long/Iraq/iraq_bkgd.pdf.
38 Rivlin (2009), 142.
39 Irwin (July 2020).
40 Metz (1988).
41 Chaudhry (October 1994).
42 Alnasrawi (1994).
43 Allawi (2007), 117.
44 For an early postwar evaluation, before the full effects of the emerging insurgency, see United Nations/World Bank, "Joint Iraq Needs Assessment," October 2003.
45 Flibbert (2013).
46 Filkins (2009).
47 Filkins (January 2017).
48 Al-Ansari (2013).
49 Lucani (December 2011).
50 Ewaid (January 2020).
51 Bernadaux (June 2021).
52 *Nuts and Dried Fruits Statistical Yearbook.*
53 Reuters, "Iran Eyes Doubling Iraq Trade to $8 billion in 2010," February 21, 2010. www.reuters.com/article/us-iraq-trade-iran/iran-eyes-doubling-iraq-trade-to-8-billion-in-2010-idUSTRE61K1PE20100221.
54 Observatory of Economic Complexity, at https://oec.world/en/profile/country/irq?compareExports.
55 World Trade Organization, at www.wto.org.

CONCLUSIONS

For a place as storied and complex as Iraq, no concluding words can be remotely definitive. Looking at the country's changes over the past hundred years, however, does suggest some general observations that have value in a national moment of stock-taking and potential transition. These claims tap into and extend the book's thematic emphasis on the importance of power, institutions, and identity in Iraqi political life, highlighting five interrelated findings that are rooted in the Iraqi experience and have ongoing relevance. They include the country's vexing "middle-state dilemma," the challenging nature of oil as both a problem and a solution, the benefits and limitations of democracy in managing political change, the persistent legacies of Iraqi state formation and nation-building, and the reality of Iraq's continued existence into the twenty-first century despite all the ordeals it has endured.

The Middle-State Dilemma

First, the foregoing chapters reveal that Iraq faces what might be called a middle-state dilemma. A middle state is a country situated in the middle rankings of several significant international categories, such as relative power, wealth, geographic size, and population. It is not among the most powerful, nor the weakest; not one of the richest, nor the poorest; not particularly large by geography, nor small in size; not included with the most populous, nor the least populated. Under the right conditions, this position generates uncertainty as to what role such a state can and should play in relation to its neighbors and the world. The most important condition generating the dilemma is a rapid upward shift in a state's power or wealth, which unmoors the state and its leadership from a stable understanding of its relative position. Driven by changing circumstances, leaders start to believe the country might not be stuck in the middle and act accordingly, often overreaching in an effort at national self-assertion.

The dilemma is acute but highly variable, making it similar to parallel circumstances like the well-known security and development dilemmas that states sometimes confront. The security dilemma occurs when a state attempts to improve its security in the face of a perceived external threat, bringing about, in so doing, the very danger it was trying to avoid. It is a dilemma, and not simply a problem or challenge, because of the uncertainty of the initial situation, which has no obvious resolution and evokes legitimate concerns about underreacting or overreacting. The middle-state dilemma is a similar, structurally induced circumstance with no self-evident remedy. It is common in that most states do not top lists of the greatest or the least in any given area, yet many find themselves rising or falling in a world of unavoidable change. It therefore offers a useful, simple account of the ever-present structural pressures animating some countries in ways that are not otherwise obvious and can lead to surprising and unfortunate outcomes.[1]

For postcolonial and developing middle states like Iraq, these pressures can be especially hard to manage, and the best national response is not evident. The growth or diminishing of relative power that accompanies a newly independent country's changing circumstances assures that such states will jostle with others for position, be fearful of missed opportunities, and jealously guard their independence. If a middle state grows in power for any reason, including fortuitous economic gains, its leaders' ambitions also tend to expand in pursuit of a larger role. Without strong international balancing mechanisms, institutional ties, normative constraints, or cautious decision-making, this easily can lead to interstate conflict, which can devolve into war if ineffectively managed. The apocryphal Hawthorne claim, that "families are always rising and falling in America," is generally even more true for developing middle states, as shifts in relative power translate into changing roles, capabilities, and statuses in their regions and in a world that is new to them.

For its part, Iraq's middle-state dilemma first became prominent and consequential after its massive economic windfall of the 1970s, which triggered both a will and a capacity to revise the country's place in the regional order. The dilemma remains apparent today in many specific ways. Iraq is a middle-ranking power in the MENA region, hemmed in by stronger states but not toothless, having outmatched a majority of its six immediate neighbors at times in the recent past. It has immense oil reserves, though its economy is best categorized as middle or even lower income due to its many deficiencies and vulnerabilities. Geographically, Iraq ranks ninth in total land area out of 21 MENA territories, seeming larger than it is because several relatively small states are in close proximity in the Gulf or Levant. It has a substantial and exceptionally fast-growing population compared to most others in the Gulf, but it is dwarfed by nearby Egypt, Iran, and Turkey. Iraq's middle-state status is even evident in being one of the oldest permanently settled territories in the world, yet fairly new as an independent country.

The Iraqi dilemma matters because, throughout its contemporary history, it has struggled to define itself as a sovereign entity and had difficulty finding its place in the MENA region. The ambiguity of its relative power, wealth, weight, and position, with leadership just out of reach but no option to stay out of the limelight, has created uncertainty and a recurring temptation to overreach in its regional relations. No contemporary Iraqi leader has resisted the call to engage forcefully with other countries, typically as a political rival, military adversary, or aspiring hegemon more than as an equal partner or ally. Iraq's future is likely to include a revisiting of this tendency, as it recovers from the travails of its experience in the Saddam Hussein era and contemplates a new place in the MENA region. Should it lead, or should it follow? Iraq, as a middle state, is not in a strong position to do either, and a Goldilocks-like middle path does not seem readily available.

Directing analytical attention to Iraq's middle-state dilemma is a useful corrective to the tendency to overemphasize the individual decision-makers and personalities in Iraqi history, particularly figures like Saddam Hussein. Saddam no doubt was dramatically important. His choices—especially some of his major war-related blunders—mattered profoundly. But given Iraq's position in the region, one has to ask, counterfactually, whether other Iraqi leaders would have been tempted to follow similar paths, or will do so in the future. Focusing on power, rather than personality, is helpful in this regard, because it has room to highlight the state in addition to individual decision-makers. Middle states take actions driven by larger structural conditions that render those at the helm less central than they might seem. The lesson in the Iraqi case is to be attentive to these circumstances, and not only the political leaders grappling with them.

Oil as Problem and Solution

A second conclusion relates to Iraq's oil wealth, which is greatly beneficial yet noteworthy for the trouble it also makes possible, even to the point of incentivizing it. Iraq's expanding fortunes are hard to exaggerate. The more than 3000-fold rise in annual state revenues, which grew from $6 million in 1945 to $21.4 billion in 1978, was as dramatic as anything of its kind.[2] By comparison, American federal receipts from various sources only grew by a factor of about nine in this same period, rising from $45.2 billion in 1945 during the last year of the Second World War to $399.6 billion in 1978.[3] Even factoring in inflation, population growth, developmental needs, and rising expectations about government services, Iraq's revenue windfall was wholly transformative for the country, at least in potential. It is easy to underestimate Iraq's wealth because so much of it was lost, and wasted, for so long. With a still-incomplete energy transition toward renewables and nonfossil fuels, and the likelihood of persistent geopolitical tensions between the United States, the Europeans, Russia, and China in the coming decades, Iraqi oil is sure to remain an extraordinary asset for the country if Iraq remains whole and stable.

The actual impact of Iraqi oil is mixed, however, because for decades it has fueled both considerable economic growth and, more prominently, ongoing conflict. Since coming into its newfound wealth, Iraq has not had a significant length of time without serious conflict, either domestic or international, with oil deeply implicated in one way or another. The second half of its century-long national existence, starting in the 1970s and coinciding with the greatest period of its rising revenues, was more conflict-ridden, tumultuous, and difficult than the first half. Much of this period was marked by Saddam Hussein's rule and included the war with Iran in the 1980s, the invasion and removal from Kuwait in the 1990s, and the even more traumatic post-2003 period of U.S.-led invasion, occupation, insurgency, and civil war. Oil made all of these conflicts more likely by shoring up the regime politically, empowering it militarily, and facilitating its WMD provocations. While its aggressive actions had complex and multiple causes, it is noteworthy that Iraqi GDP was in the process of rocketing upward in 1980 (to $52.6 billion) and 1990 (to $180.4 billion) when Iraq launched its two most consequential wars in the Saddam era.[4] In so doing, it failed to improve Iraqi lives substantially by reversing potential social and developmental gains, most of which were limited or lost over the course of four decades.

This gloomy assessment aside, it is important to avoid the facile conclusion that oil itself, or any natural resource, is inherently blameworthy or a universal "curse." In fact, the Iraqi experience lends credence to the claim that oil is not intrinsically problematic, so much as an episodic enabler of aggressive state actions. Oil is a natural substance and devoid of agency, as noted in Chapter 5. It changes both what a state can do and what it might wish to do. Just as the possession of natural resources does not dictate particular developmental choices, which are a product of more complex political and economic processes, it does not generate automatic security outcomes like bellicose international behavior. The flawed choices and missteps associated with having oil are a political function of either poor decision-making or irresistible structural incentives like Iraq's own middle-state dilemma. This was especially the case once Iraq rid itself of colonial and neocolonial control over its resources.

Democracy, Better Than the Alternatives

While resource abundance can worsen the impact of flawed leadership and state pathologies like corruption or despotism, such troubles are mitigated by good governance and responsive, accountable political institutions. This is consistent with a third finding evident in the Iraqi experience, which relates to the benefits, and the potential limitations, of democratic governance. No doubt, Iraq has suffered under decades of increasingly severe authoritarianism, single-party rule, autocracy, and sectarianism, both before and after the 1958 revolution. Yet, its present fledgling democracy—to the extent it can be categorized as such—has a better set of mechanisms to avoid the problems associated with these political forms, both domestically and internationally.

The domestic benefits of democracy for Iraq need little elaboration, despite all the shortcomings of a governance system that guarantees very little by way of optimal human development. Internationally, analysts disagree as to whether a democratic Iraq might be less inclined toward rapid, reckless actions in the security domain. While it might potentially produce a more sensible and cautious foreign policy, especially vis-à-vis other democracies, an Iraqi democracy would be subject to all the same pressures, temptations, and obligations as any other country. A democratic United States, after all, invaded and occupied Iraq itself, with no available military, institutional, or normative constraint on its decision to go to war in 2003. That said, authoritarian Iraq under Saddam, with a coup-proofed regime that only excelled at protecting itself from domestic adversaries, made choices that rendered it more vulnerable to such actions. Democratic governance would foreclose at least one path to destructive foreign policy decision-making in the errant actions of a self-interested authoritarian leader.

How this unfolds in a post–Arab Spring environment in the Middle East, still grappling with popular demands for political and economic change, will have a significant impact on Iraq itself. For better or worse, Iraqi governance prospects are tied to the outcomes in its neighbors. It is hard to imagine Iraqi democracy thriving if Syria reverts to post–civil war authoritarianism, Turkey moves further toward autocracy, Iran remains trapped between contending impulses and factions, and Saudi Arabia cannot constrain the absolutism of its monarchy. If the Arab Spring taught one lesson, it is that political, historical, and cultural connections remain powerful enough in the MENA region to cross borders and affect behaviors. The rapid wave of protests that swept the region, starting in Tunisia in December 2010, had thematic commonalities in popular demands for dignity, accountability, and economic reform, even if variations in these common themes—and dramatically different state responses—led to a wide variety of eventual, mostly disappointing outcomes.[5] Iraq need not go the way of its neighbors, but defying regional and even global trends would be a harder and more unlikely path to follow.

Critics of Iraq's post-2003 political system note its many shortcomings and promote governance alternatives, such as a radically decentralized state or a partition into autonomous Sunni, Shi'i, and Kurdish entities. Partition is politically untenable, however, because it has little support outside Kurdistan, and it is fully impractical due to the interspersal of ethnic and sectarian populations in many locales, including Baghdad. Such an approach also would exacerbate the oil revenue conundrum, since most of Iraq's oil is located in either the Kurdish north or the Shi'i-majority southeast, and sharing it across more stringently drawn borders would be especially difficult. Partition might even lead to an internationalizing of the country's domestic tensions, with external patrons like Iran or Saudi Arabia lining up behind smaller client states, or Turkey challenging the very existence of Kurdistan. Democratic governance of a single, unified state with thoughtfully considered institutions and, potentially, a federal structure remains a better choice, or perhaps the least worst option among the alternatives.

Not that Iraq's democratic prospects are entirely encouraging. The country faces a raft of ongoing political and economic challenges, including the continued use of ethnosectarian quotas to share power among elites, which has led to entrenched privilege, worsened corruption, and the alienation of large numbers of regular Iraqis. Democratic participation in elections has declined to record lows. This has been the case since the major upheaval that began with the *Tishreen* protests of October 2019 and has continued intermittently ever since. Iraq's youthful demographics and the rise of a new generation not directly experienced with the Saddamist past, or intimidated by its violence, presents both an opportunity and a risk. Young Iraqis will demand more of their leaders and their country, and they are unlikely to be satisfied with the dismal outcomes their parents suffered in the past.

This is where democracy itself offers hope, because it is not just a way to share power and authority but potentially a mechanism for distributing responsibility for solving problems and contending with challenges. If, on the one hand, enough Iraqis remain engaged in a process that allows them to participate in decision-making and address their own problems, they may be induced to continue following democratic rules and, over time, abiding by democratic norms. If, on the other hand, participation in the electoral process continues to drop out of a sense that the system simply institutionalizes elite privilege, as may be happening, Iraq's prospects grow darker. Worse still, if democratic processes allow large numbers of people to undermine the system by institutionalizing antidemocratic norms and behaviors, the possibilities become more limited.

Democratic governance is compatible with any institutional history or cultural milieu, as evidenced by the successful transitions in a significant number of countries worldwide with prior authoritarian governance. Iraqi democracy need not be as liberal and individualistic, for example, as its American counterpart. But as the U.S. case shows, democracy itself is fragile, slow to self-correct, subject to undermining by internal and external antisystem parties, and limited in its capacity to take on powerfully entrenched interests. And as Iraq's long and difficult experience demonstrates, the past shapes present circumstances in ways that cannot so easily be erased, challenging the viability of political reform.

Path Dependence in State Formation and Nation-Building

Even if democratic governance takes root in Iraq, a fourth finding is a sober appreciation of the impact of prior choices and conditions, which have been integral aspects of the country's founding decades and will continue to be influential for the foreseeable future. Iraq's experience is testimony to the power of path dependence, where choices made in one context linger into the future, often with unhelpful long-term effects that are hard to reverse, even if the circumstances change. Several unfortunate tendencies in modern Iraqi political history are deeply rooted and have path-dependent qualities, including the politicization of the military in the 1930s, the deployment of patronage politics since the advent of the monarchy, the regular resort to violence in politics that preceded even the establishment of independent Iraq, the longstanding dismal treatment of the Kurds, and the early activation and mobilization of sectarianism.

These examples of the weight of history in Iraq illustrate the enduring impact of macrohistorical processes like state formation and nation-building. In the Iraqi case, the military was given an internal, political mission rather than an external security orientation very early on, using overwhelming force to target domestic ethnic uprisings rather than foreign threats. Patronage politics and the rise of a parallel, shadow state derived from institutional weakness and leader preferences for maintaining power through social networks. Violence became part of political life even before Iraq had formal independence and sovereignty. Kurdish nationalism was an inevitable response to the establishment of an Iraqi state partly in territory home to a large, self-aware, and distinctive ethnonationalist group. Sectarianism became a normal mode of action in the early years of state weakness and again decades later when Iraqis fell back on more fundamental identities in the absence of any other means of self-protection.

What can be done? Militaries can be retrained and professionalized, corrupt forms of patronage and illicit violence can be made illegal and prosecuted under the law, Kurdish distinctiveness can be acknowledged and accommodated, and sectarian identities can be rendered less salient over time. Doing all of this at once, however, is more than difficult. While prioritizing the most important might seem tenable—eliminating state violence before corruption, for example—they all tend to go hand in hand, so Iraq needs to make progress on multiple fronts simultaneously. It needs a triple transition to move toward a rebuilt state, improved democratic governance with the protection of minority rights, and a secure regional environment. This means healthy institutions, accountable politics, and diminished international threats. Achieving all this at once has eluded most of the world, but setting a course in this direction is not too much to ask.

Surprising Unity Despite Tension and Fragmentation

Iraq's status as an unfinished state and a divided nation in a complex regional environment belies the final finding: despite its divisions and shortcomings and challenges, the country continues to hold together with surprising unity. For reasons that emanate from both internal and external sources, its domestic tensions have not led to a formal partition or permanent collapse of the country. Inside Iraq, there are enough social and political commonalities, along with shared interests, for the country to remain whole if not entirely united for the foreseeable future. The 2014 conquest of large pieces of Iraqi territory by the Islamic State did not bode well for this remaining so, but the Iraqi government's capacity to regain control, with international assistance, makes it more likely that Iraq will hold together. A range of domestic scenarios, from uncontrolled political unrest, to intensified communal tensions, to the rise of a powerful separatist impulse from the Kurdish north, for example, might change this equation. But in the meantime, Iraq is still one.

Other important reasons for Iraq's continued viability as a national state come from outside its borders, both regionally and globally. In the MENA region itself, Iraq remains part of the Arab world and partner with nearly two dozen other Arab states, which recognize its sovereignty and interact with it on that basis. Its immediate Arab and non-Arab neighbors, especially Turkey, Jordan, Saudi Arabia, and to a large extent Iran, have little to no interest in seeing Iraq fragment into multiple smaller states. None would welcome, and some would aggressively resist efforts to carve out, for example, an independent Kurdish national state in northern Iraq, or a Shi'i-dominated state in the south. The Islamic State's failure to construct a new political entity across current regional borders makes a second attempt less likely to succeed in redrawing the lines on the map. If Iraq at its weakest did not fall apart, its prospects in the immediate future are encouraging.

In an even broader sense, the Middle East puzzle is held together by the alignment of its pieces and the need for state entities to occupy spaces that otherwise would require alternative governance arrangements. The MENA states do not generally welcome dismembering Iraq or taking large parts for themselves, because this would open a Pandora's box of Middle Eastern territorial revisionism and obligate them to incorporate people and territory into their own national spaces, with all the challenges that would bring. This is not to say that regional rivals would not welcome small additions to their territory, favorable resolutions of border disputes with Iraq, privileged access to Iraqi oil and gas reserves, or a weakened Iraqi capacity to resist them. But this is a far cry from a revisionist and even revolutionary redrawing of the regional map or an active initiative to end Iraq as a national entity in the heart of the Middle East.

In addition to national and regional pressures supporting Iraq's continued unity, the global normative privileging of a world of national states makes it less likely that the international community would promote a division or partition of Iraq to end its independent existence. In fact, the international order, as constructed by the most powerful countries after the Second World War, was built on the separate and sovereign independence of individual states, as were the regional orders—even the Arab League was established in March 1945 as a club of states more than an instrument of state unification. Admittedly, norms of sovereignty are under growing stress and challenge, particularly from countervailing international human rights norms, which reject the acceptability of unconstrained state authority over citizens. But the reality of normative contention does not mandate, and has not precipitated, the wholesale disassembling of state violators of human rights. Even if such an option were considered, Iraq's greatest moment of vulnerability in this regard has passed. Partition pressure from abroad would require another calamitous international event, such as a major interstate war or a revolutionary change in a neighbor, neither of which is likely in the near term.

This is not to say that Iraq will not change, potentially for the better. Unending if uneven and erratic change is a permanent feature of the international system and all its constituent units. Several thousand years of Iraqi existence have reflected a larger human tendency toward dynamism, which is probably the only safe prediction one can make. In certain ways, the country is bigger, wealthier, and more coherently unified today than ever. Its first century has passed. Its more than 40 million people—a majority of them under age 25—will have a say over what comes next, along with a wish and an obligation to make the future as bright as possible.

Notes

1 See Jervis (1978); Flibbert (2003–2004).
2 Calculated from Rivlin (2009), 134, and Stansfield (2016), 98.
3 Office of Management and Budget, Historical Tables, Table 1.1, "Summary of Receipts, Outlays, and Surpluses or Deficits: 1789–2027," at www.whitehouse.gov/omb/budget/historical-tables.
4 See the World Bank data, at https://data.worldbank.org/indicator/NY.GDP.MKTP.CD?locations=IQ.
5 See Lynch et al. (2022).

BIBLIOGRAPHY

Abdul-Zahra, Qassim, and Bassem Mroue. "Protesters Storm Bahraini Embassy in Iraqi Capital Baghdad," Associated Press, June 27, 2019.
Aburish, Saïd K. *Saddam Hussein: The Politics of Revenge.* London: Bloomsbury, 2000.
Ahmad, Muhammad Idrees. *The Road to Iraq: The Making of a Neoconservative War.* Edinburgh: Edinburgh University Press, 2014.
Allawi, Ali A. *The Occupation of Iraq: Winning the War, Losing the Peace.* New Haven, CT: Yale University Press, 2007.
Allawi, Ali A. *Faisal I of Iraq.* New Haven, CT: Yale University Press, 2014.
Alnasrawi, Abbas. *The Economy of Iraq: Oil, Wars, Destruction of Development and Prospects, 1950–2010.* Westport, CT: Greenwood Press, 1994.
Amos, Deborah. *Eclipse of the Sunnis: Power, Exile, and Upheaval in the Middle East.* New York: PublicAffairs, 2010.
Anderson, Lisa. "Absolutism and the Resilience of Monarchy in the Middle East." *Political Science Quarterly* 106, no. 1 (Spring 1991): 1–15.
al-Ansari, Nadhir A. "Management of Water Resources in Iraq: Perspectives and Prognoses." *Engineering* 5 (2013): 667–684.
Ayoob, Mohammed, and Danielle Nicole Lussier. *The Many Faces of Political Islam: Religion and Politics in Muslim Societies.* 2nd edition. Ann Arbor: University of Michigan Press, 2020.
Ayubi, Nazih N. *Over-stating the Arab State: Politics and Society in the Middle East.* London: I. B. Tauris, 1995.
Baer, Robert. *See No Evil.* New York: Three Rivers Press, 2002.
Baker, III, James A., and Lee H. Hamilton. *The Iraq Study Group Report: The Way Forward—A New Approach.* New York: Vintage Books, 2006.
Baldwin, David. *Power and International Relations: A Conceptual Approach.* Princeton, NJ: Princeton University Press, 2016.
Baram, Amatzia. *Culture, History and Ideology in the Formation of Baʻthist Iraq, 1968–89.* New York: St. Martin's Press, 1991.
Baram, Amatzia. *Saddam Husayn and Islam, 1968–2003: Baʻathi Iraq from Secularism to Faith.* Washington, DC: Woodrow Wilson Center Press; Baltimore, MD: Johns Hopkins University Press, 2014.

Baram, Amatzia, Achim Rohde, and Ronen Zeidel, eds. *Iraq between Occupations: Perspectives from 1920 to the Present.* New York: Palgrave Macmillan, 2010.

Barker, James M., D. E. Cochran, and Robert Semrad. "Economic Geology of the Mishraq Native Sulfur Deposit, Northern Iraq." *Economic Geology* 74, no. 2 (April 1979): 484–495.

Barzani, Masoud. "Why It's Time for Kurdish Independence." *Foreign Policy*, June 15, 2017.

Bashkin, Orit. *The Other Iraq: Pluralism and Culture in Hashemite Iraq.* Stanford, CA: Stanford University Press, 2009.

Bashkin, Orit. *New Babylonians: A History of Jews in Modern Iraq.* Stanford, CA: Stanford University Press, 2012.

Batatu, Hanna. *The Old Social Classes and the Revolutionary Movements of Iraq: A Study of Iraq's Old Landed and Commercial Classes and of Its Communists, Ba'thists and Free Officers.* Princeton, NJ: Princeton University Press, 1978.

Batatu, Hanna. "The Old Social Classes Revisited," in Robert A. Fernea and William Roger Louis, eds., *The Iraqi Revolution of 1958: The Old Social Classes Revisited.* London: I. B. Tauris, 1991, 211–222.

Battle, Joyce. "Shaking Hands with Saddam Hussein: The U.S. Tilts toward Iraq, 1980–1984." *National Security Archive Electronic Briefing Book No. 82* (February 25, 2003).

Bengio, Ofra. *Saddam's Word: Political Discourse in Iraq.* New York: Oxford University Press, 1998.

Benjamen, Alda. *Assyrians in Modern Iraq: Negotiating Political and Cultural Space.* New York: Cambridge University Press, 2022.

Bernadaux, Chloé. "Cultivating Cronyism: The Collapse of Agriculture in Post-War Iraq and Syria." *Sada Journal*, June 24, 2021.

Blair, David. "U.S. Finds 'World-Class' Phosphate in Iraq." *Financial Times*, September 7, 2011.

Blaydes, Lisa. *State of Repression: Iraq under Saddam Hussein.* Princeton, NJ: Princeton University Press, 2018.

Bozo, Frédéric. *A History of the Iraq Crisis: France, the United States, and Iraq, 1991–2003.* Trans. Susan Emanuel. Washington, DC: Woodrow Wilson Center Press; New York: Columbia University Press, 2016.

Brand, Laurie A. *Official Stories: Politics and National Narratives in Egypt and Algeria.* Stanford, CA: Stanford University Press, 2014.

Braut-Hegghammer, Målfrid. *Unclear Physics: Why Iraq and Libya Failed to Build Nuclear Weapons.* Ithaca, NY: Cornell University Press, 2016.

Calabrese, John. "China–Iraq Relations Poised for a 'Quantum Leap'?" Middle East Institute, October 8, 2019.

Callaghy, Thomas M. *The State–Society Struggle: Zaire in Comparative Perspective.* New York: Columbia University Press, 1984.

Cammett, Melani, Ishac Diwan, Alan Richards, and John Waterbury. *A Political Economy of the Middle East.* 4th edition. Boulder, CO: Westview, 2015.

Carney, Stephen A. *Allied Participation in Operation Iraqi Freedom.* Washington, DC: U.S. Army, Center of Military History, 2011.

Chandrasekaran, Rajiv. *Imperial Life in the Emerald City: Inside Iraq's Green Zone.* New York: Random House/Vintage Books, 2006.

Chatham House. "Iraqi Foreign Policy: Actors and Processes." Middle East and North Africa Programme Workshop Summary, Chatham House, Washington, DC, November 26–27, 2012.

Chaudhry, Kiren Aziz. "Economic Liberalization and the Lineages of the Rentier State." *Comparative Politics* 27, no. 1 (October 1994): 1–25.

Cleveland, William L., and Martin Bunton. *A History of the Modern Middle East.* 5th edition. Boulder, CO: Westview, 2013.

Cockburn, Andrew, and Patrick Cockburn. *Saddam Hussein: An American Obsession*. London: Verso, 2002.
Cohen, Avner. *Israel and the Bomb*. New York: Columbia University Press, 1999.
Cole, Juan. "Iraq in 1939: British Alliance or Nationalist Neutrality toward the Axis." *Britain and the World* 5, no. 2 (2012): 204–222.
Cordesman, Anthony H., and Ahmed S. Hashim. *Iraq: Sanctions and Beyond*. Boulder, CO: Westview, 1997.
Coughlin, Con. *Saddam: King of Terror*. New York: HarperCollins, 2002.
Cramer, Jane K., and A. Trevor Thrall, eds. *Why Did the United States Invade Iraq?* New York: Routledge, 2011.
"Crude Oil Prices, 1861–2018," in *BP Statistical Review of World Energy*. 68th edition, 2019.
Cusimano, Joseph J. "Analysis of Iran–Iraq Bilateral Border Treaties." *Case Western Reserve Journal of International Law* 24, no. 89 (1992): 89–113.
Dahl, Erik J. "Naval Innovation: From Coal to Oil." *Joint Forces Quarterly* (Winter 2000–2001): 50–56.
Dann, Uriel. *Iraq under Qassem: A Political History, 1958–1963*. New York: Praeger, 1969.
Davis, Eric. *Memories of State: Politics, History, and Collective Identity in Modern Iraq*. Berkeley: University of California Press, 2005.
Dawisha, Adeed. *Iraq: A Political History*. Princeton, NJ: Princeton University Press, 2009.
Dodge, Toby. *Inventing Iraq: The Failure of Nation Building and a History Denied*. New York: Columbia University Press, 2003.
Dodge, Toby. *Iraq: From War to a New Authoritarianism*. London: International Institute for Strategic Studies; New York: Routledge, 2012.
Dodge, Toby, and Steven Simon, eds. *Iraq at the Crossroads: State and Society in the Shadow of Regime Change*. Adelphi Paper 354. London: IISS/Oxford University Press, 2003.
Dougherty, Beth K., and Edmund Ghareeb. *Historical Dictionary of Iraq*. 2nd edition. Lanham, MD: Scarecrow Press, 2013.
Draper, Robert. *To Start a War: How the Bush Administration Took America into Iraq*. New York: Penguin Press, 2020.
Duelfer, Charles. *Comprehensive Report of the Special Advisor to the DCI on Iraq's WMD, with Addendums*. Washington, DC: Central Intelligence Agency, 2005.
Duelfer, Charles. *Hide and Seek: The Search for Truth in Iraq*. New York: PublicAffairs, 2009.
Duelfer, Charles. "In Iraq, Done in by the Lewinsky Affair." *Washington Post*, February 24, 2012.
Dunne, Tim, Milja Kurki, and Steve Smith. *International Relations Theories: Discipline and Diversity*. 5th edition. New York: Oxford University Press, 2021.
Durkheim, Emile. *The Rules of Sociological Method*. Ed. George Catlin, trans. Sarah A. Solovay and John H. Mueller. New York: Free Press, [1895] 1964.
Enabling Peace in Iraq Center (EPIC). "The Long Game: Iraq's 'Tishreen' Movement and the Struggle for Reform." October 2021.
Ewaid, Salam Hussein, Salwan Ali Abed, and Nadhir al-Ansari. "Assessment of Main Cereal Crop Trade Impacts on Water and Land Security in Iraq." *Agronomy* 10, no. 1 (January 2020): 1–15.
Farouk-Sluglett, Marion, and Peter Sluglett. *Iraq since 1958: From Revolution to Dictatorship*. London: I. B. Tauris, 2001.
Fernea, Robert A., and Wm. Roger Louis, eds. *The Iraqi Revolution of 1958: The Old Social Classes Revisited*. London: I. B. Tauris, 1991.
Filkins, Dexter. *The Forever War*. New York: Random House/Vintage Books, 2008.
Filkins, Dexter. "Before the Flood: A Failing Dam Threatens Millions of Iraqis." *New Yorker* 92, no. 43 (January 2017): 22–28.

Flibbert, Andrew. "Iraq's Invasion of Kuwait: A Causal Analysis." Unpublished m.s., December 1990.
Flibbert, Andrew. "After Saddam: Regional Insecurity, Weapons of Mass Destruction, and Proliferation Pressures in Postwar Iraq." *Political Science Quarterly* 118, no. 4 (Winter 2003–2004): 547–567.
Flibbert, Andrew. "The Road to Baghdad: Ideas and Intellectuals in Explanations of the Iraq War." *Security Studies* 15, no. 2 (April–June 2006): 310–352.
Flibbert, Andrew. "The Consequences of Forced State Failure in Iraq." *Political Science Quarterly* 128, no.1 (Spring 2013): 67–95.
Fordham, Alice. "Iraq Settles Airline Dispute with Kuwait Ahead of Arab Summit." *Washington Post*, March 14, 2021.
Franks, Tommy. *American Soldier*. New York: Regan Books, 2004.
Gause III, F. Gregory. "The Illogic of Dual Containment." *Foreign Affairs* 73, no. 2 (March/April 1994): 56–66.
Gaventa, John. *Power and Powerlessness: Quiescence and Rebellion in an Appalachian Valley*. Urbana: University of Illinois Press, 1982.
Gilpin, Robert. *The Political Economy of International Relations*. Princeton, NJ: Princeton University Press, 1987.
Gordon, Joy. *Invisible War: The United States and the Iraq Sanctions*. Cambridge, MA: Harvard University Press, 2012.
Gordon, Michael R. "U.S. Air Raids in '02 Prepared for War in Iraq." *New York Times*, July 20, 2003, A1.
Gordon, Michael R., and General Bernard E. Trainor. *The Endgame: The Inside Story of the Struggle for Iraq, from George W. Bush to Barack Obama*. New York: Vintage Books, 2012.
Graham-Brown, Sarah. *Sanctioning Saddam: The Politics of Intervention in Iraq*. London: I. B. Tauris, 1999.
Gunter, Michael. "The KDP–PUK Conflict in Northern Iraq." *Middle East Journal* 50, no. 2 (Spring 1996): 224–241.
Haddad, Fanar. *Sectarianism in Iraq: Antagonistic Visions of Unity*. New York: Columbia University Press, 2011.
Hahn, Peter L. *Missions Accomplished? The United States and Iraq since World War I*. New York: Oxford University Press, 2012.
Hallenberg, Jan, and Håkan Karlsson, eds. *The Iraq War: European Perspectives on Politics, Strategy and Operations*. London: Routledge, 2005.
Hamilton, James D. "Historical Oil Shocks," in Randall E. Parker and Robert Whaples, eds., *Routledge Handbook of Major Events in Economic History*. New York: Routledge, 2013, 239–265.
Hashim, Ahmed S. *The Caliphate at War: Operational Realities and Innovations of the Islamic State*. New York: Oxford University Press, 2018.
Helms, Christine Moss. *Iraq: Eastern Flank of the Arab World*. Washington, DC: Brookings, 1984.
Herb, Michael. *All in the Family: Absolutism, Revolution, and Democracy in Middle Eastern Monarchies*. Albany: State University of New York Press, 1999.
Herbst, Jeffrey. *States and Power in Africa: Comparative Lessons in Authority and Control*. Princeton, NJ: Princeton University Press, 2000.
Herring, Eric, and Glen Rangwala. *Iraq in Fragments: The Occupation and Its Legacy*. Ithaca, NY: Cornell University Press, 2006.
Hiltermann, Joost R. *A Poisonous Affair: America, Iraq, and the Gassing of Halabja*. New York: Cambridge University Press, 2007.
Hinnebusch, Raymond. "Political Parties in MENA: Their Functions and Development." *British Journal of Middle East Studies* 44, no. 2 (2017): 159–175.

Huber, R. *Empire Ottoman: Division Administrative*. [S.I.: s.n., 1899]. Map. www.loc.gov/item/2007633930/.
Ibrahim, Arwa. "Iraqi Militia Attack on UAE 'a Message from Iran.'" *Al-Jazeera*, February 4, 2022.
Independent High Electoral Commission (IHEC). *al-mufawadiya al-uliya al-mustaqila lil-intikhabat*. www.ihec.iq.
International Nut and Dried Fruit Council (INC). *Nuts and Dried Fruits Statistical Yearbook 2020–2021*. Reus: INC, 53.
Irwin, Douglas A. "The Rise and Fall of Import Substitution." Working Paper 20-10, Peterson Institute for International Economics, July 2020.
Ismael, Tareq Y. *The Rise and Fall of the Communist Party of Iraq*. New York: Cambridge University Press, 2008.
Ismael, Tareq Y., and Jacqueline S. Ismael. *Iraq in the Twenty-First Century: Regime Change and the Making of a Failed State*. New York: Routledge, 2015.
al-Istrabadi, Feisal Amin. "Reviving Constitutionalism in Iraq: Key Provisions of the Transitional Administrative Law." *New York Law School Law Review* (2005–2006): 269–302.
Jackson, Ashley. *Persian Gulf Command: A History of the Second World War in Iran and Iraq*. New Haven, CT: Yale University Press, 2018.
Jervis, Robert. "Cooperation Under the Security Dilemma." *World Politics* 30 (January 1978): 186–214.
Kamrava, Mehran, ed. *Fragile Politics: Weak States in the Greater Middle East*. Oxford: Oxford University Press, 2016.
Kamrava, Mehran. *Inside the Arab State*. Oxford: Oxford University Press, 2018.
Kamrava, Mehran, and Zahra Babar. "Migrant Labor in the Persian Gulf: Comparative and Interdisciplinary Perspectives," in *Migrant Labor in the Gulf: Working Group Summary Report #2*. Qatar: Center for International and Regional Studies, Georgetown School of Foreign Service, 2011, 1–2.
Kandil, Hazem. *Soldiers, Spies, and Statesmen: Egypt's Road to Revolt*. New York: Verso, 2012.
Karsh, Efraim, and Inari Rautsi. *Saddam Hussein: A Political Biography*. New York: Free Press, 1991.
Kerr, Malcolm. *The Arab Cold War: Gamal 'Abd al-Nasir and His Rivals, 1958–1970*. 3rd edition. Oxford: Oxford University Press, 1971.
Khadduri, Majid. "The Coup d'Etat of 1936: A Study of Iraqi Politics." *Middle East Journal* 2, no. 3 (July 1948): 270–292.
Khadduri, Majid. *Independent Iraq, 1932–1958*. 2nd edition. London: Oxford University Press, 1960.
Khadduri, Majid. *Republican 'Iraq: A Study in 'Iraqi Politics since the Revolution of 1958*. London: Oxford University Press, 1969.
Khadduri, Majid. *Socialist Iraq: A Study in Iraqi Politics since 1968*. Washington, DC: The Middle East Institute, 1978.
al-Khalidi, Ashraf, Sophia Hoffmann, and Victor Tanner. "Iraqi Refugees in the Syrian Arab Republic: A Field-Based Snapshot." Occasional Paper, The Brookings Institutions–University of Bern, Project on Internal Displacement, June 2007.
al-Khalil, Samir (aka Kanan Makiya). *Republic of Fear: The Inside Story of Saddam's Iraq*. New York: Pantheon, 1989.
Khoury, Dina Rizk. *Iraq in Wartime: Soldiering, Martyrdom, and Remembrance*. New York: Cambridge University Press, 2013.
Khoury, Philip S., and Joseph Kostiner, eds. *Tribes and State Formation in the Middle East*. Berkeley: University of California Press, 1990.

Lawson, Fred H. "The Resurgence of the Arab Cold War." *Review of Middle East Studies* 49, no. 2 (August 2015): 163–172.

Lessware, Jonathan, and Zaynab Khojji. "Obituary, The Last Princess of Iraq." *Arab News*, May 11, 2020.

Longrigg, Stephen Hemsley. *'Iraq, 1900 to 1950: A Political, Social, and Economic History*. London: Oxford University Press, 1953.

Louis, William Roger. "The British and the Origins of the Iraqi Revolution," in Robert A. Fernea and William Roger Louis, eds., *The Iraqi Revolution of 1958: The Old Social Classes Revisited*. London: I. B. Tauris, 1991, 31–61.

Lucani, Paolo. *Iraq: Agriculture Sector Note*. Food and Agriculture Organization/World Bank Cooperative Programme, Report No. 4 (December 2011).

Lukes, Steven. *Power: A Radical View*, 3rd edition. London: Palgrave Macmillan, 2021.

Lynch, Marc, Jillian Schwedler, and Sean Yom, eds. *The Political Science of the Middle East: Theory and Research since the Arab Uprisings*. New York: Oxford University Press, 2022.

MacDonald, Michael. *Overreach: Delusions of Regime Change in Iraq*. Cambridge, MA: Harvard University Press, 2014.

MacDonnell, Joseph F. *Jesuits by the Tigris: Men for Others in Baghdad*. Boston, MA: Jesuit Mission Press, 1994.

Mahoney, James. "Path Dependence in Historical Sociology." *Theory and Society* 29, no. 4 (August 2000): 507–548.

Makiya, Kanan. *The Monument: Art and Vulgarity in Saddam Hussein's Iraq*. London: I. B. Taurus, 1991. New edition 2004.

Malkasian, Carter. *Illusions of Victory: The Anbar Awakening and the Rise of the Islamic State*. New York: Oxford University Press, 2017.

Mansour, Renad, and Victoria Stewart-Jolley. "Explaining Iraq's Election Results." Chatham House, October 22, 2021.

al-Marashi, Ibrahim, and Sammy Salama. *Iraq's Armed Forces: An Analytical History*. London: Routledge, 2008.

Marcus, Jonathan. "China Helps Iraq Military Enter Drone Era." *BBC News*, October 12, 2015.

Marr, Phebe, with Ibrahim al-Marashi. *The Modern History of Iraq*. 4th edition. Boulder, CO: Westview Press, 2017.

Martin, David. "Plans for Iraq Attack Began on 9/11." CBS News, September 4, 2002, in Micah L. Sifry and Christopher Cerf, eds., *The Iraq War Reader: History, Documents, Opinions*. New York: Simon & Schuster, 2003.

Matsunaga, Hideki. "The Reconstruction of Iraq after 2003: Learning from Its Successes and Failures." MENA Development Report. Washington, DC: World Bank, 2019.

Mazaheri, Nimah. "Iraq and the Domestic Political Effects of Economic Sanctions." *Middle East Journal* 64, no. 2 (Spring 2010): 253–268.

Mazarr, Michael J. *Leap of Faith: Hubris, Negligence, and America's Greatest Foreign Policy Tragedy*. New York: PublicAffairs, 2019.

McAdam, Doug, Sidney Tarrow, and Charles Tilly. *Dynamics of Contention*. New York: Cambridge University Press, 2001.

McCants, Will. *The ISIS Apocalypse: The History, Strategy, and Doomsday Vision of the Islamic State*. New York: St. Martin's, 2015.

McDowall, David. *A Modern History of the Kurds*. Revised edition. London: I. B. Tauris, 2004.

McHugo, John. *A Concise History of Sunnis & Shi'is*. London: Saqi Books, 2017.

Metz, Helen Chapin, ed. *Iraq: A Country Study*. Washington: GPO for the Library of Congress, 1988.

Migdal, Joel S. *Strong Societies and Weak States: State–Society Relations and State Capabilities in the Third World*. Princeton, NJ: Princeton University Press, 1988.

Mofid, Kamran. "Economic Reconstruction of Iraq: Financing the Peace." *Third World Quarterly* 12, no. 1 (January 1990): 48–61.

Mufti, Malik. *Sovereign Creations: Pan-Arabism and Political Order in Syria and Iraq*. Ithaca, NY: Cornell University Press, 1996.

Murray, Williamson, and Robert H. Scales, Jr. *The Iraq War: A Military History*. Cambridge, MA: Belknap, 2003.

Murray, Williamson, and Kevin M. Woods. *The Iran–Iraq War: A Military and Strategic History*. New York: Cambridge University Press, 2014.

Nakash, Yitzhak. *The Shi'is of Iraq*. Revised edition. Princeton, NJ: Princeton University Press, 2003.

National Commission on Terrorist Attacks. *The 9/11 Commission Report*. New York: W. W. Norton, 2004.

Nixon, John. *Debriefing the President: The Interrogation of Saddam Hussein*. New York: Blue Rider Press, 2016.

North, Douglas. *Institutions, Institutional Change and Economic Performance*. New York: Cambridge University Press, 1990.

Ober, Joyce A. "Materials Flow of Sulfur." Open-File Report 02-298. Reston, VA: U.S. Geological Survey, 2002.

Osman, Khalil F. *Sectarianism in Iraq: The Making of State and Nation since 1920*. New York: Routledge, 2015.

Penrose, Edith, and E. F. Penrose. *Iraq: International Relations and National Development*. London: Ernest Benn, 1978.

Pew Research Center. "The World's Muslims: Unity and Diversity." Pew Forum on Religion and Public Life, August 9, 2012.

Pfiffner, James P. "U.S. Blunders in Iraq: De-Baathification and Disbanding the Army." *Intelligence and National Security* 25, no. 1 (February 2010): 76–85.

Pfiffner, James P., and Mark Phythian, eds. *Intelligence and National Security Policymaking on Iraq: British and American Perspectives*. College Station: Texas A&M University Press, 2008.

Pincus, Walter. "Ex-Iraqi Official Unveiled as Spy, Former Envoy Worked with French, CIA." *Washington Post*, March 23, 2006.

Polk, William R. *Understanding Iraq*. New York: HarperCollins, 2005.

Przeworski, Adam. *Democracy and the Market: Political and Economic Reforms in Eastern Europe and Latin America*. New York: Cambridge University Press, 1991.

Ramazani, Rouhollah K. *Revolutionary Iran: Challenge and Response in the Middle East*. Baltimore, MD: Johns Hopkins University Press, 1986.

Rayburn, Colonel Joel D., and Colonel Frank K. Sobchak, eds. *The U.S. Army in the Iraq War, Volume 1: Invasion, Insurgency, Civil War, 2003–2006*. Carlisle, PA: U.S. Army War College Press, 2019.

Razoux, Pierre. *The Iran–Iraq War*. Trans. Nicholas Elliott. Cambridge, MA: Belknap, 2015.

Reidel, Bruce, and Katherine Harvey. "Why Is Saudi Arabia Finally Engaging with Iraq?" Brookings Institution, December 4, 2020.

Rhodes, R. A. W., Sarah H. Binder, and Bert A. Rockman, eds. *The Oxford Handbook of Political Institutions*. New York: Oxford University Press, 2006.

Ricks, Thomas E. *The Gamble: General David Petraeus and the American Military Adventure in Iraq, 2006–2008*. New York: Penguin Press, 2009.

Rivlin, Paul. *Arab Economies in the Twenty-First Century*. New York: Cambridge University Press, 2009.

Rogan, Eugene L. "The Emergence of the Middle East into the Modern State System," in Louise Fawcett, ed., *International Relations of the Middle East*. 5th edition. New York: Oxford University Press, 2019, 39–62.

Roux, Georges. *Ancient Iraq*. 3rd edition. London: Penguin Books, 1992.

Rubin, Avshalom H. "Abd al-Karim Qasim and the Kurds of Iraq: Centralization, Resistance and Revolt, 1958–63." *Middle Eastern Studies* 43, no. 3 (May 2007): 353–382.

Ryan, Curtis. "Between Iraq and a Hard Place: Jordanian–Iraqi Relations." *Middle East Report No. 215* (Summer 2000): 40–42.

Sagan, Scott D., and Kenneth N. Waltz. *The Spread of Nuclear Weapons: A Debate Renewed*. 2nd edition. New York: W. W. Norton, 2002.

Sassoon, Joseph. *Saddam Hussein's Ba'th Party: Inside an Authoritarian Regime*. New York: Cambridge University Press, 2012.

Sassoon, Joseph. *Anatomy of Authoritarianism in the Arab Republics*. New York, Cambridge University Press, 2016.

"Saudi Arabia Opens Consulate in Baghdad." *Asharq al-Awsat*, April 4, 2019.

Saudi Ministry of Commerce. "MCI, Establishing the Saudi–Iraqi Coordination Council Sets Up a New Era." Press Release, August 14, 2017.

Schuessler, John M. *Deceit on the Road to War: Presidents, Politics, and American Democracy*. Ithaca, NY: Cornell University Press, 2015.

Scott, James C. *Seeing Like a State: How Certain Schemes to Improve the Human Condition Have Failed*. New Haven, CT: Yale University Press, 1998.

Serena, Chad C. *It Takes More Than a Network: The Iraqi Insurgency and Organizational Adaptation*. Stanford, CA: Stanford University Press, 2014.

Shadid, Anthony. "The American Age, Iraq." *Granta* 116, August 30, 2011.

Silverstone, Scott A. *From Hitler's Germany to Saddam's Iraq: The Enduring False Promise of Preventive War*. Lanham, MD: Rowman & Littlefield, 2019.

Simon, Reeva Spector, and Eleanor H. Tejirian, eds. *The Creation of Iraq, 1914–1921*. New York: Columbia University Press, 2004.

Sluglett, Peter. *Britain in Iraq: Contriving King and Country, 1914–1932*. 2nd revised edition. New York: Columbia University Press, 2007.

Sly, Liz. "Baghdad Seeks to Restore Regional Role at Arab Summit." *Washington Post*, March 26, 2012.

Sly, Liz. "Iraq's Relations with Arab World Deteriorating Days after Baghdad Summit." *Washington Post*, April 4, 2012.

Smith, Niel, and Sean MacFarland. "Anbar Awakens: The Tipping Point." *Military Review* 88, no. 2 (March–April 2008): 41–52.

Spain, Ted, and Terry Turchie. *Breaking Iraq: The Ten Mistakes That Broke Iraq*. Palisades, NY: History Publishing, 2013.

Special Inspector General for Iraq Reconstruction. *Hard Lessons: The Iraq Reconstruction Experience*. Washington, DC: U.S. Independent Agencies and Commissions, 2009.

Spruyt, Hendrik. *The Sovereign State and Its Competitors: An Analysis of Systems Change*. Princeton, NJ: Princeton University Press, 1994.

Stansfield, Gareth. *Iraq: People, History, Politics*. 2nd edition. Cambridge: Polity Press, 2016.

Stewart-Jolley, Victoria. "Iraq's Electoral System: Why Successive Reforms Fail to Bring Change." Research Paper, Chatham House, Middle East and North Africa Program, October 6, 2021.

Stieb, Joseph. *The Regime Change Consensus: Iraq in American Politics, 1990–2003*. New York: Cambridge University Press, 2021.

Tarbush, Mohammad A. *The Role of the Military in Politics: A Case Study of Iraq to 1941*. London: Keegan Paul International, 1982.

Tarrow, Sidney. *Power in Movement.* 2nd edition. New York: Cambridge University Press, 1998.
Telhami, Shibley, and Michael Barnett, eds. *Identity and Foreign Policy in the Middle East.* Ithaca, NY: Cornell University Press, 2002.
Tilly, Charles. "War Making and State Making as Organized Crime," in Peter B. Evans, Dietrich Rueschemeyer, and Theda Skocpol, eds., *Bringing the State Back In.* New York: Cambridge University Press, 1985, 169–191.
Tilly, Charles. *Coercion, Capital, and European States: AD 990–1992.* Oxford: Blackwell, 1992.
TotalEnergies. "Iraq: TotalEnergies Signs Major Agreements for the Sustainable Development of the Basra Region Natural Resources." Press Release, September 6, 2021.
Trenin, Dmitri. *What Is Russia Up To in the Middle East?* Cambridge, MA: Polity, 2018.
Tripp, Charles. *A History of Iraq.* 3rd edition. New York: Cambridge University Press, 2007.
United Nations Conference on Trade and Development (UNCTAD). *State of Commodity Dependence 2021.* New York: United Nations Publications, 2021.
U.S. Senate, Select Committee on Intelligence. "Report on Postwar Findings about Iraq's WMD Programs and Links to Terrorism and How They Compare with Prewar Assessments." September 8, 2006.
Visser, Reidar, and Gareth Stansfield, eds. *An Iraq of Its Regions: Cornerstones of a Federal Democracy.* New York: Columbia University Press, 2008.
Walt, Stephen M. *The Origins of Alliances.* Ithaca, NY: Cornell University Press, 1987.
Waltz, Kenneth. *Man, the State, and War: A Theoretical Analysis.* New York: Columbia University Press, 1959.
Waltz, Kenneth. *Theory of International Relations.* Reading, MA: Addison-Wesley, 1979.
Warrick, Joby. *Black Flags: The Rise of ISIS.* New York: Anchor Books, 2015.
Wehrey, Frederic, ed. *Beyond Sunni and Shia: The Roots of Sectarianism in a Changing Middle East.* New York: Oxford University Press, 2017.
Wien, Peter. *Iraqi Arab Nationalism: Authoritarian, Totalitarian, and Pro-Fascist Inclinations, 1932–1941.* London: Routledge, 2006.
Woods, Kevin M., David D. Palkki, and Mark E. Stout, eds. *The Saddam Tapes: The Inner Workings of a Tyrant's Regime, 1978–2001.* New York: Cambridge University Press, 2011.
Woods, Kevin M., with Michael R. Pease, Mark E. Stout, Williamson Murray, and James G. Lacey. *The Iraqi Perspectives Report: Saddam's Senior Leadership on Operation Iraqi Freedom from the Official U.S. Joint Forces Command Report.* Annapolis, MD: Naval Institute Press, 2006.
Woodward, Bob. *Plan of Attack.* New York: Simon & Schuster, 2004.
World Bank. *Breaking Out of Fragility: A Country Economic Memorandum for Diversification and Growth in Iraq.* International Development in Focus. Washington, DC: World Bank, 2020.
Yergin, Daniel. *The Prize: The Epic Quest for Oil, Money, and Power.* New York: Free Press, 2008.
Younis, Nussaibah. "The Gulf between Them: What Arab Gulf Countries Can Learn from Iran's Approach to Iraq." Policy Brief, European Council on Foreign Relations, May 2021.

INDEX

Note: Page locators in **bold** represent tables on the corresponding page.

Abdullah I, King 35, 143
Abdullah II, King 153
Abdul-Mahdi, Adil 108
Abu Ghraib prison (Iraq) 103, 106
Afghanistan: anti-Soviet jihad in 140; U.S. invasion of 91
Agrarian Reform Law (1958) 50
agricultural credits 132
Ahali ("Peoples") association of reformists 29
Ahali reformers 30
Ahwar 89
al-Amn al-'Amm 67, 71, 72
al-Anfal (Spoils of War) 81
al-Aqwati, Jalal 56
al-Askari, Ja'afar 25
al-Askari shrine, destruction of 99
al-Assad, Bashar: opposition to American-led invasion of Iraq 151; relationship with Saddam Hussein 151; Russian backing for regime of 105
al-Assad, Hafez 75
al-Baghdadi, Abu Bakr 103–4, 106, 151
al-Baghdadi, Abu Omar 100
al-Bakr, Ahmed Hassan 7, 55, 56–7, 63–5, 129, 131
al-Barzani, Mullah Mustafa 51
al-Bazzaz, Abd al-Rahman 60–1
al-Bejat clan 65
al-Bu Nasir tribe 5, 65, 66, 74, 86
al-Douri, Izzat Ibrahim 88

al-Dulaimi, Naziha 51, 52
al-Duri, Izzat Ibrahim 76
al-Gaylani, Rashid Ali 6, 29, 37, 60, 117; military coup (1940) 31–2
Algiers Agreement (1975) 69, 130
al-Hakim, Mohammad Baqir 80, 97
al-Hashemi, Tareq 103
al-Hashimi, Yasin 29
al-Hikma University, Baghdad 7, 52, 68
al-Hussein, Abdullah bin 20
al-Jamali, Fadil 34
al-Jazrawi, Taha Yasin Ramadan 72, 76
al-Jubeir, Adel 150
al-Jumaila tribe 58
al-Kadhimi, Mustafa 109
al-Kailani, Sayyid Abd al-Rahman 24
al-Khoei, Abu al-Qasim 79, 90
Allawi, Ayad 98, 102, 137
Alliance, Treaty of 23
al-Majid, Ali Hasan (Chemical Ali) 81, 94
al-Maliki, Nouri 8, 102–4, 110, 146, 151, 154, 155, 182; sectarian approach to governance 152
al-Masri, Abu Ayyub 100
al-Mishraq company 166
al-Muhandis, Abu Mahdi 109
al-Qa'ida 91, 97, 140; attack on the United States 141
al-Qa'ida in Iraq (AQI) 97, 99–100, 105, 146

210 Index

al-Rashid military base 56
al-Rikabi, Alaa 110
al-Sabah, Amir Sabah al-Ahmad al-Jaber 151
al-Sabah, Sheikh Mubarak 125
al-Sa'di, Ali Salih 55, 57
al-Sadr, Ayatollah Mohammed Baqir 53, 68, 79
al-Sadr, Muqtada 101–3, 107, 109–10
al-Sa'id, Nuri 3, 7, 30–1, 36–8, 41–2, 116, 119–21, 124
al-Saud, Emir Abdulaziz 125
al-Shawaf, Abd al-Wahab 49, 123
al-Sistani, Ayatollah Ali 90, 105
al-Timman, Ja'afar Abu 29
al-Wandawi, Mundhir 56
al-Zarqawi, Abu Musab 97, 100, 146, 153, 173
American invasion of Iraq (2003) 8, 91, 93, 140–5
Ammash, Salih Mahdi 55, 57
Amn al-Amm (Public Security Directorate) 67, 72
Anatolia Project (*Güneydoğu Anadolu Projesi*, GAP) 156
Anbar Awakening (*al-Sahwa Anbar*) 100
Anglo–Iraqi Treaty of Alliance (November 1930) 23–5, 27, 117, 120; Article 4 of 31; renegotiation of 34
Anglo–Iraqi War (1941) 32, 34
Anglo–Kuwaiti Treaty (1899) 126
Anglo-Persian Oil Company 16
anti-British sentiment 31
anticolonialism 117
Arab Ba'ath Socialist Party *see* Ba'ath Party
Arab Cooperation Council (ACC) 149
Arab ethnonationalism 118
Arab–Israeli War 127–8; of 1948 118, 155; of 1967 62, 68; of 1973 71, 84, 130, 176; resolution of 137
Arab League 75, 118, 130, 187, 198; opposition to U.S. invasion of Iraq 144; summit in Baghdad (1978) 153; summit in Baghdad (2012) 149–51
Arab national identity 129
Arab nationalism 117; transnational identity politics of 114
Arab nationalist Independence Party (*Hizb al-Istiqlal*) 33
Arab nationalist movement 129
Arab Revolt 20, 22, 25, 36; British repression of 31
Arab Socialist Union (ASU) 59; single-party rule of 60

Arabs of Mandate Palestine 156
Arab Spring 8, 102–4, 150, 195
Arab Union 40
Arctic National Wildlife Refuge 177
Arif, Abd al-Rahman 60–2
Arif, Abd al-Salam 41, 48, 55, 56, 58–60, 63, 122; death of 128; distancing from Nasser's Iraqi allies 59
Arif–Bazzaz peace plan (1966) 69
Arif brothers 127–9
Armenian Genocide 18
Armenia, Republic of 18
Armistice of Mudros (1918) 17
ashrafs 20
Assyrian rebellion 28
Aswan High Dam 120
asymmetric warfare, waging of 96
Awakening Councils 100
Aziz, Tariq 78–9, 94, 139

Ba'athist militia (*al-Jaysh al-Sha'abi*) 66
Ba'ath Party 4–5, 50, 62; *al-Jihaz al-Khass* 67; bloodless coup 63; consolidation of 64–8; coup of July 1968 7, 55–8, 62–4, 129; *Far'* (Branch) 72; *Firqa* (Division) 72; founding of 37; genocidal terror campaign against the Kurdish population 81; interlude between February–November 1963 55–8; *Khaliya* (Cell) 72; Military Bureau 71; and *Mukhabarat* state 71–3; patronage networks 72; Popular Army (*al-Jaysh al-Sha'abi*) 72; *Qiyadat al-Iqlimiya* (Regional Command) 72, 76, 81; *Qiyadat al-Wataniya* (National Command) 72; as regime in transition 75–6; return of 129–31; rise to power 86; *Shu'ba* (Section) 72; slogan of "unity, freedom, and socialism" 64, 138
Baghdad College 68
Baghdad Pact (1955) 39, 50, 120, 124; withdrawal of Iraq from 124
Baghdad Railway 15
Baghdad's Revolution City (*Madinat al-Thawra*) 51, 79
Bahrain, kingdom of 152
Barzani, Ahmed 28
Barzani, Idris 75
Barzani, Masoud 89
Barzani, Mustafa 60
Barzanji, Mahmud 33
Bell, Gertrude 21
bin Laden, Osama 91, 97, 140
bin Salman, Muhammad 150
Blix, Hans 142

Boumediene, Houari 154
Bourguiba, Habib 154
"Breaking the Walls" campaign 103
Bremer, L. Paul 95, 145
British India 19
British Indian Army 14–15; XII Corps 17
British–Iraqi relations 31
British legacies, in Iraq 116–19
British Navy 16
Burma Oil 16
Bush administration 91, 101, 141, 144–6
Bush, George W. 100, 134, 144

Caliph Ibrahim 104
Camp David Accords (1978) 75, 130, 132
Central Treaty Organization 124
Chadirchi, Kamil 33
Chalabi, Ahmed 137
Chamber of Deputies (*Majlis al-Nuwwab*) 25, 40
Charge of the Knights campaign (2008) 101
chemical weapons, use of 81
China 140, 143; economic competition 157; economic cooperation with Iraq 158; as Iraq's most important energy trade partner 165; relations with Iraq 157–8
China National Petroleum Corporation (CNPC) 158
Churchill, Winston 16, 20, 32
Circle of Seven 31
civilian-dominated politics, in postwar era 32–4
civilian–military divide 66
civilian nuclear industry 130
civilizational rivalries 154
civil war of 2006–2007 96, 99–100, 151
Clinton administration 91, 137, 138
Clinton, Bill 138
coalition of the willing 144
Coalition Provisional Authority (CPA) 8, 95, 98, 145, 146, 173
Cold War: competition between the United States and the Soviet Union 120; influence on Arab–Israeli conflict 120
communist-affiliated organizations 52
Constitutional Union Party (CUP) 36, 38
Council of Ministers (*Majlis al-Wuzara'*) 99
Council of Representatives (*Majlis al-Nuwwab*) 98
coups d'état 63
COVID-19 pandemic 109
Cox, Percy 20–1

cradles of civilization 12
cross-border trade 153
cultural commonalities, among the Arab states 186

D'Arcy, William Knox 16
Da'wa party 8, 53, 75, 78, 80, 90, 98, 107, 134, 146, 173
Dean of Arab diplomacy 151
decision-making 3, 5, 19, 61, 73, 81, 87, 93, 116, 122, 145, 164, 192, 194–6
defensive unionism 128
de Mello, Sergio Vieira 97
democratic governance, in Iraq 84, 194–6
demographic and communal profile, of Iraq 170–5
dual containment, policy of 137

earnings remittances 186
economic blockade 87
economic overview, of Iraq 164–7
economic policymaking 164
economy and resource endowments, of Iraq 164–7
Eden, Anthony 121
education and social welfare 188
Egypt 12, 59; defeat in the June 1967 war 64; Free Officers military coup to end the Egyptian monarchy 35; Israel invasion of 120; Nasserist coup attempt (1965) 128; Nasserist revolution (1952) 40; Nile River valley 183; peacemaking with Israel 75
Egyptian–Israeli peace treaty (1979) 130
Eisenhower Doctrine 48
ElBaradei, Mohamed 142
electoral reforms 111
el-Nasser, Gamal Abd 35, 59, 120–3, 129
el-Qaddafi, Muammar 154
el-Sherif, Ihab 149
energy independence 177
Erdogan, Tayyip 156
ethnic and sectarian divides, in Iraq 9
ethnonationalist identity 174
Euphrates River 9, 11, 17, 19, 22, 28, 32, 106, 125, 156, 182, 183
European investment, in a Persian oil concession 15–16
European political rivalries 114
European Union 187
Europe–Iraq relationship 156–7
Export–Import Bank 132
export-led growth (ELG) 179
external rents, in Iraq 178–9

Index

Faisal I, King (Faisal bin al-Hussein al-Hashemi) 3, 6, 20–3, 25, 27, 67, 117
Faisal II, King 35, 41
"faith campaign" (*al-hamla al-imaniya*) 88
fatwa 105
fedayeen 120
female labor force participation 165
Foley, James 104
food subsidies 66
foreign assistance 186–7
fossil fuels 177
France–Iraq relationship 156–7
Free Officers group 35, 39, 48
free press, notion of 61
French nuclear deal 131

General Agreement on Tariffs and Trade (GATT) 179–80, 185
genocidal ethnic conflicts, in Bosnia and Rwanda 137
Ghaidan, Sa'dun 63–4
Ghazi, King 27, 30–1, 36, 67, 117
Gheit, Ahmed Abul 150
glasnost 133
Global Coalition to Defeat ISIS 105
global development models 179
global economic order, rules-based 185
Golden Age of Islam 1
Golden Square military allies 31
Great Britain 121; choice of a king for Iraq 20; conquest and occupation 15–17; disposition of holdings in the MENA region 20; establishment of Iraq's formal borders 13–14, 19, 23; Mandate for Mesopotamia 18; from mandate to uprising 17–19; Mesopotamian campaign (1914) 15; military occupation of Iraq 29, 117; organization of India's institutions 19; partition of India and Pakistan 19; postwar reconstruction efforts in Iraq 157; relations with Iraq 156–7; sense of self 20; Sharifian solution 20–2
Great power rivalry 55
Great Uprising of 1920 19
Great War 15
Green Zone 98
Grobba, Fritz 31
gross domestic product (GDP) 9, 164; in MENA region **168**
gross national income (GNI) 164; in MENA region **169**
Guantanamo Bay, Cuba 106
Guardians of Independence (*Haras al-Istiqlal*) 18

Gulf Cooperation Council (GCC) 149, 152
Gulf monarchies 179
Gulf War 133–5; bombing campaign against Iraq 138; Operation Desert Fox 138–9; Operation Desert Shield 133; Operation Desert Storm 133

Habbaniya (British airbase) 32
Hammadi, Sa'dun 86, 135
Harakat Imtidad (Reach Movement) 110
Hashemite Arab federation 119
Hashemite Kingdom 22–3; Jewish and Kurdish communities of 35; of Jordan 35
Hashemite monarchy 3, 36, 48, 120; assessment of 41–4; end of 37–40, 120–1; independence under 27–9; Iraqi revolution and 120–1
Hassan II, King 154
Hizb al-Da'wa al-Islamiyya see Da'wa party
HMS *Victorious* 126
honor killings, legalization of 81
House of Commons 16
Hussein, Saddam 3, 9, 50, 63, 116, 123, 129–30, 170; arrest of General Maher Abd al-Rashid 86; attempt to assassinate Qasim 123; autocratic rule of 4; Bakr's replacement by 76; birth of 65; capture of 94; claims to Presidency 73–4; in command between 1979–1988 76–8; creation of *mukhabarat* state 66; deposal of 5; execution of 94, 100; family and clan of 65; flight to Cairo 65; growth of security capabilities 67; hiding at Dora Farms, south of Baghdad 144; identity-related challenges under 78; invasion of Iran 131–3; Iran and the Shi'i challenge 78–80; Iraqi revolution in 1958 65; as Iraq's new president 76; joining of Ba'ath Party 65; Kurdish issue 69; oil and Kurdish policy 7; oil politics 68–71; overthrown by foreign military forces 87; patronage network 66; policy initiatives 68–71; popularity among his supporters 137; project to strengthen the regime 77; *Qadisiyya* 79, 85; rise of 77; social and political connections 65; strategic judgment in initiating the war 133; survival and the long stalemate (1991–2001) 87–91; sympathy for 135–40; Treaty of Friendship and Cooperation with Soviet Union 70–1
Hussein, Uday and Qusay 93

Index

identities: community-related 5; ethnic 5; role in shaping social and political outcomes 5–6; sectarian 5; social 6; tribal 5
Imperial Germany 15
imperial powers 15
import substitution industrialization (ISI) 179
Indian Cavalry Brigade 17
Indian Expeditionary Force D (IEFD) 15
Indian Muslim 17
industrial development, in Iraq 9, 179–82
infant mortality, in Iraq 172
institutions, in Iraq 4–5; political 4; State 4
insurgency and democratic development, in Iraq 96–9
inter-Arab policies 118
inter-Arab politics 128
interlude of late 1980s 84–7
International Atomic Energy Agency (IAEA) 142
International Commission of Inquiry 24
International Monetary Fund 182, 187
international trade, in Iraq 184–6
interstate cooperation 128
Intifada (1952) 35
intra-Arab political unification 118
Iran 124; coup against the nationalist Mosaddeq government 124; Iraq's invasion of 78; Islamic revolution 131; loss of U.S. arms supply and political support 131; Pahlavi dynasty 124; relations with Iraq 124; Shi'a community 79; strategic instability and weakness 79; support for the Kurds 130
Iranian–Iraqi trade 185
Iranian Revolutionary Guards 105
Iran–Iraq War (1980–1988) 7, 89, 134, 149, 180; ceasefire under UN Security Council Resolution 598 82; domestic impact of 80–2; emigration of middle-class professionals from Iraq during 90; impact on currency reserves 80; impact on Kurdistan 81; Iraqi battlefield setbacks 132; stalemate of 81–2; tanker war 132; use of chemical weapons against Iranian troops 81; war of attrition 81
Iraq: American military departure from 147; Area Command of the Ottoman Army 16; on the brink during 2001–2003 91–3; conquest by the Islamic State 197; in context of world politics 115–16; economic aims for 1990 86; foreign relations after Saddam 147–9; Governing Council 12; integration into regional labor markets 186; invasion of Kuwait 8, 87; national military of 104; noncompliance with UNSCOM inspections requirements 138; popular sovereignty in 25; protest and stalemate (2017–present) 106–10; reconstitution of an independent 104; sanctions under U.N. Security Council 88, 92; sense of national self 21; shadow state 96; significance of non-Arab debt 87; state bureaucracy in 60; state formation, deficiencies in 10; unity despite tension and fragmentation 197–8; U.S.-led invasion of 93, 134–5, 144–7, 176, 194; U.S occupation of 144–7; war-induced state failure 94; war-related genocidal campaign against the Kurds 132; in world of national states 158–9
Iraqi–Arab states relations 149–54
Iraqi Atomic Energy Commission (IAEC) 131
Iraqi Communist Party (ICP) 33, 36–7, 48, 56, 70, 124, 127
Iraqi–Egyptian relations 57, 149–50
Iraqi Free Officers 121
Iraqi governance, role of the military in 54
Iraqi Governing Council (IGC) 95, 148, 173
Iraqi Intelligence Service (IIS) 95, 140
Iraqi–Jordanian relations 153
Iraqi–Kurdish War (1961) 69
Iraqi marshes 183
Iraqi military: exposure to British military practices and training 26; self-defined mission of 26; Shi'i recruits 26; Sunni Arab–dominated officer corps 26
Iraqi Military Academy 40
Iraqi monarchy, political structure of 25
Iraqi National Accord (INA) 137
Iraqi National Alliance (INA) 102
Iraqi National Congress (INC) 91, 137
Iraqi National Oil Company (INOC) 70
Iraq–Iran border, treaty delimiting 125
Iraqi security volunteers 100
Iraqi–Syrian–Egyptian tripartite unity talks 57
Iraqiyya (Iraqi National List) 102–3
Iraq Liberation Act of 1998 (ILA) 138
Iraq Petroleum Company (IPC) 36, 51; nationalization of 130; pipeline through Syria 121
Ishraqa Kanoon 110

Islamic Action Organization (*Munazzamat al-'Amal al-Islami*) 78
Islamic Caliphate 104
Islamic Party (*al-Hizb al-Islami*) 52
Islamic State (IS) 5, 12, 114, 182; acts of violence 105; attack on the Parisian newspaper *Charlie Hebdo* 105; beheading of Egyptian Christians 106; bombings in Iraq 149; conflict zones 106; conquest of Iraqi territory 197; establishment of 53; failure to construct a new political entity 198; fight against Iraqi and Syrian militaries 105; global operations of 104–6; international coalition against 105; military campaign from 2014 to 2017 8; threat to Russia 105
Islamic State in Iraq (ISI) 100; "Breaking the Walls" and "A Soldier's Harvest" campaigns 103; Global Coalition to Defeat ISIS 105
Islamic State in Iraq and Syria (ISIS) 103
Islamic symbology 75
Islamism, transnational identity politics of 114
Israel 154–6; Arab–Israeli War (1948) 118; Arab–Israeli War (1967) 62, 68; Arab–Israeli War (1973) 71, 176; conflict with Palestine 155; invasion of Egypt 120; Islamic Jihad suicide attacks 137; movement of Iraqi Jews to 155; peacemaking with Egypt 75; Soviet Union's recognition of 37; two-state solution 137; U.S. support to 68
Israeli–Palestinian nationalist contention 119
Istakhbarat Askariyya (Military Intelligence) 72
Istiqlal Party 33, 39, 121

Ja'afari, Ibrahim 98–9
Jabr, Salih 33–4
Jesuits, in Baghdad 52, 68, 82
Jewish community, in Iraq 35, 155
Jordan 128–9; Hashemite Kingdom of 153; relations with Iraq 153
Jordanian embassy in Baghdad, bombing of 97
July 1958 revolution 6–7, 40–1, 47, 58, 84, 114, 119, 121–2
Jumaila kinsmen 58–9, 61–2

al-Kailani, Abd al-Rahman 20
Karbala, Battle of (680 CE) 173
Kazzar, Nadhim 67, 71
Kemal, Mustafa 18, 24

Khaliya (Cell) 72
Khan, Antoine Ketābči 15
Khomeini, Ayatollah 131, 173
Khor al-Zubair port 86
kinship-based patronage system 7
kinship network 74
kurdayeti 34
Kurdish community: impact of Iran–Iraq War on 81
Kurdish Democratic Party (KDP) 34, 52, 69, 175
Kurdish genocide 81
Kurdish languages, teaching of 51
Kurdish legislature and school curriculum 69
Kurdish movement 56, 75, 85; victory at the Battle of Mount Handren (1966) 60
Kurdish nationalism 197
Kurdish national self-assertion 24
Kurdish national state, in northern Iraq 198
Kurdish New Generation Movement 110
Kurdish *Peshmerga* 105–7
Kurdish referendum (2017) 106
Kurdish uprisings 28
Kurdistan Regional Government (KRG) 174
Kurdistan, Republic of: autonomous self-government zone 134; Baghdad's failure to defend 107; fight against IS in Syria 107; as threat to Iraqi territorial integrity 107
Kurdistan Workers Party (PKK) 89, 156, 175
Kuwait 66; Abd al-Karim Qasim's threat to 8, 126; Iraq's invasion of 8, 87, 133–5, 141, 150, 159, 180; oil-induced transformations of the 1970s 8
Kuwait–Saudi Divided Zone 87

labor laws 51
labor migration 163; within and to the Arab world 186
Lausanne, Treaty of (1923) 24
Law of Administration for the State of Iraq for the Transitional Period (TAL) 98
Lawrence, T. E. 20–1
League of Nations 14, 17, 19, 24, 116; Iraq's membership in 27
Lebanon 18; Hezbollah 105; political crisis 41
levels of analysis (LOA) 2
lower-income economy 165

Madinat al-Thawra (Revolution City) 51
Madrid peace conference (1991) 156
Mahabad Republic 34

al-Mahdawi, Fadhil Abbas 49
Mahdawi kangaroo court 54
Mahdi Army (*Jaysh al-Mahdi*) 101
Maktab al-Amn al-Qawmi (Bureau of National Security) 72
Maktab Askari (Military Bureau) 72
Mandate for Mesopotamia 18
March Manifesto 69
martial law 32, 48
May Day celebration (1959) 49
median age, in select countries **171**
Mesopotamia 6, 12, 18; campaign of the First World War 14
Mesopotamian Group of the Royal Air Force 19
Middle East and North Africa (MENA) region 9, 14, 21, 40, 114, 163; country areas in **167**; country populations in **167**; cultural and political connections with Iraq 148; economic transformation of 1; educational attainment in 1; gross domestic product (GDP) **168**; gross national income (GNI) **169**; Iraq in 167–70; monarchies 41; oil reserves in **168**; regional politics 137; social bonds in 1; Soviet influence in 120
middle-state dilemma 9, 191–3
al-Midfa'i, Jamil 42
MiG-21 jet fighter 123
military coup: Ba'athist coup (1968) 7, 55–8, 62–4, 129; Rashid Ali coup (1940) 31–2; Sidqi's coup (1936) 6, 29–31, 117
military dictatorship 53
military intelligence 59
Ministry of Defense 56, 63, 71
Ministry of Oil 95
modern state, creation of 13
Mohammed, Prophet 20–1, 173
monarchy, idea of 21
Mosaddeq, Mohammed 35
Mosul Dam 182
Mosul revolt (1959) 54
Mount Handren, Battle of (1966) 60
Mubarak, Hosni 78
muhasasa ta'ifiya (quota or apportionment) powersharing system 98, 108
Mukhabarat al-Amma (General Intelligence Service) 7, 71–2; Ba'athism and 71–3
multinational corporation (MNC) 178

Naqshabandi sheikh 69
Nasiriyya, battle of (1915) 16
Nasser, Gamal Abdel 62, 84, 120; Iraqi–Egyptian relations under 122
National Action Charter (1971) 70

national assembly (*al-Majlis al-Watani*) 77
national autonomy, of Iraq 27
national community-building 12
National Council of the Revolutionary Command (NCRC) 56
National Defense Council 61
National Defense Government 32
National Democratic Party (*Hizb al-Watani al-Dimuqrati*) 33, 39, 48, 52
National Guard (*al-Haras al-Qawmi*) 56–8
national identity: of Iraq 119; sense of 13
national integration, challenges of 92
National Liberation Front (FLN) 120
national oil revenues 71
national-scale government authority 13
national sense of self 18
nation-building 10; in Iraq 191; path dependence in 196–7; state formation and 13–14
natural gas markets and production 166
natural resources, non-petroleum 166–7
Nazi Germany 31
Neolithic period 11
Nixon Doctrine 130
no-fly zone, establishment of 134–5, 139
Non-Proliferation Treaty (NPT) 136
nontariff barriers (NTBs) 184
non-Turkish Ottoman territories, dismemberment of 17
North Atlantic Treaty Organization (NATO) 105, 124
North Korea 140
North Slope Alaska crude 177
nuclear program of Iraq 131
nuclear weapons capabilities, development of 131

Obama administration 102, 104
Office of Reconstruction and Humanitarian Assistance (ORHA) 145
official development agenda 91
Oil-for-Food Program 92, 137, 153, 176
oil industry 70; growth of 184
oil politics 68–71
oil sector, nationalization of 163
oil wealth of Iraq 51, 75, 162, 176–8; hydrocarbon extraction 176; impact of 193; Kirkuk oil field 176; as problem and solution 193–4; reserves-to-production ratio 176; Rumaila oil field 176; state revenues from 176; Zubair oil field 176
Old Europe 142
Operation Desert Fox 138–9
Operation Desert Shield 133
Operation Desert Storm 133

Operation Iraqi Freedom 144
Operation Southern Focus 141
"Organic Law" for Iraq 23
Organization of the Islamic Conference 187
Organization of the Petroleum Exporting Countries (OPEC) 51, 60
Osirak nuclear reactor 130
Oslo Accords of 1993 and 1995 137
Ottoman Empire 18, 29, 125–6, 153; collapse of 18
Ottoman Iraq 15, 17–18
Ottoman Sultanate, abolition of 18
Ottoman Turks 14, 17

Palestine 18, 154–6; Arab population 118; Arabs of Mandate Palestine 156; Arab support to 31; conflict with Israel 35, 155; establishment of a non-Arab state in 129; Madrid peace conference (1991) 156; *nakba* 118; support for Saddam Hussein's invasion of Kuwait 156
Palestinian Arabs 118
pan-Arabism 58, 63–4; unification project 76
Paris Exhibition (1901) 15
Paris Peace Conference 17, 119
Pasha, Fakhri 17
Patriotic Union of Kurdistan (PUK) 69, 175
Peace Partisans 49, 52
perestroika 133
permanent settled communities, rise of 11
Personal Status Law No. 188 of 1959 51
Peshmerga forces 69, 105–7, 174
petroleum refining 166
political activism 32
political authority, definition of 13
political division and trauma, legacies of 168
political economy: Iraqi state's approach to 164; meaning of 163–4
political incentives 3
Political Islam 62
political life, in Iraq 1, 4, 50, 191
political mobilization 93
political parties, creation of 41
political pluralism 102
political power: consequences of 163; of Shi'i community 173
political science and economics, disciplines of 164
political system, in Iraq 195
political violence 187
politicization of the military 40

polygamy 51
Popular Army (*al-Jaysh al-Sha'abi*) 72
Popular Mobilization Forces (PMF) 105–6
Popular Resistance militia 49
population growth, in Iraq **170**
Portsmouth Treaty (1948) 34, 120
post–civil war authoritarianism 195
postwar initiatives and retrenchment 119–20
Powell, Colin 142
power, role in Iraqi context 3–4
press censorship 32
prisoners of war (POWs) 80
pro-Nazi cabal 117
proportional representation (PR) 109
Prudhoe Bay oilfield 177
public investment 179
public sector employment 182
public security service (*al-Amn al-'Amm*) 67
Putin, Vladimir 105

Qasim, Abd al-Karim 3, 7, 40–1, 47, 48–50, 65, 84, 94, 116, 121, 122–6, 164; assessment of regime of 53–5; capture of 56; devolution into a pure military dictator 55; as Divider of Iraq 123; downfall of 55; execution of 127; first Ba'athist coup 55–8; Iraqi–Egyptian relations under 122; Iraqi foreign policy under 125; October 1959 assassination attempt 54, 65; progressive Personal Status Law 57; Ramadan Revolution (1958) 55; social orientation of 58; as "the Sole Leader" 73; threat to Kuwait 8; vision of a strong Iraqi state 55
quasi-civil war 8
quasi-democratic governance 186

Rabin, Yitzhak 137
al-Rabita (the Iraqi Women's League) 51
railroad development 15, 123, 179
Ramadan Revolution (1958) 55
al-Razzaq, Arif Abd 59
regional democracy 187
rent: concept of 178; external 178–9; non-oil forms of 178; positional 178; strategic 178
rentier state, concept of 178
Republican Guard 63, 133, 134–5; establishment of 58; tank regiment 63
resource allocation 28
Revolutionary Command Council (RCC) 40, 64, 66, 95, 133
Revolution of 1958 37–40

Index **217**

river-based agricultural system 167
river-borne trade 184
Rizgari Kurd (Liberation of Kurds) 34
Royal *Irada* (Will or Command) 25
Royal Military College 25
al-Ruba'i, Muhammad Najib 48
Rumsfeld, Donald 132, 140–2
Russia–Iraq relations 157–8

Saairun bloc 107, 109
Sabri, Naji 147
Sadat, Anwar 78; strategic realignment with the United States 84; trip to Jerusalem 130
Saddam City (*Madinat Saddam*) 79
Saddam's *Qadisiyya* 79, 85
Sahwa groups 101
Salih, Barham 108
San Remo, Italy 17, 19
Sasanian Empire of Persia 79
Saudi Arabia 128, 177; opposition to U.S. invasion of Iraq 143; U.S. military support to 130
Saudi–Iraqi Coordination Council 150
Scud ballistic missiles 129
sectarian and ethnic political struggles 90
self-defense and survival, mechanism for 96
self-determination, Wilsonian notions of 14
Sèvres, Treaty of (1920) 18–19, 24
Shah, Mozaffar al-Din 16
Shaiba, battle of (1915) 16
Shanidar Cave, in Kurdistan 11
Sharifian solution 20–2
Shatt al-Arab agreement (1937) 130
Shatt al-Arab waterway 15, 69, 85, 125, 130, 183
Shi'i Arab tribesmen 17
Shi'i-based sectarian political parties and militant groups 148
Shi'i Indigenous population 89
Shi'i population, state surveillance of 53
Shi'i protests in Karbala, repression of (1977) 75
Shi'i *'ulama* 18–19
al-Shirazi, Ayatollah Muhammad Taqi 18
Sidqi, Bakr 6, 26, 28; assassination of Jafar al-Askari 29; as Chief of the National Reform Force 29; death of 30; military coup (1936) 29–31, 117
Simele massacre 28
single-commodity trade 184
single, nontransferable vote (SNTV) 109
Sirri, Rif'at al-Hajj 35
Sistani, Ayatollah Ali 109

skilled labor force 182
Slaibi, Sa'id 58
social divisions, in Iraq 170
social elites 3
social identity, in Iraq 96, 175
Society of Ulama 53
"A Soldier's Harvest" campaign (2013) 103
Soleimani, Qassem 109, 155
Sole Leader (*al-za'im al-awhad*) 50
Soviet Union 24, 66, 68, 86, 131; development of Rumaila oilfield in southern Iraq 70; influence in Middle East and North Africa (MENA) region 120; under Joseph Stalin 124; principles of *glasnost* and *perestroika* 133; recognition of the State of Israel 37
Stalin, Joseph 124
state-building, in Iraq 3, 23–7
state bureaucracy 42
state formation: European 14; in Iraq 44, 191; and nation-building 13–14; path dependence in 196–7; processes of 4; relation with war-making 13
State of Law (SOL) party 102
state-owned enterprises 95; establishment of 163
state power, of Iraq 70, 80, 114, 159, 191–3
state revenues, growth of 130
state socialism 63
state–society divide 4
state–society engagement 28–9
state violence 87
Status of Forces Agreement (SOFA) 147
Straits of Tiran 120
Suez War (1956) 15, 84, 120–1
suicide and car bombings 96–7
Sulayman, Hikmat 29
Sunni awakening 100–2
Sunni insurgency 103
Sunni militancy, support for 101
Sunni–Shi'a divide 174
Sunni tribes 88
Supreme Council for the Islamic Revolution in Iraq (SCIRI) 80, 97, 98
al-Suwaidi, Tawfiq 33
Sykes–Picot agreement of 1916 17
Sykes–Picot border, between Iraq and Syria 104
Syria 18, 122, 129, 143; Ba'athist coup 57; relations with Iraq 150

takbir 88
Talabani, Jalal 69, 89, 98, 155
Talfah, Adnan Khairallah 74, 76, 86

218 Index

Taliban 91
Talib, Naji 61
Tanzimat period, reforms of 15
taxation of income 178
Tenet, George 142
terror attacks: Jordanian embassy in Baghdad, bombing of 97; on Parisian newspaper *Charlie Hebdo* 105; September 11, 2001 attacks 91, 140–4; on U.N. headquarters in Baghdad 146
thalweg 69, 130
Third River Project 89
Tigris River 9, 11, 17, 22, 94, 98, 104, 125, 156, 182
al-Timman, Abu 30
Tishreen (October) movement *see Tishreen* protests (2019)
Tishreen protests (2019) 8, 108, 110, 196
TotalEnergies (French company) 157, 166
trade balance 185
Transitional Administrative Law (TAL) 95
Transitional National Assembly 98
Treaty of Friendship and Cooperation with the Soviet Union (1972) 70, 130
tribal identity 5
tribal rebellions 28
Tripartite Aggression 120
Tripp, Charles 26, 96
truck bombing, of the U.N. headquarters in Baghdad 96
Truman Doctrine 125
Turkey 8, 124, 154–6; Anatolia Project (*Güneydoğu Anadolu Projesi*, GAP) 156; Kurdistan Workers Party (PKK) attacks on 156; regional cooperation with Iraq 124, 156; war of independence in Anatolia 18; water-related tensions with Iraq 156
Tuwaitha nuclear complex 131
two-state solution 137

Ukraine, Russia's invasion of 166
Umana' Saddam (Saddam's Faithful) 88
Umm al-Dunya (Mother of the Earth) 12
Umm Qasr, port of 86
unemployment, rise in 85
UNESCO World Heritage Site 183
unified legal system, establishment of 13
unified river system 184
United Arab Republic (UAR) 40, 49, 122
United Iraqi Alliance (UIA) 98–9
United National Front 39, 121
United Nations (UN): Monitoring, Verification, and Inspections Commission (UNMOVIC) 142; Special Commission on Iraq (UNSCOM) 136, 138
United States (US): Al-Qa'ida's attack on 141; Army Corps of Engineers 182; assassination of Iranian general Qassem Soleimani 109; casualty rate of the insurgency 100; counterinsurgency doctrine 100; dual containment, policy of 137; House Judiciary Committee 138; invasion of Afghanistan 91; invasion of Iraq 93, 134–5, 144–7, 176, 194; military support to Saudi Arabia 130; occupation of Iraq 144–7; oil production in 177–8; policy toward Iraq 138; Sadat's strategic realignment with 84; Status of Forces Agreement (SOFA) 147; Strategic Framework Agreement (SFA) 147; U.S. Marines 48; war on terror 142; withdrawal from Iraq 100–2
U.N. Security Council 92; Oil-for-Food Program 137; Resolution 598 132; Resolution 660 135; Resolution 661 135; Resolution 678 134–5; Resolution 687 135, 151; Resolution 688 134; Resolution 1441 141; Resolution 1483 148, 156; Resolution 1511 144; Resolutions of 1990–1991 135; sanctions against Iraq 88; support for the American hard line on Iraq 141
upper-house Senate (*Majlis al-'Ayan*) 25
USS *Abraham Lincoln* 144

velayat-e faqih, doctrine of 80
Venezuela, oil reserves of 177
Versailles, Treaty of (1919) 17

Wahabi Islamists 14
war and regime change, in Iraq 93–6
war on terror 142
wartime deprivations 81
water resources and agriculture, in Iraq 182–4
Wathbah ("The Leap") uprising (1948) 34–7, 120
weapons of mass destruction (WMD) 91, 135, 138–9, 145, 194; failure of U.S. forces to find 146
West Bank 129
White Man's Burden mentality 15, 18
Wilson, Arnold T. 20
women's rights in divorce and inheritance 51
World Bank 187
world politics, polarization in 120

World Trade Organization (WTO) 185
World War I 13, 16, 41, 118, 125, 132; Mesopotamian campaign of 14; Versailles, Treaty of (1919) 17
World War II 6, 36, 118, 125, 193; Rashid Ali coup and 31–2

Yazidi revolt (1935) 28
youth unemployment 165
Yusuf, Yusuf Salman 37

Zebari, Hoshyar 148
Zionist movement 118